AUTOMATA THEORY: MACHINES AND LANGUAGES

McGraw-Hill computer science series

RICHARD W. HAMMING
Bell Telephone Laboratories

EDWARD A. FEIGENBAUM
Stanford University

AUTOMATA THEORY: MACHINES AND LANGUAGES

RICHARD Y. KAIN
Associate Professor of Electrical Engineering
University of Minnesota

McGraw-Hill Book Company

New York   St. Louis   San Francisco   Düsseldorf   Johannesburg
Kuala Lumpur   London   Mexico   Montreal   New Delhi
Panama   Rio de Janeiro   Singapore   Sydney   Toronto

AUTOMATA THEORY: MACHINES AND LANGUAGES

Library of Congress Catalog Card Number 71–168453

07–033195–2

1234567890DODO798765432

This book was set in Times Roman, and printed and bound by R. R. Donnelley & Sons, Company. The designer was Richard Paul Kluga; the drawings were done by John Cordes, J. & R. Technical Services, Inc. The editors were Richard F. Dojny and Madelaine Eichberg. Matt Ambrosio supervised production.

to Helen

Contents

Preface

The two extremes in the spectrum of approaches to mathematical topics are: (1) Proceed from definition to theorem with all the details written out and a few examples interspersed for "motivation." (2) Use discussion and some arguments about the plausibility of the results. The former might be called "exact mathematics," the latter, "descriptive mathematics." The latter approach has the advantage that one can omit the excruciating details of complex proofs, on the assumption that the reader can fill in those details.

Most writing about automata theory has adopted the "exact" approach. This approach tends to limit the audience to those having advanced mathematical maturity. In those fields where a theory has not been widely applied, practitioners who are neither extremely curious nor mathematically mature tend to avoid taking the time to work through the exact descriptions. Thus one consequence of the exact approach might be that applications of the theory are not discovered as quickly as they would be if the theory were more accessible to "outsiders."

Three years ago the author taught some of the concepts of automata theory to electrical engineering graduate students. This text evolved from a set of notes written for that course. Because the majority of these students were interested in practical applications, an exact mathematics approach to the subject did not seem appropriate. Thus this text lies toward the descriptive end of the spectrum. But a book cannot be completely descriptive. Exactness is required especially in definitions and statements of the questions being studied. Exact definitions can be made formally or informally. In technical papers the formal approach is generally used. Therefore we often state formal definitions. However, we sometimes give informal definitions and leave the formulation of exact definitions to the problems.

In discussing some results we will omit tedious details. However, we will include statements about the types of steps which are omitted from the discussion but would be required in an exact proof. The discussion of each result will develop the arguments until the result is intuitively plausible. Readers are strongly encouraged to test each result with a simple example. This exercise should help develop their intuition about why the result holds. Some of the omitted steps are to be provided by the student as exercises in understanding detailed proofs.

The major results are collected in Appendixes 2 and 3. Appendix 2 summarizes the results relating sets of languages to each other. The answers to some unsolvability questions are summarized in Appendix 3. An annotated Bibliography, which includes some recent papers not specifically discussed in the text, is provided. Original sources are cited. References to the Bibliography are cited at the end of each chapter, in the section titled Comments. The reader is encouraged to read some of these papers. The annotations should be useful if one is looking for a specific result. Several comprehensive bibliographies have appeared recently [Rahimi (1970) and Wood (1970)]. They should be consulted if a more complete listing of the literature is required.

History Mathematical theories are often developed without regard for any applications they may have to problems which concern scientists and engineers. Other mathematical theories developed as the need arose in practical problems. Automata theory developed in both ways. Some of the theory was developed in the 1930s, well before electronic digital computers were built (in the 1940s). Most of the theory has been developed since 1953. One possible application—attempting to explain natural languages (French, English, etc.)—is a very complex problem. The motivation usually given for a study of automata theory is that its problems relate to the problems of translating the languages used to express algorithms for computing machines. Perhaps people in other disciplines will develop new applications of automata theory when they learn more about the ideas and results.

In this text we will emphasize the connection between machines and (mathematical) linguistic models because it is my conviction that most results can be discovered from a machine interpretation of the problem.   Also, many people have more intuition about the behavior of a machine than they have when they think in mathematical abstractions.

Some machine models are closely related to the data structures used in software systems.   There complex data structures can simplify the programmers' ways of thinking about the problem.   The criterion of simplicity is very complex.   A description may be simple if it is phrased in terms of complex structures.   If a person has a repertoire of structures to consider, he may be able to find simpler descriptions of his problem by using one of the more complex structures for the statement.   In our discussion we will develop a repertoire of machine structures.

We assume that the reader is not familiar with linguistic models but that he does have some knowledge of finite-state machines.   This background can be provided by a course covering sequential circuit synthesis, or by material supplementing Chapter 2.   In Sections 2.1 and 2.2 we briefly review some of the concepts from that area.   We do not assume that the reader knows anything about the relationships between machine models and linguistic models.   A knowledge of this relationship is important for intuition.   We will proceed somewhat slowly in the first six chapters, introducing linguistic and machine models and proving results about their interrelationships.   Occasionally we prove other results, either in the course of becoming familiar with the operation of a machine model or to relate the differing capabilities of the models.   As we introduce new models, we discuss some reasons why they might be interesting, often from outside the context of automata theory. Except for these insertions, the structure of each of Chapters 2 to 5 is similar: A discussion of a deterministic machine model is followed by a definition of acceptance.   A result concerning the languages accepted by the deterministic machines is proved.   Then the nondeterministic model is introduced and its relationship to the deterministic model is discussed.   Finally, the relationship between the nondeterministic model and a linguistic model is discussed.

After the relationship between machines and languages is fully developed, we proceed to results which are usually phrased in terms of the languages alone.   Even here we will use the machine formulations of the problems to prove most of the results.   This approach is taken, not to fulfill our prediction that machine models are useful, but because the proofs of many of the results can be obtained by drawing the proper picture of a machine structure.

Notice that we say that a proof is obtained by drawing a picture.   This again emphasizes that our approach is not to provide exact proofs in all the detail which some might consider desirable.   Rather, we proceed with the exact proof until a point is reached when the reader should realize the structure of the proof, so that he could complete it if he wanted to.   In Chapter 2 we discuss exactly what types of detail are omitted, and occasionally we include an exercise in which the reader should either provide a statement of

what is missing or complete the missing parts.   The latter type of exercise is
not illuminating in most cases; therefore solving one or two such exercises
should be sufficient for any reader.

Philosophy of proofs   Most of the results which relate machines to languages are proved by simulations.   The machine "mimics" the language,
and vice versa.   Often some encoding of information is required.   When the
simulations are complex, we describe them by first describing the coding to
be used and then showing a flow chart for the simulation algorithm.   Often,
if the simulation is simple, we dispense with the flow chart and use a word
description of the algorithm.   The reader is encouraged to try the simulations
on simple examples so that he can fully understand the reasons for the particular result obtained.

Chapter summaries   Since the concepts of mathematical linguistics are
probably unfamiliar to most readers, we begin in Chapter 1 with a description
of the basic concepts, rules, and problems of mathematical linguistics.   The
reader who is familiar with the work of Chomsky could skim this chapter.

In succeeding chapters we will develop models of differing complexity
and capability.   We will show the relationship between "hardware" descriptions and linguistic descriptions of computations.   Our hardware descriptions
will be limited to descriptions of structures and types of components.   We
will not discuss the detailed interconnections of any logical elements which
might be used in a particular realization of any machine.   Transition tables,
flow charts, and similar techniques are used to describe the behavior of a
machine.   We will show how the structural details of a machine can be found
from the description of any particular related language, and how the language can be found from a knowledge of the structural details of the related
machine.

The simplest machine structure is the finite-state machine.   In Chapter
2, we will see how these machines are related to particularly simple languages.
The relationships that we will consider later are easier to understand in
this simple context.   Therefore we discuss some concepts in this familiar
context, even though they might have been introduced later.

Turing machines can perform complex calculations.   In Chapter 3, we
will discuss the Turing machine model for computation and show how its
computations are related to some very general languages and mathematical
functions.

Many interesting machine models can be derived from the Turing model
by restricting the amounts of time or space used during the computation.   In
Chapter 4, we discuss the linear-bounded automaton, the simplest of the
restricted Turing machines, and relate it to a class of languages.

Pushdown automata use a data structure very similar to some data structures used in compilers, some user programs, and one family of computers. In Chapter 5, we discuss this model, relating it to languages similar to ALGOL.

The machine models introduced in Chapters 2 to 5 are not sufficient to model certain aspects of compilation problems. Modifications of the structure of a machine or the imposition of restrictions upon their operation can change the capabilities of the machine. In Chapter 6, we discuss some of these changes, which happen to be closely related to solutions for some compilation problems. We also discuss some which fit into the hierarchy of machine models in interesting ways.

The last three chapters discuss questions which are often phrased in linguistic terms, though the proofs of the results can usually be made by finding machine structures which are relevant to the question. For example, in Chapter 7, we discuss certain mappings which can be applied to the sentences of a language. By finding a machine which performs the mapping it is easy to prove some properties of the results of the mapping. In Chapters 8 and 9, we discuss some questions that might be asked about languages, such as "Does this language contain any sentences?" After discussing the simple cases—those in which the questions can be answered—in Chapter 8, we turn, in Chapter 9, to those cases where an algorithm to answer the question in all cases cannot exist. We close by showing the theoretically curious result that there is an infinite hierarchy of classes of machines (and corresponding languages) about which many questions not only cannot be answered, but also become increasingly difficult for the machines higher in the hierarchy.

Comments to readers The importance of working the problems and carefully examining the examples cannot be overemphasized. It is very easy to sit back and nod your head "yes" when proofs are discussed, but unless you try the proof or try to perform the construction in an example, you may not understand why some details are necessary. There are suggested problems at the end of almost every section of the book. The difficulty of these problems varies greatly. Some are simple exercises in executing algorithms discussed in the section. These problems are placed toward the beginning of each set of problems. Other problems are statements of questions that we believe are open at the present time. The latter problems are marked (R). Some problems discuss results that will be cited in a later section of the text. These problems are marked (P).

Comments on ordering The ordering of Chapters 1 to 5 should not be changed, except that Chapter 5 can be moved to any point after Chapter 2 (except for the material in Sec. 5.7). The materials in Sections 5.8 and 6.4 can be omitted without loss of continuity. Chapters 6 and 7 should be discussed only after the first five chapters.

The material in Chapters 8 and 9 may be interspersed with the material from Chapters 3, 4, and 5.   For example, the definition and unsolvability of the correspondence problem (Section 9.1) can be discussed after the halting problem (Section 3.6).   Then some of the unsolvable linguistic problems in Chapter 9 can be discussed after Chapter 4 and the others after Chapter 5. The solvable cases of these problems are discussed in Chapter 8, which can be left for the mature student to read without class discussion.

Audience   The more mathematical maturity the student has, the faster can the material in this book be covered.   At the graduate level for electrical engineering students, this text can require one semester, or two quarters if the students have previously studied the synthesis of sequential circuits.   At the junior or senior level, a year would be required, and the instructor should supplement the text with some background material from the theory of finite-state machines.

The Association for Computing Machinery has published some curricular suggestions for computer science programs.   This text was planned before these proposals were made, and does not exactly match any one of them.   This text material is covered in courses A1, A7, and I7 of ACM (1968) and in courses 4, 5, and 6 of McNaughton (1968).

Acknowledgments   It is difficult to single out those persons who deserve the most thanks for helping me, either directly or indirectly, with this effort. I will cite a few individuals, knowing that others who have contributed must be omitted.   What follows is a chronological listing of some of my associates, because this avoids the difficult task of ranking the persons, either by the magnitude of their influence or alphabetically.   I begin with Prof. David A. Huffman, who had the patience to advise me during my thesis research (on a problem unrelated to the present text) and caused me to pay more attention to my writing.   Next, my colleagues, past and present, Profs. F. C. Hennie, D. J. Kuck, and C. L. Liu (alphabetically!) introduced me to much of this material.   Professor R. J. Collins, as department chairman, has provided a congenial atmosphere in Minneapolis in which I could teach the course and write the notes that formed the backbone of this text.   My colleagues at the University of Minnesota contributed to that atmosphere.   One of them, Prof. O. H. Ibarra, has checked my accuracy in many places, though any errors are my own responsibility.   My students have used class-note versions of this material and have pointed out places where the discussions required changes, contractions, or expansions.

Mrs. Sharon Nelson has typed several drafts of this manuscript with extremely high accuracy.   Without this help this book would not have been completed as quickly or as easily.

My wife has been helpful with editing the text, but editing errors are my responsibility. Last, but far from least, my wife and children have put up not only with my moments at the desk with pencil and paper, but also with my daydreaming about how best to approach some of these topics. Their only compensation has been to share some elation when a thought in the shower clarified the problem.

Richard Y. Kain

Introduction

Man has long been interested in mechanical devices to alleviate mechanical, clerical, and mathematical drudgery. Large-scale utilization of mechanical aids began during the Industrial Revolution. Hollerith lightened clerical work in the late nineteenth century when he invented punched-card machines. Electromechanical computers, first constructed in the 1930s, were used to perform complex mathematical tasks for scientists and engineers. Today, electronic digital computers assist schoolchildren, housewives, and many other people with mathematical and symbolic tasks. What are the limitations of these machines? We shall discuss some mathematical theories which attempt to answer that question.

A useful computing machine is a very large finite-state machine. Since the number of states of the machine is finite, the machine's behavior can be described in finite tables or graphs called *transition tables* or *transition diagrams*.†

---

† We will review these descriptions in Chap. 2.

Useful general-purpose computers have so many states that a description by means of a transition table or transition diagram would be so large that not only would it be an enormous task to construct it, but the table would be useless. If we cannot make a list of the possible actions of the machine, how can the machine be useful? In most practical computers, the contents of less than 25 registers (the accumulator, program counter, and some memory locations) determine the behavior of the system for one memory cycle. Thus the actions of the machine are highly *structured*; the differences between the next state and the present state are determined by a small fraction of the information specifying the current state. These differences can be systematically described in the manual for a machine. Thus we have the essential information about the behavior of the machine without resorting to a complete transition table.

Suppose we have a computer inside a "black box" and are allowed to observe only the outputs and change only the inputs. Our objective is to find a "simple" description of the behavior we observe. We perform several experiments and hope to deduce a "simple" description of the machine in the box. If we do not have any idea of what might be in the box, the task will be impossible. If we know nothing about the box, we can never determine whether it is a bomb which will explode if it receives an input longer than the length of our experiment! Any finite experiment is insufficient to determine the properties of the box unless we somehow know (a priori) that our experiment has continued long enough to measure all behavior that the box might ever exhibit.

When we analyze the experiment, we must not forget that the proposed description must predict the results of future experiments on the black box. We can never know whether we meet this criterion without opening the black box. In any realistic situation the best we can do is to run a finite number of experiments and increase the complexity of the model as necessary to explain any resulting data. With some a priori information about how the box operates, what are its components, or how these components are interconnected, we can do a better job of designing the experiment and interpreting the results. Often the a priori information can be used to choose the structure of the model to represent the machine. Once the structure of the model is chosen, it is easier to determine which descriptions of the black box explain the experimental results.

Another problem in trying to find the "simplest" description of the box is that we do not know how to measure "simplicity" objectively. This difficulty is serious when we consider two finite-state descriptions of the same behavior. Suppose one description is large, but has a simple structure, and the other is small, but has a complex structure. Which is "simpler"? The difficulty is increased when two different models of the machine are considered. Our intuition tells us that the "complexity" of the description should measure both the complexity of the type of model and the complexity of the description required for the given type of model.   Unfortunately, we do not know how to formalize this intuitive notion of complexity.   Therefore we cannot prove that any one description is the "simplest" one to describe a machine.

We will avoid questions of complexity and concentrate on the different models which can be used to describe computations.   In many cases computations can be described by using some concepts of mathematical linguistics. In fact, the categorizations of languages used in mathematical linguistics and the categorizations of computing machine models are closely related.   The types of behavior which can be described within each category can be compared.   The results of such comparisons are used to establish the relationships between the categories.   Our major goal is to develop these relationships, exploiting our intuition about machines whenever possible.

1
Mathematical Linguistics

In the 1950s and 1960s many persons worked on the problem of the mechanical translation of "natural" languages, such as English, Russian, Chinese, and German. Before these languages could be translated, the structure of statements in the languages had to be understood. Consequently, Chomsky and others developed various models of linguistic structure. Some of these models are useful in solving the problem of translating computer programs.

1.1 LINGUISTIC CONCEPTS

A natural language is a combination of (1) a dictionary which gives the meanings of the various "words" in the language and (2) a set of rules that determine which combinations of words and punctuation marks form sentences in the language. The set of rules is known as the "grammar" of the language. The grammar of a language can be used to determine the structure of a sentence in the language. It can also be used to test whether a given sequence of words forms a sentence in the language.

A mathematical linguist does not use the same terms to describe a language, but he does make the distinction between meaning and structure. To him the meanings of the words and the interpretations of the meanings based on the structure are the "semantics" of the language; the structure alone is known as the "syntax" of the language. We will be primarily concerned with the structure of machines and languages. Therefore we are more concerned with the syntax of the language than with the semantics of the sentences which can be constructed within the language.

Mathematical linguistics has been extensively used in the design of programming languages and programs to translate between different programming languages. It is extremely important that the intended meaning of a statement be preserved during the translation process. It is convenient if the meaning of a statement can be easily related to its structure. Therefore the intended meanings of sentences should be considered when the structure of these sentences is studied. The syntax and the semantics are not easily separated.

Usually, we talk about only the syntax of a language. Occasionally, we will return to these interrelationships with the semantics.

This is a formal definition of a language:

A *language* is a set of strings of symbols, where:

A *string* (or *sentence*) is a finite ordered sequence of symbols.
The *length* of a string is the number of symbols in the string.
A *symbol* is a distinguishable object used in constructing the words of a language.
The *alphabet* (or *terminal vocabulary*) of a language is the set of all symbols which can appear in the strings of the language.

Notice that sentences need not end with periods, and that symbols are not restricted in form. Most of our examples will be derived from English or some computer languages; this does restrict the symbol set, but the restriction is significant only for the printer.

Strings are constructed from symbols by the operation of *concatenation*. The concatenation of two symbols x and y, written xy, is the ordered sequence of the symbols. The concatenation of two strings α and β, written $\alpha\beta$, is the string formed by writing the symbols of α and then writing the symbols of β to the right. Thus, if $\alpha = x_1x_2 \cdots x_n$ and $\beta = y_1y_2 \cdots y_m$, then $\alpha\beta = x_1x_2 \cdots x_ny_1y_2 \cdots y_m$.

Example 1

$$\text{Strings:} \quad S_1 = a$$
$$S_2 = a + b$$
$$S_3 = (a + b) - (c - d)$$
$$S_4 = Once\Delta upon\Delta a\Delta time,\Delta a\Delta big\Delta bad\Delta wolf\Delta lived\Delta in\Delta the\Delta forest.$$
$$S_5 = This\Delta is\Delta a\Delta string.$$
$$S_6 = ALGOL\Delta is\Delta a\Delta programming\Delta language.$$

(We use the symbol Δ to mark a space where it is important. Remember that a space must be a legitimate symbol in many—but not all—languages; otherwise we could not describe the separations between the individual words in an English sentence.)

Languages: $L_1 = \{a|a + b\}$
$L_2 = \{a|a + b|(a + b) - (c - d)\}$
$L_3 = \{This\Delta is\Delta a\Delta string.|ALGOL\Delta is\Delta a\Delta programming\Delta$
$language.\}$
$L_4 = \{a,b|a,c|a|b\}$

The symbol | is used to separate the individual strings which constitute the language; a comma cannot be used because some languages use a comma as one of the symbols which may appear in the strings of the language. (We assume that | may not appear in the strings of the language.) Thus language L_4 contains four strings; two of these happen to contain commas. ■†

An informal description of the forms we just used to describe languages is:

1. A language is specified by the name of the language, followed by an equals sign, followed by a pair of curly brackets (braces) which contain a list of the strings in the language.
2. A list of strings is a string, *or* a string followed by the symbol | followed by a list of strings. Finite lists of strings contain only a finite number of strings.
3. A string is any sequence of symbols not including |, {, or }. Finite strings contain a finite number of symbols.

The reader can think of other ways to describe the descriptions. This form of description has a serious drawback. Every language that we can describe in this way can contain only a finite number of distinct strings. Furthermore, since we have to list all the strings, we will never describe languages with very many strings. We need a different way to describe languages which have a very large number of strings (the number of strings may, in fact, be infinite). Any practical technique used to describe infinite sets must use a finite amount of space. Now we describe three different techniques which can be used to solve this problem.

First, consider the mathematical technique of exhibiting a generic member of the infinite set, followed by restrictions on the values of any parameters that may appear in the generic form. One simple generic form that we will use is a^n, to represent n consecutive occurrences of the symbol a. For example, we could describe the set of strings which consist of an arbitrary number of a's, and no other symbols, as

$$\{a^n|n \geq 1\}$$

† We include this symbol in the alphabet of the language used in writing this book; its appearance denotes the end of an example.

Here we use the symbol | to denote the phrase "such that," its usual mathematical meaning in this context. Note that the symbol | has two meanings. The context of its usage will always make the meaning clear, and we can conform to standards in two different fields at the same time. The mathematical meaning ("such that") is used only within this form of a language description. Another infinite set is

$$\{a^n b^m | n \geq 1, m \geq 1\}$$

which contains all strings constructed by writing an arbitrary number of a's followed by an arbitrary number of b's. On the other hand, strings in the set

$$\{a^n b^n | n \geq 1\}$$

are composed of an arbitrary number of a's followed by *exactly the same* number of b's.

A second technique is to specify a set of rules which define a procedure for testing a given string for membership in the language. For example, we could specify a language by:

Any string which contains anything but a's is not in the language.

There are formal ways to specify such tests. In the unlikely event that we wanted to list the strings in the language, we would systematically generate all strings containing the symbols of the alphabet and test each one for membership in the language.

A third technique is to specify a procedure for generating only those strings which are in the language. If one knows the generation rules, one can form testing procedures, and vice versa. Mathematical linguists often specify languages by giving generative procedures. We turn now to the details of their notations and conventions.

1.2 LANGUAGE SPECIFICATIONS

A formal description of the rules for generating strings in a language can be very intimidating; so in this section we will develop the formal rules in an informal way.

There are two types of symbols used in grammars. Terminal symbols are the only ones that can appear in the strings of the language. Nonterminal symbols are used to denote intermediate constructs in the derivations.

For example, English grammar uses concepts such as "noun phrase" and "adjectival clause." These intermediate constructs are used in derivations of English sentences. Thus each should be represented by a single nonterminal symbol. We introduce abbreviations, P for pronoun, etc., to denote the constructs by single symbols.

The terminal symbols of the English language are the letters of the alphabet, punctuation marks, and spaces.

The set of nonterminal symbols is denoted by N; the set of terminal symbols, by T. Every symbol which might arise in the generation process will be a member of the set $N \cup T$, where $\cup$ denotes set union. In this text we will use capital letters for nonterminal symbols.

The sentence symbol   One of the nonterminal symbols represents a special class of strings, usually called "sentences." Therefore it is called the "sentence symbol," and is usually denoted by S.

Rewriting rules   The set of rewriting rules is the heart of the language specification. Each rule has a left side and a right side, separated by $\rightarrow$. A rule specifies a conditional option available to the person attempting to generate a string in the language. We will call this person (or machine) the "generator of the language."

How does the generator construct a sentence? First, he begins with the sentence symbol, since that symbol denotes a sentence. Then he looks for a rule which tells him how a sentence might be formed. This must be one of the rewriting rules. For example, he might choose the rule $S \rightarrow a$, which means that the S can be replaced by a. Or he might choose the rule $S \rightarrow AB$. In this case the new string contains two nonterminal symbols; each must be replaced by other strings of symbols until all nonterminal symbols are removed. During this process the generator constructs a number of strings. The string resulting from the most recent application of a rule is the *working string* for the generator. The sequence of working strings used by the generator specifies a *derivation* of the string produced.

The rewriting rules specify how the generator may proceed from one working string of a derivation to the next working string of the derivation. Whenever the string on the left side of a rule is contained in the working string, the generator may replace it with the string which appears on the right side of the same rule. The reverse substitution is not allowed. If the rule is $S \rightarrow AB$, the generator cannot replace AB with S.

The derivation is complete when no rules can be used to modify the working string. If the final working string does not contain any nonterminal symbols, it is a sentence in the language.

Consider some simple languages.

Example 1   Terminal symbols: $\{a, -\}$; nonterminal symbols: $\{S\}$.

        Rules: $S \rightarrow a$

                   $S \rightarrow a - S$

       Let us simulate the generator of strings in this language. The sentence symbol must be the initial working string; so we write

     S

Either rule could be used to replace the S.   If we use the first rule, the new working string is

a

which is a string in the language (because it does not contain any nonterminal symbols).   However, if we choose to use the second rule, we obtain

$a - S$

Again, either rule can be applied, and we obtain

$a - a$

or

$a - a - S$

The options continue indefinitely, and the language will be

$\{X^n a | n \geq 0, X = a -\}$

using the first form of description.   ■

Rewriting rules may have several symbols on the left-hand side.   For example, consider the rule

$aA \rightarrow b$

The interpretation of this rule is that the generator may replace the sequence aA by b.   There is no inversion operation; we cannot "divide out the a" to get another rule,

$A \rightarrow a^{-1}b$

Example 2

Rules:	
$S \rightarrow AB?$	(1)
$A \rightarrow Awhich\Delta chased\Delta the\Delta rat\mathcal{L}$	(2)
$rat\Delta B \rightarrow rat\Delta which\Delta went B$	(3)
$B \rightarrow \Delta into\Delta the\Delta store$	(4)
$A \rightarrow Who\Delta saw\Delta the\Delta cat\Delta$	(5)

One derivation is

S	
$AB?$	(1)
$Awhich\Delta chased\Delta the\Delta rat\Delta B?$	(2)
$Awhich\Delta chased\Delta the\Delta rat\Delta which\Delta went B?$	(3)
$Who\Delta saw\Delta the\Delta cat\Delta which\Delta chased\Delta the\Delta rat\Delta which\Delta went B?$	(5)
$Who\Delta saw\Delta the\Delta cat\Delta which\Delta chased\Delta the\Delta rat\Delta which\Delta went\Delta into\Delta the\Delta store?$	(4)

The numbers on the right indicate which rule was used to produce the corresponding string.   Note that we could not apply rule 3 to the working string $AB?$ because the sequence $rat\Delta B$ does not occur, even though the B is present and even though the sequence $rat\Delta$ appears at the beginning of both sides of rule 3.   ■

The generator can get "stuck" by producing a working string which is not a sentence, but which cannot be modified by applying any rewriting rules.

Example 3   Take the same rules as in Example 2, but omit rule 4:

Rules:	$S \to AB?$	(1)
	$A \to A which\Delta chased\Delta the\Delta rat\Delta$	(2)
	$rat\Delta B \to rat\Delta which\Delta went B$	(3)
	$A \to Who\Delta saw\Delta the\Delta cat\Delta$	(5)

We might try the sequence

S

$AB?$	(1)
$A which\Delta chased\Delta the\Delta rat\Delta B?$	(2)
$A which\Delta chased\Delta the\Delta rat\Delta which\Delta went B?$	(3)
$Who\Delta saw\Delta the\Delta cat\Delta which\Delta chased\Delta the\Delta rat\Delta which\Delta went B?$	(5)

But we cannot proceed.   We must have made a poor choice somewhere.   Possibly by making another choice we could have derived a string of terminal symbols. But it is easy to see that the only choices we had involved continuing the use of rule 2, which would produce more copies of $which\Delta chased\Delta the\Delta rat\Delta$ after the first A.   There is no way to make this choice to keep out of the bind; we would still arrive at a point from which we could not proceed.   These rules describe a language which does not contain any strings!   ■

Some grammars have rules which shorten the length of the working string.

Example 4

Rules:	$S \to AB?$	(1)
	$A \to A\Delta which\Delta chased\Delta the\Delta rat$	(2)
	$A \to Who\Delta saw\Delta the\Delta cat B$	(3)
	$B \to \Delta which\Delta chased\Delta the\Delta mouse$	(4)
	$BB \to$	(5)

Two possible generation sequences are

S

$AB?$	(1)
$A\Delta which\Delta chased\Delta the\Delta rat B?$	(2)
$Who\Delta saw\Delta the\Delta cat B\Delta which\Delta chased\Delta the\Delta rat B?$	(3)
$Who\Delta saw\Delta the\Delta cat\Delta which\Delta chased\Delta the\Delta mouse\Delta which\Delta chased\Delta the\Delta rat B?$	(4)
$Who\Delta saw\Delta the\Delta cat\Delta which\Delta chased\Delta the\Delta mouse\Delta which\Delta chased\Delta the\Delta rat\Delta$	
$\quad which\Delta chased\Delta the\Delta mouse?$	(5)

and

S

$AB?$	(1)
$Who\Delta saw\Delta the\Delta cat BB?$	(3)
$Who\Delta saw\Delta the\Delta cat?$ ■	(5)

Summary of descriptions by generative rules   A language is described by specifying a set of terminal symbols T, a set of nonterminal symbols N, a particular nonterminal symbol S, and a set of rewriting rules R.   More formally:

A grammar is a quadruple $<T,N,S,R>$, where N,T are finite sets of symbols, $S \in N$ is the sentence symbol,† and R is a finite set of rewriting rules (or productions) of the form

$$\text{string}_1 \rightarrow \text{string}_2$$

The language L_G is the set of strings of terminal symbols which can be generated by a grammar G starting from the initial working string S, using rules from R to modify the working strings.

There are no restrictions on the forms of the two strings in a rewriting rule.

Some writers express the rewriting rules as a set of ordered pairs (S_1,S_2), where S_1 is the left-hand string and S_2 the right-hand string. We will use the form in which the two strings are connected by $\rightarrow$.

A double arrow is used to separate two strings, as in $S_1 \Rightarrow S_2$, whenever S_2 can be generated from S_1 by the single application of one rewriting rule. When several grammars are being considered, the form $S_1 \xrightarrow{G_1} S_2$ may be used to indicate that the rule used in the transformation was taken from grammar G_1. Context usually makes the subscript unnecessary.

Furthermore, the combination $\Rightarrow^*$ is used to indicate that a sequence of rewriting steps can be used to transform the left-hand string into the right-hand string. We can formally express this as:

$\alpha \xrightarrow{G_1}^* \beta$ if and only if there exists an integer k and strings $S_1, \ldots, S_k$ such that

1. $S_1 = \alpha$
2. $S_k = \beta$
3. $S_i \xrightarrow{G_1} S_{i+1}$, $1 \le i \le k - 1$

We use Greek letters to denote arbitrary strings of symbols from the "vocabulary" $V = N \cup T$. In addition, let the symbol λ denote the "empty string" (not the same as a space). For example, $ab\lambda c = a\lambda bc = \lambda\lambda abc = abc$.

Languages can be classified according to the forms of the rewriting rules used in their grammars. In the next section we state the grammatical bases for the classifications and give some examples; in later chapters we will explore the differences between the classes.

1.3 A CLASSIFICATION OF LANGUAGES

Grammars can be classified by the forms of the rewriting rules which are used in their definitions. The rules are classified by the forms of the strings on each side of each rule.

† We use $\in$ to denote set membership. Thus $S \in N$ is read "S belongs to the set N."

The classification scheme that we will use was introduced by Chomsky (1959a). In his scheme the only difference between the right and left sides of a rule can be that a *single* nonterminal symbol is replaced by a string of terminal symbols and/or nonterminal symbols.† In some cases the replacement may be allowed only if the nonterminal symbol appears in a certain context; in these cases the context is specified in the rule. The context must be the same on both sides of the rule. Thus the general form of a rewriting rule is

$$\varphi A \psi \rightarrow \varphi \alpha \psi \tag{1}$$

This rule specifies that A may be replaced by the string α whenever the A is found in the context $\varphi A \psi$. Occasionally, it is useful to name the components of the rule. We call φ the *left context*, ψ the *right context*, and α the *replacement string*. All these components may be arbitrary strings of terminal symbols and/or nonterminal symbols. They may be empty strings.

Example 1 The following rules have the proper form:

$$aAbcD \rightarrow abcDbcD$$
$$Abc \rightarrow abDbc$$
$$AB \rightarrow AbBc$$
$$AC \rightarrow A$$
$$C \rightarrow \lambda$$

The first rule specifies the replacement of A in the context $aAbcD$ by bcD. The second rule specifies a replacement which requires a right context, but no left context. The third and fourth rules require only a left context. A nonterminal symbol is erased in the fourth and fifth rules. ■

Type 0 Rules of the unrestricted form (1) are called type 0 rules. If a grammar contains only type 0 rules, it is a type 0 grammar, and the language that it specifies is a type 0 language. Since there are no restrictions on the components of type 0 rules, any rule is a type 0 rule, and any Chomsky grammar specifies a type 0 language. Type 0 languages are also called *recursive* languages.

Type 1 Type 1 rules are like type 0 rules, except that erasure of the nonterminal symbol is not permitted. The general form of a type 1 rule is

$$\varphi A \psi \rightarrow \varphi \alpha \psi \qquad \text{where } \alpha \neq \lambda \tag{2}$$

---

† In Prob. 5 of Sec. 3.3 we will see that this restriction does not cause loss of generality; the more complex rules in our previous examples can be replaced by a set of these simpler rules.

Example 2   The rules
$$aAbcD \rightarrow abcDbcD$$
$$Abc \rightarrow abDbc$$
$$AB \rightarrow AbBc$$
$$C \rightarrow wxCb$$
are type 1 rules.   The last two rules of Example 1 are not type 1 rules.   ■

Any grammar which contains only type 1 rules is a type 1 grammar. A type 1 grammar specifies a type 1 language.   Type 1 rules, grammars, and languages are often called *context-sensitive,* or *context-dependent.*

Type 2   Type 2 rules are like type 1 rules, except that there cannot be any context.   Their general form is

$$A \rightarrow \alpha \qquad \text{where } \alpha \neq \lambda \tag{3}$$

Example 3   The following are type 2 rules.
$$A \rightarrow abcA$$
$$A \rightarrow a$$
$$B \rightarrow AB$$
$$B \rightarrow xA \quad ■$$

Type 2 rules appear in the grammars of type 2 languages.   Since there is no context dependence, type 2 languages are known as *context-free* languages.

Type 3   Type 3 rules are like type 2 rules, but the replacement string is restricted to be either a single terminal symbol or a single terminal symbol followed by a single nonterminal symbol.   The general form of type 3 rules is

$$A \rightarrow \alpha \qquad \text{where } \alpha = a \text{ or } \alpha = aB \tag{4}$$

where a is a terminal symbol and B is a nonterminal symbol.

Example 4   The following rules are type 3 rules:
$$A \rightarrow bX$$
$$X \rightarrow cX$$
$$X \rightarrow d$$
$$X \rightarrow eY$$
$$Y \rightarrow f \quad ■$$

Type 3 rules are used in type 3 grammars, which specify type 3 languages.   Type 3 languages are also called *regular* languages.   We will discuss the reason for this name in Chap. 2.

We will use *type i* to represent the set of all languages of type i ($0 \leq i \leq 3$).

A language of type n is also of type m if $m < n$, since the restrictions on the form of the rewriting rules increase as the numerals increase. Thus there are at least as many type 0 languages as there are type 1 languages, etc.; that is,

Theorem 1   If $n > m$, the set of languages of type m is at least as large as the set of languages of type n. (Or $n > m$ implies *type n $\subseteq$ type m*.)

Do the increasing restrictions actually decrease the number of languages? In other words, is there a language which can be described by a type n grammar but not by a type $n + 1$ grammar? It will turn out that the answer is yes, for all applicable $n(0,1,2)$. To prove any result of this nature requires a proof that something does not belong in a specified class. It is hard to formulate and prove statements of this kind. After we have studied more of the properties of the various classes of languages, we will be able to prove this statement.

Other classifications of languages can be based upon the relationship between languages and machines. We will discuss some of these classifications after we establish the relationships between machine models and type i languages in Chaps. 2 to 5.

PROBLEMS

1. For each rewriting rule in the examples of this section, find the highest type number which can be used to classify the rule.

2. Find the highest type number which can be applied to each of the following grammars:

    (a) $G_1 = \langle T,N,S,R \rangle = \langle \{a,b,c\}, \{A,B,S\},S,R \rangle$, where R contains the rules

$S \rightarrow Aa$

$A \rightarrow c$

$A \rightarrow Ba$

$B \rightarrow abc$

    (b) $G_2 = \langle T,N,S,R \rangle = \langle \{a,b,c,d\}, \{S,A,B\},S,R \rangle$, where R contains the rules

$S \rightarrow ASB$

$S \rightarrow d$

$A \rightarrow aA$

$aaA \rightarrow aaBc$

$B \rightarrow dcb$

$A \rightarrow b$

    (c) $G_3 = \langle T,N,S,R \rangle = \langle \{a,b,c\}, \{S,X,Y\},S,R \rangle$, where R contains the rules

$S \rightarrow aX$

$X \rightarrow bS$

$S \rightarrow cY$

$Y \rightarrow bY$

$Y \rightarrow c$

$X \rightarrow a$

(d) $G_4 = \langle T,N,S,R \rangle = \langle \{a,b\}, \{S,X\},S,R \rangle$, where R contains the rules

$S \rightarrow aX$

$X \rightarrow aX$

$X \rightarrow \lambda$

(e) $G_5 = \langle T,N,S,R \rangle = \langle \{a,b\}, \{S\},S,R \rangle$, where R contains the rules

$S \rightarrow aSb$

$S \rightarrow ab$

(f) $G_6 = \langle T,N,S,R \rangle = \langle \{a,b\}, \{S\},S,R \rangle$, where R contains the rules

$S \rightarrow aS$

$S \rightarrow a$

3. Find at least three strings in each of the languages specified by the grammars of Prob. 2.

1.4 DERIVATION TREES

As we generate a sentence, we use the rewriting rules to proceed from the sentence symbol S to a string of terminal symbols. At some steps in the derivation we might be able to apply any one of several rewriting rules to the working string. If the use of any one of the rules does not affect the applicability of the other rules, the same string will be derived if the rules are used in any arbitrary sequence. The particular sequence in which the rules were applied is not important in specifying how the string was derived. The important feature of the derivation is its *structure*.

One way to specify a derivation is by writing down the sequence of working strings which are used during the derivation. This sequence contains information about the particular sequence of rule applications which was chosen. However, it does not emphasize the structure of the derivation.

Example 1 Let G have the following rewriting rules:

$S \rightarrow ASB$

$S \rightarrow a$

$A \rightarrow ($

$B \rightarrow)$

One derivation in G is

S

ASB

$(SB$

(S)

(a)

Another derivation which produces the same string is

S

ASB

AaB

$Aa)$

(a)

These derivations are basically the same. The A, S, and B of the second string become the (, a, and) of the sentence, respectively.

How can we depict only the essential structural information? For a context-free language we can use a tree structure. For example, a simple sentence diagram is a tree structure which describes the analysis of the sentence. The *derivation tree* resembles a sentence diagram. It expresses the structure of the generation process, and is useful to aid intuition. A derivation tree for one string in the language of Example 1 is shown in Fig. 1.4.1. In the tree, a line is drawn downward from a nonterminal symbol to each symbol in the sequence which replaced it in some step. When the replacement sequence contains more than one symbol, these symbols are written in order from left to right, and a line is drawn to each from the "parent" nonterminal symbol. Since we preserve the left-to-right sequencing, it is easy to read the string from left to right across the "bottom" of the tree.

The symbols in the tree are at the *nodes* of the tree; the lines joining the nodes are the *branches*. The node which does not have any predecessors is the *root* of the tree.

In a derivation D of string σ, we call a nonterminal symbol A an ancestor of symbol B if D may include a sequence of working strings such that

$$\varphi A \psi \Rightarrow^* \alpha B \beta$$

for some $\varphi, \psi, \alpha, \beta$. The derivation tree depicts this ancestral relationship, in the same way that a family tree depicts the relationships between various members of a family. In the linguistic context, we will refer to these relationships collectively as the "structure" of a string.

A symbol at a node of a derivation tree can be considered to represent the string whose derivation is depicted by the subtree having its root at that node. For example, in Fig. 1.4.1, the lowest S represents the string (a).

The meaning of a string can be made more evident by its derivation tree if the grammar is constructed so that each nonterminal symbol represents a "natural unit" of the meaning. In natural English, these units are "noun phrase," "adverbial clause," and so on. In programming languages, these units represent the results of individual sequences of computations. All compiler languages contain facilities for specifying algebraic expressions. The meaning of these expressions can be depicted by a tree structure, because the set of well-formed algebraic expressions is a context-free language.

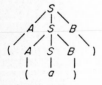

Fig. 1.4.1   Derivation tree for the string $((a))$ using the grammar of Example 1.

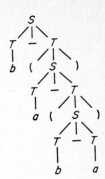

Fig. 1.4.2 Derivation tree for Example 2.

Example 2 Let G_A be a grammar with the following rewriting rules:

$$S \rightarrow T$$
$$S \rightarrow T - T$$
$$T \rightarrow a$$
$$T \rightarrow b$$
$$T \rightarrow (S)$$

Some strings in the language are

a
$a - b$
$a - (a - b)$
$b - (a - (b - a))$

The derivation tree for the last one is shown in Fig. 1.4.2.

Suppose that numeric values were assigned to a and b. The numeric value of the symbolic expression can be found by performing subtractions at places in the derivation tree which correspond to the S nodes that were replaced by using the second rule.

For example, suppose that the numeric values of a and b were 5 and 3. To evaluate the expression using the tree, first replace each symbol by the corresponding numeric value. This produces the tree of Fig. 1.4.3. Three rules are used to evaluate the expression:

1. A T node and its single descendant with a numeric value can be replaced by a single node associated with the same numeric value (Fig. 1.4.4a).

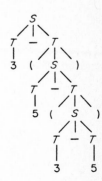

Fig. 1.4.3 Derivation tree with numeric values.

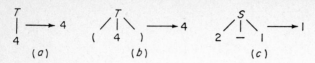

Fig. 1.4.4 Evaluation of simple subtrees in Example 2.
(a) Evaluating a term;   (b) evaluating a parenthesized term;
(c) evaluating a difference.

2. A T node and its three descendants, (, a numeric value, and), can be replaced by a single node associated with the same numeric value (Fig. 1.4.4b).
3. An S node and its three descendants, a numeric value, $-$, and a second numeric value, can be replaced by a single node associated with the difference of the two values (Fig. 1.4.4c).

Any node which does not meet the conditions of these rules cannot be "evaluated" until its immediate descendants are evaluated and the conditions met.

Each evaluation rule removes nodes from the tree. The process of evaluation is complete when the tree is reduced to a single node which is associated with the numeric value of the expression. The evaluation of our expression is shown in Fig. 1.4.5. The value of the expression is -4. ■

The evaluation rules are the semantics of the language. The evaluation rules in the example have a one-to-one correspondence with the rewriting

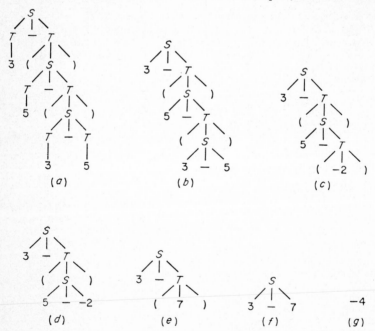

Fig. 1.4.5 Steps in the evaluation of the expression of Fig. 1.4.3.

rules of the grammar. Each evaluation rule defines the meaning of the structure created by the corresponding rewriting rule.

In the following example, this simple relationship does not hold, and the evaluation process cannot be described with the aid of the derivation tree.

Example 3   Consider G_3, a grammar with the rewriting rules

$$S \rightarrow S + S$$
$$S \rightarrow S * S$$
$$S \rightarrow a$$
$$S \rightarrow b$$

One derivation is

S
$S + S$
$S + S * S$
$S + S * S + S$
$\cdot \quad \cdot \quad \cdot \quad \cdot \quad \cdot$
$a + b * a + b$

with the tree shown in Fig. 1.4.6.

Consider a set of evaluation rules similar to those of Example 2:

1. An S node and its three descendants associated with a numeric value, $+$, and a second numeric value can be replaced by a single node associated with the sum of the two numeric values.
2. An S node and its three descendants associated with a numeric value, $*$, and a second numeric value can be replaced by a single node associated with the product of the two numeric values.

If $a = 5$, $b = 3$, the value of the expression $a + b * a + b$ is 29, using the tree of Fig. 1.4.6 and these evaluation rules. However, an evaluation using conventional† algebraic interpretations yields 23. Thus this grammar describes a language that contains only expressions which are legitimate in conventional algebra, but evaluations using a correspondence with the grammar may not yield the conventional algebraic interpretations. The problem arises because the grammar does not describe the conventional rule that multiplications are performed before additions. We conclude that this grammar is not very useful for describing algebraic expressions. ■

† We use $*$ to denote multiplication.

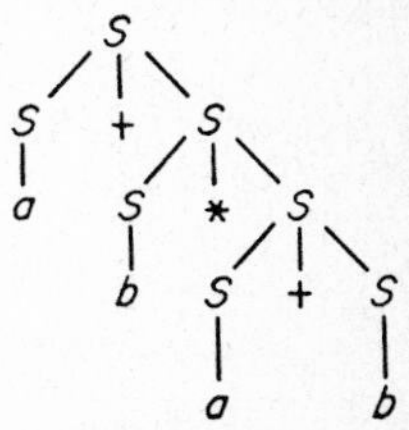

Fig. 1.4.6   Derivation tree for Example 3.

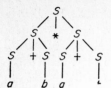

    Fig. 1.4.7 Another derivation of $a + b * a + b$ using G_3.

Ambiguity Ambiguity is an important property of a grammar and its strings. A string σ is *ambiguous in grammar G* if there exist at least two derivations of σ in G which have different derivation trees. A grammar G is *ambiguous* if there exists at least one string in the language L_G which is ambiguous in the grammar. An *unambiguous* grammar is not ambiguous.

Example 4 An ambiguous English sentence is:

    In all books examined sentences were not ambiguous.

    The ambiguity arises because "examined" may modify either "books" or "sentences." In the first case one concludes that none of the sentences in any of the books were ambiguous. In the second case there may be ambiguous sentences which did not happen to be examined. ■

Example 5 The grammar of Example 3 is ambiguous because the string $a + b * a + b$ has two derivations. One of these derivations was shown in Fig. 1.4.6. Another is shown in Fig. 1.4.7.

    If we use the derivation tree of Fig. 1.4.7 to evaluate the expression with $a = 5$, $b = 3$, we obtain a different value, 64. The important point is not that this value is conventionally incorrect, but that it differs from the value obtained from the other derivation tree. The "value" of the expression is not well defined because it is ambiguous. ■

The ambiguity of a sentence depends upon the particular grammar being used. Thus a given language might be ambiguously described by grammar G_1 and unambiguously described by grammar G_2. Suppose that we are given a language and that we want to find an unambiguous grammar to describe the language, if one exists. Thus we ask the question, "Given a language L, does there exist an unambiguous grammar of type i which describes L?" If the answer to the question is no, the language is an inherently ambiguous type i language. A language L is an *inherently ambiguous* type i language if there does not exist an unambiguous type i grammar which describes L.

Example 6 The language of Example 3 is an unambiguous context-free language because the unambiguous grammar with these rewriting rules describes it.

$S \rightarrow T + S$
$S \rightarrow T$
$T \rightarrow T * T$
$T \rightarrow a$
$T \rightarrow b$ ■

To determine whether a language or a grammar is ambiguous or un-ambiguous, we must either find the counterexample or show that it does not exist.   The sentence in Example 4 proves that the English language is in-herently ambiguous, because the sentence has two meanings whose inter-pretations require that there exist two derivation trees for the string.   In general, it is difficult to determine whether a language is inherently ambiguous.

We need to define derivation trees for context-sensitive languages if we want to define ambiguity precisely for these languages.   Since we will not discuss this case further in this book (ambiguity questions are hard enough for context-free languages), we will not define derivation trees for the context-sensitive case.   We will continue the discussion of the ambiguity and inherent ambiguity of context-free languages in Chaps. 8 and 9.

PROBLEMS

1. Draw derivation trees for the three shortest strings in the languages of Example 1 of Sec. 1.2.

2. How would you test a derivation tree against a set of rewriting rules to make sure that the rules were followed correctly?

3. How would you generate a set of rewriting rules for a context-free grammar such that all the derivation trees in a given set of trees represent derivations in that grammar? Consider the set of trees in Fig. 1.4.8.

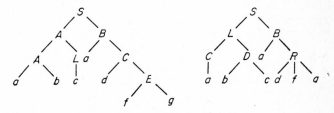

Fig. 1.4.8 A set of derivations in some language

4. Using the grammar and evaluation rules of Example 2:
   (a) Find derivation trees for the strings
   $a - b$
   $(a - b) - (b - (b - a))$
   $(a - b) - (b - (a))$
   $(b) - (a - (b - (a - (b))))$
   (b) Evaluate each of the expressions of part a when $a = 7$, $b = 22$. Be sure to use the tree in the evaluation process

5. (a) Find a context-free grammar which specifies a language containing all algebraic expressions in the variables x, y, and z, with binary operators $+$, $-$, $*$ and parentheses (and).   Do not include numeric coefficients in the expressions (see part b).   Construct the grammar so that the syntactic structure of an expression reflects the evaluation pro-cedure used in conventional algebra.

   (b) Modify the grammar of part a to include decimal (base 10) integers without leading zeros as coefficients of terms.   Be sure that your answer restricts the form of terms so that the coefficient must be the first factor in the term (forms like $x * 2 * y$ should be excluded).

(*c*) Modify the grammar of part *b* to remove the multiplication signs from the expressions. Can you do this without introducing erasing rules?

(*d*) Modify the grammar of part *c* to allow unary minus signs [as in $-a + (-b - c)$].

1.5 TESTS FOR MEMBERSHIP

Consider the following *membership question*:

Given a grammar G and a string σ, is the string σ in the language L_G generated by the grammar?

The membership question is an important question. If we could build a machine to answer the membership question, we would have a mechanical device for testing the validity of sentences. The basic portions of automata theory concentrate on the structures of machines which answer the membership question for various types of languages. This part of the theory is discussed in Chaps. 2 to 5.

Even without defining a machine, we can discuss how we could informally answer the membership question.

Consider a context-sensitive grammar G and the derivation of σ, some string in the language. Between any two steps of the derivation, the working string cannot get shorter (since erasing is not allowed). There are only a finite number of rewriting rules; hence a finite number of choices at each step of a derivation. Therefore, by performing a finite number of steps, we could derive any string in the language having length less than n, where n is any finite integer. If string σ is of length n, we can list the strings in L_G of length less than $n + 1$ and see whether σ is on the list. Hence we can answer the membership question whenever the grammar is context-sensitive. Since the sets of context-free and regular languages are subsets of the set of context-sensitive languages, the same procedure can be used with these languages.

Example 1 Consider G_3 from Example 3 of Sec. 1.4. The rewriting rules are:

$S \rightarrow S + S$
$S \rightarrow S * S$
$S \rightarrow a$
$S \rightarrow b$

We wish to determine whether $a + ab$ is a string in L_{G_3}. Since there are four symbols in the string to be tested, we must list all strings in L_{G_3} which are less than five symbols long. They are

a
b
$a + a$
$a + b$
$b + a$
$b + b$
$a * a$
$a * b$
$b * a$
$b * b$

Any other attempt to produce a derivation in G_3 will result in working strings which have more than four symbols.   For example, one attempt is

S

$S + S$

$S + S * S$

Because there are no erasing rules in the grammar, this particular attempt may be aborted after this step.

Since $a + ab$ does not appear in the list, it must not be a string in L_{G_3}.   ■

Unfortunately, we cannot always answer the membership question when the grammar is recursive.   The difficulty is that since symbols can be erased, we never know how long to keep trying to derive the string.   Therefore we might explore one sequence of choices indefinitely without ever learning the answer to the membership question.   This statement does not mean that we cannot answer the membership question for some *particular* string and a *particular* grammar; it means that we cannot build a machine which can examine any recursive grammar and any string and always tell us whether the string is in the language.

PROBLEMS

1.   Test each of the strings S_j for membership in each of the languages L_{G_i}, specified by grammars G_i, having the rewriting rules listed below.

$S_1 = aab$

$S_2 = abcd$

$S_3 = aabb$

Rules for G_1: $S \rightarrow aS$

$\qquad\qquad\quad\ S \rightarrow Sb$ aab

$\qquad\qquad\quad\ S \rightarrow a$

$\qquad\qquad\quad\ S \rightarrow c$

$\qquad\qquad\quad\ S \rightarrow cd$

Rules for G_2: $S \rightarrow AB$

$\qquad\qquad\quad\ A \rightarrow aa$

$\qquad\qquad\quad\ aB \rightarrow a$

$\qquad\qquad\quad\ A \rightarrow aA$

$\qquad\qquad\quad\ B \rightarrow bcd$

$\qquad\qquad\quad\ AB \rightarrow aB$

2.   Suppose that a given context-sensitive grammar has r rewriting rules, at most k rules with the same single nonterminal symbol being replaced on the left sides of the rules.   Also assume that every rewriting rule increases the length of the string.

(a) Derive a formula for the maximum number of steps required to derive any string of length n.

(b) Derive a formula for the maximum number of derivations which must be examined to determine the membership question for a string of length n.

(c) What additional quantities enter into the problem if rewriting rules of the form $A \rightarrow B$ are allowed in the grammar?

3. Devise a membership test for strings in the language specified by the recursive grammar with the following rewriting rules:

$$S \to AS$$
$$S \to BS$$
$$S \to CS$$
$$BC \to BcBC$$
$$C \to cC$$
$$C \to c$$
$$B \to bB$$
$$B \to b$$
$$AB \to B$$
$$AA \to aAB$$
$$A \to a$$

(*Hint:* Consider the number of b's in the string.)

1.6 TRANSFORMATIONAL GRAMMARS

Large problems can be handled more easily if they are divided into smaller parts. A useful division of a problem should be made so that (1) each piece is easy to describe (and analyze) and (2) the interrelationships between the pieces are easy to specify.

Most large computer programs are divided into a "main program" and numerous "subroutines," each subroutine using a portion of the data and performing a simply described operation on that data (the operation may be complex in detail, though it can be specified in a simple way). Many mathematical proofs are divided into lemmas, which are analogous to subroutines in computer programs. The hardware of a digital computer is divided into "functional blocks," such as adders, accumulators, memory units, etc.; these blocks are also analogous to subroutines.

In mathematical linguistics a nonterminal symbol might be considered to be a subroutine name. This association is not useful. A useful division can be made by partitioning the derivation into a "first part," "last part," and possibly a sequence of middle parts. A derivation divided in this way has the form shown in Fig. 1.6.1. The derivation in the first grammar starts with S as its initial working string and produces σ_1, a sequence of terminal symbols of G. The second portion of the derivation begins with σ_1 as the first working string, and uses the second grammar to derive σ_2, a string of terminal symbols of the second grammar. Succeeding portions of the derivation are similar. The last one produces σ, a string in the language.

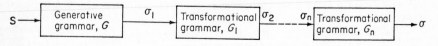

Fig. 1.6.1 The division of a derivation.

The second and succeeding grammars in this structure transform one string into another string. Therefore these grammars are known as *transformational grammars*.

The action of a transformational grammar can also be depicted in the derivation tree. The original grammar produces a top portion of the tree; succeeding transformational grammars add branches and nodes to the tree. Figure 1.6.2 shows the relationship between the derivation tree and the transformational grammars.

A transformational grammar can be specified in exactly the same way that a generative grammar is specified, except that a sentence symbol is not distinguished. Any classification scheme used for generative grammars can be used for transformational grammars.

Transformational grammars have been used to create grammars for natural languages. Simple grammars are used to generate a string describing the gross structure of a sentence (this string corresponds to σ_1 in Fig. 1.6.1), while more complex transformational grammars are used to change this structure into a word sequence.

We will use transformational grammars in some proofs, especially in Chaps. 3, 4, and 7. Usually, we will use the transformational grammar to prove certain lemmas, which provide the framework for the proof. Often we draw a parallel between the transformational grammar and a machine with nontrivial inputs and outputs.

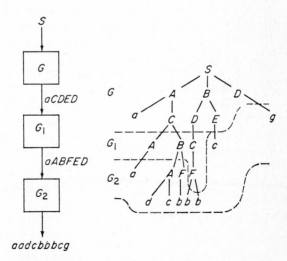

Fig. 1.6.2 A derivation of *aadcbbbcg* using two transformational grammars. (The dashed lines separate the portions of the tree added by the different grammars.)

1.7 OPERATIONS ON LANGUAGES

Many different operations can be applied to languages. Most of them fall
into two classes. The first class includes those operations which are basically
set-theoretic operations. The second class includes those operations which
operate on individual strings from one language to produce individual strings
in another language.

The set-theoretic operations that we will use are union, denoted $\cup$;
intersection, denoted $\cap$; and complement, denoted $\sim$. The union of two
languages L_1 and L_2 is a third language $L_3 = L_1 \cup L_2$, containing all strings
which were contained in either L_1 or L_2 (or both). Their intersection is the
language $L_4 = L_1 \cap L_2$, containing only those strings which were contained
in both L_1 and L_2. Finally, the complement of L_1 is the language $L_5 = \sim L_1$,
containing those strings (using the same terminal symbols as used for L_1) which
are not contained in L_1.

The second class of operations includes many which cannot be defined
until we have discussed machines (most of these are discussed in Chap. 7).
One which does not depend upon machines is the operation of reversal. Let
x's denote symbols. The reverse of $\sigma = x_1 x_2 \cdots x_n$ is $\sigma^R = x_n \cdots x_2 x_1$.
The reverse of language L is the language

$$L^R = \{\sigma^R | \sigma \in L\}$$

In later discussions we will use phraseology like "the set of type 3
languages is closed under the operation of union," or just "closed under
union." Either phrase means that the union of any arbitrarily chosen type 3
languages is also a type 3 language.

PROBLEMS

1. Prove that if a class of languages is closed under intersection and complement, then
it is closed under union.

2. Is the following statement true or false? Why?

If a class of languages is closed under intersection and union, then it may not be
closed under complement.

3. Let $L = \{1^n 2^n 1^m | m,n \geq 1\}$. Find a specification of the language $L \cap L^R$ without
using Boolean operators in your specification.

1.8 COMMENTS

In this chapter we have discussed how the mathematical linguist describes
languages by specifying the syntax of the language. Some intuitive concepts
lead to formal descriptions involving vocabularies and rewriting rules.
Grammars can be classified according to the forms of the rewriting rules.
Derivations of strings in context-free languages can be depicted in tree diagrams. The structure of the tree not only shows the derivation but may also

show the structure of the meaning of the string. When the meaning and the tree can be so closely related, it is desirable that the rewriting rules of the grammar be stated so that this relationship does hold.

When two different trees describe derivations of the same string in the same grammar, the string is ambiguous in that grammar. Unambiguous grammars are very desirable, but they may be hard to find for some languages.

In succeeding chapters we investigate the relationship between machine structures and language classifications. Regular languages and finite-state machines form the simplest case, which is the subject of Chap. 2. Turing machines and recursive languages, which are the most general case, are discussed in Chap. 3. There are many classes of languages which lie between these extremes; some of these are described in Chaps. 4, 5, and 6. Finally, in Chaps. 7, 8, and 9, we prove results which are often formulated in terms of linguistic descriptions, rather than in terms of machines. We will follow our machine orientation and prove these results in terms of machine analogs when possible.

The concepts of a grammar and language were developed extensively first by Chomsky (1959a), though similar concepts have been used by logicians for some time [see, for example, Post (1946) or Davis (1958)]. Chomsky introduced the scheme for language classification that we are using.

2
Finite-state Machines

Every actual machine can have only a finite number of components.   Therefore it can have only a finite number of states.   Thus every actual machine is a finite-state machine.

Automata theorists study many different models of machines with infinite memories, or an infinite number of states.   All these models include an infinite memory, but the machine is controlled by a finite-state machine. Thus an understanding of finite-state machines is essential to an understanding of infinite-state machines.

Many of the basic concepts related to finite-state machines are used in conjunction with the synthesis of sequential circuits.   These include not only the fundamental concept of state, but also the use of enumeration techniques to describe the behavior of machines.   Enumeration techniques are best suited to machines with small numbers of states or for use by computers, which can tolerate the tedium of the enumeration.

Large machines often can be specified by giving an algorithmic description of their behavior, as in a programmer's flow chart.   This technique is especially useful when the machine has many states but a simple structure. We will discuss this technique in this chapter so that it can be introduced in a familiar context.   We will use it to describe some machines, not because it will be the most effective technique, but because the examples will demonstrate the relationship between the various description techniques in simple cases. The technique will be quite useful in later chapters when we need to describe complex algorithms.

Because finite-state machines are familiar to most readers, we use this model as a vehicle for the introduction of some concepts which are commonly used in automata theory.   We use the finite-state model as a vehicle, not because the concepts provide new insights about the behavior of finite-state machines, but because the familiar finite-state context allows the reader to develop some insight about the concepts before we proceed to new machine models.   The most important concepts are the relationship between machine models and linguistic models, the use of tapes for inputs, and the notion of determinism.   We review the basic concepts of finite-state machines before we return to these more advanced topics.

2.1 THE MODEL

Inputs   Consider a digital circuit which has a single binary-valued input x. A clock synchronizes events.   The circuit ignores the value of x except when the clock indicates an integer value of time.   In this way the value of x is "sampled" at integer values of time; let x_t denote the value of x at time t. If x is binary, x_t will be binary (we ignore pathological cases which arise if the sampling instant happens to coincide with a change in the value of x).

Most interesting circuits do not have single binary inputs.   Either they have a number of binary-valued inputs or they have a single multivalued input.   In either case we can consider the inputs to be encoded versions of the symbols of some finite alphabet—the input alphabet.

Outputs   In a similar way we consider the outputs from the circuit to be encoded forms of symbols from an output alphabet.

States   Suppose that we want to build a circuit to produce a binary-valued output z.   Let z_t be the (sampled) value of z at time t.   We wish to design the circuit so that z_t will be 1 if and only if x_{t-1} and x_{t-2} were both 1.   If the circuit is to perform this task, it must "remember" something about the history of the sequence of x's.   We describe this memory capability by the word "state" —if two copies of a machine are in two different states, they are remembering two different things about the past.

We need not restrict our thinking about states to this history perspective.   In fact, there are two ways to think about the state of a machine: as a history of the past input behavior or as a prediction of the future output behavior. The two viewpoints are exemplified by the statements, "The input sequence ended with two 1's in a row" and "If the next input is 1, then the output will be 1 at that time." Both viewpoints are useful. The former is especially useful in deciding how the next state is to be determined; the latter, in determining what outputs the network should produce. Of course, the two viewpoints are equivalent; the above statements reflect only the predominant thinking in a human mind at certain points in the design or analysis processes.

History   Let us design a circuit to produce $z = 1$ at time t if and only if the input x had been 1 at times $t - 1$ and $t - 2$. At each time instant, the machine must determine (1) the new state of the machine and (2) the output from the machine. The two parts of the problem cannot be completely separated, because the states were introduced so that the correct outputs would be produced. Once we know what kind of historical information is required to produce the output signals, we can separate the problem into these two parts. In this example, at time t the state information must tell something about the input values at times $t - 1$ and $t - 2$. We do not need to know the values of the input signal at times before $t - 2$ to produce the proper output signals.

   Since the state information must tell something about the input sequences x_{t-2}, x_{t-1}, we begin the synthesis by assuming that the machine may have to distinguish between all four possible sequences. Thus we assign arbitrary names to these four sequences (Table 2.1.1). We should remember that at a later step, in a realistic synthesis, a procedure will be used to determine whether all four input sequences need be distinguished to produce the required output signals. We cannot make this simplification until we have determined both the state transitions and the output generation for the machine. Since the number of possible values of the input is finite and the

Table 2.1.1   The states of a sequence detector

State at time $t = s_t$	Input sequence	
	x_{t-2}	x_{t-1}
A	0	0
B	0	1
C	1	0
D	1	1

Table 2.1.2 The state transitions for the state assignment of Table 2.1.1

	x_t	
s_t	0	1
A	A	B
B	C	D
C	A	B
D	C	D

number of possible states is finite, we can specify these functions by enumerating all possible cases.

First consider the state transition function. Suppose that the machine is in state C at time t and that $x_t = 1$. What should the state be at time $t + 1$? The significant input values are $x_{t-1} = 0$ (because $s_t = C$) and $x_t = 1$. Therefore $s_{t+1} = B$. Using similar reasoning on every combination of present state and input, we can complete Table 2.1.2, specifying the "next state" for all combinations of present state and present input symbol.

Now consider the generation of the output signals. In this simple case, the output at time t does not depend upon the input at time t, and it can be described in a single column added to the transition table. In fact, the output is 1 for only one state (Table 2.1.3).

To complete the description of the machine we must specify its initial state—the state the machine is in when the first input symbol is presented to it. We arbitrarily choose $t = 0$ as the time that the first input symbol is presented to the machine. If the machine is started in state B or state D, it will produce an incorrect output at time 1 if $x_0 = 1$. Thus the initial state must be A or

Table 2.1.3 A complete description of a machine to recognize sequences ending in 11

	x_t		
s_t	0	1	z_t
$\rightarrow A$	A	B	0
B	C	D	0
C	A	B	0
D	C	D	1

C. We arbitrarily choose A. The initial state of the machine is indicated by an arrow pointing toward the row of the transition table which corresponds to the initial state. Table 2.1.3 is a complete description of an unsimplified machine to perform our task.

Prediction   The other viewpoint of state is based on considering the present state of the machine as a predictor of the machine's future behavior. Thus, if the present state and present and future inputs are known, the present and future outputs can be determined. It is important to remember that the states are a means to an end (the output signal), and not the end itself. The present state of a machine cannot be observed directly; it can only be inferred from the input-output behavior of the machine either in the future or in the immediate past.

We can use this viewpoint of state to simplify the descriptions of finite-state machines.

Suppose that we have several copies of a machine M and let S_1 and S_2 be two states of M. Perform the following experiment on two copies of M. Start one in state S_1, the other in state S_2. Give both copies the same input sequence, and observe the output sequences. There are two cases. In the first case, the two output signals are different; so the differing initial conditions must have been the cause of the difference. Thus the distinction between S_1 and S_2 is important for predicting the future behavior of machine M. In the second case, the two output sequences are the same, for any input sequence. In this case, the distinction between S_1 and S_2 is not significant for predicting the future behavior of M. We call S_1 and S_2 *equivalent* in the second case.

In the machine of Table 2.1.3, we can distinguish state D from states A, B, and C by observing the output at the initial moment. Therefore state D is not equivalent to any other state of the machine. Is there a way to distinguish states A, B, and C from each other? Suppose that the machine is in one of these three states at time 0. If $x_0 = 1$, then $z_1 = 1$ if and only if $s_0 = B$. Thus B can be distinguished from A and C. However, A and C

Table 2.1.4   A machine equivalent to the machine of Table 2.1.3

	x_t		
s_t	0	1	z_t
→A	A	B	0
B	A	D	0
D	A	D	1

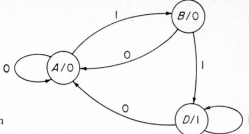

Fig. 2.1.1 The state transition graph
of the machine in Table 2.1.4.

cannot be distinguished from each other by applying an input sequence of
length 1.   After the input sequence of length 1, the machine will be in the
same state whether it started in *A* or *C*.   Thus future outputs must be identical, and *A* and *C* cannot be distinguished by observing the output.   States
A and *C* are equivalent because they "predict" the same output sequences in
response to any input sequence.   All but one of the members of a set of
equivalent states can be removed from the description of a machine.   We replace all of them by the remaining one.   The simplified machine (with *C*
removed) is described in Table 2.1.4.

The concept of equivalence can be generalized to machines.   Two
machines M_1 and M_2 are said to be equivalent if input-output experiments
cannot be used to determine whether M_1 or M_2 is the machine performing the
computation.   Procedures for performing equivalence tests are described in
detail in texts on sequential circuit synthesis.   In this book we are not concerned with simplification, but we will be concerned with two notions from
the above discussion: equivalence and the state as a predictor.

Transition graphs   The information in the transition table can be represented in a graph in which the nodes of the graph represent the states and the
(directed) branches represent the changes of state which can be caused by the
input signal at one instant of time.   Every branch is labeled with the input
symbol which will cause the transition to take place.   For example, the state
transitions of Table 2.1.4 are represented by the *transition graph* of Fig. 2.1.1.
The name of a state is written within the circle which represents that state.
The initial state is shown by drawing an arrow which does not come from
any state to the circle representing the initial state.

Outputs: Moore vs. Mealy models   In our example the output signal
at time *t* did not depend upon the input signal at time *t* and the output signal
could be associated with the state.   The finite-state-machine model which
includes this restriction was first described by Moore (1956) and is known as
the *Moore model*.   The outputs from a Moore machine can be depicted in

Table 2.1.5 A Mealy machine equivalent to the Moore machine of Table 2.1.4

	x_t	
s_t	0	1
$\rightarrow A$	$A, 0$	$B, 0$
B	$A, 0$	$B, 1$

an extra column of the transition table (as in Table 2.1.4) or within the nodes of the transition graph.   If the nodes of the transition graph are labeled, the label is placed before a separating slash and the output is placed after the slash (as in Fig. 2.1.1).

When the output at time t depends upon both the input at time t and the state at time t, the output signal cannot be associated with the state alone. The model which allows this additional complexity was first described by Mealy (1955) and is known as the *Mealy model*.   The outputs from a Mealy machine can be specified in the entries of the transition table with the next state specification.   In a transition graph the outputs are associated with the branches.   Each branch is labeled with the input and output symbols, separated by a slash (the input symbol being first).   Table 2.1.5 and Fig. 2.1.2 describe a Mealy machine, which is equivalent to the Moore machine of Table 2.1.4 and Fig. 2.1.1.

Straightforward procedures can be used to convert a Moore model of a machine into a Mealy model, and vice versa.   A change from a Mealy model to a Moore model may introduce some delay in the output signals, because the Moore model cannot give instantaneous responses to input signals.   The choice of a Moore model or a Mealy model is not important in the questions of automata theory.   Usually the Moore model is more convenient.

Formalisms   The preceding descriptions of the operation of a sequential machine are informal.   Many writers use formal definitions because they are precise.   In fact, many writers in automata theory begin discussions with formal definitions.   Therefore, whenever appropriate, we will momentarily leave our informal discussion to state formal definitions or results.   Now is

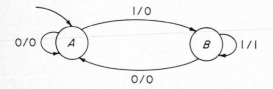

Fig. 2.1.2 Transition graph of the machine in Table 2.1.5.

the time to state a formal definition of a finite-state machine. We use the Moore model. The formal definition of the Mealy model is left as an exercise (Prob. 1).

A finite-state machine has a finite set of states $S = \{S_1, S_2, \ldots, S_m\}$, a finite set of input symbols $I = \{I_1, I_2, \ldots, I_n\}$, and a finite set of output symbols $O = \{O_1, O_2, \ldots, O_p\}$. The behavior of the machine is described by two functions; one maps the ordered pair (input, state) into a new state, the other maps states into outputs. The set of ordered pairs {(input, state)} is the cartesian product of the sets I and S, written $I \times S$. For the sets I and S above,

$$I \times S = \{(I_1, S_1), (I_1, S_2), \ldots, (I_1, S_m), (I_2, S_1), \ldots, (I_n, S_m)\}$$

The two functions can be represented as mappings, as follows:

$$f: I \times S \to S$$
$$g: \quad S \to O$$

This mathematical formalism expresses the mappings by stating the domain (the set of permissible values of the argument set) and the range (the set of permissible values of the result of applying the function to a permissible combination of arguments). The formalism implies nothing about the properties of the mapping itself.

A concise formal definition of a (Moore model of a) finite-state machine is:

A *finite-state machine* is a sextuple $\langle I, O, S, S_0, f, g \rangle$
where I = a finite set of input symbols
O = a finite set of output symbols
S = a finite set of states
$S_0 \in S$ = the initial state S_0
and f and g are mappings:
$$f: I \times S \to S$$
$$g: \quad S \to O$$

Flow charts   The Mealy and Moore models of finite-state machines are the enumerative frameworks for specifying the actions of those machines. Enumeration is not a practical technique when the number of states is very large. Thus these models, though exact, do not provide useful frameworks for describing the actions of large machines. Flow-chart descriptions of the behavior of large machines are exact and can be useful if the machine's behavior is structured.

The flow-chart description is based on the observations that every digital computer is a finite-state machine and that every finite-state machine can be considered as a digital computer. Flow charts can be used to describe the behavior of the digital computer; hence they can also be used to describe the behavior of finite-state machines. The flow-chart technique is useful in complex, but structured, cases for two reasons: First, the pictorial representation of the structure is more compact, and second, the structure of the computations is more evident.

Our flow-chart conventions are similar to the conventions used in flow charts for computer programs. They are:

1. Data can be stored in locations whose names consist of letters and numerals, but not numerals alone.
2. Names may be subscripted, but the number of allowable subscripts must be finite.
3. Data are stored by replacement operations, indicated by ←.
4. Precise word descriptions of operations may be used.
5. Conditional branching is indicated by specifying the test within a diamond-shaped box. The paths leaving the box are labeled with the conditions under which they are taken.
6. Unconditional operations are specified within rectangular boxes; only one branch leaves any rectangular box.
7. The sequence of operations follows the direction of the directed branches.

Example 1   The flow chart of Fig. 2.1.3 describes a finite-state machine M which simulates another finite-state Moore machine M'. The transition table of M' is stored in the array $t(s,x)$, where s is the number of the state and x is the number of the input symbol. The vector $u(s)$ contains the output of M' when M' is in state s. ■

Example 2   *Problem:* Design a finite-state machine which has a single binary input x, such that the output will be 1 at time t whenever the equation

$$(2x_{t-6} + x_{t-5})^2 = 8x_{t-4} + 4x_{t-3} + 2x_{t-2} + x_{t-1}$$

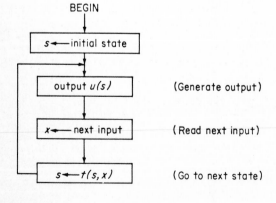

Fig. 2.1.3 A flow chart for a simple simulator of a Moore machine.

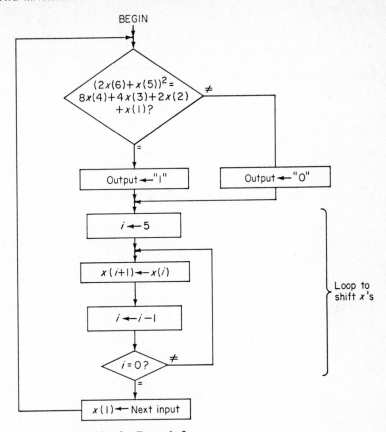

Fig. 2.1.4 Machine for Example 2.

is satisfied (i.e., whenever the previous four bits are the binary representations of the square of the two bits before them), and 0 otherwise. Let $x(i)$ contain at time t the value of the input signal x_{t-i}. The flow chart of Fig. 2.1.4 describes the machine.

The flow chart is not too complex, but the machine it describes has 64 states; so a transition-table description would require 128 entries.

Note that the machine can be considered as a squarer of numbers, in the sense that it can answer questions of the form "Is $n^2 = m$?" With only a single binary input and a single binary output (the latter is interpreted as "yes" or "no"), complicated functions can be "computed." ■

A programming language can be developed to express the computations described in the flow chart. This technique is equivalent to the flow-chart description; straightforward procedures can be used to translate between the flow-chart description, the program description, and the transition-table description of the same machine. We will not use a programming language in this book.

PROBLEMS

1. Give a formal definition of the Mealy model for a finite-state machine.

2. Construct a Mealy machine which is equivalent to the Moore machine in Table 2.1.6.

Table 2.1.6   A Moore machine

Present state	Next state		Output
	$x = 0$	$x = 1$	
$\rightarrow 0$	3	1	0
1	1	2	1
2	2	3	
3	3	0	0

3. (*a*) Define equivalence between Moore and Mealy models of machines to perform the same task. Be sure to state the time relationships between corresponding outputs.

(*b*) Describe a procedure to derive an equivalent Moore machine from a given Mealy machine.

4. Modify the simulator of Example 1 so that it can detect when the output is 1 and halt after that step.

5. Describe a finite-state machine with a single binary input x whose output is 1 at time t if and only if the number of 1's in the sequence $x(1) \cdots x(t - 1)$ has a remainder of $x(t - 3)x(t - 2)x(t - 1)$ (interpreted as a binary integer) upon division by 8.

6. A machine M simulates another machine M' in real time if M performs the same computations as M' in the same time interval. Suppose that the simulator of Example 1 were used to simulate a finite-state machine M' in real time. How much time can M use to perform the computations in the loop of Fig. 2.1.3? Assume that M' reads an input symbol every second.

7. Let $x(t)$ be the input sequence of binary bits to a machine. The machine should produce an output of 1 at time $t + 1$ if t is a multiple of 3 and the input sequence $x(1) \cdots x(t/3)$ considered as binary integer is the sum of the binary integers $x(t/3 + 1) \cdots x(2t/3)$ and $x(2t/3 + 1) \cdots x(t)$; otherwise the output should be 0.

(*a*) Can this job be performed by a finite-state machine? Explain.

(*b*) Give an exact proof of your answer to part *a*.

2.2 RELATIONSHIPS BETWEEN MACHINES AND LANGUAGES

In Sec. 1.5 we discussed the membership question (whether a given string was in the language defined by a given grammar). We found that it is possible to answer the membership question whenever the grammar is context-sensitive. However, we did not define the structure of the machine we would have to construct to answer the membership question. In Chaps. 2 to 5, we will be exploring the following questions: (1) Given a grammar, what is the simplest structure of a machine which will examine input strings and determine which ones are sentences in the language specified by the grammar? (2) Given a machine, find a grammar which describes the set of strings "accepted" by the machine.

The notion of a machine which "recognizes" a set of strings is important in both of these questions. A schematic representation of such a machine is shown in Fig. 2.2.1. To precisely discuss the two questions, we must have an exact definition of the operation of the "recognizer" and the rules for interpreting its behavior.

A *recognizer* (or *acceptor*) of strings with vocabulary T is a machine whose input set I is T and whose output set has two members, which we arbitrarily denote 0 and 1. Whenever the machine produces an output of 1, it *accepts* a string.

Since we are discussing Moore models, we can associate the outputs with internal states. Thus we define some states to be accepting states:

A state of a recognizer which produces a 1 output is an *accepting state*. The states of the recognizer which produce 0 outputs are *nonaccepting states*.

Now we can define the first recognition problem. We are given a grammar G. We would like to design a machine M_G which has an input alphabet T (the same as the terminal vocabulary of the grammar). Whenever the input sequence is in the language L_G, and the machine was started in its initial state, the machine should reach an accepting state; otherwise, the machine should reach a nonaccepting state.

The precise form of the second (inverse) recognition problem is the following. Given a machine M with an input alphabet T and a binary output, construct a grammar G such that the strings of L_G are exactly those which cause M to reach an accepting state if M is started in its initial state.

How is the input sequence given to the machine? Two input mechanisms are used with different models for recognizers. In one, the machine reads the input sequence from a prepared tape. In the other, the machine receives the sequence of input symbols in time sequence at the "input terminal" of the machine. The two kinds of inputs require different machine structures, since a machine to read an input tape must have a reading head.

Fig. 2.2.1 Recognizer of strings in a language.

In some models the machine can control the motions of the reading head. The description of each recognizer must describe its input mechanism.

An input terminal receiving a time sequence of symbols is not commonly used when the recognizer is not a finite-state machine. Any finite-state acceptor which uses a time-sequence input can be modified to use a tape input (Prob. 2). For the time being, we restrict our discussion to machines using time-sequence (or *real-time*) inputs. The operation of such a machine is defined as follows:

> If the input string σ from time 0 to time t is a string in the language L_G, then M_G should be in an accepting state at time $t + 1$ if it is started in its initial state at time 0. We say that M_G is a *recognizer* for the language L_G and that any string σ which causes M_G to reach an accepting state one time unit after the string was completed is *accepted* by M_G, if the state of M_G before σ began was its initial state.

The delay of one time unit is included to allow Moore models to be used for the recognizers.

We can extend the relationship between a language and a machine to a relationship between a set of languages and a set of machines. Thus we will be interested in the set of languages which are accepted by finite-state acceptors. This set is denoted *1DFSA*. Formally,

> $1DFSA = \{L | L$ is a language and there exists a finite-state acceptor which accepts $L\}$

We can use the notion of accepting states (often called *final* states) to remove the outputs from the definition of a finite-state acceptor. Formally,

A finite-state acceptor is a quintuple $\langle I,S,S_0,f,F \rangle$
where $\quad I = $ a finite set of input symbols
$\qquad S = $ a finite set of states
$\qquad S_0 \in S = $ the initial state
$f: I \times S \rightarrow S = $ the next-state function
$\qquad F \subseteq S = $ the set of final states

Class relationships We are interested in classifying machines and languages. Suppose that we could show that a finite-state recognizer could be constructed for any regular language. Furthermore, suppose that we could construct a regular language to describe the set of strings accepted by any given finite-state recognizer. Then we would have shown that the same types of actions can be described by either a finite-state recognizer or by a regular grammar; we might say that finite-state recognizers and regular languages have the same *power*.   Eventually, we will develop a power hierarchy relating types of machine models and types of languages.

We are interested in proving statements about the relationships between classes of languages, between a class of languages and the class of sets (of strings) accepted by a class of machines, and between the classes of sets accepted by two classes of machines.

The possible relationships between two classes of languages C_{L_1} and C_{L_2} can be enumerated as follows:

$$C_{L_1} \subseteq C_{L_2} \quad \text{(for every } L \in C_{L_1}, L \in C_{L_2})$$
$$C_{L_1} \supseteq C_{L_2} \quad \text{(for every } L \in C_{L_2}, L \in C_{L_1})$$
$$C_{L_1} = C_{L_2} \quad (C_{L_1} \supseteq C_{L_2} \text{ and } C_{L_1} \subseteq C_{L_2})$$
$$C_{L_1} \subset C_{L_2} \quad (C_{L_1} \subseteq C_{L_2} \text{ and there exists at least one } L \in C_{L_2} \text{ such that } L \notin C_{L_1})$$
$$C_{L_1} \supset C_{L_2} \quad (C_{L_1} \supseteq C_{L_2} \text{ and there exists at least one } L \in C_{L_1} \text{ such that } L \notin C_{L_2})$$

C_{L_1} and C_{L_2} are incomparable

(there exist $L_a \in C_{L_1}$ and $L_b \vdash C_{L_2}$ such that $L_a \notin C_{L_2}$ and $L_b \notin C_{L_1}$)

Discussion   Before we proceed to the major job of establishing the relationship between grammars, languages, and machines, let us pause to discuss the relationship between these questions and practical issues.   Before the reader becomes too hopeful of finding practical applications for these theories, we must say that the theory is now under development and, as is to be expected during the formative stages of a theory, its applications are limited.   We will briefly mention some of the reasons why the applications are limited.

First, the machines considered in automata theory are almost always acceptors.   Therefore their outputs are limited to a sequence of yes and no answers.   In fact, most of the models produce only a single yes or no for each input sequence.   Practical computers produce much more output information for each input sequence.   Therefore the acceptor model is an awkward first approximation to the practical situation.   A slightly better approximation can be obtained by placing the possible answer in the input sequence and considering the machine as a question answerer, as in Example 2 of Sec. 2.1. This approximation is very awkward and not very interesting.

Second, the theoretical models which have interesting properties have an infinite memory.   This might be a realistic approximation to some practical situations, but the interesting properties of our theoretical models disappear if the infinite storage is made finite.   Then why do we study these models?   Because the structure of the infinite storage in the model may suggest techniques for the effective utilization of the finite storage available in a real machine.

Finally, the applications are limited because the theory, in its infancy, concentrates on those questions which are most easily answered. These questions necessarily involve simplified descriptions of actuality. Significant applications might arise if the theory or similar techniques could be extended to more complex situations. In any case the basic (i.e., simplified) theory must be understood first.

PROBLEMS

1. Construct a Moore recognizer with input alphabet $\{a,b\}$ such that the machine accepts the language $\{a^n b | n \geq 1\}$. Be sure to specify the initial state of the recognizer.

2. The definition of acceptance given in the text applies to the finite-state model with real-time inputs. In this problem we will develop a definition of acceptance for a model with tape input. Consider a particular string $\sigma = x_0 x_1 \cdots x_n$, where the x's represent individual input symbols. We represent σ on a tape by dividing the tape into "squares," each containing one symbol, and writing $x_0, x_1, \ldots, x_n$ in successive squares from left to right. Every time interval the machine's reading head moves one square to the right, so that at time t the reading head is over the square which contains x_t. The input symbol at time t is the symbol written in the square under the reading head.

    (*a*) How would you define the starting conditions for the machine?

    (*b*) How would you define the accepting conditions for the machine?

    (*c*) Give a complete definition of the acceptance by M of a string σ.

3. Consider a fixed two-symbol alphabet $\{a,b\}$, and let C_j denote the class of languages over that alphabet which are accepted by finite-state recognizers having not more than j states ($j > 1$).

    (*a*) Prove: $C_{i+1} \supseteq C_i, i > 1$.

    (*b*) What must be shown to prove $C_{i+1} \supset C_i$? Can you prove this?

2.3 FINITE-STATE RECOGNIZERS

In this section we will discuss ways to describe the behavior of finite-state recognizers, first in terms of languages and then in terms of "regular expressions." Specifically, we discuss the questions, "Given a finite-state recognizer, find a grammar that describes the language it recognizes" and "Given a finite-state recognizer, find a closed-form description of the strings in the language it recognizes." The answers to these questions are algorithms which produce a grammar or a closed form from a transition table or diagram describing the recognizer. If the recognizer is described by a flow chart (or software description), more complex algorithms are required. We will not discuss them here. No generality is lost by this omission because any software description is equivalent to a transition-table description.

To simplify the descriptions of finite-state recognizers, we adopt the following conventions:

1. Final states are represented in transition diagrams by double circles and in transition tables by encircled numerals.

2. If for some state S_j no transition is shown for input $I_k \in I$, it is assumed that there exists a transition to a "dead state" S_d. The dead state is described by:

$f(i,S_d) = S_d$, for every $i \in I$, and S_d is not a final state

In other words, the machine gets "trapped" in the dead state and can never reach a final state after that time.

2.3.1 GRAMMARS FROM FINITE-STATE RECOGNIZERS

The first problem is to derive a grammar from the specification of a finite-state recognizer.

A Recognizer   We observed in Sec. 2.1 that if we knew the state of the machine at time t, then we could predict future outputs from future inputs. In particular, we can determine which sequences of future input symbols will lead to an acceptance of the entire input string.   For example, if the machine of Fig. 2.1.1 is in state B at time t, we know that any input string consisting of 1's from time t to time τ will produce a 1 output at time $\tau + 1$.   (These are not the only strings which will produce a 1 output at time τ.)

We also observed that the knowledge of the state of a machine at time t gives us some information about the sequence of input symbols before time t.   For example, if the machine of Fig. 2.1.1 is in state B at time t, we know that the input symbol at time $t - 1$ could not have been a 0.

We can combine these two intuitive notions of state to find the algorithm which determines a grammar from a given finite-state recognizer.   The formal argument follows.

Let $L_i(t)$ denote the set of input strings of length t which will place the machine in state i at time t, given that the machine started in its initial state at time 0.   Time 0 is defined as the time when the first symbol of the input string is presented to the machine.   Similarly, let R_i denote the set of input strings such that, if $x \in R_i$ is the input sequence beginning at time t and ending at time τ, then the machine will be in an accepting state at time $\tau + 1$. Note that R_i is not a function of t, since the machine's description is independent of time.   Any input string in the set $L_i(t)R_i = \{\alpha\beta | \alpha \in L_i(t), \beta \in R_i\}$ will be in the language accepted by the machine, since this set is composed of strings having an initial segment α which puts the machine in state i at time t and a final segment β which puts the machine in an accepting state, given that it was in state i.

The set union

$$\bigcup_{t=0}^{\infty} L_i(t)R_i$$

will contain all strings which will be accepted if the machine passes through state i at some point in the recognition process. We can factor the expression

$$\left[\bigcup_{t=0}^{\infty} L_i(t)\right] R_i$$

and call the bracketed portion L_i:

$$L_i = \bigcup_{t=0}^{\infty} L_i(t)$$

Now L_i is a set containing every sequence (of any length) which places the machine in state i when it is started in the initial state. If m is the index of the last state in the machine, the set union

$$\bigcup_{i=1}^{m} L_i R_i$$

is the set of all strings in the language accepted by the machine.

If the initial state is also a final state, an acceptance output is produced before any input symbols are presented to the machine. In that case we say that the machine accepts the empty string λ. To simplify the statements of results, we restrict finite-state recognizers by adding the condition $S_0 \notin F$ to the definition of an acceptor. This condition prevents the empty string from appearing in the language accepted by the machine.

A grammar   Consider a derivation of a string in a regular language. Remember that any nonterminal symbol occurring in a working string in the derivation can be considered to represent a set of strings. If each nonterminal symbol is replaced by some string from its set (by using a sequence of the rewriting rules), a string in the language is produced. This observation is extraordinarily similar to the observation that the knowledge of the present state of an acceptor tells us what strings can be used to complete the input sequence in an acceptable way. Our construction will draw an exact parallel between the states in the recognizer and the nonterminal symbols in the grammar.

An example   Consider the finite-state recognizer described by the transition diagram in Fig. 2.3.1. Some sequences which are contained in the L_i and R_i sets are

$$1 \in L_3$$
$$101 \in L_3$$
$$1 \in R_1$$
$$01 \in L_1$$

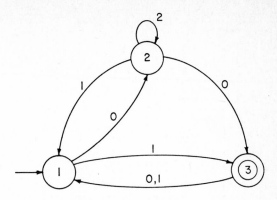

Fig. 2.3.1 A finite-state recognizer.

We could continue this enumeration process, but it is tedious and not very illuminating. We need a systematic method if we want to find the members of the various sets. Such a method will be developed in the next section. The major goal of this section is to develop the relationship between the recognizer and a grammar. Fortunately, we do not need to enumerate the strings to find the desired result. However, we do need to express the relationships between the various sets to achieve our goal.

To find a grammar to generate the language recognized by our machine, we associate a nonterminal symbol N_i in the grammar with each set R_i (and therefore with each state in the machine). Now, if the machine is in state 1 at time t, a string σ_1 from the set N_1 (or R_1) must begin at time t if the machine is to reach a final state when σ_1 is completed. Examining our machine, we find that two input symbols might occur at time t without forcing the machine to the dead state. If the input is 0, the machine will go to state 2, and any member of N_2 can then complete the acceptable input. Therefore we know that N_1 must include the set† $0N_2$. The grammar must reflect this relationship by containing the rewriting rule

$$N_1 \rightarrow 0N_2$$

If the machine is in state 1 at time t and the input signal at time t is 1, the input will be accepted. The grammar must include the rewriting rule

$$N_1 \rightarrow 1$$

After the input signal was 1 at time t, the machine reaches state 3 at time $t + 1$, and a final state can be reached at a later time by continuing the input

---

† The concatenation of a symbol x and the name of a set S denotes the set of strings formed by concatenating x with each string in S.

sequence with a member of R_3. The grammar must also include the rewriting rule

$$N_1 \to 1N_3$$

These three rules are the only rules in the grammar with N_1 on the left side, since we have examined all possible actions of the machine when it is in state 1. We will complete this discussion in Example 1.

Procedure   The general procedure for finding the rewriting rules of the regular grammar which is equivalent to a given finite-state machine is as follows:

For each transition leading from state i to state j when the input symbol is I_{ij}:

1. Include the rewriting rule

$$N_i \to I_{ij}N_j$$

2. If state j is an accepting state, include the rewriting rule

$$N_i \to I_{ij}$$

These steps determine all the rewriting rules of the grammar. The set of strings in the language is the set of strings which can follow after the machine is in its initial state. Thus the nonterminal symbol which corresponds to the initial state must be the sentence symbol in the grammar.

Note that each rule has the form

$$A \to aB$$

or

$$A \to a$$

which are precisely the forms allowed in regular grammars.

Example 1   The rewriting rules of the grammar which corresponds to the recognizer of Fig. 2.3.1 are

$$N_1 \to 0N_2$$
$$N_1 \to 1N_3$$
$$N_1 \to 1$$
$$N_2 \to 2N_2$$
$$N_2 \to 1N_1$$
$$N_2 \to 0N_3$$
$$N_2 \to 0$$
$$N_3 \to 0N_1$$
$$N_3 \to 1N_1$$

Since S_1 is the initial state, N_1 is the sentence symbol.

The following table illustrates the relationship between the operation of the acceptor and the derivation in the grammar for the string 021101, which is a sentence in the language.

Time	Input symbol	State	Working string
			N_1
0	0	S_1	$0N_2$
1	2	S_2	$02N_2$
2	1	S_2	$021N_1$
3	1	S_1	$0211N_3$
4	0	S_3	$02110N_1$
5	1	S_1	021101
		S_3	

Discussion   We have shown that, for any given finite-state machine, we can write a grammar which seems to describe the language accepted by the machine. However, we have not shown that the grammar exactly describes the language, because we do not have a proof that the grammar and the machine work in "parallel" ways. A rigorous proof of the desired result must include proofs of the following two statements:

1. For every string of input symbols which produces machine acceptance, there exists a sequence of steps in a derivation from the grammar such that the derivation produces the accepted string.
2. For every derivation in the grammar producing a string σ, there exists a sequence of transitions in the machine when σ is the input sequence such that the machine reaches a final state when the string is completed.

These two statements can be proved by showing that each machine step can be placed in one-to-one correspondence with a derivation step, and vice versa. Then an induction step completes the proofs. The details of such proofs are extremely tedious and not illuminating (since they usually require an exhaustive analysis of all possible cases), so we will not prove such statements in this text. Rather, we concentrate on establishing the parallelism on an intuitive basis. The interested reader can provide the detailed proofs whenever he feels the need.

Subject to the above discussion, we have shown that, for every finite-state recognizer, there exists a regular language which contains exactly the same strings that are recognized by the recognizer. Formally stated, $1DFSA \subseteq type\ 3$. In Sec. 2.5 we prove that there exists a finite-state recognizer that will recognize every string in any given regular language. This will prove the equivalence of the two sets.

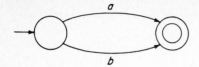

Fig. 2.3.2 A simple recognizer.

2.3.2 REGULAR EXPRESSIONS FROM FINITE-STATE RECOGNIZERS

We now describe another technique for representing the behavior of finite-state recognizers. The preceding representation produced a regular grammar; this representation will give a "closed-form" description of the set of strings recognized by the recognizer. We begin by discussing the operators to be used in the closed form. We use examples of simple situations to find the operators we will need in the expressions. We print all regular expressions in boldface to distinguish them from strings of symbols.

In the first example a recognizer has two parallel paths to the accepting state.

Example 1 Consider the recognizer of Fig. 2.3.2. The machine accepts the strings a and b. We use + (some writers use the set-theoretic $\cup$) to denote set union. This recognizer accepts the set **a + b**. ■

The second example contains a path two branches long.

Example 2 The recognizer of Fig. 2.3.3 accepts a string of two symbols: a followed immediately by b. We denote this sequence by concatenating the symbols:
ab ■

The last basic configuration is a cycle (or loop).

Example 3 The recognizer of Fig. 2.3.4 will accept a string of any length if every symbol in the string is an a. Since the initial state is the final state, the recognizer accepts the null string. We denote the set of sequences consisting of any number of a's by
a*

Another definition of **a*** is

$$\mathbf{a*} = \bigcup_{i=0}^{\infty} a^i$$

where a^0 conventionally denotes the null string λ. ■

Expressions of the form **aa*** arise frequently enough so that the special notation **a⁺** is used for them. Thus

$$\mathbf{a^+} = \bigcup_{i=1}^{\infty} a^i = \mathbf{aa*}$$

Fig. 2.3.3 A concatenation recognizer.

Fig. 2.3.4 A closure recognizer.

A closed-form expression for the set of strings accepted by a finite-state machine can be found by using rules derived from these examples to remove states from the state diagram until only the initial and final states remain. We leave this technique as an exercise for the reader. We will discuss a purely algebraic technique which is similar to this method.

Expressions, Sets The closed-form expressions we will use are known as regular expressions. A regular expression is a compact means of expressing the same type of information about a set of strings that is specified by a description such as $\{a^n b^m | n \geq 0, m \geq 1\}$. A formal recursive definition of a regular expression is:

1. Any terminal symbol and the symbols λ and φ are regular expressions.
2. The set union of two regular expressions **x** and **y**, denoted by **x + y**, is a regular expression.
3. The concatenation of two regular expressions **x** and **y**, denoted by **xy**, is a regular expression.
4. The iteration (or closure) of a regular expression **x**, denoted by **x***, is a regular expression.
5. If **x** is a regular expression, then so is **(x)**. The appearance of parentheses may influence the order of evaluation of the expression (see below).
6. There are no regular expressions that cannot be constructed by a finite number of applications of rules 1 to 5.†

These rules describe the sequences of symbols which can form a regular expression, but they do not tell us anything about how we relate the regular expression to a set of strings. To define this relationship, we must discuss the "evaluation" of a regular expression. We placed the word *evaluation* in quotation marks because its usual meaning and the implications of that meaning do not apply in the context of regular expressions; usually, evaluation implies that there is a unique value for the entity being evaluated, whereas here evaluation is the process of finding one string in the set of strings which the expression represents.

The evaluation of a regular expression proceeds from the iterations to the concatenations and, finally, to the unions. This ordering is similar to

---

† Regular expressions may contain the form **x⁺**, where x is a regular expression, because any occurrence of **x⁺** may be replaced by **xx***, which is a regular expression according to this definition.

the ordering in algebra of the operators for exponentiation, multiplication, and addition.   As in algebra, parentheses may be used in a regular expression to alter this ordering of the evaluation; an expression within parentheses must be completely evaluated before it can be used as an operand for a succeeding operator.

A specification of the evaluation procedures for each of the operators in the expression will complete the evaluation procedure.   Let x and y denote regular expressions.   The evaluation procedures are:

1. A string in $x + y$ is a string from x or a string from y.
2. A string in xy is a string from x followed by a string from y.
3. A string in $x*$ is a string in $xx \cdots x$ (n times), for some $n \geq 0$.
4. The set φ contains no strings.
5. The set λ contains only the empty string.

In the third rule x is evaluated n times, each evaluation being independent of the others.   For example, the set represented by the expression $(a + b)*$ contains the string *aba*.

Since we know how to find individual strings in the sets represented by regular expressions, we can enumerate the set of these strings.   Such a set of strings is a regular set:

A *regular set* is any set of strings which can be represented by a regular expression.

We should note in passing that there are many interesting and useful sets (such as the set of all well-formed regular expressions!) which are not regular sets.   We are not equipped with sufficient information to prove this statement at this point.

Example 4   *Problem:* Find the two sets represented by the two expressions

$a + bc$
$(a + b)c$

Each set contains two strings; the second one has two symbols in each of its strings.   ■

Example 5   Given

$x = (a + b)*$
$y = a* (ba*)*$

Do x and y represent the same set?   Set x contains all strings of any length which contain only a's and b's.   The strings of set y are of the form

1. A sequence of a's (possibly null), followed by
2. Any number of occurrences of sequences consisting of a b followed by some a's (again, possibly no a's)

Any sequence of a's and b's can be divided into subsequences such that each subsequence (except possibly the first) begins with a b and has no other b in the subsequence. For example, using commas to indicate the divisions, we have

a,b,b,baaa,b
,baa,ba,baa
aaa,b,b,b

Thus any sequence of a's and/or b's can be placed in the form described by the expression for **y**. Therefore the two expressions are equivalent. (See Prob. 7.) ■

Equations   Any expression can be turned into a function of one or more variables by replacing some of the operands in the expression by variables. For example, the expression **a + bc** can be transformed to the function **a + bx**, where **x** is a variable. In this algebra, expressions, variables, and functions all denote sets of strings. Two expressions, variables, or functions can be related by equations, such as

$$\mathbf{a + bx = x}$$

If a set of equations contains as many equations as variables and the set is "consistent," the set of equations specifies the sets of possible "values" of the variables. Some sets of equations will specify variables which are regular sets, but other equations may require that the variable denote a nonregular set. For example, the equation

$$\mathbf{x = a + bx}$$

has a regular set for a solution, but the equation

$$\mathbf{x = a + bxc}$$

does not have a regular solution. (We are not at the point where we can prove these statements.)

In this section we will discuss how we write and solve a set of equations which describe the behavior of a given finite-state recognizer. It will turn out that these equations will have regular sets for their solutions.

When we write these equations, we will use **u** and **v** to denote known regular sets and **x**, **y**, and **z** to denote unknowns, and other symbols will always denote terminal symbols. (Note that digits are terminal symbols.) For example, $\mathbf{x = 0x + 1}$ is an equation with one unknown **x** and two terminal symbols, 0 and 1.

Our procedure for writing the equations parallels our procedure for writing the productions for the grammar of the language. Thus we associate an unknown $\mathbf{x}_i$ with each state S_i of the machine except the dead state. The unknowns x_i represent the set of input sequences which will move the recognizer from state S_i to an accepting state (similar to N_i and R_i). There is one equation for each state of the machine. It is constructed as follows:

1. The left side of the ith equation is x_i.
2. For each branch from state S_i to some state S_j, with input symbol $T_{i,j}$, add the following terms to the right side of the ith equation:

    a. $\mathbf{I}_{i,j}x_j$.
    b. $\mathbf{I}_{i,j}$, if S_j is an accepting state.

Note that each branch to an accepting state yields two terms, while the other branches produce only one term.

Example 6 For the recognizer of Fig. 2.3.1, the equation which describes the activity when the machine is in state 1 is

$$x_1 = 0x_2 + 1x_3 + 1 \qquad \blacksquare$$

The arguments of Sec. 2.3.1 can be used to show that the equations which are generated by this algorithm do express the relationships between the unknowns that are required to describe the given machine. To find the expressions which describe the set of strings accepted by the machine, we must solve these equations.

Solutions We have the following problem: Given a set of equations of the form

$$x_i = \sum_j a_{i,j}x_j + \sum_j b_{i,j} \tag{1}$$

find the sets x_i.

We cannot use conventional algebraic operations to solve the equations because there is no inversion operation in this algebra and because our "multiplication" is not commutative. Let us study a single equation in a single unknown first.

Suppose we have

$$x = ux + v \tag{2}$$

where $\mathbf{u}$ and $\mathbf{v}$ represent sets of strings. Let us interpret this equation in terms of sets. The equation says that the set $\mathbf{x}$ is composed of the union of two sets, $\mathbf{ux}$ and $\mathbf{v}$. The first set contains all strings constructed by taking a member of $\mathbf{u}$ and concatenating a member of $\mathbf{x}$ to the right, while the second contains only strings from the set $\mathbf{v}$. Considering the equation as a recursive definition of the set **x**, we can generate the solution by successive substitutions.   First

$$\mathbf{v} \subseteq \mathbf{x}$$

Thus we get

$$\mathbf{uv} \subseteq \mathbf{x}$$
$$\mathbf{uuv} \subseteq \mathbf{x}$$
$$\mathbf{uuuv} \subseteq \mathbf{x}$$

and so on.   Intuitively, the solution must be **u*v**.

To prove that **u*v** is a solution to Eq. (2), we can substitute it for every **x** in the equation to obtain

$$\mathbf{u^*v} \stackrel{?}{=} \mathbf{uu^*v} + \mathbf{v}$$

Factoring on the right, we have

$$\mathbf{u^*v} \stackrel{?}{=} (\mathbf{uu^*} + \lambda)\mathbf{v} \tag{3}$$

We cannot cancel out the **v** (why?).   But if we could show that

$$\mathbf{u^*} = \mathbf{uu^*} + \lambda \tag{4}$$

we would be able to make a substitution and prove the equality.

We prove Eq. (4) by substituting the definition of **u*** for its appearances:

$$\sum_{i=0}^{\infty} \mathbf{u^i} \stackrel{?}{=} \mathbf{u} \sum_{j=0}^{\infty} \mathbf{u^j} + \lambda$$

$$= \sum_{j=0}^{\infty} \mathbf{u^{j+1}} + \mathbf{u^0}$$

$$= \sum_{j=0}^{\infty} \mathbf{u^i}$$

Thus Eq. (4) is true and can be used to reduce Eq. (3) to an equality, proving that **u*v** is a solution to Eq. (2).

Though we have shown that **u*v** is a solution of Eq. (2), we do not know whether it is the unique solution of Eq. (2).   The uniqueness proof requires the proof of two statements:

1. Any **x** satisfying Eq. (2) must satisfy $\mathbf{x} \supseteq \mathbf{u^*v}$.
2. Any **x** satisfying Eq. (2) must satisfy $\mathbf{x} \subseteq \mathbf{u^*v}$, if $\lambda \notin \mathbf{u}$.

Proof of statement 1   We prove this statement by induction, based on the sets $\mathbf{R_q} = \sum_{i=0}^{q} \mathbf{u^i v}$.   From Eq. (2), we find

$$\mathbf{x} \supseteq \mathbf{uy} + \mathbf{v} \text{ for any } \mathbf{y} \subseteq \mathbf{x} \tag{5}$$

The basis for the induction is that $R_0 = v \subseteq x$. This is verified by setting $y = \varphi$ in Eq. (5). To make the induction step, assume that $R_j \subseteq x$ and set $y = R_j$ in Eq. (5), giving

$$x \supseteq uR_j + v = u \sum_{i=0}^{j} u^i v + v = \sum_{i=0}^{j} u^{i+1} v + v = \sum_{i=0}^{j+1} u^i v = R_{j+1}$$

Thus $x \supseteq R_{j+1}$ and, by induction, $x \supseteq R_\infty = u^*v$.

Proof of statement 2   Since we know from statement 1 that $x \supseteq u^*v$, assume that $x = u^*v + w$, where w is some nonempty set of strings which does not contain any string from u^*v (w may not be a regular set). Let r denote the shortest string in w, and let k be the length of r. (If there are several shortest strings in w, let r be one of them.) Substitute the assumed solution into the equation

$$u^*v + w \overset{?}{=} u(u^*v + w) + v$$
$$u^*v + w \overset{?}{=} uu^*v + uw + v = u^*v + uw$$

The string r appears in the w on the left side of the equation, as part of w, and not in u^*v. Where is the matching string r in the sets on the right side? Not in u^*v. Can it be in uw? If u does not contain λ, every string in uw must contain at least $k + 1$ symbols. Since r contains k symbols, it cannot be in uw. Therefore the set w must be empty if the equation is to be satisfied.

We have completed the proof that the solution $x = u^*v$ is the unique solution of the equation if $\lambda \notin u$. The uniqueness condition can be extended to a set of equations by straightforward techniques. When a set of equations is generated to describe the actions of a finite-state recognizer by following the algorithm that we have described, the uniqueness conditions will be satisfied (why?).

In Prob. 9 the form of the solution of Eq. (2) when $\lambda \in u$ is discussed.

A set of equations can be solved by successively eliminating variables

Example 7   The recognizer of Fig. 2.3.1 is described by the equations

$$x_1 = \qquad 0x_2 + 1x_3 + 1$$
$$x_2 = 1x \;\; + 2x_2 + 0x_2 + 0$$
$$x_3 = (0 + 1)x_1$$

Remember that 0, 1, and 2 are terminal symbols, not numeric coefficients!
        By substitution we remove x_3 to obtain

$$x_1 = 1(0 + 1)x_1 + 0x_2 + 1$$
$$x_2 = [1 + 0(0 + 1)]x_1 + 2x_2 + 0$$

For the moment consider x_1 to be a "constant." The second equation gives x_2 in terms of x_1:

$$x_2 = 2*\{[1 + 0(0 + 1)]x_1 + 0\}$$

Substituting this expression in the first equation, we obtain:

$$x_1 = \{1(0 + 1) + 02*[1 + 0(0 + 1)]\}x_1 + [02*0 + 1]$$

so that

$$x_1 = \{1(0 + 1) + 02*[1 + 0(0 + 1)]\}*[02*0 + 1]$$

This expression describes the set of strings in the language accepted by the given recognizer if state 1 is the initial state. If we want to find the language recognized by the same machine for some other initial state, we can back-substitute and determine the other x's. In this way we find

$$x_2' = 2*\{[1 + 0(0 + 1)]\{1(0 + 1) + 02*[1 + 0(0 + 1)]\}*[02*0 + 1] + 0\}$$
$$x_3 = (0 + 1)\{1(0 + 1) + 02*[1 + 0(0 + 1)]\}*[02*0 + 1]$$

If we had removed x_3 and x_1 and then solved for x_2, our answers would have looked quite different. For example, the expression for x_2 would have been

$$x_2 = \{[1 + 0(0 + 1)][1(0 + 1)]*(0) + 2\}*\{[1 + 0(0 + 1)][1(0 + 1)]*1 + 0\}$$

The two expressions for x_2 both represent the set of strings accepted by the machine when state 2 is the initial state. Therefore they must be equivalent regular expressions. ■

Is there any algebraic method for testing two regular expressions for equivalence? Unfortunately not; every known test for the equivalence of two regular expressions is equivalent to synthesizing two reduced finite-state machines to recognize the sets and then testing those machines for equivalence.

PROBLEMS

1. Find a grammar for the language accepted by the machine described by Table 2.1.4.

2. Give the details of a proof that every finite-state recognizer recognizes a regular set of strings.

3. Discuss how you might prove that any regular set can be recognized by a finite-state machine.

4. Find a procedure for deriving regular expressions for grammatical descriptions of languages without constructing a recognizer for the language.

5. Find a regular expression for the set of strings accepted by
  (a) The machine in Table 2.1.4
  (b) The machine in Table 2.1.5
  (c) The machine in Table 2.3.1

6. Modify the procedure for constructing the equations so that it can be used when a Mealy model describes the recognizer. Use your procedure on the Mealy machine of Table 2.3.1.

Table 2.3.1 A Mealy recognizer

	x_t		
S_t	0	1	2
→ 1	2/0	4/0	3/1
2	1/1	1/0	4/1
3	3/1	1/1	2/0
4	2/0	2/1	3/0

7. In Example 5 an argument was used to make it plausible that two sets of strings are equal. A rigorous proof of this fact might be constructed from the argument "If $\mathbf{x} \supseteq \mathbf{y}$ and $\mathbf{y} \supseteq \mathbf{x}$, then $\mathbf{x} = \mathbf{y}$." Provide such a proof for the sets $\mathbf{x}$ and $\mathbf{y}$ in Example 5.

8. In the text, the equations for the set of strings accepted by a finite-state machine were developed by relying upon a correspondence between the states and the sets R_i. The equivalent grammar was derived by the same argument.

(*a*) Find a procedure to generate a grammar whose language is equivalent to the set of strings accepted by a given finite-state recognizer, using a correspondence between the states and the sets L_i. Be sure to identify the sentence symbol.

(*b*) Describe a procedure which can be used to find a set of equations based upon the correspondence between S_i and L_i. Note that these equations do not have the exact form of those in the text. How are these solved?

(*c*) Use the procedures developed in parts *a* and *b* to find a regular expression denoting the language accepted by the machine of Table 2.1.5.

9. Show that $\mathbf{x} = \mathbf{u}*(\mathbf{v} + \mathbf{w})$ is a solution to the equation

$$\mathbf{x} = \mathbf{ux} + \mathbf{v}$$

if $\lambda \in \mathbf{u}$ for any set $\mathbf{w}$ (even a nonregular set).

10. For each regular expression below, find all strings of length 5 or less which are included in the set that the expression denotes.

(*a*) $\varphi*$
(*b*) $(01 + 10)*$
(*c*) $(11 + 0)(00 + 1)*$
(*d*) $(2 + 0)*(2 + 1)^+$
(*e*) $1(11)*$
(*f*) $(01)* + (10)*$

11. Let lowercase letters denote arbitrary regular sets. Which of the following identities are true? Why?

(*a*) $\mathbf{a}* = \mathbf{a}*\mathbf{a}*$
(*b*) $(\mathbf{a} + \mathbf{b})* = \mathbf{a}* + \mathbf{b}*$
(*c*) $(\mathbf{a} + \mathbf{b})* = \mathbf{a}*(\mathbf{a} + \mathbf{b})*$
(*d*) $\mathbf{a}^+ = \mathbf{a}^+\mathbf{a}^+$
(*e*) $\mathbf{a} + (\mathbf{a} + \mathbf{bc})* = (\mathbf{a} + \mathbf{bc})*$
(*f*) $(\mathbf{a}(\mathbf{a} + \mathbf{b})* + \mathbf{c})* = (\mathbf{a} + \mathbf{b} + \mathbf{c})*$

12. (*a*) Find a grammar which specifies a language containing all regular expressions using the terminal symbols x, y, and z. Construct the grammar so that the syntactic structure of an expression reflects the evaluation procedure. (See Prob. 5 of Sec. 1.4.)

(*b*) Show how the expression $(\mathbf{x} + \mathbf{y})*(\mathbf{z} + \mathbf{yx})$ would be derived by your grammar.

(*c*) Give a procedure for "evaluating" a regular expression which is specified by its derivation tree in your grammar.

(*d*) Do you think your grammar is ambiguous? Why? (A rigorous proof of your answer is not required.)

2.4 NONDETERMINISTIC FINITE-STATE MACHINES

To show that there is a grammar equivalent to a given machine, we find rewriting rules which are similar to the moves of the machine. Thus, if the machine contains the transition $S_i \rightarrow S_j$ with input I_{ij}, we place a rule $N_i \rightarrow I_{ij}N_j$ in the grammar. To show that there exists a machine to recognize the language specified by a given grammar, we could try to reverse that process. For example, if the grammar contained the rule $N_1 \rightarrow I_1N_2$, we would place a transition $S_1 \rightarrow S_2$ with input I_1. But suppose that the grammar also contained the rule $N_1 \rightarrow I_1N_1$. There should also be a transition $S_1 \rightarrow S_1$ with input I_1. If we allow both of these transitions, we have a problem, because when the machine is in state S_1 with input I_1, it has two possible moves!

Determinism vs. nondeterminism   The basic incompatibility between the sequence of operations of the machine and the sequence of steps in a derivation in the language is that of *determinism*: at every step in the machine's operation the input symbol and current state uniquely determine the next state, and the state, in turn, uniquely determines the output.

The machine operates by checking each input symbol against a set of rules as it arrives. It can do this because the set of rules is specified in a deterministic way.

Suppose the set of rules were specified by a grammar. For example, consider the grammar with rewriting rules

$$S \rightarrow aS$$
$$S \rightarrow aA$$
$$A \rightarrow bB$$
$$A \rightarrow b$$
$$B \rightarrow bB$$
$$B \rightarrow b$$

Consider a machine which tests strings against these rules by checking each input symbol as it arrives. Suppose the input string is *ab*. When the *a* arrives, the machine must decide whether it should look for a string from S or from A to complete the input. If it decides (incorrectly) to look for a string from S, it will not determine that *ab* is a string in the language. Either the machine must make the choice between S and A without knowing what the succeeding symbols of the input string will be or it must be constructed in some way which is not similar to the structure of the rewriting rules of the grammar.

In this section we define nondeterministic finite-state machines so that (1) we can use them as recognizers, and (2) their structures will be similar to the structures of the rewriting rules of the corresponding grammars. We will show that for every nondeterministic finite-state recognizer there exists an equivalent (though more complex) deterministic finite-state recognizer. In Sec. 2.5 we will use these concepts to prove that there exists a finite-state recognizer for every regular language.

Definitions Informally, a nondeterministic machine is a machine for which some moves may not be uniquely determined by the input symbol and the present state. Formally,

A *nondeterministic finite-state machine* is a sextuple $\langle I,O,S,S_0,f,g \rangle$, where

1. I is the (finite) set of input symbols, denoted by $I_1, \ldots, I_n$.
2. O is the (finite) set of output symbols, denoted by $O_1, \ldots, O_p$.
3. S is the (finite) set of states, denoted by $S_0, \ldots, S_m$.
4. $S_0 \in S$ is the initial state.
5. f is a mapping,† $f: I \times S \to 2^S$.
6. g is the output mapping, $g: S \to O$.

[Note that we arbitrarily choose to discuss the Moore model, and that the output is a deterministic function of the state (Prob. 3).]

The mapping f determines a nonempty set of states. Any one of the states in the set $f(s,i)$ is a possible next state when the machine is in state s, with input i. Thus, if $f(S_1,I_1) = \{S_1,S_2,S_3\}$ and the machine is in state S_1 receiving input I_1, it has three choices for its next state.

When the mapping f produces a set with exactly one member for every (state, input) combination, the machine is deterministic. In previous sections we have discussed deterministic machines, though many of the results that we discussed are true for nondeterministic machines as well.

When a nondeterministic machine is used as an acceptor, the set of output symbols and the output function are replaced by a set of final states F.

How do we interpret the operation of a nondeterministic acceptor?

We say that a nondeterministic machine M accepts a string σ if there exists at least one sequence of states beginning with the initial state and ending with an accepting state, such that the state changes in the sequence are consistent with the input sequence and the machine description. The set of strings which are accepted by a nondeterministic acceptor M is the language accepted by M. Let *1NFSA* denote the set of languages which are accepted by nondeterministic finite-state acceptors.

† 2^S denotes the set of all nonempty subsets of S.

Table 2.4.1 A nondeterministic acceptor

	$x = 0$	$x = 1$
→ 1	1,2	3
2	2	1
③	1	3,2

Table 2.4.2 The box simulation of the machine of Table 2.4.1

t:	0	1	2	3	4	5	6
x:	0	0	1	1	1	0	
M_1	1	1	1	(3)	2	1	1
M_2							2
M_3					(3)	2	2
M_4					(3)		1
M_5			2	1	(3)	2	2
M_6						(3)	1
M_7		2	2	1	(3)	2	2
M_8						(3)	1

We must realize that a nondeterministic machine is not something that we will ever build, and the intuitive notions tied up with determinism must not be applied to nondeterministic models. Though a nondeterministic machine does not have unique moves, it does not contain a random device to choose its moves. Rather than make a probabilistic guess and possibly obtain the wrong answer to the membership question for a particular string, the machine should explore all move sequences which are consistent with the input sequence. If at least one of these sequences leads the machine to an accepting condition, it must accept the input string.

We can visualize what is happening when a nondeterministic finite-state acceptor M is testing a string by considering a box containing copies of M. Therefore, suppose that we have a large supply of copies of a nondeterministic machine M. We start one machine in its initial state S_0 and the other machines are "turned off." We present the input sequence to all the machines. Whenever any machine has a choice of next states, extra copies of M are started in operation ("turned on") in such a way that at least one is in each one of the possible states of M. Thus each machine is exploring a possible sequence of choices. As more choice points are encountered, more machines may be called into action. The string σ is accepted by M if at least one of the operating machines reaches an accepting state when σ is completed. Example 1 illustrates this mechanism.

Example 1 A nondeterministic acceptor is described by the transition table 2.4.1, where each entry shows the set of possible next states for a given combination of state and input symbol. Let us number the machines in the box M_1, M_2, ... Now consider an experiment in which the input sequence is 00111. We depict the operation in a chart (Table 2.4.2), where we show a state for a machine only if that machine is operating.   Whenever a nondeterministic move is reached, a new machine is started.   Dotted lines show which machine was started at which choice.   Final states are circled.   We see that the strings 001, 0011, and 00111 are accepted by M.   ■

Equivalence   Are nondeterministic finite-state acceptors more powerful than deterministic finite-state acceptors?   No!   We prove this statement by constructing a deterministic acceptor which simulates the behavior of any given nondeterministic acceptor, and vice versa.   In general, the deterministic machine will have many more states than the equivalent nondeterministic machine.

It is easy to prove the second part of the statement (that $1DFSA \subseteq 1NFSA$).   Any deterministic machine is a special case of a nondeterministic one; so any language that could be accepted by a deterministic machine could be accepted by a nondeterministic one.   (Indeed, by the same machine!)

The first part of the statement (that $1NFSA \subseteq 1DFSA$) is harder to prove.   Consider the box containing copies of a nondeterministic machine M and suppose that M has m states.   What is the maximum number of copies of M that we really need?   Suppose that we examine the machines in the box at some instant and find two that are in the same state.   Since both of these machines will exhibit the same future behavior, one of them is redundant.   Thus we never need more than m copies of M inside the box.

Example 2   The simplified simulation of the machine of Table 2.4.1 is shown in Table 2.4.3.   ■

Since the box contains a finite number of finite-state machines, the whole box is a finite-state machine.   We could bound the number of states of this composite machine by some function of m.   Such bounds are not significant; the important fact is that the number of states is finite.

We must show that the box operates deterministically.   The details of this construction require that we modify the insides of the machines within

Table 2.4.3   The simplified box simulation of the machine of Table 2.4.1

t:	0	1	2	3	4	5	6
x:	0	0	1	1	1	0	
M_1	1	1	1	③	2	1	1
M_2		2	2	1	③	2	2
M_3						③	

Table 2.4.4 A deterministic machine
equivalent to the nondeterministic
machine of Table 2.4.1

	$x=0$	$x=1$
⟶ (1)	(1,2)	(3)
(2)	(2)	(1)
⟨(3)⟩	(1)	(2,3)
(1,2)	(1,2)	(1,3)
⟨(1,3)⟩	(1,2)	(2,3)
⟨(2,3)⟩	(1,2)	(1,2,3)
⟨(1,2,3)⟩	(1,2)	(1,2,3)

the box or abandon the notion that the box contains copies of M with some interconnecting logic. We use the second approach.

An equivalent deterministic machine What is the essential information about what is happening inside the box? Answer: a list of the states of the operating machines. This list is equivalent to a list of the possibilities open to the nondeterministic machine. Therefore we construct a deterministic finite-state machine M' whose states correspond to the subsets of the set of states of the nondeterministic machine M. To emphasize this relationship we will use n-tuples whose elements are chosen from the states of M to represent the states of M'. The transition table for M' can be constructed in a straightforward way.

Example 3 *Problem:* Construct the transition table of a deterministic machine to simulate the behavior of the machine in Table 2.4.1. We begin by using each nonempty subset of the states of M as a state of M'. We construct the transition table of M' (Table 2.4.4) by listing in the next state n-tuple any state which could have succeeded one of the states in the present state n-tuple.

The reader should determine how the initial and final states of M' were determined.

This procedure may generate a table that contains states which cannot be reached from the given initial state for any input sequence. A shorter table (without these extra states) can be found directly if we begin from the initial state of M', which is the set containing the known initial state of M. We add states to the present state column only if they appear as a next state entry. In this particular example state (2) is not needed. ▪

The details of these constructions and the determination of the initial and final states of the deterministic machine is our next topic.

Formal results   The constructions we have been informally describing can be formally included in the proof of a theorem concerning the equivalence of the models:

Theorem 1 $1DFSA = 1NFSA$.

    Proof   (a) The deterministic acceptor is a special case of the nondeterministic acceptor.   Therefore $1DFSA \subseteq 1NFSA$.

      (b) Given a nondeterministic finite-state acceptor M with m states $S_1, \ldots, S_m$, construct a finite-state acceptor M' with $2^m - 1$ states whose labels are the sets $(S_1), \ldots, (S_m), (S_1,S_2), \ldots, (S_1,S_m)$, $(S_2,S_3), \ldots, (S_2,S_m), \ldots, (S_{m-1},S_m), (S_1,S_2,S_3), \ldots, (S_{m-2}, S_{m-1},S_m), \ldots, (S_1, S_2, \ldots, S_m)$.   We denote these sets by the symbols $S_i'(1 \leq i \leq 2^m - 1)$.   The input alphabets of M and M' are identical.   The accepting states of M' are determined as follows: State S_i' is an accepting state of M' only if some S_j in S_i' is an accepting state of M.   The state transition function f' is constructed such that S_l is in the set $f'(S_i',I_j)$ if and only if $S_l \in f(S_m,I_j)$ for some $S_m \in S_i'$.   The initial state of M' is (S_k), where S_k is the initial state of M.

      We must show that:

1. M' is deterministic.
2. M' accepts any input sequence that M will.
3. M accepts any input sequence that M' will.

Now we prove these three statements.

1. The state transition function for M' produces one result for each (state, input) pair.   Therefore M' is deterministic.
2. The set S_i' is the set of possible states of M.   The transition function of M' is constructed so that S_i' contains all possible states of M at the next move.   Therefore M' keeps track of the possibilities open to M.   Furthermore, M' reaches an accepting state whenever there is at least one sequence of transitions in M which lead to an accepting state.   Thus M' accepts any string which M accepts.
3. If M' accepts a string, it must reach a final state which includes in its set a final state of M.   For any state S_k in the set S_i' there exists a sequence of choices of moves of M which would place M in state S_k at the same time that M' was in S_i'.   Thus, if M' accepts the string, there must exist a sequence of moves by M leading to acceptance of the same string.   Q.E.D.

PROBLEMS

1. Let M be described by Table 2.4.5.

    (a) Find a regular expression describing the language accepted by M.

    (b) Find a deterministic acceptor which is equivalent to M.

Table 2.4.5 A nondeterministic finite-state machine

	a	b
→ (S_1)	S_1	S_2
S_2	S_2	S_1, S_2

2. Find a deterministic acceptor equivalent to the acceptor of Table 2.4.6.

Table 2.4.6 A nondeterministic acceptor

	x	y
→ S_1	S_1, S_2	S_3
S_2	S_1	S_2
(S_3)	S_2	S_1, S_2

3. Let M be a nondeterministic finite-state machine with outputs.

    (a) Write a formal definition of M as a six-tuple $\langle I, O, S, S_0, f, g \rangle$, where

$$f: I \times S \to 2^S$$
$$g: I \times S \to 2^O$$

    (b) Write a formal definition of M as a five-tuple $\langle I, O, S, S_0, f \rangle$, where

$$f: I \times S \to 2^{S \times O}$$

    (c) Using the definition of part a, find a regular expression for the set of output strings which could be produced by the machine of Table 2.4.7 if the input string is restricted to the set **b***.

Table 2.4.7 A nondeterministic finite-state machine

	a	b
→ S_1	S_1/R	S_2/R
S_2	S_2/R	$\left\{ \begin{matrix} S_1 \\ S_2 \end{matrix} \right\} / \left\{ \begin{matrix} R \\ L \end{matrix} \right\}$

(*d*) Using the definition of part *b*, find a regular expression for the set of output strings which could be produced by the machine of Table 2.4.8 if the input string is restricted to the set **b***.

Table 2.4.8 A nondeterministic finite-state machine

	a	*b*
→ S_1	S_1/R	S_2/R
S_2	S_2/R	$\left\{\begin{matrix} S_1/R \\ S_2/L \end{matrix}\right\}$

(*e*) Do the expressions found in parts *c* and *d* represent the same sets? Explain.

4. Prove: Any nondeterministic finite-state acceptor whose initial state is nondeterministically chosen from a specified set of initial states is equivalent to a deterministic finite-state acceptor.

5. Write a formal definition of a nondeterministic finite-state acceptor in which the final state determines acceptance of the input string.

2.5 NONDETERMINISTIC FINITE-STATE ACCEPTORS FOR REGULAR LANGUAGES

We now show that a nondeterministic finite-state acceptor can be constructed to recognize any given regular language (*type 3* $\subseteq$ *1NFSA*). This result completes the proofs of the equivalence between finite-state acceptors and regular languages. At the end of the section we will extend the equivalence to include regular expressions.

Given a regular grammar G describing language L, we want to construct a nondeterministic finite-state acceptor that will recognize strings from that language. Let the nonterminal symbols of G be $N_1, \ldots, N_n$. Let the acceptor have states $S_d, S_0, S_1, \ldots, S_n$. Let S_d be the "dead state" and let S_0 be the only accepting state. We will establish a correspondence between the states and the nonterminal symbols:

$$S_i \leftrightarrow N_i \qquad 1 \leq i \leq n$$

(Note that S_0 and S_d do not require corresponding nonterminal symbols in the grammar.) Furthermore, assume without loss of generality that N_1 is the sentence symbol for the grammar. Then S_1 will be the starting state of M.

We construct the machine reversing the process used in Sec. 2.3 to construct a grammar from the specification of an acceptor. In particular, for each rewriting rule of G include a transition in M as follows:

1. If $N_i \to I_j N_k$ is a rewriting rule in G, include the transition $S_i \to S_k$ for input symbol I_j in M.
2. If $N_i \to I_j$ is a rewriting rule in G, include the transition $S_i \to S_0$ for input symbol I_j in M.
3. If there are no rewriting rules in G with N_i on the left side which include I_j on the right side, include the transition $S_i \to S_d$ for input symbol I_j in M.
4. Also include $S_0 \to S_d$ and $S_d \to S_d$ for all $I_j \in I$ in M.

Transitions created by rule 1 keep the machine following the possible derivations of sequences which are not completed sentences but which might be completed to form an acceptable string. Transitions created by rule 2 may be made when the final symbol of a sentence is read. Thus the machine should be able to make transitions to the accepting state for each of these cases. Rule 3 handles the case when there is no way to continue this sequence of input symbols to form an acceptable sentence. The machine goes to a dead state S_d. Rules 4 force the machine to the dead state after producing an output and ensure that the machine can never reach an accepting state after it has reached the dead state.

This construction produces a nondeterministic finite-state machine which will recognize strings in the language described by an arbitrary regular grammar. Since we already know $1DFSA = 1NFSA$ and $1DFSA \subseteq type\ 3$, we have shown

Theorem 1 $1DFSA = 1NFSA = type\ 3$. (The sets of regular languages, the languages accepted by deterministic finite-state acceptors, and the languages accepted by nondeterministic finite-state acceptors are identical.)

Regular expressions Can we construct a recognizer for a language specified by a regular expression? If so, regular expressions are equivalent to type 3 languages. We will show how one can construct a type 3 grammar to define the same set of strings that is described by a given regular expression.

Consider a grammar with sentence symbol S which contains the rewriting rule $S \to aB$. Suppose that this rule is the only rule with S on the left side and a followed by a nonterminal symbol on the right side. Every string in the language which begins with a must be completed by a string in the set denoted by B. If we had a way to find the regular expression for B from the regular expression for S, we could apply the same technique to B and find more of the rewriting rules of the grammar. If the procedure terminates after a finite number of steps, we have a grammar for the language.

These considerations lead us to define the derivative of a regular expression:

The *derivative of a regular expression* R with respect to a terminal symbol a is the set

$$D_a[R] = \{u \mid au \in R\}$$

Let R and S be two regular expressions.   Straightforward computations yield

$$D_a[R + S] = D_a[R] + D_a[S]$$
$$D_a[RS] = (D_a[R])S + \delta(R)D_a[S]$$
$$D_a[R*] = (D_a[R])R*$$
$$D_a[a] = \lambda$$
$$D_a[b] = \varphi \qquad \text{for any terminal symbol } b \neq a$$
$$D_a[\lambda] = \varphi$$
$$D_a[\varphi] = \varphi$$

where

$$\delta(R) = \begin{cases} \lambda & \text{if } \lambda \in R \\ \varphi & \text{otherwise} \end{cases}$$

The definition of the derivative can be extended to the derivative of a set R with respect to a string $\sigma = a_1 a_2 \cdots a_n$:

$$D_\sigma[R] = D_{a_n}[D_{a_1 a_2 \cdots a_{n-1}}[R]]$$

Let $A = \{a_1, a_2, \ldots, a_n\}$ be the set of terminal symbols, let R be a regular expression using symbols from A, and let R_s denote $D_s[R]$.   Every nonempty string in R must start with some member of A.   Thus

$$R = \sum_{i=1}^{n} a_i D_{a_i}[R] + \delta(R)$$

Similarly,

$$D_s[R] = \sum_{i=1}^{n} a_i D_{Sa_i}[R] + \delta(D_s[R])$$

for any $S \in A*$.   By taking more derivatives in this manner until no new ones arise, we can construct a set of equations describing R.   Will the process of constructing the equations ever terminate?   Only if the number of distinct nonempty derivatives is finite.

It can be shown [Brzozowski (1964a)] that the number of distinct derivatives of R is finite.   The proof† is based on an induction on the number

---

† For completeness we include Brzozowski's proof in the text.   The reader may skip the proof.

of operators in $\mathbf{R}$. Let k be the number of operators. *Basis:* If $k = 0$, $\mathbf{R}$ is a single symbol and has not more than three derivatives. *Induction step:* Assume that $\mathbf{P}$ and $\mathbf{Q}$, which contain not more than k operators, have n_P and n_Q distinct derivatives, where n_P and n_Q are finite. Now consider the structure of $\mathbf{R}$, having $k + 1$ operators.

Case 1 $\quad \mathbf{R} = \mathbf{P} + \mathbf{Q}$

Then $\mathbf{D_S[R]} = \mathbf{D_S[P]} + \mathbf{D[Q]}$

Thus $\quad n_R \leq n_P n_Q$

Case 2 $\quad \mathbf{R} = \mathbf{PQ}$

By successively applying the relation for the derivative of a product, we obtain

$$\mathbf{D_S[R]} = (\mathbf{D}_{a_1 a_2 \ldots a_n}[\mathbf{P}])\mathbf{Q} + \delta(\mathbf{D}_{a_1 a_2 \ldots a_{n-1}}[\mathbf{P}])\mathbf{D}_{a_n}[\mathbf{Q}]$$
$$+ \delta(\mathbf{D}_{a_1 a_2 \ldots a_{n-2}}[\mathbf{P}])\mathbf{D}_{a_{n-1} a_n}[\mathbf{Q}] + \cdots$$
$$+ \delta(\mathbf{D}_{a_1}[\mathbf{P}])\mathbf{D}_{a_2 a_3 \ldots a_n}[\mathbf{Q}] + \delta(\mathbf{P})\mathbf{D_S[Q]}$$

Thus $\quad n_R \leq n_P 2^{n_Q}$

Case 3 $\quad \mathbf{R} = \mathbf{P}*$

An expansion yields

$$\mathbf{D_S[R]} = \{\mathbf{D_S[P]} + \delta(\mathbf{D}_{a1}[\mathbf{P}])\mathbf{D}_{a_2 a_3 \ldots a_n}[\mathbf{P}]$$
$$+ \delta(\mathbf{D}_{a_1 a_2 \ldots a_{n-1}}[\mathbf{P}])\mathbf{D}_{a_n}[\mathbf{P}]\}\mathbf{P}*$$

Thus $\quad n_R \leq 2^{n_P} - 1$

This completes the induction step and the proof that the number of distinct nonempty derivatives is finite.

If we establish the relationship $\mathbf{R} \leftrightarrow N$ between expressions R and nonterminal symbols N, the corresponding rewriting rules can be found by the steps:

1. For each i such that $\mathbf{D}_{a_i}[\mathbf{R}] \neq \varphi$, $\mathbf{D}_{a_i}[\mathbf{R}] \neq \lambda$, write $N \rightarrow a_i N_i$.
2. For each i such that $\delta(\mathbf{D}_{a_i}[\mathbf{R}]) = \lambda$, write $N \rightarrow a_i$.

The N_i are new nonterminal symbols which correspond to the regular sets $\mathbf{D}_{a_i}[\mathbf{R}]$. Since the number of distinct nonempty derivatives is finite, the number of nonterminal symbols in the grammar will be finite.

Example 1 Find a grammar for the set $R = (ab + bc)(b + c)*$. The derivatives are

$$R_a = b(b + c)* \qquad \delta(R_a) = \varphi$$
$$R_b = c(b + c)* \qquad \delta(R_b) = \varphi$$
$$R_c = \varphi$$
$$R_{aa} = \varphi$$
$$R_{ab} = (b + c)* \qquad \delta(R_{ab}) = \lambda$$
$$R_{ac} = \varphi$$
$$R_{ba} = \varphi$$
$$R_{bb} = \varphi$$
$$R_{bc} = (b + c)* = R_{ab}$$
$$R_{aba} = \varphi$$
$$R_{abb} = (b + c)* = R_{ab}$$
$$R_{abc} = (b + c)* = R_{ab}$$

The rewriting rules of the grammar are

$$N \to aN_a \qquad N_{ab} \to bN_{ab}$$
$$N \to bN_b \qquad N_{ab} \to b$$
$$N_a \to bN_{ab} \qquad N_{ab} \to cN_{ab}$$
$$N_a \to b \qquad N_{ab} \to c$$
$$N_b \to cN_{ab}$$
$$N_b \to c$$

Since there exists a regular grammar for every regular set, we have regular sets = regular grammars = *1NFSA* = *1DFSA* = *type 3*.

PROBLEMS

1. Grammar G generates language L. It has sentence symbol S and the following rewriting rules:

$$S \to bA \qquad A \to b$$
$$S \to bB \qquad A \to bS$$
$$A \to aA \qquad B \to aA$$
$$A \to aB \qquad B \to a$$
$$A \to a$$

(a) Construct a nondeterministic machine M to recognize the strings in the language generated by G.

(b) Find a deterministic machine M' which is equivalent to M.

(c) Find another grammar for L from the description of M'.

2. Find a finite-state recognizer for each of the following regular sets, using the derivatives of the expression to define the states of the machine.

(a) $a*b + b(a + bb)*a$

(b) $(0 + 12)(01 + 12)*$

(c) $(a + b*a + cc)*cb*$

3. In this problem we consider finite-state machines having an input line labeled S which is used for a "start pulse," other input lines used to receive the input symbol, and one binary output. If the start input of a machine receives a 1 at time t, the machine will behave as though it were in its initial state at time t, and the input symbol at time t will be the first symbol in the input sequence to the machine. For example, a machine to recognize the symbol x whenever it occurs at the same time as a start signal is shown in

Fig. 2.5.1. The start pulse may occur at an arbitrary number of distinct times, *nondeterministically* "resetting" the machine to its initial state each time. Every machine that we discuss behaves this way with respect to its start pulse. Furthermore, every

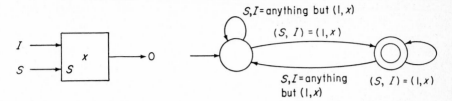

Fig. 2.5.1 A recognizer for the symbol *x*.

machine must produce a 0 output at time *t* if it has not received a start pulse at some time $\tau < t$. In this problem we wish to construct a machine with a start input which will recognize a given regular set. The strings to be tested will be presented as a time sequence of symbols with a start pulse accompanying only the first symbol of the sequence.

The machine to recognize a regular set **R** will be constructed from smaller machines which themselves have start inputs and which recognize "simpler" regular sets. The regular set which a machine recognizes will be written within the box denoting the machine. The machine of Fig. 2.5.2 recognizes the set **ab**.

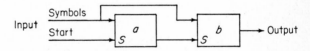

Fig. 2.5.2 A recognizer for the set **ab**.

(*a*) Construct nondeterministic recognizers for **a** + **b** and **a*** from recognizers for **a** and **b**.

(*b*) Construct a nondeterministic recognizer for the set **[(01 + 11)* + 10(0* + 1)]* 1** from recognizers for **0** and **1**.

(*c*) Show how a nondeterministic finite-state machine can be built to recognize the set specified by a given regular expression, by structuring the machine like the "structure" of the regular expression.

4. (*a*) Prove: If *L* is a regular language, then L^R is also a regular language. (*Hint:* Show how to construct a recognizer for L^R, given a recognizer for *L*.)

(*b*) Using the result of part *a*, show that grammars containing only rules of the form

$$A \rightarrow Ba$$

or

$$A \rightarrow c$$

describe regular languages. (*Note:* If the kinds of productions are mixed, as in $A \rightarrow Ba$; $B \rightarrow cA$, the language may not be regular.)

5. (P) Let *M* be an *m*-state acceptor and let *x* be a string of length *n* which is accepted by *M*. (*M* may accept other strings, too.)

(*a*) Prove: If n is sufficiently large, then there must exist a decomposition $x = uvw$ such that $v \neq \lambda$ and $uv^q w$ is accepted by M for all $q > 1$. (*Hint:* If n is large enough, the machine must cycle through some set of states while accepting x.)

(*b*) Find a function $f(m,p)$, where p is the size of the input alphabet, such that the statement of part *a* is true for all x having more than $f(m,p)$ symbols.

(*c*) Prove the statement of part *a* by arguing from the forms of the derivation trees of strings in the language. (*Hint:* Consider the repetitions of nonterminal symbols in the sequence of working strings which describe the derivation.)

6. (P) Show that $L_1 \cup L_2$, $L_1 \cap L_2$, and $\sim L_1$ are regular languages if L_1 and L_2 are regular languages. (*Hint:* Use the fact that *type 3 = 1NFSA*. You also may want to use one of De Morgan's rules:

$$L_1 \cup L_2 = \sim [(\sim L_1) \cap (\sim L_2)]$$

or

$$L_1 \cap L_2 = \sim [(\sim L_1) \cup (\sim L_2)]$$

though they are certainly not necessary.)

7. Show that $\{a^n b^n | n \geq 1\}$ is not a regular language. (*Hint:* See Prob. 5.)

2.6 TWO-WAY FINITE-STATE ACCEPTORS

Finite-state acceptors can be constructed so that they read the input sequence from a tape. When the machine has the input on a tape, it can take its time to read the sequence. It could "think" about the past events for a while and then continue to the next input symbol when it chose to. (If the input is a time sequence, the machine must read every symbol when it is presented; so it cannot pause to "think.") Furthermore, a machine with an input on a tape might be allowed to move both ways on the tape. Such a machine can back up and reexamine the input an arbitrary number of times.

Can a finite-state acceptor with either of these options recognize a nonregular language? No. In this section we discuss these results.

First we must define the model of a finite-state acceptor with an input tape (Figure 2.6.1). The tape is divided into "squares," each containing a single symbol. The end squares of the tape contain "endmarkers," ϕ at the left end, $ at the right end. The sequence of symbols between the endmarkers is

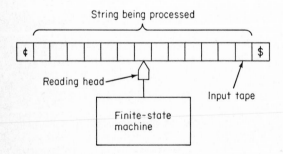

Fig. 2.6.1 A two-way finite-state acceptor.

the input string (read from left to right). The machine has a reading head which can examine a single square of the input tape at one time. The action of the machine during one move is determined by both the symbol under the reading head and the state of the machine. In a single move the machine goes to a new state and instructs the reading head to move one square to the left or right. The machine accepts the input string if it moves the reading head over the right endmarker of the tape while the machine is in an accepting state. A formal definition of a two-way finite-state acceptor is

A *nondeterminstic two-way finite-state acceptor* is a quintuple

$$\langle I,S,S_0,f,F \rangle$$

where

$I =$ a finite set of input symbols
$S =$ a finite set of states
$S_0 \in S =$ the initial state
$f\colon I \times S \to 2^{S \times \{L,R,N\}} =$ the function which specifies the set of possible pairs of the next state and the direction of motion ($L =$ left, $R =$ right, $N =$ no move)
$F \subseteq S =$ the set of accepting states

If f is a single-valued function, the two-way acceptor is *deterministic*. The acceptor is started in the initial state with the reading head over the left endmarker. The string on the input tape is accepted if the acceptor moves the reading head to the right endmarker while the machine is in an accepting state. Let *2DFSA* (*2NFSA*) denote the set of languages which are accepted by two-way deterministic (nondeterministic) finite-state acceptors.

Null moves Can a two-way finite-state acceptor which uses null (N) moves recognize any language which cannot be recognized by a machine without null moves? To answer this question, we ask another one: What can a finite-state acceptor do during a null move? Only go to a new state. Thus, suppose that a machine makes a null move from state S_a to state S_b with input symbol i. What does the machine do next? Symbol i is still under the reading head; so the machine now moves to S_c as specified by symbol i and state S_b. But if it had moved to state S_c in the first place, the null move would not have been required and the same future behavior would occur. In this way every null move can be removed without losing any capability. Finite-state machines cannot do anything more if they are allowed to sit still and "think."

One-way acceptors A finite-state acceptor which cannot move to the left is a one-way finite-state acceptor. Is the one-way finite-state model equivalent to the model of finite-state acceptors with time-sequence inputs? Yes, because null moves do not extend the power of the machine.

A two-way machine

Example 1   A two-way machine is described by the transition table 2.6.1.   (Remember our previous convention that any unspecified entry is to be read as a transition to the dead state.)

Let us consider the operation of the machine when the input tape in Fig. 2.6.2 is presented to the machine.

In Fig. 2.6.3 we show the sequence of motions and states by using a number to indicate the state; the position of the number to indicate the position of the reading head; and arrows to indicate the move sequence.   ■

Equivalence   Now we show how to construct a one-way deterministic machine M_1 which is equivalent to a given two-way deterministic machine M_2. This will prove that $1DFSA = 2DFSA$.   The nondeterministic case is left as an exercise for the reader (Prob. 5).

A one-way machine M_1 can make only as many moves as there are symbols in the input string, while the two-way machine M_2 will make more moves if it ever moves to the left ("backs up").   Therefore M_1 cannot simulate the given M_2 on a move-to-move basis.

The one-way machine suffers from the restriction that it can look at each input symbol only once, while the two-way machine can always go back and take another look at the input sequence.   The one-way machine must determine enough information the first time through, so that it does not have to look back.   The key to this construction is to determine what information M_1 must remember to avoid looking back at the input sequence.

Three ways to remember enough information are:

1. Remember the symbols on the input tape.
2. Remember the sequence of moves that M_2 might make.
3. Remember enough information to predict the actions of M_2 whenever it chooses to back up.

We consider each technique separately to see whether the necessary information can be generated and stored by M_1.

Table 2.6.1   A two-way acceptor

Present state		Symbol Read		
		0	1	¢
→ (S_1)	1	$2R$	$3R$	$1R$
(S_2)	2	$4L$	$3L$	
(S_3)	3	$3R$	$4R$	
(S_4)	④	$2R$	$3L$	

Tape-square no: | 1 | 2 | 3 | 4 | 5 | 6 | 7 | 8 |

Tape: | ¢ | 0 | 1 | 0 | 1 | 0 | 1 | $ |

Fig. 2.6.2 An input tape.

Case 1 Let m be the number of states of M_1 and let n be the number of symbols in the input alphabet. If M_1 has read p symbols of the input sequence, it must remember which one of all possible p-symbol sequences was read. Since there are n^p such sequences, the machine must have at least n^p states. If the input sequence has r symbols and $n^r > m$, the machine must run out of memory before the input sequence has been completely read. Since the length of the input sequence cannot be limited when M_1 is designed, we cannot design a one-way machine which can remember the input sequence for all input tapes.

Case 2 The one-way machine cannot remember the sequences of moves that M_2 would make because the number of sequences depends upon the length of the input string and M_1 will run out of memory.

Case 3 Since M_1 cannot keep the complete move sequences of M_2, we must extract the significant information from the move sequences and determine whether this amount of information is small enough so that M_1 can remember it. Note that the intermediate states of either acceptor are never directly observed; the only relevant states are the initial state of the acceptor and the state which the machine is in when (and if) it reaches the right endmarker. By similar reasoning, the important information about a sequence of moves is (1) the locations of the reading head at the beginning and end of the sequence and (2) the states of the machine before and after the sequence. Consider the sequence of moves between the time that M_2 moves left from a square and the time that it returns to that square. The important information about the sequence is the state (S_1) in which the backing up began and the state (S_2) in which M_2 returns to the square from which it backed up.

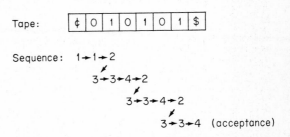

Fig. 2.6.3 An operating sequence of a two-way machine.

This information will be denoted by the pair (S_1, S_2). The details of the sequence (of states and moves) which takes M_2 from S_1 to S_2 are not relevant. We now show that the information about terminal conditions which might result from all possible backing-up move sequences can be computed and remembered by M_1 as it moves from left to right.

States   Suppose that M_2 is reading the symbol on square i. It might move from that square to the left or to the right. If it moves to the left, entering state S_j, what state will it be in when it next moves right into square i? Since the answer to this question depends upon the symbols on the tape to the left of square i, that answer must be remembered by M_1 as it moves into square i. Thus M_1 must determine the answers to two types of questions:

1. What state will M_2 be in the first time its reading head reaches square i of the tape?
2. For each state S_j of M_2, what state will M_2 be in when it next enters square i if it had moved to the left from square i into square $i - 1$ while entering state S_j?

A special case arises if M_2 never reaches the square at the time that its state should be examined to answer the question. We say that it reaches the square in the dead state S_d when in fact it never reaches the square. Let the states of M_2 be $S_1, S_2, \ldots, S_m$, and assume that none of these is the dead state (this assumption does not affect our argument, but makes our counting precise). Then there are $m + 1$ different conditions for which a state of M_2 must be remembered by M_1.

The state of M_1 must include all these $m + 1$ items of information; so we represent each state of M_1 by an $(m + 1)$-tuple. The first component of the tuple is the state of M_2 when it first reaches square i; the remaining components are pairs (S_j, S_k), where S_k is the state in which M_2 returns to square i if it moves left from square i to square $i - 1$ while moving into state S_j. [By requiring that the pair (S_j, S_k) be the $(j + 1)$st entry of the tuple, we can make the S_j's redundant, but we will still include them in our descriptions, for clarity.] For example, if M_2 had states S_1, S_2, S_3, and S_4, one of the states of the equivalent M_1 would be denoted $(S_2, (S_1, S_2), (S_2, S_d), (S_3, S_3), (S_4, S_2))$. There are $(m + 1)^{m+1}$ such states.

If the sequence of states of M_1 for a particular input tape is known, the sequence of operation of M_2 on the same tape can be constructed. Consider Fig. 2.6.4. Under square i of an input tape we depict the state of M_1 when it reaches square i by showing segments of paths which summarize the behavior of M_2 on the squares to the left of square i. In the figure we show M_1 in state $(S_2, (S_1, S_2), (S_2, S_d), (S_3, S_3), (S_4, S_2))$ on square 2 of the tape from

Fig. 2.6.3.   The (S_2, S_d) case is shown by a path which does not return to the boundary of square 2.

How do we determine the state transitions of M_1 from the transition table of M_2?

Informal construction   The major problem in constructing the transition table of M_1 is finding the backup pairs.   In this section we will informally discuss one procedure which can be used to find the transition table.   We will develop the procedure by considering some cases which arose in Example 1.   We will consider the different situations which affect the computation of the backup information.   Thus we will study only some of the moves which occurred in that example, and see how M_1 can determine the correct information in each case.

We will begin the construction from the initial state and then find which states can be reached from that known state on any possible input tape.   If we enter only those states into the table, the table will be smaller than if we considered all $(m + 1)^{m+1}$ possible states of M_1 without regard for whether they can be reached from the known initial state.

The initial state of M_2 is S_1.   If M_2 ever moved left from the initial square (which is the one containing the left endmarker), it would halt.   Therefore the initial state of M_1 must be $(S_1, (S_1, S_d), (S_2, S_d), \ldots, (S_m, S_d))$.

To begin the construction we start with the known initial state of M_1 and find the next states of M_1 for all possible input symbols in the first square.   Then we continue with the new states, finding which states they

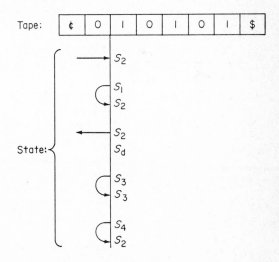

Fig. 2.6.4   The state information of the one-way machine.

may move to for various possible input symbols.   For this machine the constructions are not particularly interesting until we reach later squares; so we will skip to an interesting case.   We should realize that all cases are handled in similar ways.

One case is shown in Fig. 2.6.4.   The machine has reached the second square in state $(S_2, (S_1, S_2), (S_2, S_d), (S_3, S_3), (S_4, S_2))$, and there is a 1 in the square.   The paths in the figure show the effects of the various backup possibilities which might arise (this information is held in the present state of M_1).   What should the state of M_1 be when it reaches the next square?   One way to find this state is to construct segments of the possible paths of M_2 as it crosses the square.   These are shown in Fig. 2.6.5.   First consider the path of M_2 the first time it reaches this square.   From the state of M_1 we know that M_2 would be in state S_2 at that time.   To extend the path we have to determine the next action of M_2 when it is in state S_2 reading a 1.   From Table 2.6.1, we find that M_2 moves left into state S_3.   This path segment is shown in Fig. 2.6.5.   Since this motion was to the left, we still do not know the state of M_2 the first time it reaches the third square of the tape.   What we know is that M_2 turns left, moving into state S_3, and that at some later time it returns to this square while moving into state S_3 (this is because there is a path $S_3 \rightarrow S_3$ in the present state of M_1).   We must determine the next action of M_2 by finding out what it would do when it reached this square in state S_3.   The table tells us that it moves right into state S_4.   Therefore the state of M_2 the first time it reaches the third square of the tape is S_4, and S_4 should be entered as the first component of the next state of M_1.

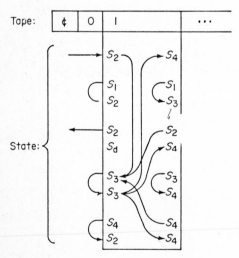

Fig. 2.6.5   Updating the state information in M_1.

To complete the determination of the next state of M_1, we must consider the possibilities which might arise if M_2 were to back up to this square from the next square to the right. If it were moving into state S_1 as it backed up, it would leave this square by moving right and changing to state S_3. Similarly, if it were changing to state S_3 as it entered this square, it would move to the right and enter state S_4. These two path segments can be added to the figure. Now suppose that M_2 returned to this square while changing to state S_2. It would then leave this square by moving to the left and changing into state S_3. From the present state of M_1 we know that M_2 would later return to this square while entering state S_3. At that time it would leave this square by moving right and entering state S_4. Therefore the first time that it reaches the next square after returning to this square (when changing to state S_2) it would be changing to state S_4. This path is shown in the figure. The last possibility is that M_2 might back up to this square while entering state S_4. The actions in this case are identical with those which would follow a return to this square while entering state S_2. Therefore it would be entering state S_4 the next time it moved to the next square on the input tape. When we add this path segment to the figure, we have completed the enumeration of all possible segments of paths of M_2 while reading the symbol in this square, given the information about the previous squares which was contained in the present state of M_1 when it entered the square. Therefore we have completed the determination of the next state of M_1. That state can be read from the right-hand edge of the block shown in the figure. It is state $(S_4, (S_1,S_3), (S_2,S_4), (S_3,S_4), (S_4,S_4))$.

Another important case is illustrated in Fig. 2.6.6. When M_2 first reaches this square while changing into state S_4, it moves left and changes to state S_3. Later it returns to this square while changing to state S_4. This time it again moves left, and again it changes to state S_3. Therefore it has entered a loop which cannot be broken. Since M_2 will never move right from this square, it will never reach the next square of the input tape. Thus we say that M_2 reaches the next square in the dead state S_d. The other portions of the state of M_1 are not significant because they describe how M_2 would behave if it had returned to this square from the right; we know that this cannot happen because M_2 never reaches any square to the right of this one.

By following similar reasoning for all combinations of the present state of M_1 and its input symbols,† we construct a set of blocks (dominoes) which is equivalent to the transition table of M_1.

The blocks shown in Figs. 2.6.5 and 2.6.6 specify the actions of M_2 during its possible visits to a square of the tape. They also specify the action of M_1 during its single visit to the same square. Note that the top edge of

† Remember that we can omit those states which cannot be reached from the known initial state on any input tape.

each block is labeled with the symbol in the square on the input tape, and the leftmost edge is labeled with the state of M_1 as it enters that square. The right edge is labeled with the state of M_1 as it moves to the next square. Since the state as it moves to the next square must be the same as the state when it enters the next square, the action of M_1 in the next square must be specified by a block whose left edge matches the right edge of this block. Continuing this argument, we conclude that the actions of M_1 on a tape can be determined by playing a domino game in which the left edge of the leftmost block must be the state of M_1 when it starts on the first square of the tape, the sequence of symbols along the top edge of the row of dominoes must match the input tape, and the adjacent edges of the dominoes must match. If we play this game with the entire input tape, starting with the initial state of M_1, the path segments on the blocks can be examined to find the complete details of the move sequence of M_2 on the same tape. The state of M_2 when it leaves the segment by moving off the right end can be read from the upper right edge of the rightmost block.

How can we determine whether M_2 accepts an input tape? We play this domino game starting with the proper initial state for M_1, which is $(S_1, (S_1, S_d), (S_2, S_d), \ldots, (S_m, S_d))$. Then we must determine whether M_2 halts over the right endmarker in a final state. It is possible that M_2 enters the last square several times before halting there; so we must be careful about defining the final states of M_1. An easy way to define them is to consider another machine, M_2', which is the same as M_2, except that whenever M_2 halts on the right endmarker in a final state, M_2' moves to the right in a

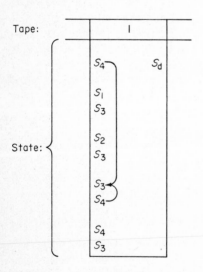

Fig. 2.6.6 Updating the state of M_1.

Table 2.6.2 A one-way acceptor equivalent to the machine of Table 2.6.1

	0	1	¢
→ $(S_1, (S_3, S_d), (S_4, S_d))$	$(S_2, (S_3, S_3), (S_4, S_2))$	$(S_3, (S_3, S_4), (S_4, S_d))$	$(S_1, (S_3, S_d), (S_4, S_d))$
$(S_2, (S_3, S_3), (S_4, S_2))$	$(S_3, (S_3, S_3), (S_4, S_2))$	$(S_4, (S_3, S_4), (S_4, S_4))$	
$(S_3, (S_3, S_4), (S_4, S_d))$	$(S_2, (S_3, S_3), (S_4, S_2))$	$(S_4, (S_3, S_4), (S_4, S_d))$	
$(S_4, (S_3, S_4), (S_4, S_4))$	$(S_3, (S_3, S_3), (S_4, S_2))$		
$(S_3, (S_3, S_3), (S_4, S_2))$	$(S_3, (S_3, S_3), (S_4, S_2))$	$(S_4, (S_3, S_4), (S_4, S_4))$	
$(S_4, (S_3, S_4), (S_4, S_d))$	$(S_2, (S_3, S_3), (S_4, S_2))$		

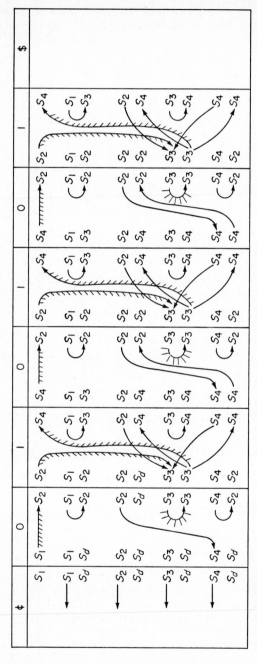

Fig. 2.6.7 The solution of the domino game for the one-way machine equivalent to the two-way machine of Table 2.6.1. The path followed by M_2 is crosshatched (compare with the path shown in Fig. 2.6.3).

final state. There are no other conditions under which M_2' moves to the right of the endmarker. Machine M_2' will first run off the right endmarker in a final state only if M_2 accepts the string on the input tape. Thus the final states of M_1 must be those which would produce a next state of M_1' (based on M_2') in which the first component of the tuple is a final state of M_2'. More details of this determination are considered in Prob. 6.

The result of the domino game for the machine derived from Example 1 is shown in Fig. 2.6.7.

If the two-way machine never enters a certain state while moving to the left, the equivalent one-way machine will not have to know what the two-way machine would do under these circumstances. Therefore the backup pair which corresponds to that state can be omitted from the description of the states of the equivalent one-way machine. This observation can reduce the size of the table for the equivalent one-way machine. For the machine in our example, states S_1 and S_2 meet the condition; so they can be omitted as candidates for backing up. Using this observation, we derive the one-way machine of Table 2.6.2, which is equivalent to the two-way acceptor of Table 2.6.1.

The machine of Table 2.6.2 could be further reduced to a four-state machine by conventional reduction algorithms. This reduction is not necessary for our argument, however, because we are interested in the existence of the equivalent one-way machine, and not in its complexity (as long as the number of its states remains finite).

Since there is a one-way finite-state machine which is equivalent to any given two-way deterministic finite-state machine we have shown:

Theorem 1 *2DFSA = type 3.* (Two-way deterministic finite-state acceptors accept precisely the regular languages.)

This result states that finite-state recognizers with input tapes do not gain additional power by being allowed to move both directions on the input tape. More complex machines usually gain additional power if they are allowed two-way motions.

PROBLEMS

1. (*a*) Find the domino patterns of the one-way machine of Table 2.6.2.

(*b*) Use the dominoes to find the path as the machine checks 01001.

2. Construct a two-way machine to recognize the language $L \in \{a,b,c\}*$ that contains those strings in which a sequence from the set **a(ab)*** is found between every pair of c's and the string begins and ends with c's.

3. Find the simplest one-way acceptor which is equivalent to the acceptor of Table 2.6.3.

Table 2.6.3　A two-way acceptor

	a	b	$\mathcal{c}$
$\longrightarrow$ S_1	S_2R	S_2L	S_1R
S_2	S_3R	S_1R	S_3R
$\textcircled{$S_3$}$	S_2L	S_3L	

4. In the definition of a two-way machine, a single function f was used to describe both the next-state and move choice.

　(*a*) When the machine is deterministic, show that the mapping

$$f: I \times S \rightarrow 2^{S \times \{L,R\}}$$

can be replaced by

$$f: I \times S \rightarrow S$$
$$h: I \times S \rightarrow \{L,R\}$$

without changing the set accepted by the machine.

　(*b*) Why is the replacement in part *a* not possible in a nondeterministic acceptor without changing the language it accepts? Give an example.

5. Would the construction in the text have to be modified to find a one-way finite-state machine which accepts the same set of strings as a given two-way nondeterministic finite-state machine? Why? If so, how?

6. To change M_1 in the construction in the text so that it enters the last square in a final state, we must define the final states of M_1 to be those which correspond to move sequences of M_2 such that, if M_1 reaches the last square in the proper way, there will exist a way to construct an accepting move sequence for M_2. Thus there must be some "looking ahead" to define the final states of M_1. Give a description of an algorithm for finding the final states of M_1.

2.7　COMMENTS

The concept of state as applied to digital systems appeared for the first time in Huffman (1954). Moore (1956) discusses many identification and equality questions for sequential circuits. Mealy (1955) introduces the Mealy model.

　The notion of regular expressions was introduced by Kleene (1956), who showed the equivalence between regular expressions and the computations of finite-state machines. Arden (1960) discusses the uniqueness of the solutions of equations of the form $\mathbf{x} = \mathbf{ax} + \mathbf{b}$; the uniqueness of the solutions of equations which have more complex structures is discussed by Bodnarchuk (1965b).

　The equivalence between two-way and one-way finite-state machines was proved by Shepherdson (1959). Rabin and Scott (1959) discuss many results concerning finite-state machines with input tapes.

3
Turing Machines

Turing machines are at the high end of the hierarchy of complexity and power.
A Turing machine has an infinite memory, though the amount of memory
used during any terminating computation must be finite. All machine models
discussed in later chapters have an infinite memory with restricted access.
The models differ in the restrictions on their access to the contents of the
infinite memory.

The Turing machine model is important because the set of calculations
which can be performed by Turing machines is believed to include all calculations which any machine can perform. This assertion cannot be proved,
because the phrase "any machine" includes machines not yet proposed.
However, one can show that Turing machines can compute all partial-recursive functions; mathematicians believe that this class includes all functions
which can be computed. We will concentrate on the relationship between
the machine model and the set of languages; the reader is referred to Minsky
(1967) for the details of the equivalence between Turing machines and partial-
recursive functions.

The Turing machine model imposes only a few restrictions on the access to the infinite memory. This makes it easier to study than models with more restrictions, but it is difficult to obtain many constructive results concerning its properties. The model is useful in automata theory, not only as the most general model but also as a general model which can be restricted in theoretically simple ways to obtain models with less power.

3.1 TURING MACHINE MODELS

The Turing machine model has a finite-state machine connected to a read/write head which moves on an infinite tape (Fig. 3.1.1). The infinite tape is divided into "squares," each containing a single symbol chosen from some set $T = \{T_1, \ldots, T_n\}$, where T_1 (often written b) denotes the blank symbol. At any time, all but a finite number of squares of the tape will be blank (contain b). The read/write head can examine and change the contents of one tape square at a time. The action of the machine during a move is determined by the symbol under the read/write head and the internal state (a member of the finite set $S = \{S_1, \ldots, S_m\}$). The action may include a change of the state of the machine, of the symbol under the read/write head, and of the position of the read/write head on the tape. In Turing's model all these changes may be made in each move.

Many machine models with infinite tapes can be constructed by modifying Turing's model. In this section we will discuss some of those models which are equivalent to the Turing machine and prove those equivalences. Other equivalent models will be discussed in Secs. 3.4 and 3.5.

The other models are constructed by (1) restricting the types of actions during one step, (2) adding more tapes and/or read/write heads, or (3) changing the tape format.

3.1.1 TURING'S MODEL

The machine has one tape which is infinite in both directions, with one read/write head which examines one square at a time. In one step the machine

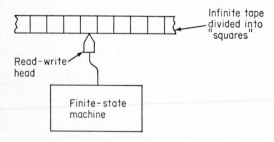

Fig. 3.1.1 A Turing machine.

Table 3.1.1   A Turing machine

State	Input		
	b	1	2
$\rightarrow S_1$	$2LS_2$	$1RS_1$	
S_2	bRS_3	$1LS_2$	$2LS_2$
S_3		bRS_4	bRS_5
S_4	$1RS_5$	$1RS_4$	$2RS_4$
S_5	$1LS_2$		

examines the symbol under the read/write head and the current state to determine:

1. A new symbol to be written on the tape in the square under the read/write head (this is the same square from which the input symbol was read).
2. A motion of the reading head along the tape; either the head moves one square left (L) or one square right (R).
3. The next state of the finite-state machine.
4. Whether to halt or not.

Since any Turing machine has a finite number of states and a finite tape alphabet, it can be described by a transition table, transition graph, or flow chart. Each transition must specify the new symbol in the square under the read/write head, the direction of motion of the read/write head, and the new state. We retain the convention that the machine halts whenever it encounters a combination not specified in the machine's description.

Example 1   Table 3.1.1 describes a five-state Turing machine with three symbols in its tape alphabet. Suppose that it is started in state S_1 reading the leftmost 1 on the tape of Fig. 3.1.2. Figure 3.1.3 shows "snapshots" of the machine after each of its first four moves. The internal state is written within the box representing the control unit. After 27 moves the machine halts in the configuration shown in Fig. 3.1.3*f*.   ■

The information in the transition table can be enumerated by listing each possible move as a quintuple $\langle S_i, T_j, T_k, \begin{Bmatrix} H \\ L \\ R \end{Bmatrix}, S_l \rangle$. The first two elements of the quintuple are the present state and the symbol under the read/write head. If the first two elements of a quintuple describe the actual conditions, then its final three elements indicate the actions to be performed; they are written in the order the actions are performed: T_k is the new symbol, the

{ b | b | b | I | I | b | b | b | b }| **Fig. 3.1.2**   The initial tape for Example 1.

L or R specifies left or right motion by the read/write head, and S_i specifies the next state of the machine. An H in the move position means that the machine halts after this step. For example, one quintuple in the description of the machine of Table 3.1.1 is $\langle S_2,b,b,R,S_3 \rangle$. Usually, we write, move quintuples, without punctuation, as $S_2 b b R S_3$.

As a convenience in the discussions to follow, we will refer to any machine described by Turing's original formulation as a Q-machine.

Functions   A Turing machine starts with a given initial tape and performs a transformation on that tape. If the machine halts, the result of that transformation is the contents of the tape at the time the machine halted. If the machine never halts, the result is not defined. Often it is convenient to define these transformations as mathematical functions. We define the

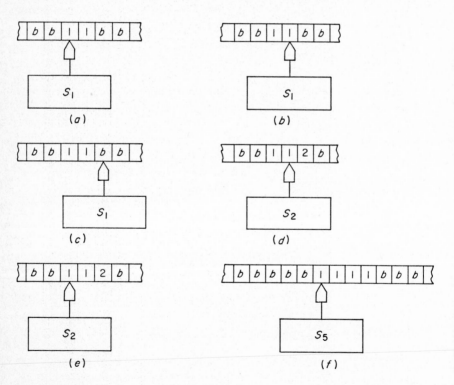

Fig. 3.1.3   The Turing machine of Table 3.1.1 in action.   (a) Initial; (b) 1 move; (c) 2 moves; (d) 3 moves; (e) 4 moves; (f) 27 moves.

transformation as a function from the nonnegative integers to the nonnegative integers if several conditions are met:

1. The initial tape contains n 1's in consecutive squares and is blank otherwise.
2. The machine is started with its read/write head over the leftmost 1 and its control unit in a specified initial state.
3. When the machine halts, its tape contains only 1's and blanks.

Conditions 1 and 2 define the "standard starting conditions." The operation of the machine is defined as the computation of an integer function of an integer argument, where the number of 1's on the initial tape is the value of the argument and the number of 1's on the final tape is the result. If the machine does not halt, or halts with other symbols on the tape, the function is undefined for the argument which was provided. Since the result is not defined for all arguments, the function is called a *partial function*. If the result were defined for all arguments, the function would be a *total function*.

Example 2   The Turing machine of Example 1 computes $f(n) = 2n$.
   We can argue that the machine computes $f(n) = 2n$ by observing the effects of the actions of the machine when it is in various states. Initially, in state S_1, it moves to the right and writes a 2 at the right end of the original sequence of 1's. The remaining states form a loop in which one 1 is erased to the left of the 2 and then two 1's are written to the right of the 2. In states S_2 and S_3 the machine finds and erases the leftmost 1. In states S_4 and S_5 the machine finds the right end and adds two 1's. The machine halts in state S_5, with the read/write head over the leftmost 1 of the answer. The machine halts in almost standard conditions (though not, of course, in state S_1, for then it would be in an "infinite loop"). ■

Recursive functions   Is there a mathematical characterization of the functions which can be computed by Turing machines? (Remember that these are functions of nonnegative integers into nonnegative integers.)
   A recursive definition of a primitive recursive function is given by the following rules:

1. The zero function $Z(x) = 0$ is a primitive recursive function.
2. The successor function $S(x) = x + 1$ is a primitive recursive function.
3. The generalized identity function of n variables $I_{i,n}(x_1, x_2, \ldots, x_n) = x_i$ $(1 \le i \le n)$ is a primitive recursive function for any finite value of n.
4. If $f_1, f_2, \ldots, f_n$ are n primitive recursive functions of m variables and g is a primitive recursive function of n variables, then the function h defined by

$$h(x_1, \ldots, x_m) = g(f_1(x_1, \ldots, x_m), f_2(x_1, \ldots, x_m), \\ \ldots, f_n(x_1, \ldots, x_m))$$

is a primitive recursive function. This is the composition of the functions $g, f_1, f_2, \ldots, f_n$.

5. If f is a total function of n variables and g is a total function of $n + 2$ variables, then the function h defined by

$$h(0, x_1, x_2, \ldots, x_n) = f(x_1, \ldots, x_n)$$
$$h(y + 1, x_1, x_2, \ldots, x_n) = g(y, h(y, x_1, \ldots, x_n), x_1, \ldots, x_n)$$

is a primitive recursive function. This is the operation of primitive recursion.

6. Every primitive recursive function can be constructed by a finite number of applications of rules 1 to 5.

Example 3 The function $f(y,x) = y + x$ is a primitive recursive function. It is defined as follows:

$$f(0,x) = I_{1,1}(x)$$
$$f(y + 1, x) = S(I_{2,3}(y, f(y,x), x))$$

To evaluate the sum $2 + 3$ using this definition, we substitute as follows:

$$
\begin{aligned}
f(2,3) &= S(I_{2,3}(1, f(1,3), 3)) \\
&= S(f(1,3)) \\
&= S(S(I_{2,3}(0, f(0,3), 3))) \\
&= S(S(f(0,3))) \\
&= S(S(3)) \\
&= S(4) \\
&= 5
\end{aligned}
$$

■

Every primitive recursive function is a total function. Every primitive recursive function can be computed by a Turing machine which halts whenever the input tape is in standard format. To prove the statement that every primitive recursive function can be computed by a Turing machine, we must exhibit a Turing machine which performs each of the operations of steps 1 to 5, and show how these machines can be combined to obtain the desired result. To prove that these machines always halt, we must use an induction proof (Prob. 3).

The set of partial-recursive functions is formed from the set of primitive recursive functions by introducing the minimalization operator, by adding the following rules:

7. Any function obtained by applying rules 1 to 5 to partial-recursive functions is a partial-recursive function.

8. If f is a total function of $n + 1$ variables, then the function

$$h(x_1, \ldots, x_n) = \mu_y(f(y, x_1, \ldots, x_n))$$

is a partial-recursive function. The minimalization function μ_y has the value which is the least (nonnegative integer) value of y such that $f(y, x_1, \ldots, x_n) = 0$ for the given values of $x_1, \ldots, x_n$.

9. Every partial-recursive function can be constructed by a finite number of applications of rules 7 and 8.

Turing machines can compute partial-recursive functions, but might not halt, because there may not exist a value of y satisfying a minimalization operator. If it turned out that such a value did not exist, the machine would try indefinitely to find it. It might seem reasonable that a machine could be constructed to detect whether a value of y exists and to cause the search to be aborted when it does not exist. Unfortunately, such a machine does not exist (Prob. 4 of Sec. 3.6).

Conversely, every Turing machine computation can be described by a partial-recursive function. A proof of this statement is complex and is omitted from this text.

Instantaneous descriptions   Snapshots of a machine in action are very useful for describing the behavior of the machine. In Example 1 we depicted the machine's conditions by drawing pictures of the machine. The instantaneous description of a machine represents the same information using a string of symbols. Strings are easier to write than pictures are to draw, and the string representation is quite useful when proving statements about the set of languages which a set of machines accepts. For these reasons, as each machine model is introduced, we also introduce the rules for forming the instantaneous description of any machine within that class.

The *instantaneous description* of the configuration of a Turing machine is a string of symbols constructed as follows:

1. Write down the symbols currently contained on the smallest contiguous portion of the tape which includes all nonblank squares and the square where the read/write head is located.
2. Immediately to the left of the symbol in the square under the read/write head, write a symbol indicating the current state of the machine. (To avoid ambiguity, the symbols used to indicate the states must be distinct from the symbols which may appear on the tape.) If the tape is blank, the instantaneous description consists of the symbol representing the internal state of the machine followed by a single b.

Each instantaneous description has finite length, since the machine cannot visit more than a finite number of squares in finite time.

Example 4   The instantaneous description
$$T_4T_1T_2T_1T_2T_2S_3T_1T_4T_2$$
represents the machine in Fig. 3.1.4.   ■

A sequence of instantaneous descriptions depicting the conditions after each move made by a machine will be useful when we discuss the relationships between the operation of a Turing machine and the derivation of the string it is accepting.

Example 5   The following sequence of instantaneous descriptions describes the computation discussed in Example 1.

```
     S₁  1   1                        S₂  b   1   2   1   1
     1   S₁  1                        S₃  1   2   1   1
     1   1   S₁  b                    S₄  2   1   1
     1   S₂  1   2                    2   S₄  1   1
     S₂  1   1   2                    2   1   S₄  1
S₂   b   1   1   2                    2   1   1   S₄  b
     S₃  1   1   2                    2   1   1   1   S₅  b
     S₄  1   2                        2   1   1   S₂  1   1
     1   S₄  2                        2   1   S₂  1   1   1
     1   2   S₄  b                    2   S₂  1   1   1   1
     1   2   1   S₅  b                S₂  2   1   1   1   1
     1   2   S₂  1   1           S₂   b   2   1   1   1   1
     1   S₂  2   1   1           S₃   2   1   1   1   1
     S₂  1   2   1   1                S₅  1   1   1   1
```

3.1.2   QUINTUPLE RESTRICTIONS

Other machine models that are equivalent to Q-machines and that use a single read/write head on a single infinite tape can be created by placing restrictions on the combinations of actions which can be performed in one move. Any one of the following restrictions can be imposed, and the class of machines which meets the restriction will be equivalent to the class of Q-machines.

1. Allow the machine not to move the read/write head.
2. The machine must change state and may either write or move, but not both.
3. The machine must move and may either change state or write, but not both.
4. The machine must write and may either move or change state, but not both.

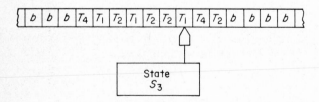

Fig. 3.1.4   A Turing machine during a computation.

5. The machine may perform only one action: move or write or change state.

In this section we will prove that the first two classes of machines are equivalent to the class of Q-machines. The second result will be used later. Proofs of the equivalence for classes 3 and 4 are discussed in Probs. 9 and 10. We will not discuss class 5 [see Fischer (1965a)].

Options not to move   Now we give the machine the option not to move the read/write head in a move. Whenever the machine should exercise this option, we write N in the move position of the quintuple. We denote these machines as *N-machines*. It is easy to show that the sets of Q-machines and N-machines are equivalent. Let Q denote the set of Q-machines and N the set of N-machines. A set inclusion relation such as $Q \subseteq N$ is satisfied if, for every Q-machine, there is an equivalent N-machine. If $Q \subseteq N$ and $Q \supseteq N$, then $Q = N$. Now we prove $Q = N$:

1. $Q \subseteq N$, since any Q-machine is automatically an N-machine. (It does not happen to use the option not to move.)
2. $N \subseteq Q$, since we can construct a Q-machine Q' equivalent to a given N-machine N' by inserting additional states for every N move, as follows:
    The set of quintuples of Q' includes every quintuple from N' in which the move is L or R. If the quintuple $S_i T_j T_k N S_l$ appears in N', add state S_i^* to the set of states of Q' and include the quintuples

    $$S_i T_j T_k L S_l^*$$

    and

    $$S_i^* T_p T_p R S_l \qquad \text{for } 1 \le p \le n$$

    in the description of Q'. The effect is that Q' simulates no move by moving to the left one square and then back to the right without changing the symbol in the neighboring square. Since every N-move has been eliminated from the description, the machine constructed is a Q-machine.

Always change state   Now we restrict the machine to change state and either write or move, but not both, in a single step. The machine can be described by quadruples in which the third entry is either a new symbol or an L or R representing the motion. We will call machines in this class *F-machines*. We show the equivalence between F- and N-machines by construction:

1. $F \subseteq N$: Construct a machine N' equivalent to a given machine F' as follows:

    a. If $S_iT_jT_kS_l$ is in F', put $S_iT_jT_kNS_l$ in N'.
    b. If $S_iT_jLS_k$ is in F', put $S_iT_jT_jLS_k$ in N'.
    c. If $S_iT_jRS_k$ is in F', put $S_iT_jT_jRS_k$ in N'.
2. $N \subseteq F$: Construct a machine F'' equivalent to a given N'' as follows:
    a. If $S_iT_jT_kNS_l$ is in N'', put $S_iT_jT_kS_l$ in F''.
    b. If $S_iT_jT_kLS_l$ is in N'', put both $S_iT_jT_kS_{i,j}$ and $S_{i,j}T_kLS_l$ in F''.
    c. If $S_iT_jT_kRS_l$ is in N'', put both $S_iT_jT_kS_{i,j}$ and $S_{i,j}T_kRS_l$ in F''.

In this simulation F'' first writes the proper new symbol in the square and then goes into a state in which it remembers the state-symbol combination which initiated the sequence. In the next step the machine moves the head to the proper square and enters the correct state.

3.1.3 TAPE RESTRICTIONS

The Turing model uses a single tape which is infinite in both directions. Equivalent models can be defined with a tape which is infinite in only one direction or with an arbitrary finite number of infinite tapes.

    To prove an equivalence between two machine models using different storage formats we must introduce mappings which translate information from one format to the other. We must be very cautious with these proofs because we might perform computations (during the process of translating the tape into the new format) which aid the machine! Restrictions must be introduced so that arbitrary translations are not allowed. For Turing machine models it is enough to require that each of these mappings be simple enough so that it can be performed by a Turing machine.

    Note that if a Turing machine translation were applied to the input tape of a finite-state acceptor, and the translator did the bulk of the decision task, we might conclude that the finite-state acceptor could accept any set of strings acceptable by a Turing machine. This conclusion is false

One-way infinite tapes A tape which is infinite in only one direction is called a *one-way infinite tape*; a tape which is infinite in both directions is called a *two-way infinite tape*. To show the equivalence between machines with one-way and machines with two-way infinite tapes, we need to simulate a machine with a two-way infinite tape on a machine with a one-way infinite tape. The reverse inclusion is trivial. Therefore we must show (1) that a two-way infinite tape can be mapped onto a one-way infinite tape, and (2) that the finite-state control can be modified so that a machine M_1 with the one-way infinite tape can be constructed to simulate the behavior of a given machine M_2 which uses a two-way infinite tape.

    The one-way tape has an end square in the direction in which it is not infinite. We assume that this end square is at the left end of the tape.

Suppose we number the squares of both tapes: on the one-way tape begin with 1 at the leftmost square; on the two-way tape, begin with some square arbitrarily chosen to be square 0. The remaining squares are numbered with successive integers increasing toward the right. The squares of the two-way tape are mapped onto the squares of the one-way tape as follows: Let n and m be the numbers of corresponding squares on the one-way and two-way tapes, respectively. Then

$$n = \begin{cases} 2m + 2 & \text{for } m \geq 0 \\ -2m + 1 & \text{for } m < 0 \end{cases}$$

Figure 3.1.5 illustrates the mapping. This mapping amounts to folding the two-way tape at square 0 and then placing the symbols from the upper and lower folds in alternate squares on the one-way tape. Note that the first square of the one-way tape is not used for symbols from the original tape; we will use it for a special marker to tell the one-way machine that it has reached the end and must turn around; let this marker be the symbol $*$, some symbol which is not in the tape-symbol set of M_2.

The simulation proceeds as follows:

1. The one-way machine moves twice as many squares as the two-way machine would have when it encountered the same state-symbol combination, unless it encounters the endmarker $*$. To know whether "right" motion on the two-way tape corresponds to right motion on the one-way tape, M_1 must know whether M_2 is to the right or left of the fold. To remember the position of M_2 relative to the fold, M_1 must have at least two states for each state of M_2.
2. Whenever M_1 reaches the endmarker $*$, it reverses its interpretation of L and R and moves to the proper square to begin on the other fold of the tape.

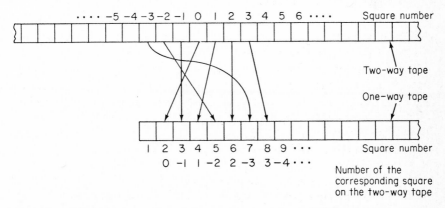

Fig. 3.1.5 Mapping a two-way infinite tape onto a one-way infinite tape.

Details   Let M_2 be a quintuple Turing machine with a two-way infinite tape.   Let M_1 be a quintuple Turing machine with a one-way infinite tape. The problem is to simulate the operation of machine M_2 on machine M_1. First, create a tape for M_1 by mapping the symbols from M_2's tape onto M_1's tape with the mapping described above.†   Without loss of generality, assume that square 0 on M_2's tape is the square initially scanned by M_2.   Place the symbol $*$, not in the vocabulary of machine M_2, in square 1 of M_1's tape.

Let $T = \{T_1, T_2, \ldots, T_n\}$ be the set of tape symbols of M_2.

The quintuples of M_1 are constructed as follows: If $S_i T_j T_k D S_l$ is in M_2 (where D is L or R), place in M_1 the following quintuples (where D' is the reverse of D, that is, if D is L, D' is R, and vice versa):

$$\left.\begin{array}{l} S_i T_j T_k D S_{l,D} \\ S_{l,D} T_m T_m D S_l \end{array}\right\} \text{for } 1 \le m \le n \left.\begin{array}{l} \text{double move in forward} \\ \text{interpretation} \end{array}\right.$$

$$\left.\begin{array}{l} S_i' T_j T_k D' S_{i,D}' \\ S_{l,D}' T_m T_m D' S_l \end{array}\right\} \text{for } 1 \le m \le n \left.\begin{array}{l} \text{double move in reverse} \\ \text{interpretation} \end{array}\right.$$

$$S_i' * * R S_i \qquad\qquad\qquad\quad \}\text{reverse-forward transition}$$

$$S_{i,L} * * R S_{i,R}' \qquad\qquad\qquad \}\text{forward-reverse transition}$$

Note that S_i' is state S_i when the machine is on the other "fold."

If M_2 is started in state S_i scanning square 0, then M_1 is started in state S_i scanning square 2.

Flow-chart description   We will also describe this simulation in a flow chart.   In later sections, we will use either flow charts or quintuples, but not both, choosing on the basis of ease of understanding.   Usually the flow-chart description will be chosen.

The simulation of machine M_2 by machine M_1 is described by the flow chart of Fig. 3.1.6.   The array $t(i,j)$ contains triples (u,D,s) describing the next move of M_2 when the state is S_i and the symbol is T_j.   After the triple is read into x, the three components are addressed as $x(1)$, $x(2)$, $x(3)$.

Multitape machines   Another model gives the machine a finite-number of tapes, with an independent read/write head on each tape.   At every step, the actions of the machine are determined by the n symbols read from the n tapes and the present state of the machine.   While performing a single step, the machine may write on any one tape and move the read/write head on that tape.   The machine then enters a new state.   The description requires $(n + 5)$-tuples.   (Why?)

† Note that the symbols themselves are unchanged in the mapping process.

Fig. 3.1.6   Simulation of a machine with a two-way infinite tape by a machine with a one-way infinite tape.

BEGIN

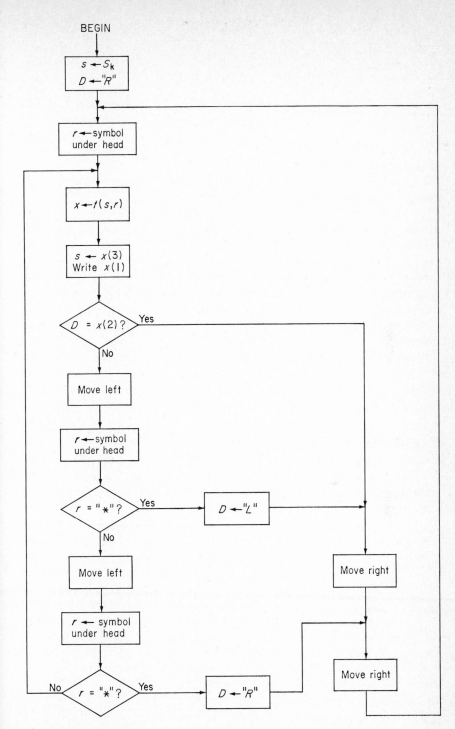

95

Can the operation of an n-tape machine be simulated by a one-tape machine? Now we show that the answer is yes.

How do we code the information from the n tapes onto a single tape? There are several ways to encode multiple tapes onto a single tape. We will use a conceptually simple way in which we use n consecutive squares on the single tape to represent the symbols in the set of squares of the n tapes which have the same square number. Thus square p on tape m is mapped into square $np + m$ on the single tape.

The detailed construction of the simulator is complex. We will indicate the general nature of the construction.

First, notice that the n squares under the n read/write heads of the n-tape machine are not at the same position on the tapes, and therefore not in a set of adjacent squares on the tape of the one-tape machine. Then the one-tape machine cannot use the position of its one read/write head to indicate the positions of the n read/write heads. Rather, it must use its tape to remember the locations of the n heads. It can do this by marking those symbols which are under the n read/write heads of the n-tape machine. Before it can simulate a step, the one-tape machine must hunt for those marked symbols and accumulate the total input information. Some "flag" information must be kept so that the machine knows which direction to move to find the next marked symbol.† After reading all n relevant symbols, it can simulate the moves of the n-tape machine in a straightforward manner (Prob. 16).

PROBLEMS

1. Give a formal description of Turing's model for Turing machines (using a sextuple and mappings).

2. Find the sequence of instantaneous descriptions as the machine of Table 3.1.2 computes $f(2)$. What function does this machine compute?

3. Define standard starting conditions for a machine which computes a function of n arguments $x_1, \ldots, x_n$ to be an instantaneous description of the form

$$S_1 \quad 1^{x_1} \quad b \quad 1^{x_2} \quad b \quad 1^{x_3} \quad b \cdots b \quad 1^{x_n}$$

(a) Prove that the primitive recursive functions of rules 1 to 4 can be computed by Turing machines.

(b) Prove that the primitive recursive function of rule 5 can be computed by a Turing machine.

(c) Prove that the machines constructed in parts a and b always halt.

4. Prove that partial-recursive functions formed by rule 8 can be computed by Turing machines (see Prob. 3 for tape formats).

5. Using only the constructions of Prob. 3, describe a Turing machine which computes the function $f(x,y) = x + y$. (*Hint:* See Example 3.)

---

† Without these flags, the one-tape machine might search indefinitely in the wrong direction for a marked symbol.

Table 3.1.2 A Turing machine

Present state	Input		
	b	1	2
$\to S_1$	$2LS_2$	$1RS_1$	
S_2	$1RS_3$	$1LS_2$	
S_3		bRS_4	
S_4	$1LS_5$	$1RS_4$	$2RS_4$
S_5	bLS_6	$1LS_5$	$2LS_5$
S_6	bLS_8	$1LS_7$	
S_7	$1RS_8$	$1LS_7$	
S_8	bRS_9	$1RS_8$	
S_9	bRS_9	bRS_4	$1LS_{10}$
S_{10}	$1LS_{10}$	$1LS_{11}$	
S_{11}		$1LS_{11}$	

6. Construct N- and F-machines equivalent to the Q-machine of Table 3.1.1
   (*a*) By using the constructions from the proofs.
   (*b*) By working from the description of the function computed by the machine.

7. In the proof that $N \subseteq F$, new states $S_{i,j}$ were introduced (refer to the proof for the definitions). Show that the proof would not work in all cases if the new states were $S_{i,k}$.

8. Show that if a deterministic machine is simulated by the technique used in Sec. 3.1.2, the simulator is also deterministic.

9. An M-machine is a Turing machine which in one step may move the read/write head and either change its state or write a new symbol, but not both. Show that $M = Q$. (*Hint:* To simulate a step in which both a new state and a new symbol are created, have the simulator enter a new state only, then write the new symbol, and then enter the desired state.)

10. A W-machine is a Turing machine which in one step may write a new symbol and either change its state or move, but not both. Show that $N = W$. (*Hint:* Create new symbols which contain information about the move which needs to be made. Then make the move in the next step.)

11. Construct a Turing machine with a one-way infinite tape which simulates the machine in Table 3.1.2.

12. Fill in the details of the simulation of an n-tape Turing machine (modification in Sec. 3.1.3) by a one-tape Turing machine. It may be helpful to consider the following points:
   (*a*) Every square with a read/write head on it might be marked with the number of the read/write head.
   (*b*) If the leftmost and rightmost squares which are under reading heads are marked to indicate that fact, it will be easier for the one-tape machine to locate all the markers.
   (*c*) Extra information in a square can be represented easily if the square is considered to contain an m-tuple, with each component selected from a preselected alphabet. For example, (1,3) could represent a single symbol (Prob. 15).

13. (P) (a) Show that a Turing machine with a two-symbol tape alphabet is equivalent to a Turing machine with an m-symbol tape alphabet. (*Hint:* Encode the symbols into binary numbers.)

(b) Find a two-symbol Turing machine T' which is equivalent to the Turing machine T of Table 3.1.1. What encoding must be performed on the input tape before it is presented to T'?

14. (P) Let a deletion-insertion Turing machine be a Turing machine in which the operations of deleting the square being read or adding a new square with specified contents immediately to the right of the read/write head are allowed. Show that these machines are equivalent to Q-machines.

15. (P) Another way to map a two-way infinite tape onto a one-way infinite tape is to expand the alphabet of tape symbols so that a single square on the one-way tape can contain an ordered pair of the symbols from the alphabet of the two-way tape. For example, if the alphabet of the two-way tape were $\{0,1\}$, the alphabet of the one-way tape would be $\{(0,0), (0,1), (1,0), (1,1)\}$. We could visualize the one-way tape as having two "tracks," one containing the symbols from squares to the left of square 0 of the two-way tape, the other containing the symbols from square 0 and the squares to its right. We could introduce functions $r_1((w,x)) = w$ and $r_2((w,x)) = x$, which describe reading from one track only, and functions $w_1((u,v),y) = (y,v)$ and $w_2((u,v),y) = (u,y)$, which describe writing on one track only. Describe in detail how a machine with a two-way infinite tape can be simulated by a machine with a one-way infinite tape, using the tape mapping specified above.

16. Let machine M have n tapes, with m read/write heads on each tape. In one move mn symbols are examined but only one is changed and only one read/write head is moved.

(a) Give a formal description of M.

(b) Prove that the operations of M can be simulated by a one-tape machine with one read/write head and a one-way infinite tape.

17. Another n-tape Turing machine model restricts the actions during a single move so that they depend upon the symbol read from only one of the tapes. The state of the control unit determines which tape will be read and rewritten during the next move.

Prove that this model is equivalent to the n-tape model in which all tapes can be read in any move but only one tape is changed and one read/write head is moved (Prob. 16).

18. Let $(p_1, \ldots, p_n)$ be the first n prime integers. An n-tuple of nonnegative integers $(i_1, i_2, \ldots, i_n)$ can be encoded into a single integer by using the one-to-one mapping $G(i_1, \ldots, i_n) = \prod_{j=1}^{n} p_j^{i_j}$. This mapping is known as a *Gödel mapping*.

(a) Construct a Turing machine to compute the function $F(k,g) = i_k$, where i_k is the kth component of a vector $(i_1, \ldots, i_n)$ used in forming $g = G(i_1, \ldots, i_n)$. In other words, i_k is the power of the kth prime in the prime factorization of g.

(b) Show that any integer function of n integer variables is equivalent to some function of one integer variable.

3.2 TURING MACHINE ACCEPTORS

The string to be tested by a Turing machine acceptor must be written on the tape before the machine begins the recognition process. The result of the test is determined from the contents of the tape or the internal state when the machine halts (if it does). One definition of acceptance is the following:

A Turing machine tests a string σ if it is started in its initial state reading the left endmarker of a tape containing $\text{¢}\sigma\$$, where ¢, $\$$ are endmarkers not in the alphabet of σ. The machine accepts σ if it halts in an accepting state. The machine does not accept σ if it either halts in a non-accepting state or does not halt.

There are many other equivalent definitions of acceptance by Turing machines. Some of these are discussed later.

Let *DTMA* denote the class of languages accepted by deterministic Turing machine acceptors. Also, let an *F*-acceptor denote an *F*-machine used as an acceptor.

Example 1 In the Turing machine below, S_1 is both the starting state and the accepting state. The machine accepts all strings which contain an even number of 1's.

S_1 ¢ ¢ R S_1
S_1 1 b R S_2
S_2 1 b R S_1

Example 2 In the Turing machine below, S_1 is the initial state and S_9 is the final state. The machine accepts strings consisting of a sequence of 1's followed by the same number of 2's, followed by the same number of 3's. This set of strings is $\{1^n 2^n 3^n | n \geq 1\}$.

S_1 ¢ ¢ R S_1 } move off endmarker
S_1 1 b R S_2 } erase first 1
S_2 1 1 R S_2 ⎫
S_2 b b R S_2 ⎬ move right to first 2, erase it
S_2 2 b R S_3 ⎭
S_3 2 2 R S_3 ⎫
S_3 b b R S_3 ⎬ move right to first 3, erase it
S_3 3 b R S_4 ⎭
S_4 3 3 L S_5 } more 3's on tape
S_4 $\$$ b L S_8 } no more 3's on tape
S_5 b b L S_5 ⎫ are there more 2's?
S_5 2 2 L S_6 ⎭
S_6 2 2 L S_6 ⎫
S_6 b b L S_6 ⎬ are there more 1's?
S_6 1 1 L S_7 ⎭
S_7 1 1 L S_7 ⎫ move to leftmost 1 to start over
S_7 b b R S_1 ⎭
S_8 b b L S_8 ⎫ accept string if all symbols are erased from original string
S_8 ¢ b N S_9 ⎭

The algorithm followed by this machine may be difficult to follow; try tracing the operation for some short strings, such as 112233, 1233, 11223, and 1112233, or draw a flow chart describing the algorithm.

The language L accepted by the machine in Example 2 is not a regular language. In Prob. 5 of Sec. 2.5 it was proved that in a regular language any string longer than some number of symbols can be broken into three strings $x = uvw$ such that $v \neq \lambda$ and all strings of the form $uv^k w$ for any $k \geq 1$ must be in the language. To show that L does not meet this condition, one must enumerate the various ways that a nonempty v might be selected from a long string in L. In all cases the string $uv^2 w$ will not be in L. Therefore L is not regular.

In this chapter we will show that Turing machine acceptors accept recursive languages. This result and the fact that L is not regular prove that there exist recursive languages which are not regular.

PROBLEMS

1. Can the machine in Example 2 be simplified? How? (*Hint:* Perhaps the tests made while the machine is in states S_4, S_5, and S_6 are not necessary. If they are not needed, show where the nonacceptable strings they were designed to catch will be detected.)

2. (P) In the text we defined Turing machine acceptance of a string in terms of the state of the machine when it halts.

(*a*) Define acceptance in terms of the machine halting with a specified symbol under the read/write head.

(*b*) Show that the definition in part *a* is equivalent to the one given in the text. (*Hint:* You must show that, for every acceptor using one definition of acceptance, there exists an acceptor for the same language using the other definition of acceptance.)

3. Consider an n-tape Turing machine processing a string which was originally written (with endmarkers) on one of the tapes.

(*a*) Create a reasonable definition of the acceptance of the string by the machine. Be sure to specify the initial conditions.

(*b*) Show that an n-tape acceptor as you defined it in part *a* is equivalent to a one-tape acceptor as defined in the text.

4. (P) Let M be a Turing acceptor with tape alphabet $T = \{T_1, T_2, \ldots, T_n, \mathcal{c}, \$\}$.

(*a*) Show that an acceptor M' with tape alphabet

$$T' = \{T_1, T_2, \ldots, T_n, \mathcal{c}, \$, \vdash, \dashv \}$$

can be constructed such that it meets both of the following conditions:

(i) M' accepts the same language as M.

(ii) M' keeps the markers $\vdash (\dashv)$ on the leftmost (rightmost) tape square which is adjacent to the leftmost (rightmost) square that must be included in the instantaneous description of M at the corresponding step of the computation. (This condition may be violated only when M' is moving an endmarker.) For example, if the instantaneous description of M is

$$10\mathcal{c}11021\$1bS_2b$$

then the instantaneous description of M' at the corresponding move should be

$$\vdash 10\mathcal{c}11021\$1bS_2b\dashv$$

(*b*) Show that any M' which meets the conditions of part *a* can be modified to construct an acceptor which first tests a string for acceptance and then erases the entire tape if the string is acceptable. (During the erasing stage, condition ii should be satisfied.) Thus any language accepted by a Turing acceptor according to the definition in the text can be accepted by a Turing acceptor which leaves the tape blank.

(*c*) The purpose of this part is to prove that, for every acceptor M' using endmarkers (as described in part *a*), there exists an equivalent *M* without endmarker symbols which accepts the same language as *M'* does. This proof proceeds in several steps.

(i) Show that any Turing acceptor *M* can be modified to form *M''*, which first spreads out the input sequence so that the symbols which were written in squares 1 to *n* are now written in $2n$ squares (squares $n + 1$ to $3n$ may be convenient), the odd-numbered squares containing the symbols and the even-numbered squares being blank.

After spreading out the input sequence, *M''* should ignore the even-numbered squares and simulate *M* on the odd-numbered squares.

(ii) Suppose that an endmarker ($\vdash$ or $\dashv$) is represented by a nonblank symbol in an even-numbered square. Show that, for any acceptor using endmarkers, there exists an equivalent acceptor not using separate endmarker symbols.

(*d*) Using the equivalence from the results of parts *a*, *b*, and *c*, prove that the following two definitions of Turing machine acceptance are equivalent to the one stated in the text. The starting conditions are the same in all three cases. The two accepting conditions are:

1. The machine halts with a blank tape.
2. The machine halts in a specified state with a blank tape.

(*Hint:* The endmarkers are required to test whether the tape is blank.)

3.3 RECURSIVE-LANGUAGE DESCRIPTIONS OF TURING MACHINE ACCEPTORS

We now prove that for every Turing machine acceptor there exists an equivalent recursive language. This will prove *DTMA* $\subseteq$ *type 0*. The grammar constructed will generate a language containing exactly those strings accepted by the machine. In Sec. 3.5 we will show that, for any recursive language, we can construct a Turing machine which will accept the strings in that language; i.e., *type 0* $\subseteq$ *DTMA*.†

In Sec. 3.1 we discussed several equivalent formulations of a Turing machine. If we show that we can generate a recursive language from a given acceptor described by one formulation, we will know that we can generate a recursive language for any Turing machine acceptor, however formulated. We arbitrarily choose to discuss the *Q*-machine in this section.

In Probs. 2 and 4 of Sec. 3.2 we discussed several equivalent definitions of acceptance conditions for Turing machine acceptors. We need prove the equivalence between acceptors and languages for only one definition of acceptance. For convenience in the discussions to follow, we will prove the equivalence for acceptors which accept only if they stop in a specified state, leaving the tape blank. Without loss of generality, we assume that S_2 is the accepting state and that S_1 is the initial state. In the remainder of this chapter, every acceptor will be assumed to be defined that way, unless explicitly specified otherwise.

† This equivalence is the basis for naming type 0 languages "recursive."

The proof that $DTMA \subseteq type\ 0$ is divided into two steps. First we show (Lemma 1) that we can construct a recursive transformational grammar G describing the analysis algorithm followed by a given Turing acceptor Q. The transformational grammar will describe the analysis process in the sense that it permits a derivation of string x from string y, where x and y are instantaneous descriptions of the Turing machine, if the machine has a sequence of moves leading it from x to y. Any string σ which is accepted by Q will be mapped by the acceptor into an instantaneous description $S_2 b$. We construct the grammar such that it maps σ into S if and only if σ is accepted by Q.

Second, we prove that the rewriting rules of the transformational grammar can be "turned around" to produce a set of rewriting rules for a recursive generative grammar which describes the generation of the strings in the language.

Lemma 1   Given a Q-acceptor Q, there exists a recursive transformational grammar G which transforms any string σ accepted by Q into the string S.

Proof   The operation of the acceptor can be described in terms of the sequence of its instantaneous descriptions as it analyzes σ. For example, we might have the following sequence of instantaneous descriptions:

$$S_1 \notin T_1 T_2 T_1 T_2 T_2 T_1 \$$$
$$\notin S_1 T_1 T_2 T_1 T_2 T_2 T_1 \$$$
$$\notin T_1 S_2 T_2 T_1 T_2 T_2 T_1 \$$$
$$\notin T_1 b S_2 T_1 T_2 T_2 T_1 \$$$
$$\vdots$$

To simplify the details of the proof, the working strings which the transformational grammar will use will be the instantaneous descriptions of the Turing machine with ending brackets ([and] for the left and right ends). The working string in the grammar corresponding to the instantaneous description $S_1 \notin T_1 T_2 T_1 T_2 T_2 T_1 \$$ is $[S_1 \notin T_1 T_2 T_1 T_2 T_2 T_1 \$]$.

First we find a set of rewriting rules for a transformational grammar G' which will transform the string $[S_1 \notin \sigma \$]$ to the string $[S_2 b]$ if and only if Q accepts σ. Every production of G' will be context-dependent, since the action of the machine is determined by two pieces of information—the present state and the symbol being scanned—and those are not encoded into the same symbol in the instantaneous description. Even though the input information can be tested in one rewriting rule, all the actions of one machine step cannot be performed in one step of the grammatical derivation, because the rules for the construction of rewriting rules allow changing only a single nonterminal symbol into a (possibly empty) string of terminal and/or nonterminal symbols in one step of the derivation. There are two ways to get around this problem. One is to write a sequence of rewriting rules such that the sequence must be chosen in proper order and the sequence performs the correct transformation on the instantaneous description. The other way is to prove that the capability of the grammar is not expanded by allowing rewriting rules of the form $string_1 \rightarrow string_2$. One such rule can be used to perform all the changes made by one move of the machine. In Prob. 5 we prove that these more general rules can be used in recursive grammars. In our proof of the equivalence between recursive languages and Turing machine acceptors we will use the general rules.

Details The enumeration of the rewriting rules of the grammar is accomplished by classifying various cases. First, what kind of move is made by the machine? Second, is the length of the instantaneous description changed (because an end square was erased or a new square was used)?

Let S denote the set of the acceptor's states.

1. Moves:
   a. No move
   Q contains the quintuple $S_i T_j T_k N S_l$
   The consecutive instantaneous descriptions contain the sequences

   $$---S_i T_j---$$
   $$---S_i T_k---$$

   The rewriting rule is

   $$S_i T_j \rightarrow S_i T_k$$

   b. Right move
   Q contains the quintuple $S_i T_j T_k R S_l$
   The consecutive instantaneous descriptions contain the sequences

   $$---S_i T_j---$$
   $$---T_k S_l---$$

   The rewriting rule is

   $$S_i T_j \rightarrow T_k S_l$$

   c. Left move
   Q contains the quintuple $S_i T_j T_k L S_l$

The consecutive instantaneous descriptions contain the sequences

$$---T_mS_iT_j---$$
$$---S_lT_mT_k---$$

where T_m is the symbol in the square to the left of the read/write head before the move.

A set of rewriting rules is needed to cover all possible symbols T_m in the square to the left. They are

$$T_mS_iT_j \rightarrow S_lT_mT_k \qquad \text{for all } T_m \in T$$

2. Length changes

   a. Left end

   There are two cases, depending upon whether the instantaneous description becomes longer or shorter.

   It will become longer if the machine moves left to a blank square. In such a case the move $S_iT_jT_kLS_l$ is being executed when the read/write head is at the left end of the instantaneous description. This case can be detected by the proximity of the left bracket. Thus the consecutive working strings begin

$$[S_iT_j---$$
$$[S_lbT_k---$$

The rewriting rule is

$$[S_iT_j \rightarrow [S_lbT_k$$

There is one of these rules for each left-move quintuple of Q.

The instantaneous description should be shortened whenever a blank occurs next to the left bracket. Then the blank should be deleted by the rule

$$[b \rightarrow [$$

   b. Right end

   Again there are two cases. We must shorten the instantaneous description when a blank appears next to the right bracket, provided that this blank is not under the read/write head. The set of rewriting rules

$$T_ib] \rightarrow T_i] \qquad \text{for all } T_i \in T$$

accomplishes this shortening.

The string must be lengthened when the machine moves to a new square at the right end. The set of rewriting rules which will accomplish this is

$$S_i] \rightarrow S_ib] \qquad \text{for all } S_i \in S$$

A complete proof that the grammar constructed by this procedure describes the analysis process must include a proof that the grammar cannot produce sequences of strings which do not correspond to analysis sequences of the machine. In keeping with the discussion in Sec. 2.3.1, we will not include proofs of such statements in the text.

Grammar G' transforms the string $[S_1 \not c \sigma \$]$ into the string $[S_2 b]$ if and only if machine Q accepts σ. To complete the proof of the lemma, we must add rewriting rules to G' to change σ into $[S_1 \not c \sigma \$]$ and to change $[S_2 b]$ into S.

The latter transformation is trivial; it can be accomplished by the rewriting rule

$$[S_2 b] \rightarrow S$$

The transformation of σ is accomplished by a simple set of rewriting rules, but their interpretation requires some discussion. The rules are

$$T_i \rightarrow [S_1 \not c T_i$$
$$T_i \rightarrow T_i \$] \quad \text{for all nonblank } T_i \in T$$

Clearly, these rules can be applied at many points in a derivation using the grammar G (G contains the rules of G' and these initial and final rules). If they are not applied at the right time and position, the transformation of σ into S will not be possible. Why? Because

1. These rules introduce brackets.
2. Brackets are never removed except in pairs by the rule which transforms $[S_2 b]$ to S.
3. S does not appear on the left side of any rule of G.
4. Symbols which occur outside a pair of brackets can never be moved inside the pair.

As a consequence of these statements, the only way to obtain a single S is never to allow brackets to appear except at the ends of the working string. Thus there does not exist a way of transforming σ to S that does not correspond to a legitimate move sequence of the acceptor.

Q.E.D.

Proof of theorem   With this lemma, the proof of the theorem is simple. We construct a transformational grammar G from the description of the acceptor Q. Then we construct the generative grammar G'' with the inverse rewriting rules which are constructed by reversing the arrows. If Q accepts σ, there exist derivations $\sigma \underset{G}{\Longrightarrow}^* S$ and $S \underset{G''}{\Longrightarrow}^* \sigma$.

Example 1 The Turing machine of Example 1 of Sec. 3.2 was described by three quintuples:

$$S_1 \quad \text{¢} \quad \text{¢} \quad R \quad S_1$$
$$S_1 \quad 1 \quad b \quad R \quad S_2$$
$$S_2 \quad 1 \quad b \quad R \quad S_1$$

If S_1 is both the starting and accepting state, this machine accepts any string containing an even number of 1's. We wish to find the grammar which generates this language. One could examine the problem statement and immediately write down the rewriting rules:

$$S \rightarrow \lambda$$
$$S \rightarrow 11S$$

However, we wish to use the procedure just discussed. (Note that the inspection technique cannot be used unless there is some way to get a description of the language from the description of the machine. Usually this is not possible.)

For each quintuple in the acceptor we must find the corresponding production in the transformational grammar which simulates the analysis process:

Q-acceptor	Analysis grammar
$S_1 \quad \text{¢} \quad \text{¢} \quad R \quad S_1$	$S_1\text{¢} \rightarrow \text{¢}S_1$
$S_1 \quad 1 \quad b \quad R \quad S_2$	$S_1 1 \rightarrow bS_2$
$S_2 \quad 1 \quad b \quad R \quad S_1$	$S_2 1 \rightarrow bS_1$

These are the rewriting rules for the cases in which the length does not change. The transformational grammar must also include the blank manipulation rules and the bracket manipulation rules. They are:

$$[b \rightarrow [$$
$$bb] \rightarrow b]$$
$$1b] \rightarrow 1]$$
$$S_1] \rightarrow S_1 b]$$
$$S_2] \rightarrow S_2 b]$$
$$[S_2 b] \rightarrow S$$
$$1 \rightarrow [S_1\text{¢}1$$
$$1 \rightarrow 1]$$

By reversing the arrows in these 11 rules we obtain the rewriting rules for the generative grammar describing the language accepted by the machine. ∎

PROBLEMS

1. Find the derivation of the string 11 using the grammar developed in Example 1.

2. Find the rewriting rules of a grammar for the language accepted by the Turing acceptor in Example 2 of Sec. 3.2.

3. If we use the procedure of this section to construct a generative grammar to describe the language accepted by a Turing machine, will we ever obtain a context-sensitive grammar? Explain.

4. The purpose of this problem is to clarify a minor technical error in the proof of this section. The construction used in the proof creates a recursive grammar in which some of the rewriting rules change some of the terminal symbols of the language. Describe how to introduce a new nonterminal symbol corresponding to each terminal symbol such that the terminal symbols are not changed by the rewriting rules. Be sure to add rules to change the new nonterminal symbols back to the original terminal symbols at the end of the derivation.

5. (*a*) Show that a grammar containing rewriting rules of the form

$$\varphi\alpha\psi \rightarrow \varphi\beta\psi$$

where α is a string of nonterminal symbols and β is a string of nonterminal symbols and/or terminal symbols, generates a recursive language.

(*b*) If length (α) $\leq$ length (β) in all rules in the grammar, show that the grammar generates a context-sensitive language.

3.4 NONDETERMINISTIC TURING MACHINES

The concept of nondeterministic machines makes equivalence proofs easier. In particular, the proof that there exists a machine to recognize a given language is more straightforward if a nondeterministic acceptor is used. For example, it was easy to show that there was a nondeterministic finite-state machine for every regular language; our previous proof that nondeterministic finite-state machines are equivalent to deterministic finite-state machines then completed a cycle of inclusions from which we inferred the equivalence of all members of the cycle. We are going to proceed in the same way to show the equivalence of Turing machines with recursive grammars.

In this section we will define nondeterministic Turing machines and show that they are equivalent to deterministic Turing machines.

A *nondeterministic Turing machine* is a Turing machine in which there may be several possible actions for any state-symbol combination.

A string σ is accepted by a nondeterministic Turing machine if there exists a sequence of moves leading from the initial instantaneous description $S_1\,\text{¢}\sigma\$$ to an accepting condition. Let $NTMA$ denote the set of languages accepted by nondeterministic Turing machines.

We now show that the set of languages accepted by nondeterministic Turing machines is a subset of the set of languages accepted by deterministic Turing machines ($NTMA \subseteq DTMA$). Since any deterministic Turing machine is a nondeterministic Turing machine, the two sets of languages are equivalent ($NTMA = DTMA$).

As before, we demonstrate the inclusion by constructing a deterministic machine to mimic the behavior of a given nondeterministic machine. In other words, we will describe a procedure by which one can construct a deterministic Turing machine to simulate a given nondeterministic Turing machine M. We will not give the details of the construction, but simply outline the general sequences of actions which the deterministic machine must follow.

Tape formats   To prove a similar result for finite-state machines (Sec. 2.4) we demonstrated that the deterministic machine could keep track of all the possible states of the nondeterministic machine within its finite-state control. This was useful because only some limited information about the finite-state machine is needed to determine acceptance.   Since a Turing machine can rewrite its tape, its choice sequence determines not only a position and a state but also a tape configuration.   A finite-state control unit cannot remember all tape configurations which could result from various sequences of choices. Therefore a deterministic Turing machine which is simulating a nondeterministic Turing machine must keep track of an arbitrarily large, but finite, number of tape configurations.   The tape, with its capacity for arbitrarily large amounts of information, is the only place where the information about the possibilities could be stored.

Each possibility can be described by specifying the instantaneous description of the machine which would result if that possibility were selected. The tape of our simulating machine will contain a sequence of instantaneous descriptions, separated by special marking symbols *, as depicted in Fig. 3.4.1.

Search strategies   How does the deterministic machine search through the possibilities and find whether there is a path to an accepting condition?

Let us depict the sequences of choices which face the nondeterministic machine in a tree structure.   Place the initial instantaneous description at the root of the tree.   From each instantaneous description, draw a branch for each possible next move to a node representing the instantaneous description after that move has been made (Fig. 3.4.2).   The task of the deterministic machine is to search the tree and determine whether there exists a path leading to acceptance of the string.   Many strategies can be used to search trees; two commonly used ones will be discussed here.

One strategy used in some tree-searching computer programs—for example, in syntax-directed compilers—is to search the leftmost possibilities until a "failure" occurs and then to "back up" to a choice point (a node with more than one successor) and search the leftmost of the remaining possibilities.   If no possibilities remain at the choice point, another backing-up move is made.   If one backs up to the root of the tree with no untried choices remaining, there is no "success" node in the tree.   Let us call this "strategy $L\text{-}R$" (for "left-right").

A second strategy is to examine all next choices for step i before pro-

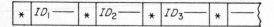

Fig. 3.4.1   Tape format for a deterministic Turing machine simulating a nondeterministic machine.

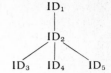

Fig. 3.4.2   A tree of instantaneous descriptions for a nondeterministic Turing machine.

ceeding to step $i + 1$.   This way the tree is examined from the top (its root) to the bottom, rather than left to right.   Call this "strategy *T-B*."

Remember that there is no guarantee that a Turing machine performing any given computation will halt.   Furthermore, there is no way to test whether a computation will terminate or not (this is the famous *halting problem*—see Sec. 3.6.2).   There may be an infinitely long path in the tree, which is a form of "failure" that cannot be detected.   The deterministic machine could spend forever chasing down an infinite path without detecting success or failure unless its search strategy is carefully chosen.   In particular, if the deterministic machine is to produce, in finite time, the same results that the nondeterministic machine produces in finite time, the deterministic machine must be sure to examine every finite sequence of choices in finite time. Therefore it must not follow an *L-R* strategy, but rather a *T-B* strategy.

Simulation procedure   Assume without loss of generality that the nondeterministic machine has a one-way infinite tape.   For the moment we will assume that the simulation has been in progress; we will describe the initial conditions later.   The simulation will be divided into *cycles*; one cycle will include the simulation of one step of the nondeterministic machine and the creation of a list of the choices for the next instantaneous descriptions.   Remember that the tape of the deterministic machine contains a sequence of instantaneous descriptions separated by ∗, as shown in Fig. 3.4.1.   We can correlate the sequence of instantaneous descriptions with the tree of choices of the nondeterministic machine.   In the tree of choices there is a node for each possible move of the nondeterministic machine.   For example, Fig. 3.4.2 shows the choice tree of a nondeterministic machine which started with instantaneous description ID_1, had no choice, and produced a new instantaneous description ID_2.   Then ID_2 gave three alternatives called ID_3, ID_4, and ID_5.

The numbering convention used above is the following: (1) label the initial configuration ID_1.   (2) Whenever a move is made add tree branches from the node from which the move is made; for each possible next configuration a branch will lead to a node placed on the next level of the tree.   (3) Start to number the nodes at the root of the tree, numbering from left to right on a given level.   When every node on a level is numbered, the numbering continues on the next level at the left side.   The number associated with a node by this procedure is the position of the corresponding instantaneous description on the tape of the deterministic simulator.

The operation of one cycle of the simulator is as follows:

1. Examine the current instantaneous description ID_j.
2. Let $n = 1$.
3. Determine the nth possible next configuration of the nondeterministic machine, and write the corresponding configuration on the right end of the tape. Repeat this step for $n = n + 1$ until no possibilities remain.
4. If any next configuration is an accepting configuration, the simulator enters an accepting state and halts. Otherwise, let $j = j + 1$ and go to step 1.

To start the deterministic simulator we put a copy of the initial configuration of the nondeterministic machine on the tape, surround it with the asterisk markers, and start the simulator reading the leftmost ∗.

The details of the construction of the simulator are exceedingly tedious, so we will not give them here. A flow-chart description using several subroutines is the easiest form of description for an algorithm of this complexity.

This construction shows that, for every nondeterministic Turing machine, one can construct a deterministic Turing machine which accepts the same set of strings. Therefore we have completed the proof that nondeterministic Turing machines have the same power as deterministic Turing machines.

PROBLEMS

1. A nondeterministic Turing machine N is described by the quintuples:

$S_1¢¢RS_1$	S_310RS_3
S_101RS_3	S_311LS_3
S_110RS_2	S_311RS_4
S_110RS_3	S_400RS_4
S_200RS_3	S_411RS_5
S_210RS_2	S_511LS_2
S_301LS_3	S_511RS_4
S_301LS_4	

Machine N is started in the configuration

    $S_1¢10110\$$

The machine accepts a string if it halts in state S_4. Assume that a deterministic simulator D of N is constructed using the algorithm given in this section. Assume that the simulator marks those instantaneous descriptions which have been examined for their successors by changing the ∗ immediately following the ID to +. When the + is written, the symbols in the preceding ID have their original forms.

(a) The simulator runs until it either runs out of possible choices or it creates an accepting condition. What is the contents of the tape of the simulator when it halts?

(b) Is the sequence 10110 accepted by N?

2. Let L_1 and L_2 be two languages accepted by Turing machine acceptors. Show that Turing machine acceptors can be constructed which accept the languages $L_1 \cap L_2$ and $L_1 \cup L_2$. (*Hint:* What search strategy must be used in the $L_1 \cup L_2$ cases?)

3. How must the simulation of an N-machine by an F-machine (Sec. 3.1.2) be modified if the N-machine is nondeterministic? (*Hint:* What do you need to do if both $S_1 T_1 T_1 L S_2$ and $S_1 T_1 T_1 R S_3$ are quintuples of the N-machine?)

3.5 TURING MACHINE ACCEPTORS FOR RECURSIVE LANGUAGES

We now show that if a recursive grammar G is given, a Turing machine acceptor for the language L_G can be constructed; thus *type 0* $\subseteq$ *NTMA*.

  We prove the statements in two parts. First we consider a nondeterministic Turing machine that can examine any portion (of the nonblank part) of the tape in one move and choose its next actions based on whether certain subsequences of symbols ("patterns") can be found on the tape. We then show that such a "pattern machine" has the same capabilities as the other formulations of Turing machines.

  Finally, we show that a nondeterministic pattern machine can be constructed to recognize the strings in the recursive language which was specified by the given grammar G. Thus the set of recursive languages and the set of languages recognized by Turing machine acceptors are the same (*type 0* = *DTMA* = *NTMA*).

Pattern machines First we define our new Turing machine formulation:

  A *P-machine* (pattern machine) is a nondeterministic Turing machine specified by a pair $\langle T, P \rangle$, where T is the set of symbols on the tape and P is a finite set of pairs of sequences in T^*.

  During one "step," a P-machine examines the tape to find any occurrence of a set of consecutive squares whose contents match the sequence in the first position of some pair in P. The sequence found is replaced by the second sequence of that pair. Since the replacement sequence is of arbitrary length, the length of the nonblank portion of the tape may change. Of course, there may be many occurrences of matches with the leftmost sequences of the pairs; in this case, one of the corresponding replacements is chosen nondeterministically. When the tape does not contain a matching subsequence for any pair in P, the machine halts. (COMIT and SNOBOL are two programming languages based upon similar "pattern-matching" operations.)

  A P-machine accepts a string σ if there is some sequence of replacements starting from the original string with endmarkers (the tape ¢σ\$) such that the machine halts with only one square of the tape not blank and with

that square containing a designated symbol A.   A P-machine used in this
way is called a P-acceptor.

Example 1   A P-acceptor has the symbol set $T = \{0,1,A,\text{¢},\$\}$, and the pattern pairs
$P = \{(01,11), (011,1), (11,A), (\text{¢}A\$,A)\}$.   Figure 3.5.1 shows some of the possible
replacements for the initial strings 0011, 01010, and 001001.   Since the strings
0011 and 001001 can be transformed to a single A, these strings are accepted by
the machine.   However, since 01010 cannot be mapped into an A by the machine,
it is not accepted.   ■

Equivalent Turing machine   Next we show that, for every P-acceptor,
there exists a nondeterministic Turing machine N which accepts the same

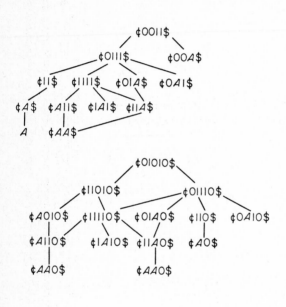

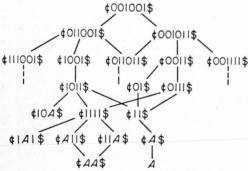

Fig. 3.5.1   The operation of a P-acceptor.

set of strings. We show this by simulating a single replacement step of the
P-machine by a sequence of steps of *N*. First, the *N*-machine can search to
find an occurrence of any one of a finite number of sequences by simple tree-
search techniques. (One of the nondeterministic choices in the pattern-
matching algorithm of the *N*-machine must be the choice to not begin the
match at the present square.) When one of the sequences is found, it can be
replaced by the second finite sequence. The remainder of the tape may have
to be rewritten if the lengths of the two sequences differ (Prob. 14 of Sec.
3.1). After the replacement has been made, the *N*-machine must back up to
the left endmarker and start the next cycle. We leave the details as an exercise
for the reader (Prob. 2).

We have shown

Theorem 1   For every *P*-acceptor there exists a nondeterministic Turing
machine acceptor which accepts exactly the same set of strings.

A *P*-acceptor for every language   Now we show that there is a *P*-
acceptor for every recursive language. This step is trivial because we only
need to "turn around" the productions of the grammar to obtain a set of
pairs which specify a *P*-acceptor. In other words, we make a transformational grammar which maps any string in the language into the sentence symbol. Then we construct a *P*-acceptor to act in the same way. When it
transforms the input sequence into the sentence symbol, it accepts the string.
Two details remain: (1) The *P*-acceptor must erase the endmarkers, so we
add $(\text{¢}S\$,A)$ to the description of the machine, where S is the sentence symbol
of the grammar. (2) The machine should check the input tape to verify that
the initial string contains only terminal symbols of the language. If the
initial strings are all in T^*, this second problem does not exist; otherwise,
the machine simulating the *P*-acceptor must start with a search of the tape
for symbols which are not in the terminal alphabet. Since this is easily
arranged, we have

Theorem 2   For every recursive language there exists a *P*-acceptor which
accepts the strings in the language.

Example 2   Specify a *P*-acceptor to accept strings from the language generated by the
grammar with the following rewriting rules:

$$S \rightarrow cBbS$$
$$S \rightarrow aSbSc$$
$$S \rightarrow aBb$$
$$cBb \rightarrow dBb$$
$$cBb \rightarrow db$$
$$B \rightarrow ef$$

The patterns for the machine are found by reversing the arrows in the grammatical productions and adding the pair to erase the endmarkers.

$P = \{(cBbS,S), (aSbSc,S), (aBb,S), (dBb,cBb), (db,cBb), (ef,B), (¢S\$,A)\}$

All the symbols used in the patterns must be included in the alphabet of the machine, so

$T = \{a,b,c,d,e,f,A,B,S,¢,\$\}$

The machine will leave a single A on the tape when it accepts the original string. ■

In summary, we have shown, by a multiple-step proof, that the set of languages accepted by Turing machines and the set of recursive languages are the same ($TMA = type\ 0$). First we showed that languages accepted by Turing machine acceptors could be described by recursive grammars. Then, by introducing nondeterministic machines and P-machines, we showed that, for every recursive grammar, there exists a Turing machine acceptor to recognize the strings in the language generated by the grammar.

PROBLEMS

1. Let G be a recursive grammar having the following rewriting rules:

$$S \to 11S$$
$$S \to S00$$
$$S \to 22AB$$
$$AB \to 2B$$
$$B \to 0B$$
$$B \to 0$$

Find a P-acceptor for L_G. (*Warning:* The acceptance symbol should not be a symbol used in the grammar.) S is the sentence symbol.

2. The steps required in the simulation of a P-machine by an N-machine can be divided into four subroutines:

1. Find the first occurrence of a pattern.
2. Replace the pattern, as specified by the pattern pairs of the machine.
3. Does the tape contain only A? If so, halt.
4. Move to the left end and go to step 1.

Draw flow charts describing the steps required to perform each of these four tasks.

3. Use a grammatical argument to show that $L_1 \cup L_2$ is a recursive language if L_1 and L_2 are recursive languages. (Also see Prob. 2 of Sec. 3.4.)

4. Show that the set of recursive languages is closed under the operation of reversal.

5. (P) A Post normal system is another way to specify transformations on strings. Each rule of the Post normal system specifies the action possible during one step in the transformation. In one step a sequence of symbols (α) from the left end of the working string is removed and a specified (possibly null) sequence of symbols (β) is appended to the right end of the sequence. We write this rule (α,β). If there exists a derivation starting with a specified sentence symbol S which derives the sequence of symbols #σ#, where # is a specified endmarker, we say that σ is in the language generated by the Post normal system.

(a) Show that there exists a Turing machine which accepts the language generated by a given Post normal system. Your answer should give a procedure for constructing the Turing machine. The procedure must work for any arbitrary Post normal system.

(b) Show that, for every Turing acceptor, there exists a Post normal system which generates the language accepted by the machine. (*Hint:* Let lowercase letters represent the symbols in the Turing machine's tape alphabet T and let symbols S_i represent the states of the Turing machine. Form a string by taking the instantaneous description of the Turing machine and adding #'s as endmarkers at each end. The working strings in the Post normal system will be strings of this form or cyclic rotations of these strings. Show that each of the productions below produces the indicated effect.

$$\begin{matrix} (T_i,T_i) \\ (\#,\#) \end{matrix} \quad \text{for all } T_i \in T \quad \Big\} \text{ rotate description}$$

(S_iT_j,S_iT_k) rewrite symbol; change state

$(T_mS_iT_j,S_iT_mT_k)$ for all $T_m \in T$ rewrite, move left, change state

What is the production for moving right? Relate these productions to those used in Sec. 3.3.)

3.6 UNSOLVABLE PROBLEMS

Many interesting questions about acceptors and languages cannot be answered. This means that an algorithm for a Turing machine does not exist which will always answer the question. It is important to discover exactly where the boundary between the solvable questions and the unsolvable questions lies; if a problem is unsolvable, one should not spend his time trying to solve it. Also, we can use the solvability or unsolvability of certain questions about the members of subsets to divide sets of sets (such as the set of languages) into subsets.

In recursive-function theory similar statements can be made about whether certain functions can be computed (i.e., are partial recursive); an important boundary separates those functions which can be computed from those which cannot.

Most unsolvability results are proved by showing that the assumption that a problem is solvable leads to the conclusion that another problem is solvable; but the second problem is already known to be unsolvable, and thus a contradiction results. Therefore the first problem must be unsolvable. We do need at least one unsolvability result to start the chain of proofs. Other techniques must be used to establish the contradictions to prove the first unsolvability results.

In this section we will discuss two unsolvability results. The first is a simple example of a nonrecursive function, which is shown to be nonrecursive by first assuming otherwise. The second problem is the *halting problem*. The unsolvability of this problem can be used to start a chain of proofs leading to the other unsolvability results of automata theory. We will use it in Chap. 9 to prove the unsolvability of the *Post correspondence problem*, which is the basis of most of the unsolvability results of that chapter.

3.6.1 THE MODIFIED BUSY-BEAVER PROBLEM

Are there any noncomputable functions? Now we demonstrate such a function.

Consider the class C_m of Turing machines having m states and the tape alphabet $\{b,1\}$. We restrict our attention to machines described in the same formalism; quintuples are usually chosen for this problem. Suppose we start a machine $M \in C_m$ in standard starting conditions on a tape containing m 1's. If the machine does not halt, we discard it; otherwise we count the number of 1's on the tape when the machine stops. Among all machines in C_m there will be some maximum number n of 1's left on the tape by a halting machine. (We can find n from the set of halting machines because that set is finite.) Now define a function $f(m)$ such that $f(m)$ is that maximum number of 1's left on the tape by a halting machine in C_m:

$$f(m) = n$$

Can we construct a Turing machine F to compute the function f? A machine F which answers the question should transform a tape with m 1's on it to a tape with $f(m)$ 1's on it, for any positive m.

We now show that we cannot construct a machine to compute f by establishing a contradiction. Assume that a machine F which computes f exists. If F uses more than two symbols on its tape, use the procedure of Prob. 13 of Sec. 3.1 to construct an equivalent machine F' which uses only two symbols on its tape. Suppose we combine F' with another machine, as follows: First, machine F' computes $f(m)$, given m. But instead of halting, F' starts machine G, which writes one more 1 on the tape and then halts. The composite machine $F'G$ computes

$$g(m) = f(m) + 1$$

Let t be the number of states in $F'G$. Now ask $F'G$ to compute $g(t)$. From the definition of the machine, the answer is $g(t)=f(t) + 1$. However, since $F'G$ is a t-state machine in C_t, it cannot leave more than $f(t)$ 1's on the tape when it halts, because otherwise it would be the winner in the "contest" and the value of $f(t)$ would have to be changed. Then we have

$$g(t) \leq f(t)$$

by the definition of $f(t)$.

But since

$$g(t) = f(t) + 1$$

we have

$$f(t) + 1 \leq f(t)$$

Our contradiction can be resolved only by assuming one of our hypotheses false; the only hypothesis is that a machine to compute f exists. Mathematically, we say that there is no algorithm to compute f, or that f is a noncomputable (or nonrecursive) function.†

This problem is called the *busy-beaver problem* because the objective is to see how busy a Turing machine can be when the numbers of its states and symbols are limited.

3.6.2 THE HALTING PROBLEM

One might wonder why the busy-beaver function is not computable; we could envision a Turing machine which would simulate the behavior of each m-state machine and keep track of the maximum number of 1's left on the tape by a halting machine. This strategy does not work, however, because the simulator will have trouble deciding whether the machine being simulated will ever halt. If it cannot make this basic decision, it might simulate a machine indefinitely, always hoping that that simulated machine will eventually halt. There never would be an answer from the machine computing $f(m)$—an unacceptable condition.

Thus we are led to consider the solvability properties of the halting problem.

Halting problem: Given a description of a machine (an encoded list of its quintuples) and its instantaneous description, will the machine ever halt? We must be careful to define what would constitute an acceptable solution to the problem.

A problem is *recursively unsolvable* if there is no Turing machine which will answer the problem for all possible values of the parameters.

In this question the parameters are a machine and an instantaneous description. The acceptable solution is a machine H which will accept the description of an arbitrary machine M and an instantaneous description I of M's configuration and tell whether M ever halts when started with that instantaneous description. We require that H halt when it has come to a decision.

Now consider a restricted version of the problem.

Restricted halting problem: Given a machine M, will it halt if given its own description on its tape?

† Other noncomputable functions can be derived from the same experiments; instead of counting the number of squares containing 1's, we could count the number of moves that a machine makes before stopping, or the number of tape squares visited by the machine before it halts. See Rado (1962) for more details and Brady (1966) for some values of similar functions.

If we cannot solve this restricted problem, we cannot solve the general halting problem.

Let the machine to solve the restricted halting problem be H'. If we had a copy of H', we could modify it to form H'' as follows: (1) Whenever H' is about to halt, having decided that M halts, let H'' enter an infinite loop; then H'' will not halt if M does when M is given its own description. (2) Whenever H' is about to halt, having decided that M does not halt, then H'' halts. Thus H'' will halt if and only if M does not when M is given its own description.

The required contradiction is obtained by giving H'' its own description: It will halt if it does not halt, and vice versa. As before, we look for the hypothesis which must not have been valid—the existence of H'. Therefore H could not exist, and the halting problem is recursively unsolvable.

Note the common structure of these two proofs of the nonexistence of a machine. First, we assume that the machine M exists. Second, we make a small addition to M to construct M'. Finally, we obtain a contradiction about M' by giving it itself as the parameter of the computation.

PROBLEMS

1. Show that the complement of a recursive language may not be recursive. (*Hint:* The recognizer may never halt if it is given a string which is not in the language.)

2. By reducing it to the halting problem, show that the following problem is recursively unsolvable:

Printing Problem: Does machine M with instantaneous description I ever print symbol T_j on the tape?

3. Consider the function s giving the maximum number of steps executed by a halting Turing machine in C_m: $s(m) = n$, where n is the maximum number of steps executed by a halting machine in C_m before it halts, if it is started in the initial configuration $S_1 1^m$.

(*a*) Show that if $s(m)$ were computable, then $f(m)$ would be, where $f(m)$ is the function defined in the text.

(*b*) Is $s(m)$ computable? Explain.

4. In this problem we will prove that there exist partial-recursive functions which are not recursive.

(*a*) Show how the instantaneous description of a Turing machine can be encoded into a unique positive integer. [*Hint:* Encode the individual symbols into unique integers and combine these by using either Gödel numbering (Prob. 18 of Sec. 3.1) or positional notation.]

(*b*) Show that each move of a Turing machine can be described by a partial-recursive function operating on the integer you found in part *a*.

(*c*) Given that a halting Turing machine can be described by a recursive function, prove that there exists a partial-recursive function which is not recursive. (*Hint:* If not, would the halting problem be unsolvable?)

3.7 THERE ARE RECURSIVE LANGUAGES WHICH ARE NOT CONTEXT-SENSITIVE LANGUAGES

We now show that there exists at least one language which is accepted by a Turing machine (and thus is recursive) but which is not a context-sensitive language. We will need two schemes, one for enumerating all possible strings over a fixed alphabet, the other for enumerating all possible context-sensitive languages. Both schemes must use the same alphabet of terminal symbols. Also, we require the knowledge that the membership problem can be solved for context-sensitive languages (Sec. 1.5). We do not require a detailed knowledge of the enumeration schemes.

Let V be the alphabet of terminal symbols. Let there be some function f for deriving a context-sensitive language from a string $x \in V^*$. We require that f have the following properties:

1. For every string $x \in V^*$, $f(x)$ is a context-sensitive language.
2. For every context-sensitive language L there exists at least one $y \in V^*$ such that $f(y) = L$.

Even though a given context-sensitive language may be specified by more than one string in V^*, every context-sensitive language is specified by at least one string.

Existence of f   It may not be clear that there exists a function satisfying the above conditions. Therefore we digress momentarily to discuss the existence of such a function. The details of this section are not essential to the arguments that follow, except for the result that there exists a function having the desired properties.

We shall now exhibit one function which meets the requirements. Let $V = \{a|\,;|\rightarrow|\,:\}$. Also, let $g(x)$ be a mapping which transforms a sequence $x \in V^*$ into a sequence in $V_1^* = \{a|\,;\}^*$, defined by:

1. Let $g(x)$, for $x = v \in V$, be defined by

    $g(a) = a$
    $g(;) = aa$
    $g(\rightarrow) = aaa$
    $g(:) = aaaa$

2. For $x = v_1 v_2 v_3 \cdots v_n$, $n \geq 2$, $g(x) = g(v_1 v_2 v_3 \cdots v_{n-1}); g(v_n).$†

Example 1 $g(a \rightarrow aa;:) = a;aaa;a;aa;aaaa$ ▪

---

† Note that the semicolon is a symbol in the string $g(x)$.

We interpret a sequence in V_1^* as the specification of a grammar, according to the following rules:

1. A rewriting rule is represented by a sequence of the form $aaaa;L;aaa;R;$ $aaaa$, where $;L;$ and $;R;$ denote sequences which do not contain subsequences of the form $;aaaa;$ or $;aaa;$. If L contains more semicolons than R, this sequence is ignored. (This restriction eliminates recursive rewriting rules.)

2. Within $;L;$ and $;R;$ determined from rule 1, the subsequence a^n occurring between semicolons represents the nth symbol, as follows:

$$a^1 \leftrightarrow a$$
$$a^2 \leftrightarrow ;$$
$$a^3, a^4 \qquad \text{illegal, by rule 1}$$
$$a^n \leftrightarrow N_n \qquad \text{a nonterminal symbol of the grammar for } n \geq 5$$

3. The subsequence $;;$ represents the sentence symbol of the grammar.
4. Any subsequences not in the form specified in rule 1 are ignored.
5. The rewriting rules of the grammar are specified by rules 1 to 4 only.

We shall define the language $f(x)$ from the grammar defined by a string $x \in V_1^*$ as follows: Any string in the regular set $(\mathbf{a;} + \mathbf{aa;})\mathbf{*}(\mathbf{a} + \mathbf{aa})$ is in the language $f(x)$ if it can be derived from the string $;;$ using rewriting rules which are determined from x by rules 1 to 5 above.

Example 2 The string $x = aaaa;;aaa;a;aaaa;;aaa;a;;aaaa$ represents the grammar with rules

$;;\rightarrow a$
$;;\rightarrow a;;$

The diagonal construction   Let $L = \{x \mid x \in V_1^*, x \notin f(x)\}$ be a language. We will show that L is not a context-sensitive language, but that a Turing machine can answer the membership question for L, so that L is a recursive language.

First, L is not a context-sensitive language, because for any string $x \in V_1^*$, $x \in L$ if and only if $x \notin f(x)$. Thus L differs from the context-sensitive language $f(x)$. Since the set $\{f(x) \mid x \notin (a, ;)^*\}$ includes all context-sensitive languages using vocabulary V_1, L is not a context-sensitive language, because it differs from each one in at least the membership of one string.

Second, L is a recursive language. A Turing machine can be designed so that, when it is given a string x, it can test x for membership in language $f(x)$. Since $f(x)$ is a context-sensitive language, the machine always halts. The Turing machine then gives the opposite answer to the one obtained for the membership question. Thus L is a recursive language which is not context-sensitive.

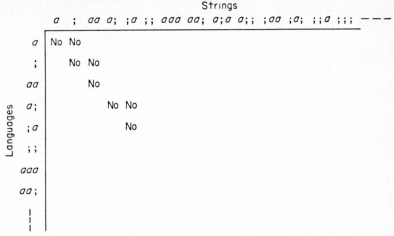

Fig. 3.7.1 The array of answers to context-sensitive membership questions.

This construction is known as a *diagonal construction* because it uses the diagonal elements of an array. Consider a two-dimensional array in which the rows are labeled with languages and the columns are labeled with strings. Identify each language $f(x)$ by the string x (Fig. 3.7.1). The answer to the question "Is string j in language i?" is written in the jth column of row i. Thus the entries in row i answer all membership questions about language i. Language L is specified by the complements of the entries along the diagonal of the array; hence the name.

PROBLEMS

1. Why does the above proof work properly without requiring any statements about the size of the terminal vocabulary of the language?

2. Explain the error(s) in the following argument:

> Consider the proof in this section that a diagonal language can be constructed which is different from all the languages which were enumerated. Suppose that the length restriction in rule 1 of the interpretation scheme is removed. The recursive languages are thus enumerated, and the remainder of the proof could be used to show that there exists a language accepted by a Turing machine which is not recursive.

3.8 COMMENTS

Turing machines were introduced in Turing (1936). Post normal systems were introduced in Post (1936). Various models of the Turing machine and proofs of their equivalence are summarized in Fischer (1965a). The equivalence between Turing machines and recursive languages was shown via recursive functions in Chomsky (1959a).   For a discussion of the relationship between Turing machines and recursive functions, see Davis (1958), Minsky (1967), or Rogers (1967).

The first problem in the machine domain shown to be unsolvable was the *halting problem* shown unsolvable by Turing (1936).   Rado (1962) introduced the *busy-beaver problem* in looking for a noncomputable function which was "easy" to describe.

4
Linear-bounded Automata

The capabilities of the Turing machine and the finite-state machine are vastly different.   For example, essentially every question about finite-state machines is solvable, whereas many interesting questions about Turing machines are not.   To find machine models whose capabilities are in between these two, we must at the same time generalize the finite-state model and restrict the Turing model.   To generalize the finite-state model, we must have an infinite memory; to restrict the Turing model, we must somehow restrict the uses of the infinite memory.   In this chapter we discuss a simple form of restriction on the use of the infinite memory.

   The linear-bounded model is significant for two reasons: (1) the set of languages accepted by machines in this class is the set of context-sensitive languages, and (2) the infinite storage is restricted in size, but not in accessibility, compared with the Turing machine.   The latter point may seem inconsistent with our condition that the amount of memory be infinite; this is not quite the correct conclusion, because the amount of memory is limited, not to a fixed number of locations (which would, after all, give a finite-state model)

but to a fixed *function* of the length of the input sequence. Certain changes
in the function which limit the length will lead to different capabilities in the
machine model. To obtain the equivalence with context-sensitive languages,
we limit the length of the tape to a linear function of the length of the input
sequence. We will show that the capabilitity of the class of machines is the
same for all length bounds which are linear functions of the length of the
input sequence. Because a linear function is used to bound the length of
the tape, machines in this class are called *linear-bounded machines.*

If the number of squares used by machines in a certain class is limited
to a computable function of the length of the input string, the membership
question for the languages in the class accepted by those machines must be
solvable (Prob. 3 of Sec. 4.1). Since this question is solvable, the set of languages accepted by such machines must be smaller than the set of recursive
languages.

In this chapter we define the linear-bounded model and show some
equivalence results relating the capabilities of the model to sets of languages.
The question of whether the deterministic and nondeterministic versions of
this model are equivalent has not been answered. One major result equates
the languages accepted by nondeterministic linear-bounded automata with
the context-sensitive languages.

The study of context-sensitive languages may be important for practical
problems because it may be true that many compiler languages lie between
context-sensitive and context-free languages.

4.1 THE MODEL

A linear-bounded automaton (LBA) is a Turing machine in which the tape
is not infinite, but rather its length is bounded by a linear function of the
length of the input sequence. Thus, if n is the length of a given input sequence, the sequence can be recognized by an LBA if it can be recognized by

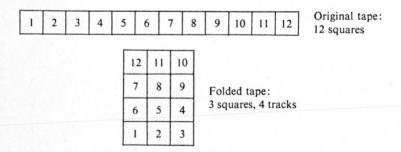

Fig. 4.1.1 Folding the tape for $n = 3, k = 4$.

Track no.

	T_1	T_1	T_2	T_1		4
	T_2	T_3	T_2	T_3		3
*					*	
	T_1	T_2	T_1	T_2		2
	T_3	T_2	T_1	T_3		1

Fig. 4.1.2 A k-track tape.

a Turing machine which uses no more than kn squares of its tape, where k is a constant specified in the description of the machine. The easiest way to specify the model formally is to append the preceding sentence to the definition of a Turing machine. The initial conditions must be specified, particularly regarding the location of the input sequence on the finite tape. We will assume that the input sequence is at the leftmost end of the tape; that it is enclosed with endmarkers ¢, $; and that the remainder of the tape is blank. The machine is started reading the leftmost endmarker on the tape. To determine the allowed length of tape, we count both the endmarkers and the symbols in the input sequence. The value of the constant k is a property of the machine, and may not depend on the particular input string presented to the machine.

In this section we will show that the value of k is immaterial if it is greater than or equal to 1. In other words, given a machine with $k > 1$, there exists a machine with $k = 1$ which simulates its behavior. In Prob. 2 we show another model for LBA's which has some meaning when $k < 1$, and we show that even for these values, changing the value of k does not change the capabilities of the model. In later sections we will assume $k = 1$, and thereby shorten some proofs.

We now show that, for any linear-bounded automaton, having bound kn, $k > 1$, there exists a linear-bounded automaton with bound $n + 2$ which performs equivalent calculations. We will assume, without loss of generality, that k is an integer; otherwise we could bound the space by a k having the next highest integral value. The construction is based on folding the nk-square tape into k folds, each n squares long. Then we place the symbols from the jth fold onto the jth track of the n-square tape. A sample tape is shown in Fig. 4.1.1.

The simulator will use endmarkers to detect the end of the tape. When the simulator detects an endmarker, it will turn around and consider the symbols on the next track. The endmarker is represented by ∗, and is written in an additional square at each end of the tape (Fig. 4.1.2).

Simulation with $k = 1$ We must show that the operation of the one-track machine can be simulated by the k-track machine. The details are very similar to the details of the simulation of a Turing machine with a doubly infinite tape by a Turing machine with a singly-infinite tape. A register within the finite-state control is used to hold the number of the track being read. When the asterisk endmarkers are encountered, the contents of this counter are changed by 1.

To give precise details of the simulation, we must precisely specify the machines and their symbol sets. Let the original machine be M, with states $\{S_1, S_2, \ldots, S_m\}$ and symbols $\{T_1, \ldots, T_p\}$. Let the new machine, with $k = 1$, be M'. We will represent the symbols of M' by k-tuples $(T_{i1}, T_{i2}, \ldots, T_{ik})$. If the k-tuples represent the (composite) symbol in the ith square of the tape of M', $T_{i,j}$ is the symbol in the ith square of the jth track (see Prob. 15 of Sec. 3.1 for a similar construction). If the tape had four tracks and contained symbols as shown in Fig. 4.1.2, the symbols, left to right, would be (T_3, T_1, T_2, T_1), (T_2, T_2, T_3, T_1), (T_1, T_1, T_2, T_2), and (T_3, T_2, T_3, T_1).

To simplify the formalism, we define a set of functions r_i which operate on k-tuples and give as a result the ith element of the k-tuples. In other words, r_i *reads* the ith component of the k-tuple. Thus $r_1((T_3, T_1, T_2, T_1)) = T_3$. Also, let $w_i(x,y)$ be the k-tuple obtained by taking the k-tuple x and replacing its ith component by the element y. In other words, w_i *writes* into the ith track of the tape, changing the ith component of the k-tuple. For example, $w_3((T_3, T_1, T_2, T_1), T_1) = (T_3, T_1, T_1, T_1)$.

The details of the simulation are described in Fig. 4.1.3. In the simulator, l contains the track number being used, k is the multiplier for the simulated machine, and t contains the transition-table information for the simulated machine, following the format used in Sec. 3.1.3. We assume that both M and M' are started on the leftmost square of the input tape and that S_1 is the initial state of M.

Since we can construct a linear-bounded automaton with $k = 1$ to simulate the behavior of a linear-bounded automaton with $k > 1$, we henceforth discuss only the case $k = 1$.

No extra capability is introduced if we consider the tape to have some fixed number of squares u in addition to the number allowed by the linear bound. The contents of such squares could be stored in the control unit, keeping the tape length within the linear bound. But since the extra squares on the tape can sometimes be used to simplify descriptions, we will use bounds of the form $n + u$ in the remainder of the chapter.

PROBLEMS

1. A linear-bounded machine M with $k = 3$ and initial state S_1 has the quintuples

$S_1 \cent\cent R S_1$
$S_1 0 1 R S_2$
$S_1 1 1 L S_1$
$S_2 1 0 R S_2$
$S_2 0 1 L S_1$
$S_2 \$ 0 R S_2$

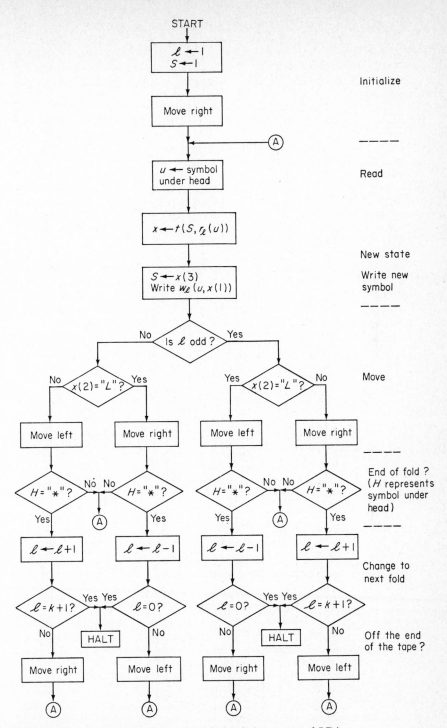

Fig. 4.1.3 Simulation for a $k = 1$ LBA simulating a general LBA.

Construct an equivalent machine M' with $k = 1$. Simulate the behavior of M' operating on an input sequence 010 (assume that 0 is the blank symbol).

2. Consider a linear-bounded machine model (Fig. 4.1.4) defined according to the following rules:

(i) There is one input tape, on which there is a reading head which never writes and never moves left.

(ii) There is a working tape, whose length is k times the length of the input tape. A read/write head can modify the contents of the squares on the working tape in arbitrary ways.

(iii) The operation of the machine is determined by the two symbols being read (from the two tapes) and the internal state of the control unit. In one step the machine can perform any or all of the following operations: move the input reading head one square right, write a new symbol on the working tape, move the read/write head one square in either direction, enter a new state, halt.

(a) Show that this model is equivalent to the one discussed in the text. Consider copying the input sequence onto the working tape before doing anything else.

(b) Let the length of the working tape be the least integer not less than kn. Show that fractional values of k (even when $k < 1$) do not change the power of the model.

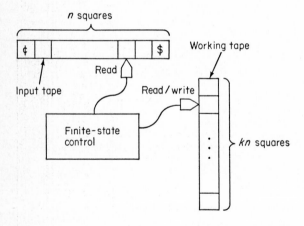

Fig. 4.1.4 An alternative structure for a linear-bounded automaton.

3. Consider a class C_f of Turing machine acceptors which use less than $f(n)$ tape squares if they halt, where n is the length of the input sequence and f is a recursive function. [If f is a recursive function, then a Turing machine F can be constructed to compute $f(n)$ such that F halts for all values of n.] Show that

(a) The halting problem is solvable for machines in C_f.

(b) The membership question is solvable for machines in C_f.

4. Describe the construction of a linear-bounded simulator with $k = 1$ using a quintuple form of description for the simulator and for the simulated machine (with $k > 1$).

5. In Sec. 3.1 and Probs. 9 and 10 of Sec. 3.1 we described several modifications to the formulation of a Turing machine. Which of the modifications can be applied to linear-bounded machines without affecting the capability of the model? Explain.

4.2 LINEAR-BOUNDED ACCEPTORS

Now we restrict the discussion to linear-bounded machines which produce acceptance or rejection outputs when given a string to test:

A linear-bounded acceptor is a Turing machine which is given a tape containing the sequence σ surrounded by endmarkers $\cent$, \$. There are no squares on the tape not used for the input sequence. The machine is started in its initial state S_1 reading the left endmarker. If the machine halts over the right endmarker in a final state, the machine is said to accept the string σ. On the other hand, if the machine halts over the left endmarker, or over the right endmarker in a nonfinal state, the string σ is rejected. Also σ is rejected if the machine never halts or if it runs off the tape.

The nondeterministic linear-bounded acceptor is a linear-bounded acceptor which may have choices of its next move for any state-symbol combination.

Let *DLBA* (*NLBA*) denote the set of languages accepted by (non-) deterministic linear-bounded acceptors.

Is *DLBA* = *NLBA*? There is no proof that the two sets are equal, and there is no counterexample to the assertion. This question is still open.

Intersections Now we discuss the effects of Boolean operations on the sets of languages accepted by linear-bounded automata.

First we prove that the class of languages accepted by linear-bounded automata is closed under intersection. An acceptor M_3 for $L_3 = L_1 \cap L_2$ can be constructed as follows (Fig. 4.2.1): The tape of M_3 is divided into two tracks. First the machine copies σ onto the second track of the tape and uses the second track to test the string for membership in L_1. If this test fails, the string is rejected. On the other hand, if the string is in L_1, the machine enters a second set of states, where it tests σ for membership in L_2, using the copy of σ which remains on the first track. (Why was the copying step required?) If this second test succeeds, the string is accepted. Notice that if the machines to test for membership in L_1 and L_2 are deterministic, the machine testing for membership in $L_1 \cap L_2$ will also be deterministic.

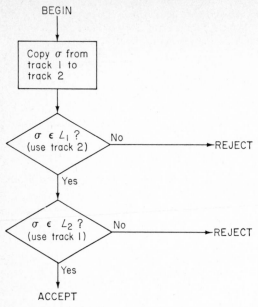

Fig. 4.2.1   The algorithm for recognizing the intersection of two linear-bounded languages.

Theorem 1   The sets *DLBA* and *NLBA* are closed under intersection.   In
other words,

  (*a*) If $L_1, L_2 \in DLBA$, then $L_1 \cap L_2 \in DLBA$, and
  (*b*) If $L_1, L_2 \in NLBA$, then $L_1 \cap L_2 \in NLBA$.

Complements   We now show that the class *DLBA* is closed under complementation.   The complement of a language is defined with respect to all
strings over the same alphabet, so that if T is the alphabet of L_1, then $\sim L_1 = T^* - L_1$; $\sim L_1$ contains exactly those sequences which are not in L_1 but
which are composed of symbols from T.   To show that *DLBA* is closed under
complementation, we must construct a deterministic linear-bounded acceptor
to accept $\sim L_1$, whenever L_1 is in *DLBA*.   The general strategy is to build
a machine M' which simulates a deterministic acceptor M.   As M' simulates
M, it also counts the number of moves that M has made.   An upper bound
for the number of moves, based on the assumption that M is not in an infinite
loop, can be found.   If this bound is exceeded, M' can conclude that M is
in an infinite loop.   Either M halts or this bound is exceeded; in either case
M' knows the outcome of M's calculations and M' can give the opposite of
M's answer.

Let M be a deterministic linear-bounded acceptor which accepts L_1 and let M' denote the machine we will construct. Also let n, m, and p denote the length of the input sequence, the number of states of M, and the number of symbols used by M, respectively. Note that n is dependent upon the particular input sequence, but both m and p are parameters of the machine.

The simulator M' detects the occurrence of any one of the conditions which causes M to reject the input. There were four ways that M could reject σ. First, it could halt, not at the right endmarker. Second, it could halt at the right endmarker in a nonaccepting state. Third, it could run off the end of the tape. Finally, it might never halt. For the first three cases it is not difficult to construct M' to detect the rejection of the string by M. The only difficult case is to show that M' can detect when M will never halt. We will show that this can be accomplished by having M' count the moves of M. We will need a bound on the number of different configurations of M.

Suppose M is given the string σ of length n. The number of possible configurations of symbols on the tape is p^n. Furthermore, the read/write head might be in any one of the n positions on the tape, and the machine could be in any one of m states. Therefore the maximum number of different configurations of the machine is mnp^n.

If M's calculation continues for $mnp^n + 1$ steps, then some configuration must have occurred at least twice and the machine must be in an infinite loop. Suppose that machine M' simulates the operation of M and counts the number of steps used by M. If that count reaches $mnp^n + 1$, the conclusion must be that M is in an infinite loop and that M would reject the input sequence. In this case M' must accept the input.

After we show that the required maximum count can be fitted into the limited space, we will discuss the details of how the machine M' makes a move simulating M and then increments the counter. Since any one of p different symbols may appear in any one of the n squares, the symbols in one track can represent all integers between 0 and $p^n - 1$. The additional factor is mn, but we use m^n instead. This is not less than mn (unless $m = 1$), and m^n can be represented on another track by using one of m symbols in each of the n squares.†

The details of the construction of M' are exceedingly tedious. We will exhibit a tape format, the structure of the algorithm, and a flow-chart description of the simulator. The tape will have $n + 2$ squares,‡ including not only the endmarkers of M, but also the additional endmarkers for M'.

The tape has four tracks, as shown in Fig. 4.2.2. Each track on the tape contains symbols from its own distinct alphabet. Track 1, which

† This coding may be criticized in terms of its inefficiency of space, but the same construction must work for all n, and those codings which are efficient for large values of n do not work for small values of n.

‡ See Sec. 4.1 for comments about how the two additional squares can be removed.

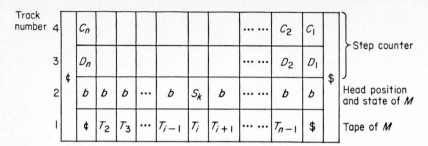

Fig. 4.2.2 The tape for machine M', recognizing the complement of the language recognized by M.

contains a duplicate of the contents of the tape of M, uses the same alphabet as M, namely, $T = \{T_1, T_2, \ldots, T_p, \phi, \$\}$. Track 2, which records the position of the read/write head of M and the internal state of M, uses alphabet $S = \{S_1, S_2, \ldots, S_m, b\}$, where b is a blank symbol and the S_i's represent the states of M. Tracks 3 and 4 contain numbers representing the count of the number of moves which M has made. They use alphabets $C = \{0, 1, \ldots, p - 1\}$ and $D = \{0, 1, \ldots, m - 1\}$, respectively. Note that the numbers in the last two alphabets begin with zero; this convention simplifies the discussion. Also note that the highest integers in C and D are related to the numbers of states and symbols of M.

The counting procedure is based on the following interpretation of the contents of tracks 3 and 4:

1. Track 4 contains a base-p integer N_4, with its most significant digit on the left end of the tape. Thus, if the symbol in track 4 in the ith square from the right endmarker is denoted by c_i, then $N_4 = \sum_{i=0}^{n-1} c_{i+1}p^i$.
2. Track 3 contains a base-m integer N_3, with its most significant digit on the right end. If d_i is the symbol in track 3 in the ith square from the right, then $N_3 = \sum_{i=0}^{n-1} d_{n-i}m^i$.

The counting strategy is to use N_4 to count up to p^n; when that overflows, count one in N_3, which counts up to m^n. If N_3 overflows, M is in a loop and M' should accept the string.

Track 1 is a copy of the tape of M, and track 2 is blank except for the square under the read/write head of M. This square contains a symbol representing the state of M. Whenever M' wishes to simulate a move of M, it finds the nonblank square in track 2. Then both the present state of M and the symbol read by M are under the read/write head of M', and a move of M can be chosen. If the chosen move does not require motion of the read/write head of M, the new symbol and next state can be written onto the tape of M'. If the chosen move requires motion of the read/write head of M, the new symbol is written (erasing the symbol in track 2), the move is made, and the new state is then written in track 2. Each new configuration of M must be examined to determine whether a halting condition has been reached. If the new configuration is not a halting one, the move counter is incremented and tested for overflow before simulating the next move. Figure 4.2.3 shows the structure of this process.

The simulator can be broken into two parts: The part actually simulating the moves of M, and the part which counts the number of moves simulated. The part directly simulating M is almost a copy of M. The structure of the counting part depends only upon the numbers of states and symbols in M; therefore this part will be the same for many different machines M.

Example 1   Consider the machine which accepts the complement of the set accepted by the machine described in Example 2 of Sec. 3.2. The initial tape contents and the contents after one and six moves are shown in Fig. 4.2.4.   ■

The construction above has shown that machine M', which simulates a linear-bounded acceptor M, is also a linear-bounded acceptor and that M' accepts a string whenever M rejects that same string. Therefore the languages L_M and $L_{M'}$ are complements of each other. Thus we have shown that the class *DLBA* is closed under the operation of complementation.

Using *De Morgan's theorem*, the set *DLBA* is also closed under union. We have shown

Theorem 2   The set *DLBA* is closed under union, intersection, and complementation.

Nondeterministic complements   The complement of L is defined such that a string which is not in L is in $\sim L$. However, if we use the algorithm of Fig. 4.2.3 to construct a recognizer M' for a nondeterministic machine M, any string for which there is a sequence of choices leading to nonacceptance by M will be accepted by M'. Let $\sim_M L_M$ denote the set of strings accepted by M'. Note that a string can simultaneously be in L_M and $\sim_M L_M$. In fact, we have

$$L_M \cup \sim_M L_M = \mathbf{T^*}$$

but

$$L_M \cap (\sim_M L_M) \supseteq \varphi$$

Since languages and their complements $\sim_M$ are not necessarily disjoint, we cannot make simple statements about unions via De Morgan's theorem for the nondeterministic case.

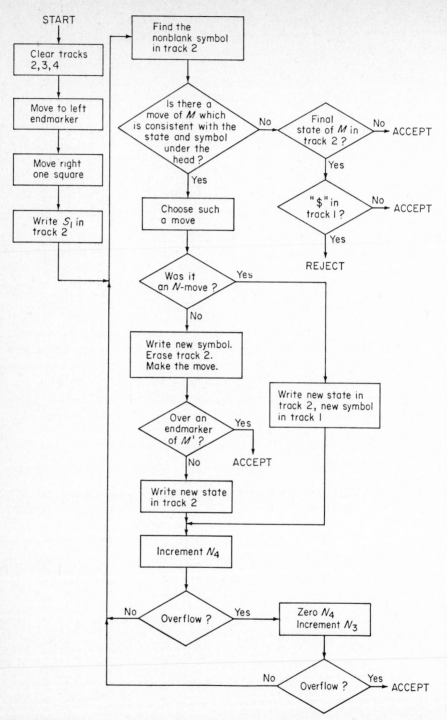

Fig. 4.2.3 Flow chart of the simulation algorithm to recognize the complement of an LBA language.

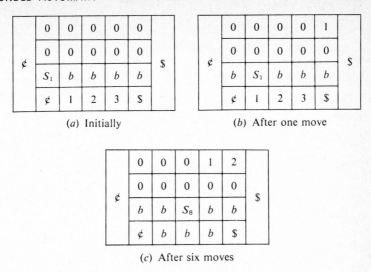

(a) Initially   (b) After one move

(c) After six moves

Fig. 4.2.4 Contents of the tape of a simulator.

We can show that *NLBA* is closed under union by a direct construction. Given two languages L_1 and L_2, both in *NLBA*, their union will be accepted by a nondeterministic linear-bounded acceptor whose first move is a nondeterministic choice between L_1 and L_2. If L_1 is chosen and the string is in L_1, it will be accepted. Similarly, the string will be accepted if it is in L_2, and L_2 is chosen on the first move. Therefore

Theorem 3 The set *NLBA* is closed under union.

It is not known whether the class *NLBA* is closed under complementation; it would be if the classes of deterministic and nondeterministic LBA's were equivalent, and might be even if they were not.

PROBLEMS

1. Let M be a linear-bounded machine which recognizes language L_M.

(a) What are the standard starting conditions for M?

(b) We want to build a machine M' to recognize the complement of L_M. The starting conditions for M' should be the same as those for M. In particular, the alphabet of initial tape symbols should be the same as for M. Write a sequence of quintuples for M' which will replace tape symbols such as T_i by $(T_i,b,0,0)$, so that M' can then function as described in the text. After completing the sequence described by the quintuples you construct, the machine M' should be prepared to simulate the first step of M.

2. In Prob. 1, M' does not have any more squares on its tape than M does. In particular, the endmarkers on M's tape are not separately considered. How must the simulation of M by M' be modified to cover those cases in which M reads an endmarker?

Your answer should include:

1. A description of the representation used on the tape of M' for the special configurations of M
2. A description of how the quintuples (or algorithms) that are required for those special cases are constructed from the description of M
3. A description of the halting conditions for M'

3. Suppose that a machine M' is recognizing the complement of the language L_M accepted by machine M which has m states and p-tape symbols. Let M' be given an input sequence such that M will enter an infinite loop. What are the contents of tracks 3 and 4 of the tape of M'

    (*a*) Just after simulating the last step of M before M' decides that M is in a loop?

    (*b*) When M' halts?

4. Does the set *NLBA* form a Boolean algebra? Why?

5. Prove that, if M is a deterministic linear-bounded acceptor, there exists another deterministic linear-bounded acceptor M' such that M' halts for every input tape, and M' accepts the same set of strings that M does.

6. What are the errors in the following argument?

> Every linear-bounded acceptor is a Turing machine. Since the halting problem for Turing machines is unsolvable, the halting problem for linear-bounded machines is unsolvable. Therefore a machine cannot be built to accept the complement of a language in the set *DLBA*.

4.3 THE SETS ACCEPTED BY LINEAR-BOUNDED ACCEPTORS ARE CONTEXT-SENSITIVE LANGUAGES

In this section we will show that there exists a context-sensitive grammar to generate the strings accepted by a given deterministic linear-bounded automaton (*DLBA* $\subseteq$ *type 1*). The argument is essentially the same as the argument regarding recursive languages and Turing machines (Sec. 3.3). But now we must make sure that the grammar we develop will not contain productions which decrease the length of the string. If this constraint is not satisfied, the constructed grammar will be recursive, which is not the desired result.

Recall the arguments used in Sec. 3.3. First we showed that there existed a transformational grammar which paralleled the analysis process followed by the machine. Then we showed that the productions of this grammar could be turned around to give a grammar which generated the language. This second step depended upon the fact that the productions describing the analysis had certain forms.

Our argument for the linear-bounded case will produce a generative grammar using endmarkers. We will then show that, for every context-sensitive language generated with endmarkers, there exists another context-sensitive grammar (with more nonterminal symbols) which will generate the same language without endmarkers. Therefore we will have shown that

there exists a context-sensitive grammar without endmarkers which generates
the language accepted by the linear-bounded acceptor. The endmarkers
simplify the proof since they fix the length of the instantaneous description of
the machine.

The two steps will be presented in three lemmas.

Lemma 1   Let S_F be the accepting state of a linear-bounded acceptor M.
There exists a recursive transformational grammar G_M which describes
the analysis process followed by M, such that G_M derives S_F from
$S_1 \not{c} \sigma \$$ whenever M accepts the string $\sigma \in T^*$.

This lemma is very similar to Lemma 1 of Sec. 3.3, and the same construction can be used in the proof of the two lemmas.   However, the way we
have defined linear-bounded acceptors, they can accept the input string, leaving an arbitrary sequence of symbols on their tapes when they halt.   The
complete transformational grammar describing the analysis process should
derive the sentence symbol from the initial instantaneous description.   But
if the grammar simply parallels the operation of the acceptor, it will produce
a string of the form $\not{c} T_1 T_2 \cdots T_n S_F \$$.† We must add productions to the
transformational grammar (which is generated by the procedure used in the
proof of Lemma 1 of Sec. 3.3) so that this string is reduced to S_F.   The
following additional rules will perform the task:

$$T_i S_F \$ \to S_F \$ \qquad \text{for all } T_i \in T$$
$$\not{c} S_F \$ \to \not{c} S_F$$
$$\not{c} S_F \to S_F$$

Lemma 2   Let $\hat{G}$ be a grammar derived from a given grammar G by reversing
the arrows in all the productions of G. If G is the transformational
grammar constructed in Lemma 1, such that G describes the analysis
process of a linear-bounded acceptor, then $\hat{G}$ is a context-sensitive
grammar.

In Sec. 3.3 we proved that the reversal of the productions describing the
actions of a Turing machine acceptor also generated a recursive language.
In the linear-bounded case we can restrict the productions of the original
grammar sufficiently so that, when they are reversed, they will be context-
sensitive productions.   We recall that the only difference between recursive
and context-sensitive grammars is that, in the former, the right-hand side of a
production may be shorter than the left side.   This situation occurs only if
the unreversed grammar contains productions which increase the length of

---

† In these proofs we will assume that the acceptors never rewrite the endmarkers.   This
assumption does not lose generality (Prob. 3).

the string. In the grammar of Lemma 1, the only changes of length are the shortenings which occur in the set of rules which erase symbols from the instantaneous description after the machine has reached an accepting condition. Therefore the productions of G never increase the length of the description, and moreover, the final instantaneous description is S_F. When these productions are reversed to form $\hat{G}$, a context-sensitive grammar results which describes the language accepted by the linear-bounded acceptor, with S_F the sentence symbol of that grammar.

Now we have shown that, for any given linear-bounded acceptor, we can construct a context-sensitive grammar which describes the language accepted by the machine. To complete the relationship we must show

Lemma 3 If G is a context-sensitive grammar with endmarkers, there exists a context-sensitive grammar G' without endmarkers which generates the same language.

This result is obtained by a simple trick; we introduce extra symbols which incorporate the marker information. Let ${}^{\varphi}T_i$ represent symbol T_i occurring just to the right of the left endmarker; similarly, $T_i{}^{\$}$ represents T_i just to the left of the right endmarker. We need rules to preserve the endmarkers: If $T_i\beta T_j \rightarrow T_k\alpha T_l$ is a rewriting rule in G, where α, β are strings of terminal and/or nonterminal symbols, then place the four rules

$$T_i\beta T_j \rightarrow T_k\alpha T_l$$
$$T_i\beta T_j{}^{\$} \rightarrow T_k\alpha T_l{}^{\$}$$
$$\varphi T_i\beta T_j \rightarrow \varphi T_k\alpha T_l$$
$$\varphi T_i\beta T_j{}^{\$} \rightarrow \varphi T_k\alpha T_l{}^{\$}$$

in G'.

However, if $T_i(T_j)$ is $\varphi(\$)$, a different replacement must be used. For the first case, $\varphi T_i\beta T_j \rightarrow \varphi T_k\alpha T_l$ is a rewriting rule in G, and G' must contain the two rewriting rules

$$\varphi T_i\beta T_j \rightarrow \varphi T_k\alpha T_l$$
$$\varphi T_i\beta T_j{}^{\$} \rightarrow \varphi T_k\alpha T_l{}^{\$}$$

The reader can provide similar details for the other cases (Prob. 7). We also need to remove the special symbols. This is accomplished by the rewriting rules

$$T_i{}^{\$} \rightarrow T_i$$

and

$$\varphi T_i \rightarrow T_i \qquad \text{for all } T_i \text{ in the terminal alphabet of the language}$$

Finally, we must create the endmarkers. For the initial symbol, use $\text{¢}S\$$ and include the rewriting rules

$$\text{¢}S\$ \to \text{¢}T_i\alpha T_j\$$$
$$\text{¢}S \to \text{¢}T_i\alpha T_j$$
$$S\$ \to T_i\alpha T_j\$$$

in G' if $S \to T_i\alpha T_j$ is a rewriting rule in G, where α is a sequence of terminal and/or nonterminal symbols. (What rules must be added if $S \to N_i$ is a rewriting rule in G?)

Since the endmarkers can be encoded in the end symbols and then removed without changing the length, the languages generated without endmarkers are identical with those generated with endmarkers.

Therefore we have

Theorem 1 *DLBA $\subseteq$ type 1.* (For every linear-bounded acceptor there exists a context-sensitive grammar generating the language accepted by the machine.)

PROBLEMS

1. Find the grammar describing the language accepted by the linear-bounded acceptor described by the quintuples

$S_1\text{¢}\text{¢}RS_1$	$S_3\$\$LS_1$
S_110RS_2	$S_2\text{¢}\text{¢}RS_4$
S_101LS_2	S_400LS_4
S_211LS_1	S_410RS_4
S_201RS_3	$S_4\$$ halt and accept
S_311RS_3	S_301RS_3

2. (*a*) Simulate the machine of Prob. 1 as it accepts the string 01.

(*b*) Show how the grammar you constructed in Prob. 1 derives the string 01.

(*c*) Show how the steps of the machine (part *a*) and the grammar (part *b*) parallel each other.

3. Describe the modifications which are necessary to transform a linear-bounded acceptor M which halts on the rightmost endmarker into an acceptor M' which halts with a blank tape. Be sure you consider the following cases:

(*a*) M may not accept because it erases the tape (in particular, it may erase the endmarkers).

(*b*) M may accept the tape by modifying the endmarker without erasing it, and later restoring it to the original endmarker symbol. Are some restrictions required to cover this case completely? Do these restrictions cause a loss of generality?

4. Why are the modifications described in Prob. 3 never actually made to a machine description?

5. State an additional fact which must be proved to show that the modifications of Prob. 3 do not alter the capabilities of the machine model.

6. The proof in this section really works only for the case $k = 1$. Indicate the steps required to prove that a context-sensitive grammar exists to describe any linear-bounded automaton.

7. Lemmas 2 and 3 are not quite complete to provide the result described. In particular, the symbol representing the state of the acceptor must be erased from the instantaneous description. Give the details of the constructions necessary to remove the need for the symbols denoting the state. (*Hint:* How were the endmarkers removed?)

8. Suppose that a Turing machine operates on a tape whose length is bounded by $f(n)$, where n is the length of the input sequence. Let $C_{f(n)}$ represent the class of languages accepted by machines having the fixed functional bound $f(n)$.

(*a*) Define the acceptance and rejection conditions for these machines by paralleling the $f(n) = kn$ case.

(*b*) Why can we not use a folding argument with $k = f(n)/n$ to reduce all $f(n)$-bounded machines to the linear-bounded case?

(*c*) Show that $C_{f(n)}$ forms a Boolean algebra, for any fixed $f(n) < \infty$, if the machines are deterministic.

4.4 NONDETERMINISTIC LINEAR-BOUNDED ACCEPTORS FOR CONTEXT-SENSITIVE LANGUAGES

To show the remaining relationship between linear-bounded acceptors and context-sensitive languages, we prove that there is a nondeterministic linear-bounded acceptor for each context-sensitive language (*type 1* $\subseteq$ *NLBA*). To prove this result we must show that, for any given context-sensitive language, a linear-bounded acceptor can be constructed which will recognize the strings in the language.

The argument that we used for Turing machine acceptors and recursive languages can be adapted to linear-bounded acceptors and context-sensitive languages. We will show that a nondeterministic machine which recognizes patterns can be constructed such that it satisfies the linear bound on the tape length. Also, we show that one of these machines can be made to follow the reverse of the generation process of a context-sensitive grammar. This produces an analysis of the input sequence.

First we define a linear-bounded P-machine:

> A *linear-bounded P-machine* is a nondeterministic linear-bounded automaton specified by a pair $\langle T,P \rangle$, where T is the set of symbols on the tape and P is a finite set of pairs of sequences in T^* such that in each pair the second string is not longer than the first string.

The operation of a linear-bounded P-machine is similar to the Turing P-machine: The machine examines the tape to find an occurrence of the first sequence of some pair. If the sequence is found, it may be replaced by the second sequence of the pair. When no more replacements are possible, the machine halts. We say that the machine accepts a string σ if there exists some sequence of replacements such that the machine halts with a blank tape and with the machine in a specified final state S_F, having been started in its initial state, with the read/write head scanning the left endmarker of a tape containing $\mathop{\mkern0mu}\text{¢}\sigma\$$.

Due to the length constraint on the pairs describing the P-machine, it is obvious that the machine does indeed obey the constraint of linear-bounded-ness with $k = 1$. Furthermore, it should be easy to see that the pairs can be the inverted versions of the productions of a context-sensitive grammar, since the length constraint corresponds to the nonerasing constraint in the definition of the grammar. (How is the result of Prob. 5 of Sec. 3.3 helpful?)

The only step remaining is to show the exact construction of a P-machine to accept strings from a given language. Two steps are required. First, the machine must check that the given string contains only terminal symbols of the language; this can be done deterministically. Second, the machine must attempt, nondeterministically, to reduce the given string to the sentence symbol by following the reverse productions. Both of these steps exactly parallel the operation of a Turing machine P-acceptor, so we will not discuss the details further. We have shown

Theorem 1 For every context-sensitive language, there exists a nondeterministic linear-bounded acceptor accepting exactly the strings in the language.

PROBLEMS

1. Prove that a linear-bounded P-machine does not accept a language that cannot be accepted by a linear-bounded machine described by conventional quintuples.

2. Show that $\{0^m 1^{g(m)} | m \geq 1\}$ is a context-sensitive language if $g(m)$, which is fixed for the language, can be computed from m by performing only additions and/or multiplications. [*Hint:* How much tape space is required to compute $g(m)$?]

4.5 COMMENTS

The results of this chapter can be summarized as follows: Context-sensitive languages and the set of languages accepted by nondeterministic linear-bounded acceptors are identical (*type 1 = NLBA*). However, the question of the equivalence of the set of context-sensitive languages and the set of languages accepted by deterministic linear-bounded acceptors is still open.

In Sec. 5.7 we will show that deterministic linear-bounded acceptors can accept all context-free languages, so the power of these acceptors probably lies between context-sensitive languages and context-free languages.

The linear-bounded model was introduced by Myhill (1960). Some closure properties are found in Kuroda (1964). Other early results are in Landweber (1963).

Linear-bounded models are only one example of the use of time or space bounds to limit the operations of a Turing machine. One can determine other time or space bounds on the calculations required for Turing machines to perform certain recognition tasks. Occasionally, these bounds can be used to show set-inclusion results. A number of papers covering these areas are listed in the Bibliography.

5
Pushdown Automata

If the existence of practical applications were the major criterion for inclusion in automata studies, we would study only the pushdown machine and some of its variants. Other models would be regarded as theoretically curious changes to the pushdown model. Before we move to theoretical consideration of pushdown machines, we will digress for some comments regarding the usefulness of the pushdown model.

Computer programming languages, such as FORTRAN, ALGOL, and PL/1, allow many constructions which do not resemble the basic operations directly performed by the hardware of most machines. A compiler, which is a computer program itself, is used to translate from the programming language to the computer's language. Mathematical expressions may appear in statements in most programming languages. When a mathematical expression is used in a statement, the compiler has to perform three major tasks: (1) test the structure of the statement for acceptability, (2) determine the meaning of the statement, and (3) translate that meaning to the language of the machine which is to execute the program. The three processes can be related easily when the units of structure are the same as the units of meaning (Sec. 1.4). In this chapter we emphasize the structural properties of the language. We assume that the meaning is simply related to that structure and does not require separate consideration, though we will discuss the meaning in conjunction with some examples.

We concentrate on those programming-language statements which resemble mathematical expressions. Parentheses may be mixed with the conventional algebraic operators ($+$, $-$, $*$, $/$, exponentiation) to affect the order of evaluation of an expression. Theoretically, these parentheses can be nested to arbitrary depth. At the same time the left and right parentheses must occur in balanced pairs. A finite-state machine cannot determine which sequence of parentheses are legal and which are not (a consequence of Prob. 5 of Sec. 2.5). Therefore a machine with infinite storage is required to perform the recognition process even for the simplest forms of algebraic expressions. When parenthesis checking is the only job to be performed, a machine with a counter for its infinite storage can be used (Prob. 4 of Sec. 6.3). A counter is a special case of a pushdown storage, but a counter machine is not sufficiently powerful to perform the translation of algebraic statements. The pushdown machine is sufficient for the recognition of single statements, but it cannot perform the recognition process for most programming languages.

Many programming languages impose restrictions on the types of operands which can be used in certain contexts. For example, in FORTRAN II, an integer quantity cannot be added to a floating-point quantity. In languages where "mixed-mode" arithmetic is allowed, the compiler must detect when these cases occur and produce a translation dependent upon what "declarations" were made concerning the modes of the quantities appearing in the expression. The compiler cannot perform this task without having access to a table which contains the type information which was declared at the beginning of the program. A pushdown machine cannot perform this task; thus one should consider generalizations of pushdown machines which can perform it. We will examine some of these in Chap. 6.

In this chapter we describe the pushdown model and prove its relationship with context-free languages. In addition, we show some examples illustrating the processing of mathematical expressions by compiler to show that this task can be performed by a pushdown machine. Finally, we demonstrate some results relating pushdown acceptors and linear-bounded acceptors.

5.1 THE MODEL

A pushdown automaton has two tapes and a finite-state control (Fig. 5.1.1). One tape, the *input tape*, contains the input sequence and is read by a reading head. The second tape, the *pushdown tape*, is infinite in one direction only,

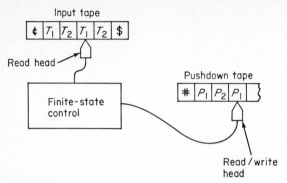

Fig. 5.1.1   A pushdown machine during a computation.

say to the right.†   A read/write head moves on the pushdown tape, but with the restriction that whenever it moves left, it erases the square it is leaving. Furthermore, whenever it moves right, it writes a new symbol in the square it enters.   Thus the only nonblank squares of the pushdown tape lie between the read/write head and the fixed left end of the tape.

For convenience we assume that the symbols on the pushdown tape are distinct from those on the input tape.   Let $P = \{P_1, P_2, \ldots, P_p\}$ be the set of pushdown-tape symbols, $T = \{T_1, T_2, \ldots, T_n\}$ be the set of input-tape symbols, and $S = \{S_1, S_2, \ldots, S_m\}$ be the set of internal states.

In one step the machine examines (1) the input symbol in the square under the reading head, (2) the pushdown symbol in the square under the read/write head, and (3) the internal state, to determine:

1. A motion of the input reading head (right or null)
2. An action on the pushdown tape, either
   a. Do nothing, or
   b. Erase the symbol under the head, then move left, or
   c. Move the head right and write symbol P_k *in the new square*
3. A new internal state
4. Whether to halt

If the choice of the move depends on the input symbol, the reading head must move right during the move; in other cases the reading head does not move, and we write λ for the input symbol in the description of that move.   If we follow this convention, we do not need to specify the motion of the reading head on the input tape, because it can be inferred from the value of the input

† Conventionally, the pushdown tape is pictured vertically, with the fixed end of the tape at the bottom.   We show the pushdown tape horizontally, with the fixed end at the left, so that the pictures of the machines resemble their instantaneous descriptions.

symbol which determined the action.   Since the finite-state control can store the last symbol read from the input tape, this convention does not cause loss of generality.

A move of the pushdown machine can be expressed as a quintuple of the form $T_iP_jS_kP_lS_m$, where T_i, an input symbol or λ, P_j, a pushdown symbol, and S_k, an internal state, determine the move, and P_l, a pushdown symbol or N or E, and S_m, an internal state, specify the actions taken during the move (motion on the input tape is specified if T_i is not λ).   A machine is specified by a list of the quintuples describing all possible moves.   The machine halts if a combination of $T_iP_jS_k$ occurs which does not appear in the quintuple list.

The input tape has endmarkers, denoted by $\cent$ and $\$$.   In some cases a move to the endmarkers can initiate special actions, but in many cases the endmarkers can be eliminated from the model without restricting the power of the class of machines.   The pushdown tape has an endmarker $\#$ which is always at the (fixed) left end of the pushdown stack.   This endmarker cannot be eliminated from the model, since the fact that the pushdown stack is empty cannot be detected without it.   This endmarker could be written on the pushdown tape during the first move made by the machine, but usually one assumes that the endmarker is permanently written on the pushdown tape. Sometimes we call the pushdown tape a "stack," whose "top" is the symbol under the read/write head and whose "bottom" is the endmarker.

When a pushdown machine is started, the read head will be placed on the left endmarker of the input tape and the pushdown tape will contain only its endmarker, with the read/write head over the endmarker.   The initial state of the finite-state control is specified as part of the description of the machine.

The instantaneous description of a pushdown machine is constructed from two concatenated strings, the first representing the contents of the input tape, the second the pushdown tape, with the endmarker of the pushdown tape to the left.   The endmarkers $\$$ and $\#$ separate the two strings.   A symbol representing the state of the machine is written immediately to the left of the symbol from the input tape which is under the reading head.

Example 1   Consider the pushdown machine with initial state S_1 which is described by the list in Table 5.1.1.   The table entries are interpreted as follows:

1. The first three columns contain the information which determines the next action.
2. The fourth column specifies the action with the pushdown store: N means do nothing; E means erase the symbol on the tape (and move the read/write head one square toward the $\#$ square); a pushdown tape symbol indicates that that symbol, say P_n, will be added to the right end of the pushdown stack (by moving the read/write head one square to the right and writing P_n in the new square).

Table 5.1.1 A pushdown machine's transition table

T_i	P_j	S_k	Pushdown tape	S_m
¢	#	S_1	N	S_2
1	#	S_2	P_1	S_2
1	P_1	S_2	P_1	S_2
1	P_2	S_2	P_1	S_2
2	#	S_2	P_2	S_2
2	P_1	S_2	P_2	S_2
2	P_2	S_2	P_2	S_2
3	#	S_2	N	S_3
3	P_1	S_2	N	S_3
3	P_2	S_2	N	S_3
2	P_2	S_3	E	S_3
1	P_1	S_3	E	S_3
$	#	S_3	Halt	S_3
Other cases			Halt	S_2

3. The fifth column specifies the next state.

    Suppose the machine is presented with the input tape ¢112131211\$. The sequence of instantaneous descriptions will be

S_1¢112131211\$#
¢$S_2$112131211\$#
¢1$S_2$12131211\$#P_1
¢11$S_2$2131211\$#P_1P_1
¢112$S_2$131211\$#$P_1P_1P_2$
¢1121$S_2$31211\$#$P_1P_1P_2P_1$
¢11213$S_3$1211\$#$P_1P_1P_2P_1$
¢112131$S_3$211\$#$P_1P_1P_2$
¢1121312$S_3$11\$#P_1P_1
¢11213121$S_3$1\$#P_1
¢112131211S_3\$#

Pushdown machines as compilers   In conventional mathematical notation, also known as *infix* notation, each binary operator is written between the two operands that it operates on. In *reverse polish*, or *postfix*, notation the binary operator is written following its two operands. For example, Table 5.1.2 shows pairs of expressions having equivalent meanings. Parentheses are not necessary in postfix notation, since the ordering of the symbols is sufficient to determine the order of evaluation.

    To determine the value of an expression written in postfix form, first replace each symbol by the corresponding value. Anywhere that an operator is preceded by two values, that operator can be applied to those two values; the result of this application replaces the two values and operand.

Table 5.1.2 Some mathematical expressions in both infix and postfix forms

Infix	Postfix
$a + b$	$ab +$
$a + b * c$	$abc * +$
$(a + b) * c$	$ab + c *$
$(a + b)/(c + d)$	$ab + cd + /$

The evaluation of $ab + cd + /$ with $a = 3, b = 7, c = 2, d = 3$ might proceed as follows:

$37 + 23 + /$
$(10)23 + /$
$(10)5 /$
2

where we use parentheses to group those symbols which represent single values.

In infix expressions the order of evaluation is specified by parentheses and by (often unwritten) "precedence" rules that state the order of evaluation in otherwise ambiguous situations. For example, the algebraic precedence rules are that multiplications and divisions are evaluated before subtractions, which are evaluated before additions. Thus we say that addition has lowest precedence and exponentiation the highest precedence. Table 5.1.3 lists typical precedence values for arithmetic operators. A sequence of operators of the same precedence is evaluated from left to right. Thus $3 + 4 - 2 + 1 = 6$ and $3 * 4/2 * 3 = 18$. Parentheses may be used to change the ordering of the evaluation steps.

A pushdown list can be used, not only to evaluate expressions written in postfix notation, but also to translate from the infix form of an expression to the equivalent postfix form. We now illustrate these two applications, using a flow-chart description of the pushdown machines. In these examples single symbols are used to represent single variables.

Table 5.1.3 Operator precedence in mathematical expressions

Operator	Precedence
$+, -$	1
$*, /$	2
$\uparrow$ (exponentiation)	3

Example 2 *Evaluation of Postfix Expressions* The input tape of the pushdown machine contains a postfix expression with a numeric value or an operator in each square of the tape.   Two values, which can be considered to be the top two values on the pushdown stack, are stored in the control unit.   Let a and b be the names of the cells which hold those values.

The strategy is as follows: Whenever a value is read, it is placed on the stack, and whenever an operator is read, the top two values on the stack (in a and b) are used as the operands for performing the indicated operation.   The result of the operation replaces the value in a.   The value in b has been used, and a new value for b is read off the pushdown list (Fig. 5.1.2).

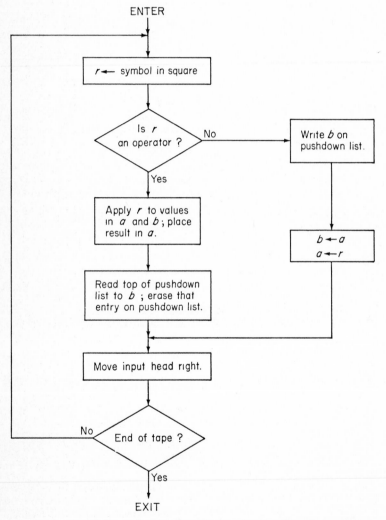

Fig. 5.1.2 A pushdown machine to evaluate well-formed postfix expressions.

Exceptional cases arise whenever the pushdown list becomes empty, or when the input sequence is not a well-formed postfix expression. The latter case is not handled by the flow chart (Prob. 7).

Consider the evaluation of $3 - 5 * (7 + 9)$, which is equivalent to $3579 + * -$ in postfix notation. The input to the pushdown machine is $(3)(5)(7)(9)(+)(*)(-)$, where the parentheses enclose separate values but are not written on the input tape. We indicate the position of the input head of the machine by the symbol S when writing instantaneous descriptions of the machine. In the right column we show the contents of the pushdown list and the registers a and b, with the top of the pushdown list on the right. The sequence of instantaneous descriptions at the end of each step as the machine evaluates the expression is

(pushdown list) (b) (a)

$S¢(3)(5)(7)(9)(+)(*)(-)\$\#$	
$¢S(3)(5)(7)(9)(+)(*)(-)\$\#$	
$¢(3)S(5)(7)(9)(+)(*)(-)\$\#$	(3)
$¢(3)(5)S(7)(9)(+)(*)(-)\$\#$	(3)(5)
$¢(3)(5)(7)S(9)(+)(*)(-)\$\#(3)$	(3)(5)(7)
$¢(3)(5)(7)(9)S(+)(*)(-)\$\#(3)(5)$	(3)(5)(7)(9)
$¢(3)(5)(7)(9)(+)S(*)(-)\$\#(3)$	(3)(5)(16)
$¢(3)(5)(7)(9)(+)(*)S(-)\$\#$	(3)(80)
$¢(3)(5)(7)(9)(+)(*)(-)S\$\#$	(−77)

The next example illustrates the process of translating from infix to postfix notation. Since an output sequence will be produced, we require a mechanism for outputs. A simple mechanism—an output terminal, where a time sequence of symbols is observed—will be used.

Example 3 *Translation from Infix to Postfix Notation*   In the evaluation problem, the pushdown list was used to store sequences of operands. In the translation problem, operators are stored on the pushdown list. An enumeration of all possible cases can be used to prove that the sequence of operands in an infix expression is the same as in the equivalent postfix expression. The translation problem reduces to the problem of placing the operators in the sequence at the proper places. Thus, as the translator reads the input sequence from left to right, it saves an operator until its second operand has been output, then it outputs the operator. The end of the second operand is detected by the occurrence of a matching right parenthesis, an operator having equal or lower precedence (for example, an addition appearing after a multiplication), or the end of the input string (denoted by the endmarker $). Left parentheses must be stored on the stack to delimit those operators which were enclosed within parentheses in the infix form. Whenever the machine reaches a right parenthesis on the input, it knows that back to the matching left parenthesis the operators have complete second operands.

When a new operator is read, the translator must decide whether some operators from the top of the stack should be output. After all have been inserted in the output sequence, the new operator is placed on the top of the stack. Figure 5.1.3 shows a flow-chart description of the translator.

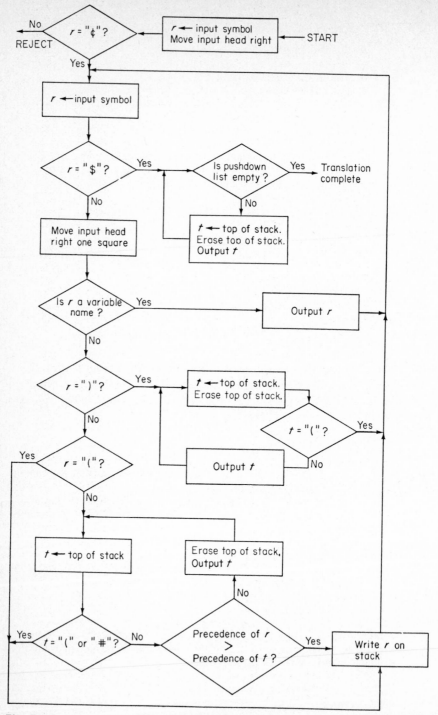

Fig. 5.1.3 Flow chart describing the translation of mathematical expressions from infix to postfix form.

The sequence of instantaneous descriptions below indicates the process of translating $(a*b+c)+a*c$ to postfix form. The output sequences are shown to the right; the leftmost symbol of a sequence is the first one sent to the output terminal.

ID	Output symbol
$S¢(a*b+c)+a*c\$\#$	
$¢S(a*b+c)+a*c\$\#$	
$¢(Sa*b+c)+a*c\$\#($	
$¢(aS*b+c)+a*c\$\#($	a
$¢(a*Sb+c)+a*c\$\#(*$	
$¢(a*bS+c)+a*c\$\#(*$	b
$¢(a*b+Sc)+a*c\$\#(+$	$*$
$¢(a*b+cS)+a*c\$\#(+$	c
$¢(a*b+c)S+a*c\$\#$	$+$
$¢(a*b+c)+Sa*c\$\#+$	
$¢(a*b+c)+aS*c\$\#+$	a
$¢(a*b+c)+a*Sc\$\#+*$	
$¢(a*b+c)+a*cS\$\#+*$	c
$¢(a*b+c)+a*cS\$\#$	$*+$

The output (postfix) expression is $ab*c+ac*+$. ■

PROBLEMS

1. Simulate the behavior of the pushdown machine in Example 1 of Sec. 5.1 when presented with each of the following input sequences:

(a) $¢1121131121\$$

(b) $¢12131211\$$

(c) $¢121131211\$$

2. The machine in Example 2 performs some unnecessary manipulations of the stack. For instance, a value might be read from the stack (and erased) in one step and then written back onto the stack in the next step without any change. Modify the machine to eliminate the unnecessary busywork. (*Hint:* It may be helpful to use two bits to indicate when registers a and b contain useful information.)

3. Where does the machine in Example 2 leave the result of the evaluation?

4. Simulate the machine in Example 3 as it translates $a*b/(c+d*e-(f*a-b))$ to postfix form.

5. Modify the machine in Example 3 so that it can correctly translate expressions containing unary minus signs, such as $-a+b$. You will need different symbols ($-$ and $-_1$, for example) for binary and unary minus in the postfix expression but not in the infix expression. (Why?)

6. Prefix notation is similar to postfix notation, except that each operator precedes its operands. Describe a machine which reads an infix expression from right to left and translates it to an equivalent prefix expression.

7. The machines in Examples 2 and 3 do not check the input for proper structure. For example, $a++b$ would be translated to $ab++$ by the machine of Example 3. Modify each machine so that it checks the structure of the input expression in addition to performing the proper translation or evaluation.

5.2 PUSHDOWN ACCEPTORS

A pushdown acceptor is presented with a string σ surrounded by endmarkers ¢, $. The machine is started on the left endmarker of the input tape in its initial state. The pushdown tape initially contains only its endmarker, which is under the read/write head when the machine starts. The machine accepts the string if it halts in one of its accepting states, with the reading head reading the right endmarker on the input tape and the pushdown tape read/write head over its endmarker. The machine rejects the string if it halts in a non-accepting state, if it halts in an accepting state with the reading head not on the right endmarker, if it halts with the pushdown tape nonempty, if it never halts, or if it tries to erase the endmarker on the pushdown tape. Let $1DPDA$ ($INPDA$) denote the set of languages accepted by one-way (non-)deterministic pushdown acceptors.

Note that, according to the way we have defined pushdown machines, one could loop indefinitely without moving the reading head on the input tape.

Example 1 Let the machine in Example 1 of Sec. 5.1 be an acceptor, with S_3 the accepting state. It accepts the language

$$L = \{\alpha 3 \alpha^R | \alpha \in \{1,2\}^*\}$$

Informally, the machine first copies α onto the pushdown tape (while the machine is in state S_2); then, when the 3 is read, the machine begins to compare the remainder of the input with the sequence stored on the pushdown tape. Since the pushdown tape is read in the reverse order from that in which it was written, the last part of the input sequence must match the first part in reverse order. ■

Sentences which read the same if the letters are read in reverse order are known as *palindromes*. For example, the sentence "Able was I ere I saw Elba" is a palindrome. This palindrome has an odd number of symbols; so the center one is not matched by another symbol. It is known as the *centermarker* if it is a letter which can never appear in the other positions of the string. Language L consists of palindromes with centermarkers. Note that as a string in L is read from left to right, the position of the center is known from the appearance of a 3. If there were no centermarker, one would have to count the symbols in the string to find its center. The acceptor of Example 1 used the appearance of the centermarker to change to state S_3 and begin the check that the second half of the input string was a mirror image of the first half.

An important palindrome language is the language

$$L_1 = \{1^n 3 1^n | n \geq 0\}$$

over two symbols. This language cannot be recognized by a finite-state machine. (Suppose L_1 were recognized by a finite-state machine M. Then M must recognize $1^n 3 1^n$ for n arbitrarily large. But by Prob. 5 of Sec. 2.5,

M must also recognize either 1^p31^n or 1^n31^p for some $p > n$, when n is larger than some limit. The latter strings are not in L_1.) Since L_1 is accepted by a deterministic pushdown acceptor (the one in Example 1 of Sec. 5.1), we have

Theorem 1   *1DPDA ⊃ type 3*.   (Deterministic pushdown acceptors are more powerful than finite-state acceptors.)

In the next section we show that, for any deterministic pushdown acceptor M, there exists a context-free grammar generating the language accepted by M (*1DPDA ⊆ type 2*). Then we introduce nondeterministic pushdown acceptors, and eventually we show that there is a nondeterministic pushdown acceptor for every context-free language (*type 2 ⊆ 1NPDA*). We will show that nondeterministic pushdown acceptors are more powerful than deterministic ones, so the classes are not all equivalent. Symbolically, we have

$$1DPDA \subset 1NPDA = type\ 2$$

PROBLEMS

1.   (P) A rigorous proof of Theorem 1 requires a proof that there exists a deterministic pushdown acceptor to accept any language accepted by a finite-state acceptor. Show that there is a deterministic pushdown acceptor for every regular language. (*Hint:* Do not use the pushdown tape.)

2.   State all the results needed to prove

$$Type\ 2 \supset 1DPDA \supset type\ 3$$

5.3 CONTEXT-FREE LANGUAGE DESCRIPTIONS OF PUSHDOWN ACCEPTORS

We now show that there exists a context-free grammar to generate the language accepted by a pushdown acceptor (*1DPDA ⊆ type 2, 1NPDA ⊆ type 2*). To prove this we will construct a generative grammar such that sequences of working strings in the derivation of a string σ will parallel the operation of the acceptor, in the sense that the terminal symbols of σ are generated in the order that the acceptor reads them (from left to right). The major step in constructing the grammar is finding an appropriate set of nonterminal symbols and specifying the relationship between the operation of the machine and those nonterminal symbols.

Relationships   As a pushdown machine processes an input string σ, symbols may be stacked on the pushdown tape. If the machine accepts σ, it must erase each of these symbols in some later step. Consider a sequence of input symbols which is read by the acceptor between the time a pushdown symbol is written and the time that particular symbol is erased. That sequence is a member of the set of strings which can occur whenever that pushdown symbol is written. Therefore it is natural to associate a nonterminal symbol in the grammar with each pushdown symbol in the machine. An example will show that this simple relationship will not produce enough nonterminal symbols.

Example 1   Consider the pushdown machine with initial state S_1 described by the following list of quintuples:

¢	#	S_1	N	S_2
1	#	S_2	P_1	S_2
1	P_1	S_2	P_1	S_2
1	P_2	S_2	P_1	S_2
2	#	S_2	P_2	S_2
2	P_1	S_2	P_2	S_2
2	P_2	S_2	P_2	S_2
3	#	S_2	N	S_3
3	P_1	S_2	N	S_3
3	P_2	S_2	N	S_3
4	#	S_2	N	S_6
4	P_1	S_2	N	S_6
4	P_2	S_2	N	S_6
2	P_2	S_3	E	S_3
1	P_1	S_3	E	S_3
1	#	S_3	P_1	S_4
2	#	S_3	P_2	S_4
3	#	S_3	N	S_5
1	P_1	S_4	P_1	S_4
1	P_2	S_4	P_1	S_4
2	P_1	S_4	P_2	S_4
2	P_2	S_4	P_2	S_4
3	P_1	S_4	N	S_5
3	P_2	S_4	N	S_5
1	P_1	S_5	E	S_5
2	P_2	S_5	E	S_5
$	#	S_5	(accept)	
1	P_1	S_6	E	S_6
2	P_2	S_6	E	S_6
$	#	S_6	(accept)	

This machine is a simple modification of the machine of Example 1 of Sec. 5.1; it accepts the language

$$\{\alpha 3 \alpha^R \beta 3 \beta^R | \alpha, \beta \in \{1,2\}^*\} \cup \{\alpha 4 \alpha^R | \alpha \in \{1,2\}^*\}$$

If we associate a nonterminal symbol with the set of strings which can occur, given that P_2 is placed on the pushdown list, we have a problem. The symbol P_2 could be erased from the list when the machine is in any one of three states, depending upon the centermarker symbol and whether the P_2 was written for a symbol in the first or second palindrome (if 3 was the centermarker). The machine remembers (in its internal state—states S_3 or S_6) whether a 3 or 4 was the centermarker for the first palindrome. If the centermarker was a 3, a second palindrome must follow to make the string acceptable. Otherwise the string must end after the first palindrome. If these three cases are not distinguished in the grammar, the grammar will also define derivations of strings like $\alpha 4\alpha^R \beta 3\beta^R \gamma 3\gamma^R$, which are not accepted by the machine and therefore should not be in the language. ◼

The nonterminal symbol must convey some information about the state of the machine at the time the symbol is erased from the pushdown stack. A similar argument can be used to show that the state at the time the symbol was written on the pushdown stack is significant. The nonterminal symbols also must convey some information about the symbol written on the stack. Thus we associate the nonterminal symbols of the grammar with sets of strings as follows:

Let N_{S_i,S_j,P_k} be the nonterminal symbol which represents the set of sequences such that, if the reading of one of the sequences in N_{S_i,S_j,P_k} begins when the machine is state S_i with P_k on the top of the pushdown list, then the machine will be in state S_j and will have just erased the same P_k when the sequence is completed. For the case $P_k = \#$, let $N_{S_1,S_2,\#}$ represent the set of strings in the language, where S_1 is the starting state and S_2 is the accepting state of the machine.†

Example 2   Consider the machine of Example 1. Since the machine does not erase the pushdown symbol when it is in states S_1, S_2, or S_4, the sets N_{S_i,S_1,P_j}, N_{S_i,S_2,P_j}, and N_{S_i,S_4,P_j} are empty for all S_i and P_j. The set N_{S_2,S_3,P_2} contains strings of the form $\alpha 3\alpha^R 2$ for $\alpha \in \{1,2\}^*$. ◼

Construction   The rewriting rules of the grammar G of the language describing the set accepted by a given pushdown machine M can be constructed by the following process:

1. If M contains the move

   $T_i P_j S_k P_l S_m$

   place the rewriting rule

   $N_{S_k,S_p,P_j} \rightarrow T_i N_{S_m,S_q,P_l} N_{S_q,S_p,P_j}$ in G for all S_p, S_q in S

2. If M contains the move

   $\lambda P_j S_k P_l S_m$

---

† This requires that we modify the correspondence by replacing the erasure of the P_k by the halting of the machine for $N_{S_1,S_2,\#}$ only.

place the rewriting rule

$$N_{S_k,S_p,P_j} \rightarrow N_{S_m,S_q,P_l} N_{S_q,S_p,P_j} \text{ in } G \text{ for all } S_p, S_q \text{ in } S$$

3. If M contains the move

$T_i P_j S_k E S_l$

place the rewriting rule

$N_{S_k,S_l,P_j} \rightarrow T_i$ in G

4. If M contains the move

$\lambda P_j S_k E S_l$

place the rewriting rule

$N_{S_k,S_l,P_j} \rightarrow \lambda$ in G

5. If M contains the move

$T_i P_j S_k N S_l$

place the rewriting rule

$N_{S_k,S_p,P_j} \rightarrow T_i N_{S_l,S_p,P_j}$ in G for all S_p in S

6. If M contains the move

$\lambda P_j S_k N S_l$

place the rewriting rule

$N_{S_k,S_p,P_j} \rightarrow N_{S_l,S_p,P_j}$ in G for all S_p in S

7. Place the rewriting rule $S \rightarrow N_{S_i,S_j,\#}$ in G, where S_i is the starting state, for every S_j in the set of accepting states.

8. If M contains the move

$\$\#S_k$(halt)

and S_k is an accepting state, then place the rewriting rule

$N_{S_k,S_k,\#} \rightarrow \$$ in G

Consider the first rule. The production states that, to get from S_k to S_p with P_j on the stack, the machine must get from S_m to some intermediate state S_q with P_l on the stack; then it must erase the P_l and continue from S_q to S_p with the same P_j on the stack. In the latter subsequence, the machine may write additional symbols on the stack, but these possibilities are covered in the N_{S_q,S_p,P_j} set.

The other rules have similar interpretations, with the exception of rule 7, which provides the starting conditions, and rule 8, which provides the stopping conditions.

Example 3 The rewriting rules of the grammar generating the language accepted by the acceptor of Example 1 of Sec. 5.1 are as follows:

Quintuple	Productions
—	$S \rightarrow N_{S_1,S_3,\#}$
$\mathcal{c}\#S_1NS_2$	$N_{S_1,S_1,\#} \rightarrow \mathcal{c}N_{S_2,S_1,\#}$
	$N_{S_1,S_2,\#} \rightarrow \mathcal{c}N_{S_2,S_2,\#}$
	$N_{S_1,S_3,\#} \rightarrow \mathcal{c}N_{S_2,S_3,\#}$
$1\#S_2P_1S_2$	$N_{S_2,S_1,\#} \rightarrow 1N_{S_2,S_1,P_1}N_{S_1,S_1,\#}$
	$N_{S_2,S_1,\#} \rightarrow 1N_{S_2,S_2,P_1}N_{S_2,S_1,\#}$
	$N_{S_2,S_1,\#} \rightarrow 1N_{S_2,S_3,P_1}N_{S_3,S_1,\#}$
	$N_{S_2,S_2,\#} \rightarrow 1N_{S_2,S_1,P_1}N_{S_1,S_2,\#}$
	$N_{S_2,S_2,\#} \rightarrow 1N_{S_2,S_2,P_1}N_{S_2,S_2,\#}$
	$N_{S_2,S_2,\#} \rightarrow 1N_{S_2,S_3,P_1}N_{S_3,S_2,\#}$
	$N_{S_2,S_3,\#} \rightarrow 1N_{S_2,S_1,P_1}N_{S_1,S_3,\#}$
	$N_{S_2,S_3,\#} \rightarrow 1N_{S_2,S_2,P_1}N_{S_2,S_3,\#}$
	$N_{S_2,S_3,\#} \rightarrow 1N_{S_2,S_3,P_1}N_{S_3,S_3,\#}$
$\vdots$	$\vdots$
$3\#S_2NS_3$	$N_{S_2,S_1,\#} \rightarrow 3N_{S_3,S_1,\#}$
	$N_{S_2,S_2,\#} \rightarrow 3N_{S_3,S_2,\#}$
	$N_{S_2,S_3,\#} \rightarrow 3N_{S_3,S_3,\#}$
$\vdots$	$\vdots$
$1P_1S_3ES_3$	$N_{S_3,S_3,P_1} \rightarrow 1$
$\$\#S_3$(halt)	$N_{S_3,S_3,\#} \rightarrow \$$

To see how the derivation of a string parallels the operation of the machine as it accepts that string, consider the machine with input $\mathcal{c}12321\$$. Compare the instantaneous descriptions of the machine with the working strings in a derivation of the string:

Machine	Derivation
	S
$S_1\mathcal{c}12321\$\#$	$N_{S_1,S_3,\#}$
$\mathcal{c}S_212321\$\#$	$\mathcal{c}N_{S_2,S_3,\#}$
$\mathcal{c}1S_22321\$\#P_1$	$\mathcal{c}1N_{S_2,S_3,P_1}N_{S_3,S_3,\#}$
$\mathcal{c}12S_2321\$\#P_1P_2$	$\mathcal{c}12N_{S_2,S_3,P_2}N_{S_3,S_3,P_1}N_{S_3,S_3,\#}$
$\mathcal{c}123S_321\$\#P_1P_2$	$\mathcal{c}123N_{S_3,S_3,P_2}N_{S_3,S_3,P_1}N_{S_3,S_3,\#}$
$\mathcal{c}1232S_31\$\#P_1$	$\mathcal{c}1232N_{S_3,S_3,P_1}N_{S_3,S_3,\#}$
$\mathcal{c}12321S_3\$\#$	$\mathcal{c}12321N_{S_3,S_3,\#}$
(accept)	$\mathcal{c}12321\$$

Note that (1) the terminal symbols to the left of the reading head match the terminal symbols in the corresponding working string, (2) the sequence of final subscripts on the nonterminal symbols matches the contents of the pushdown stack, and (3) the first subscript on the first nonterminal symbol is the present state of the machine. ▪

One discrepancy between the grammar and the machine remains.   The machine examines tapes of the form $\textcent\sigma\$$, where σ does not contain $\textcent$ or $\$$. Though we define the machine to accept strings of the form $\alpha 3\alpha^R$, it actually accepts all tapes of the form $\textcent\alpha 3\alpha^R\$$.   Since the grammar parallels the machine, it describes the language containing all strings of the form $\textcent\alpha 3\alpha^R\$$. We must modify the grammar to remove the endmarkers (Prob. 2).

Rule 4 generates productions which are not allowed in context-free grammars.   Thus the grammar just constructed is not a context-free grammar.   If we can show that the presence of erasing rules in a context-free grammar does not increase the capability of the grammar, then we will have a proof that, for every pushdown acceptor, there exists a context-free language to describe the set of strings accepted by the machine.†   Therefore we now show that the use of erasing productions does not increase the capability of context-free grammars.

Erasing rules   Given a context-free grammar containing erasing rules, we will show that there exists a context-free grammar, not containing erasing rules, which generates the same set of nonnull strings.

The restriction to nonnull strings is required because an erasing grammar could contain the rule $S \to \lambda$ (or a set of rules having the same effect), and the language would contain the null string.   If erasing is not allowed, every string must contain at least one symbol.

The first step in producing an equivalent nonerasing grammar is to find the set of all nonterminal symbols which can be transformed into the null string.‡   Whenever a sequence of these nonterminal symbols appears on the right side of a production, we replace that production by more than one production; the extra productions will cover the possibilities that that sequence of nonterminal symbols might be erased in a future step of a derivation in the erasing grammar.   The following example will help clarify the procedure.

Example 4   Consider a grammar having the following rewriting rules:

$S \to AS$
$S \to B$
$A \to aBC$
$B \to bB$
$B \to \lambda$
$C \to cC$
$C \to \lambda$

---

† We have shown only the construction.   A complete proof must show that sequences in the grammar and sequences in the acceptor's operation can be placed in a one-to-one correspondence.   (See Prob. 3 and Sec. 2.3.)
‡ The grammar generates the null string if and only if S is in this set.

One derivation is

S
AS
AB
$aBCB$
aCB
aC
acC
ac

We wish to remove productions with null right sides from the grammar and produce an equivalent grammar. We must allow not only for the possibilities $B \Rightarrow^* \lambda$ and $C \Rightarrow^* \lambda$, but also for $BC \Rightarrow^* \lambda$. As far as the $A \to aBC$ production is concerned, these cases can be covered by replacing the original production with four productions:

$A \to a$
$A \to aB$
$A \to aC$
$A \to aBC$

The last three productions cover those cases in which either B or C is transformed into a nonnull string. If the production $A \to aBC$ were the only one in the grammar having B or C on the right side, the productions $B \to \lambda$ and $C \to \lambda$ could be removed from the grammar after the original production had been replaced by the four shown above. Since there are other productions with B or C on the right-hand side, they will have to be treated similarly before the rules $B \to \lambda$ and $C \to \lambda$ can be removed from the grammar.

The nonerasing grammar which is equivalent to the complete grammar has the following rewriting rules:

$S \to AS$
$S \to B$
$S \to A$
$A \to a$
$A \to aB$
$A \to aC$
$A \to aBC$
$B \to bB$
$B \to b$
$C \to cC$
$C \to c$

Our problem of finding an equivalent nonerasing grammar will be completely solved when we describe a procedure for finding the set of nonterminal symbols which might be transformed into the null string. Define a sequence A_i of sets of nonterminal symbols as follows:

1. $N_j \in A_1$ if and only if $N_j \to \lambda$ is a rewriting rule in G.
2. $N_j \in A_{i+1}$ if and only if $N_j \in A_i$ or $N_j \to \varphi$ with $\varphi \in A_i^*$ is a rewriting rule in G.

The second part of the second rule covers the case when the nonterminal symbol is replaced by a sequence of nonterminal symbols, each of which can be transformed into the null string. One computes these sets until two sets are identical; since $A_m = A_n$ for $m > n$, where n is the number of nonterminal symbols in the grammar, not more than n iterations will be required (why?).

To write the equivalent grammar without erasing rules:

1. Remove every production of the form $N_j \rightarrow \lambda$.
2. Keep every production in which the right side does not contain any nonterminal symbols in A_n.
3. The remaining productions contain at least one $N_j \in A_n$ on the right side. Replace each production by a set of productions in which the nonterminal symbols from A_n are erased and kept in all combinations.

The new grammar will generate the same language as the original one, with the possible exception of the null string. Furthermore, the null string is missing only if $S \in A_n$.

Since we can write an erasing context-free grammar for every pushdown acceptor, and since there is a nonerasing context-free grammar equivalent to every erasing context-free grammar (with the exception of the null string), we have

Theorem 1†   There exists a context-free grammar describing the set of strings accepted by a deterministic pushdown acceptor, except that if the acceptor accepts the null string, it will be absent from the language described by the grammar.

Symbolically stated, the theorem is:

If $L \in 1DPDA$, then $L - \{\lambda\} \in type\ 2$

PROBLEMS

1.   Grammar G has the following rewriting rules:

$$S \rightarrow 0S0$$
$$S \rightarrow 1S1$$
$$S \rightarrow A$$
$$A \rightarrow 2B3$$
$$B \rightarrow 2B3$$
$$B \rightarrow \lambda$$
$$B \rightarrow 3$$

(a) Find a nonerasing grammar equivalent to G.

(b) Describe the language L generated by G by exhibiting a typical string in L and specifying any constraints on parameters in the string.

(c) Find a deterministic pushdown acceptor which accepts L.

† Some writers—Ginsburg, for example—define context-free and regular languages to allow erasing productions, making the statement of such theorems slightly simpler.

2. The procedure described in this section produced a grammar which defined a language with each string containing endmarkers. How should the procedure be modified so that the grammar produces strings without endmarkers?

3. Let M be a pushdown acceptor and let the grammar G be constructed from M by the procedure described in this section.

(*a*) Show that, for every sequence of moves of the acceptor which leads to acceptance, there exists a sequence of strings produced by the grammar leading to a sentence in the language.

(*b*) State and prove the converse of part *a*.

4. (P) Let a generalized pushdown acceptor be a pushdown acceptor which can write a finite sequence of symbols on the pushdown tape in one step. Each single step is described by a tuple of the form

$$T_i P_j S_k (P_m P_n \cdots P_q) S_l$$

The sequence $P_m P_n \cdots P_q$ is written on the pushdown tape so that P_q is on the top of the stack when the move is completed.

(*a*) Show that generalized pushdown acceptors are equivalent to pushdown acceptors as defined in the text.

(*b*) A replacing pushdown acceptor is a generalized pushdown acceptor, except that the sequence of pushdown symbols *replaces* the symbol on the top of the pushdown tape. Show that replacing pushdown acceptors are equivalent to pushdown acceptors.

5.4 NONDETERMINISTIC PUSHDOWN AUTOMATA

A nondeterministic pushdown automaton is a pushdown automaton which may have several next moves for some combination of present state, input symbol, and pushdown symbol. A string is accepted by a nondeterministic pushdown machine if there exists a sequence of choices that lead to the machine halting in an accepting condition after the machine was started in standard starting conditions.

In this section we will give examples which show that the nondeterministic pushdown acceptor is more powerful than the deterministic pushdown acceptor. We will exhibit a language accepted by a nondeterministic pushdown acceptor, but not accepted by any deterministic pushdown acceptor. We will not prove the latter part of this statement until later (Sec. 7.6), because it is easier to prove using other linguistic devices. In this section we argue its plausibility. In the next section we will show that there exists a nondeterministic pushdown acceptor for each context-free grammar. Together, these results show that the set of deterministic pushdown-acceptor languages is smaller than the set of context-free languages. Problem 1 of Sec. 5.2 showed that there is a deterministic pushdown acceptor for each regular language, so the set of languages accepted by deterministic pushdown acceptors is definitely positioned between the sets of regular and context-free languages.

Without further ado, we state that the palindrome language without centermarker

$$\{\alpha\alpha^R | \alpha \in \{1,2\}^*\}$$

is context-free and can be recognized by a nondeterministic pushdown acceptor, but not by a deterministic pushdown acceptor.

To show that this statement is plausible, we first show a nondeterministic pushdown acceptor for the language. The acceptor of Example 1 of Sec. 5.1 (with S_1 the starting state and S_3 the accepting state) accepts odd-length palindromes with centermarkers. When this machine is in state S_2, it copies the first part of the string onto the pushdown list. The centermarker indicated that the machine should enter state S_3 and begin to check the second half of the input string against the pushdown list. When there is no centermarker, the acceptor cannot deterministically decide when it has reached the (unmarked) center. A nondeterministic acceptor can decide that it is at the center, enter state S_3, and then begin checking the (supposed) second half of the string. If it chooses the center properly, the remainder of the input will match the pushdown tape and the string will be accepted. The machine is described by the following quintuples:

$$
\begin{array}{lll}
\text{\cent} \# S_1 N S_2 & 1 P_2 S_2 P_1 S_2 & 2 P_1 S_2 P_2 S_3 \\
1 \# S_2 P_1 S_2 & 1 P_2 S_2 P_1 S_3 & 2 P_2 S_2 P_2 S_2 \\
1 \# S_2 P_1 S_3 & 2 \# S_2 P_2 S_2 & 2 P_2 S_2 P_2 S_3 \\
1 P_1 S_2 P_1 S_2 & 2 \# S_2 P_2 S_3 & 2 P_2 S_3 E S_3 \\
1 P_1 S_2 P_1 S_3 & 2 P_1 S_2 P_2 S_2 & 1 P_1 S_3 E S_3 \\
& & \$ \# S_3 (\text{halt})
\end{array}
$$

In state S_2 the machine copies the input onto the pushdown tape; then it moves to state S_3 and compares the remainder of the input sequence with the sequence on the pushdown tape. If the machine chooses to move to S_3 at exactly the middle of the input sequence, an accepting condition will be reached if and only if the second half of the input sequence is indeed the reflection of the first half of the sequence. If the machine chooses to move to state S_3 at some position which is not the center of the input sequence, the second part of the input sequence will not match the sequence on the pushdown tape, because the two will have different lengths. Thus the input sequence would not be accepted by that choice of moves.

Since the length of the input sequence is arbitrary, a deterministic pushdown machine cannot determine when to start looking for the reflection; it cannot accept the language.

Hence it is plausible that the following theorem is true.

Theorem 1 $1DPDA \subset 1NPDA$.   (The set of languages accepted by deterministic pushdown acceptors is strictly smaller than the set of languages accepted by nondeterministic pushdown acceptors.)

A simple but rigorous proof of this theorem requires some additional concepts which are introduced in Chap. 7; the rigorous proof of the theorem is deferred until Theorem 2 of Sec. 7.6.

PROBLEMS

1. (*a*) Find a context-free grammar to generate the palindrome language without centermarkers which is described in the text:

(i) By examining the forms of the strings contained in the language

(ii) By applying the procedure of Sec. 5.3 to the acceptor described in the text

(*b*) Compare the operation of the acceptor examining the tape ¢12211221$ with the derivations of the string 12211221, using the grammars of part *a*.

2. Show that there exists a context-free grammar which describes the language accepted by any given nondeterministic pushdown acceptor.

3. The machine described in this section accepts strings which are palindromes of even length over the alphabet $A = \{1,2\}$.

(*a*) Describe the language L containing palindromes of odd length, but without centermarker, over A.

(*b*) Find a nondeterministic pushdown acceptor for L.

5.5 NONDETERMINISTIC PUSHDOWN ACCEPTORS FOR CONTEXT-FREE LANGUAGES

Now we prove that the set of context-free languages is the same as the set of languages accepted by nondeterministic pushdown acceptors ($INPDA = $ *type 2*). Recall the procedure used in Sec. 5.3 to construct a context-free grammar to describe the language accepted by a given pushdown acceptor. That procedure can be used on nondeterministic machines as well as deterministic machines. In Prob. 4 of Sec. 5.3 the equivalence between pushdown acceptors and replacing pushdown acceptors was proved. This result also applies to nondeterministic pushdown acceptors (Prob. 4). In this section we complete the cycle of relationships by showing that there exists a nondeterministic replacing pushdown acceptor which accepts any given context-free language.

The nondeterministic acceptor will test a string by attempting to find a way it could be derived using the grammatical description of the language. The algorithm is depicted in flow-chart form in Fig. 5.5.1.

First the machine writes the sentence symbol on the pushdown tape and moves the input head off the endmarker. Then it attempts to derive the input string using the pushdown tape for temporary storage. As terminal symbols are derived, they are checked against the input sequence. Thus, whenever the top symbol on the pushdown tape corresponds to a terminal symbol, it is compared with the input symbol; if they correspond to each other, the symbol on the pushdown tape is erased and the input head is advanced. If they do not correspond, the process terminates and the string

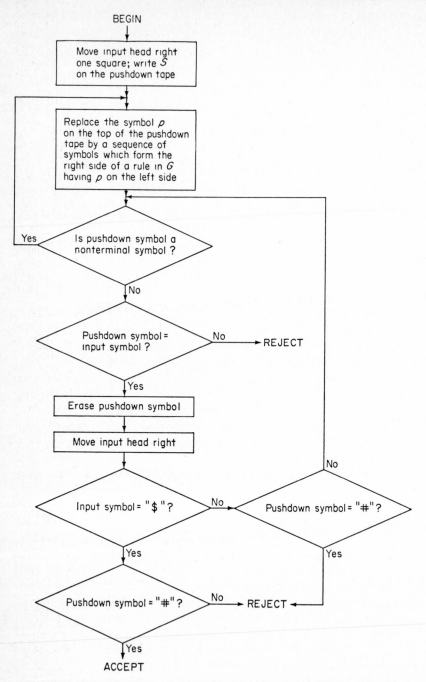

Fig. 5.5.1 Flow chart describing a nondeterministic acceptor for a context-free language L with grammar G.

is rejected. Whenever the top symbol on the pushdown tape corresponds to a nonterminal symbol in the grammar, it is nondeterministically *replaced* by the sequence on the right-hand side of one of the productions of which it was the left-hand side. The replacement is made so that the leftmost symbol (of the sequence on the right side of the production) is on the top of the pushdown list after the replacement.

The machine will halt with the pushdown tape empty and with the input reading head on the right-hand endmarker only if (1) the input string was in the language defined by the grammar and (2) the acceptor made a sequence of choices paralleling a sequence of choices which could be used to derive that string in that grammar. Therefore the machine indeed accepts the given language.

Since pushdown machines in which sequences may replace single symbols on the pushdown tape in one step are equivalent to those in which only a single symbol can be written or erased in one step (Prob. 4), the argument shows that, for every context-free language, there exists a nondeterministic pushdown acceptor which accepts the language.

Detailed quintuples A quintuple description of a nondeterministic pushdown machine M which accepts the language defined by a given context-free grammar can be obtained by the following procedure:

Let G be a context-free grammar generating a language L_G. Let $T = \{T_1, T_2, \ldots, T_n\}$ be the set of terminal symbols of G. Let $N = \{N_1, N_2, \ldots, N_m\}$ be the set of nonterminal symbols of G, and let $S \in N$ be the sentence symbol. The machine will have an input tape alphabet $T \cup \{\mathcal{c},\$\}$ and a pushdown symbol alphabet $\{P_{T_1}, P_{T_2}, \ldots, P_{T_n}, P_{N_1}, \ldots, P_{N_m}\}$. We associate P_{T_i} with T_i, and P_{N_j} with N_j. The quintuples are constructed as follows:

1. The states of the acceptor are S_1 and S_2, with S_1 the initial state and S_2 the accepting state.
2. The machine includes the replacing quintuples

   $\mathcal{c}\#S_1(\#P_S)S_2$ (write the sentence symbol on the pushdown tape)
   $\$\#S_2$(halt)   (the final step in an accepting sequence)

3. If G contains the production $N_i \to A_1 A_2 \cdots A_n$, where the A_i are from either N or T, the machine must have the replacing quintuple

   $\lambda P_{N_i} S_2 (P_{A_n} \cdots P_{A_2} P_{A_1}) S_2$

   (See Prob. 4 of Sec. 5.3 for an explanation of the notation.)
4. For each $T_i \in T$, the machine must have the quintuple

   $T_i P_{T_i} S_2 E S_2$ (match and erase terminal symbols)

5. There are no quintuples not arising from rules 2, 3, and 4.

Example 1   Given the context-free grammar with the following rewriting rules:

$$S \to 1S1$$
$$S \to SA$$
$$S \to 4$$
$$A \to 1A2$$
$$A \to 3$$

Find a nondeterministic pushdown acceptor for the language.   The quintuples are listed below.   The rule numbers indicate how each quintuple was generated.

Rule	Production	Quintuple
2	—	$\text{¢}\#S_1(\#P_S)S_2$
	—	$\$\#S_2(\text{halt})$
3	$S \to 1S1$	$\lambda P_S S_2 (P_1 P_S P_1) S_2$
	$S \to SA$	$\lambda P_S S_2 (P_A P_S) S_2$
	$S \to 4$	$\lambda P_S S_2 P_4 S_2$
	$A \to 1A2$	$\lambda P_A S_2 (P_2 P_A P_1) S_2$
	$A \to 3$	$\lambda P_A S_2 P_3 S_2$
4	—	$1 P_1 S_2 E S_2$
	—	$2 P_2 S_2 E S_2$
	—	$3 P_3 S_2 E S_2$
	—	$4 P_4 S_2 E S_2$

The sequence of instantaneous descriptions as this machine recognizes the sequence 141321 is

$S_1 \text{¢} 141321 \$ \#$
$\text{¢} S_2 141321 \$ \# P_S$
$\text{¢} S_2 141321 \$ \# P_1 P_S P_1$
$\text{¢} 1 S_2 41321 \$ \# P_1 P_S$
$\text{¢} 1 S_2 41321 \$ \# P_1 P_A P_S$
$\text{¢} 1 S_2 41321 \$ \# P_1 P_A P_4$
$\text{¢} 14 S_2 1321 \$ \# P_1 P_A$
$\text{¢} 14 S_2 1321 \$ \# P_1 P_2 P_A P_1$
$\text{¢} 141 S_2 321 \$ \# P_1 P_2 P_A$
$\text{¢} 141 S_2 321 \$ \# P_1 P_2 P_3$
$\text{¢} 1413 S_2 21 \$ \# P_1 P_2$
$\text{¢} 14132 S_2 1 \$ \# P_1$
$\text{¢} 141321 S_2 \$ \#$
(accept)

The reader will probably have suspected that the steps in which the machine does not use up an input symbol could be avoided by a sufficient amount of looking ahead.   In Sec. 5.8 we will show a related result in the grammatical framework; that result can be used to find a machine which uses up an input symbol in every move (Prob. 3 of Sec. 5.8).

In this section we have shown

Theorem 1 $1NPDA = type\ 2$.   (The set of context-free languages is equivalent to the set of languages accepted by nondeterministic pushdown acceptors.)

This result does not locate deterministic pushdown acceptors in the hierarchy; the results of Prob. 1 of Sec. 5.2, with Theorem 1, place the set of deterministic pushdown-acceptor languages between the sets of context-free and regular languages, but not equivalent to either set.

PROBLEMS

1.   Even though we are not prepared to prove that a pushdown acceptor for a context-free language can be constructed so that it reads an input symbol in every move, we can eliminate some of the waste moves of the construction given in this section.   Specify a procedure to find a nondeterministic replacing pushdown acceptor for a context-free language which reads an input symbol during every move in which it uses a rewriting rule whose right-hand side begins with a terminal symbol.   Use your procedure on the grammar of Example 1.

2.   Consider a context-free grammar G and the nondeterministic pushdown acceptor generated from G by the procedure described in this section.   Describe precisely the relationships between the instantaneous descriptions of the acceptor and the strings in the derivations of G.   [*Hint:* Consider the string obtained from the instantaneous description by (*a*) deleting the sequence of symbols beginning with S_2 and ending with $\#$ and (*b*) reversing the order of the symbols beyond $\#$.]

3.   A set-replacing pushdown acceptor is a pushdown acceptor in which each move is described by a quintuple of the form $\langle T_i R_j S_k R_l S_m \rangle$, where R_j and R_l are specified regular sets.   In one move the machine nondeterministically deletes some string in R_j from the top of the stack and replaces it by some string in R_l.   This move can be made only if the input symbol is T_i, the present state is S_k, and the sequence beginning at the top of the stack is a string in R_j.   The next state will be S_m.

The machine accepts string σ if the machine, when started in the initial configuration $S_1 \not\!c \sigma \$ \#$, has a sequence of moves taking it to a final configuration $\not\!c \sigma S_n \$ \#$, where S_n is an accepting state.

Find an algorithm which can be used to prove that the set of context-free languages is equivalent to the set of languages accepted by set-replacing pushdown acceptors.

4.   Find an algorithm which can be used to prove that nondeterministic replacing pushdown acceptors are equivalent to nondeterministic pushdown acceptors (Prob. 4 of Sec. 5.3).

5.   Show: $\{x2y \,|\, x,y \in \{0,1\}^*,\ x \neq y\} \in 1NPDA$.

5.6   CLOSURE PROBLEMS IN SETS OF LANGUAGES ACCEPTED BY PUSHDOWN ACCEPTORS

In this section we discuss questions regarding the closure of the sets of languages accepted by deterministic and nondeterministic pushdown acceptors under Boolean operations.   First we show the trivial result that the union of two type i languages is a type i language for $0 \leq i \leq 2$. Then we demonstrate a language which is not context-free. Finally we prove that the set $INPDA$ is not closed under either complementation or intersection.

Union   It is easy to show that $L_1 \cup L_2$ is a type i language if L_1 and L_2 are type i languages, for $0 \leq i \leq 2$. Suppose that G_1 and G_2 are type i grammars, that G_1 defines L_1 and G_2 defines L_2, and that S is the sentence symbol in each grammar. Create a new grammar G_1' by replacing S by S_1 (a new nonterminal symbol) everywhere in G_1. Similarly, create G_2' from G_2, with S_2 replacing S and with nonterminal symbols renamed such that $N_1' \cap N_2' = \varphi$, where N_1' and N_2' are the sets of nonterminal symbols used in G_1' and G_2'. Now construct a grammar G with sentence symbol S as follows:

1. Include all productions from G_1' and G_2'.
2. Include $S \rightarrow S_1$ and $S \rightarrow S_2$.
3. Include no productions not arising from steps 1 and 2.

The first step of a derivation in G must use one of the rules in step 2; this choice determines from which language the string will be derived. In succeeding steps we use productions from the chosen grammar to derive the string. The sets of nonterminal symbols must be mutually exclusive to make this work properly, for otherwise a production from G_1' might be used after choosing to derive a sentence from L_2. This could result in the derivation of a string which is in neither L_1 nor L_2.

Note that when one is constructing the union of two regular grammars, he cannot use the above procedure, because the productions $S \rightarrow S_1$ and $S \rightarrow S_2$ are not legal in regular grammars. In Chap. 2 another method was used to construct a finite-state recognizer for the union of two regular languages, proving that the class of regular languages is also closed under union. Thus we have

Theorem 1   The union of two type i languages is also a type i language, for $0 \leq i \leq 3$.

A characterization of context-free languages   To discuss the other closure problems, we will need an important lemma characterizing context-free languages. A similar result for regular languages is that there exists an integer n such that any string u of length greater than n which is in the language can be decomposed $u = wxy$, such that $x \neq \lambda$ and every string of the form $wx^p y$ ($p \geq 1$) is also in the language (Prob. 5 of Sec. 2.5). We will use the lemma for context-free languages to show that $\{1^n 2^n 3^n | n \geq 1\}$ is not a context-free language. The latter result can be used to prove that the set of context-free languages is not closed under intersection or complementation.

In the remainder of this section we will use the lowercase letters $(s, t, \ldots, z)$ to represent strings of terminal symbols and $u', v', \ldots, z'$ to represent strings of terminal and/or nonterminal symbols.

Lemma 1   For every context-free language L there exist integers m and n such that every string $s \in L$ with length$(s) > n$ can be decomposed in the form

$$s = uvwxy$$

where $vx \neq \lambda$ and length $(vwx) \leq m$ and such that all strings of the form

$$uv^kwx^ky \qquad k \geq 1$$

are in the language.

In other words, for every string in the language longer than a certain minimum length (n), there is an infinite set of other strings which also must be in the language (since it cannot be the case that both v and x are null). This result can be used to prove that certain languages are not context-free because it imposes a structure on the set of strings if that set is to be a context-free language.   Whenever we can show that a language does not have this structure, we know that it is not a context-free language.

The notion of a simplified grammar for a context-free language is convenient for the proof.   A grammar is simplified if it does not contain any production of the forms $N_i \to N_j$ or $N_i \to \lambda$.   For every context-free grammar G there exists a simplified context-free grammar G' describing the same language.   To construct G', first use the procedure for removing erasing productions (Sec. 5.3) to remove the erasing productions.   In addition, we must eliminate productions of the form $N_i \to N_j$.   Suppose that the production $N_i \to N_j$ is included in grammar G.   Then, for any production in G which has N_i on the right side, add productions to G' in which the N_i's in the original production are changed to N_j's in all possible ways.   When this procedure has been used on all productions with N_i on the right side, the $N_i \to N_j$ production can be removed.   When all such productions are removed, a simplified grammar which describes the same language is obtained. Now we proceed with the proof of the lemma, assuming that the language has a simplified grammar.

Proof   The proof of the lemma is based on counting the number of levels in the derivation tree for s, the string in the statement of the lemma. Let p be the number of nonterminal symbols in the simplified grammar of L.   If there are more than $p + 1$ levels in the derivation tree for s, then there must be a path in the tree from the sentence symbol to a terminal symbol which contains more than p nonterminal symbols. Since there are only p different nonterminal symbols, that path must contain at least two occurrences of at least one nonterminal symbol.

Now let A be a nonterminal symbol which occurs at least twice in some path down the tree. Thus, for some z' containing A, $A \Rightarrow^* z'$ is a derivation in the grammar. Because the grammar is simplified, z' must contain more than one symbol. Therefore let $z' = v'Ax'$; we know that $v'x' \neq \lambda$. Also, $v'x'$ may contain nonterminal symbols. The nonterminal symbols in v' and x' can be replaced by sequences of terminal symbols (which are subsequences of s) such that the sequence v' becomes v, and x' becomes x, where v and x contain only terminal symbols. There also exists a derivation $A \Rightarrow^* w$, where w is a string of terminal symbols (Fig. 5.6.1).

We know that $s = uvwxy$ is in the language L, because this string is produced by the original derivation tree. Since $A \Rightarrow^* v'Ax' \Rightarrow^* vAx$, we must have $A \Rightarrow^* v^kAx^k$, for all $k \geq 1$. Because the original string was derived by $S \Rightarrow^* uAy \Rightarrow^* uvAxy \Rightarrow^* uvwxy$, there must also exist derivations of the form $S \Rightarrow^* uAy \Rightarrow^* uv^kAx^ky \Rightarrow^* uv^kwx^ky$, for all $k \geq 1$. Therefore all strings of the form uv^kwx^ky ($k \geq 1$) must be in L.

Q.E.D.

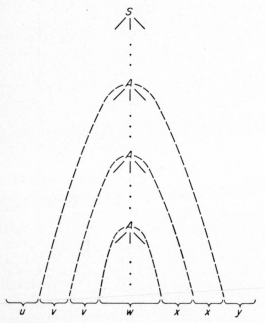

Fig. 5.6.1 The derivation for a string in a context-free language.

In the proof we did not compute bounds on m and n, but we only need to know that both are finite for the proof to work (Prob. 2).

A language which is not context-free Next we demonstrate a language which is not context-free.

Lemma 2 The language $L_1 = \{1^n 2^n 3^n | n \geq 1\}$ is not a context-free language.

Proof Assume that L_1 is context-free. We will use Lemma 1 to arrive at a contradiction. By Lemma 1 there exists some integer m such that every sentence s which is longer than m can be divided into five strings u, v, w, x, and y, with $w \neq \lambda$ and $vx \neq \lambda$, such that, for all k, $uv^k wx^k y$ is in the language. Let $M = [m/3] + 1$, where $[x]$ denotes the least integer greater than x. Then $1^M 2^M 3^M$ is longer than m characters and must be decomposable, as above. Now we show that w cannot contain any 1's, 2's, or 3's. We consider each case separately.

1. Assume w contains a 1. Either (*a*) v is null or (*b*) v contains at least one 1.
   a. v is null. Then x is nonnull and must contain either 1's or 2's or both 1's and 2's. The language must contain the string $z = uv^2 wx^2 y$. If $x = 1^p 2^q$, $p > 1$, $q > 1$, then in z there exists a 1 which follows a 2; this cannot occur in any string in L_1. If x contains only 1's, then $1^p 2^M 3^M$ must be in the language for some $p > M$; but this cannot occur in any string in L_1. Similarly, if x contains only 2's, then $1^M 2^p 3^M$ must be in the language for some $p > M$. But there are no strings of this form in L_1. Hence, if w contains a 1, v cannot be null.
   b. v is nonnull. Then v must contain at least one 1, and $z = 1^p 2^M 3^M$ would be in L_1, for some $p > M$. Contradiction. Thus case 1 cannot occur.
2. Assume w contains a 2. This case is similar to case 1, though there are a few more subcases which have to be considered.
3. Assume w contains a 3. This case is symmetric to case 1. Therefore it cannot occur.

Since w cannot contain any of the terminal symbols, it must be null. But Lemma 1 states that w cannot be null if L_1 is a context-free language. Therefore L_1 cannot be a context-free language. Q.E.D.

Other closure results Now we can use Lemma 1 to prove the next closure result concerning context-free languages:

Theorem 2   The set of context-free languages is not closed under intersection.

Proof   Consider the languages $L_2 = \{1^n2^n3^m|n \geq 1, m \geq 1\}$ and $L_3 = \{1^m2^n3^n|n \geq 1, m \geq 1\}$.   Both L_2 and L_3 are context-free (Prob. 3). However,

$$L_4 = L_2 \cap L_3 = \{1^n2^n3^n|n \geq 1\}$$

is not context-free, by Lemma 2.   Q.E.D.

An immediate consequence of this theorem is

Theorem 3   The set of context-free languages is not closed under complementation.

Proof   If a set were closed under both union and complementation, then by De Morgan's law it must be closed under intersection.   Since the set of context-free languages is closed under union, but not under intersection, it cannot be closed under complementation.   Q.E.D.

Note that the complement of a context-free language and the intersection of two context-free languages are both context-sensitive, because every context-free language is in the set $DLBA$.   We prove this fact in the next section.

PROBLEMS

1.   Prove that w in the proof of Lemma 2 cannot contain a 2.

2.   Find an upper bound to the length n in Lemma 1, given that there are p nonterminal symbols in the simplified grammar and that no production has more than r symbols on its right side.

3.   Show that the language $\{1^n2^n3^m|n \geq 1, m \geq 1\}$ is context-free.

4.   (P) (*a*) Prove that $1DPDA$ is closed under the operation of complementation. (*Hint:* Construct an acceptor which duplicates the accepting algorithm and then gives the opposite answer.)

(*b*) Prove that $1DPDA$ is not closed under union.

5.   Prove that the language $\{w2w^R2w|w \in \{0,1\}^*\}$ is not context-free.

6.   Let a simplified context-sensitive grammar be a grammar in which, at every step of the derivation, either the length of the working string or the number of terminal symbols in the working string increases.   Show that there exists a simplified context-sensitive grammar which is equivalent to any given context-sensitive grammar.

5.7 DETERMINISTIC LINEAR-BOUNDED ACCEPTORS FOR CONTEXT-FREE LANGUAGES

Now we show how to construct a deterministic linear-bounded acceptor for any given context-free language. Since $DLBA$ is closed under complementation and intersection (Sec. 4.2) while the set of context-free languages is not, there must be at least one language in $DLBA$ which is not context-free ($\{1^n2^n3^n|n \geq 1\}$). Therefore the hierarchy is

$$1DPDA \subset 1NPDA = type\ 2 \subset DLBA \subseteq NLBA = type\ 1$$

with a question on the equality $DLBA = NLBA$.

General comments The deterministic linear-bounded acceptor must accept strings without making any choices. One way to show that a nondeterministic job (the job of the nondeterministic pushdown machine) can be done deterministically is to show that a deterministic machine can simulate the behavior of the nondeterministic machine on a step-by-step basis, keeping track of the choices. This approach is difficult because the deterministic machine must operate within a very limited space on its tape (Prob. 4). A deterministic linear-bounded machine can be constructed to perform an "analysis by synthesis" of a given context-free language L. It will try to derive the given string using the rewriting rules of the grammar for L. The machine will keep track of the choices it makes during the derivation. If a sequence of choices does not lead to the desired string, the machine will try a different sequence of choices. All possible sequences of choices will be systematically tried. The information required to perform this algorithm can be stored within the linear-bounded amount of space available on the tape.

We discuss three details before moving on to the proof. First, we will assume that the context-free language is specified by a simplified grammar. We have already shown (in Sec. 5.6) that, for every nonsimplified context-free grammar, there exists a simplified context-free grammar describing the same language, with the possible exception of the null string. Therefore there is no loss in generality in using a simplified grammar. In the simplified grammar each production either increases the length of the string or changes a nonterminal symbol to a terminal symbol. Therefore, if a string is of length n, not more than $2n$ steps could have been used in its derivation.

Second, since the grammar is context-free, the final result of the derivation does not depend upon the particular sequence in which the nonterminal symbols are replaced when a point in a derivation is reached where there are several nonterminal symbols in the working string. In particular, any string which can be derived following the rules of the grammar can be derived by a procedure in which at any step in the derivation the leftmost nonterminal symbol in the working string is the one to be replaced. Since the derivation tree is generated from left to right, these derivations are known as *left-to-right derivations*.

Finally, we associate numbers with the productions of the grammar, using the integers from 0 to $p - 1$. Any left-to-right derivation can be described by a sequence of numbers in which the ith number is the number of the rule used in the ith step of the derivation. Since each step of the derivation is a replacement of the leftmost nonterminal symbol in the working string, there is no ambiguity about where the production is applied. If n is the number of symbols in the string, there cannot be more than $2n$ numbers in the sequence describing the derivation. Therefore a $2n$-position base-p number represents the derivation, with the ith-digit position from the left containing the number of the production used in the ith step of the derivation. Every legal derivation is represented by such an integer, but not all integers will represent a legal derivation.

Example 1   Consider the context-free grammar with the following rewriting rules:

$$S \rightarrow 1S1 \tag{0}$$
$$S \rightarrow SA \tag{1}$$
$$S \rightarrow 4 \tag{2}$$
$$A \rightarrow 1A2 \tag{3}$$
$$A \rightarrow 3 \tag{4}$$

(This grammar appeared in Example 1 of Sec. 5.5.) The left-to-right derivation of the string 141321 is

S	
$1S1$	(0)
$1SA1$	(1)
$14A1$	(2)
$141A21$	(3)
141321	(4)

The numbers to the right identify the rewriting rule used to produce the corresponding string. This derivation is described by the number 01234.

The number 013 cannot describe a legal derivation. The first two steps are

S	
$1S1$	(0)
$1SA1$	(1)

Rule 3 cannot be applied to the leftmost nonterminal symbol in this string.   ▪

Details   There will be five tracks on the tape of the deterministic linear-bounded machine. The first track will hold the string being tested. The second track will hold the working string for the derivation. The third and fourth tracks will hold the base-p number which represents the choices of productions to be used in the derivation. The fifth track will contain a marker indicating which element of tracks 3 and 4 is being used in the next step of the derivation (in other words, which step of the derivation is being simulated).

	*	0	0	0	0	0	0		marker
	0	0	0	0	0	0	0		counter
¢	0	0	0	0	0	0	0	$	
	S	0	0	0	0	0	0		attempt at derivation
	1	2	1	2	3	1	1		input sequence

Fig. 5.7.1 An initialized tape.

To start a test, the machine writes the sentence symbol in track 2, clears tracks 3 and 4, and places the marker in track 5 over the first position of the number in tracks 3 and 4. A typical configuration after this initialization process is shown in Fig. 5.7.1.

To simulate a single step of the derivation, the machine examines the symbol under the marker to determine which production should be used in the next step of the derivation (Fig. 5.7.2). Then it examines the string on track 2 to see whether the indicated production can be applied to the leftmost nonterminal symbol in the string. If the production can be applied, the transformation is made. If the string on track 2 does not contain any nonterminal symbols, it is compared with the input string on track 1. If the two strings match, the string is accepted. If the working string still contains nonterminal symbols, the marker is moved to the next position of the counter, and another step in the derivation is simulated.

The machine must try to find a different way to derive the given string if track 2 contains a string of terminal symbols which does not match the input sequence, or if the indicated production cannot be applied. The value of the count defines the derivation. A new derivation is described by the next higher count. Thus the machine should increment the counter. If the counter does not overflow, the new count is a code for another way that the string could be derived. The machine writes the sentence symbol on track 2 and then moves the marker on track 5 to the first position to start a new derivation. The machine then attempts another replacement step. On the other hand, if the counter overflows, all derivations which might lead to an input sequence of length n have been tried, and since none were successful in deriving the input sequence, the input string must be rejected.

The machine described in Fig. 5.7.2 accepts strings in the given language; so we have constructed a deterministic linear-bounded acceptor for a given context-free language. Hence we have

Theorem 1 *Type 2 $\subset$ DLBA $\subseteq$ NLBA = type 1*

As we have noted in Sec. 4.5, the question of the equality of the sets *DLBA* and *NLBA* is unresolved.

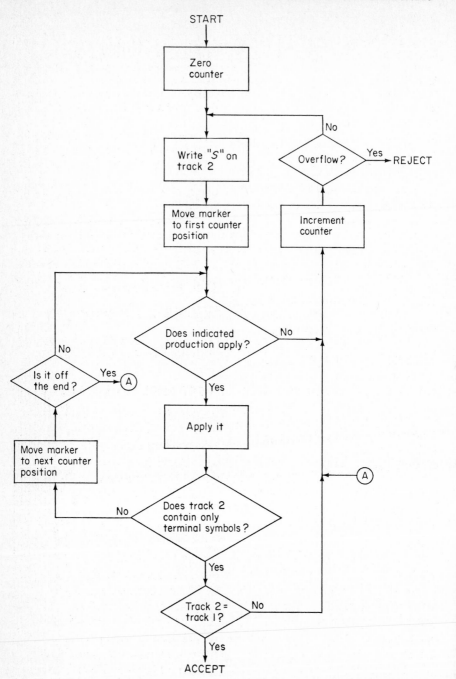

Fig. 5.7.2 Flow chart for the algorithm followed by a linear-bounded machine recognizing a context-free language.

PROBLEMS

1. Use the integers assigned to the rewriting rules of the grammar G in Example 1 and find the integers which describe the derivations of the strings 411322 and 11413113211322. Consider the deterministic linear-bounded acceptor M constructed to recognize L_G by following the algorithm described in this section. Assume that the machine does not erase any square on the tape between the time the generation is completed and the time the machine halts. Find the final contents of the tape of M after it accepts each of these strings.

2. Find an algorithm which can be used to show that a deterministic Turing machine can accept a context-sensitive language without using more than n^2 tape squares, where n is the length of the input string. (*Hint:* Consider an analysis by synthesis, and use the result of Prob. 6 of Sec. 5.6.)

3. Repeat Prob. 2, with a space bound of $kn[\log_r n] + n$, where r is a fixed integer. (*Hint:* A count can be encoded into a base-r integer.)

4. In this problem we explore the possibility of constructing a deterministic linear-bounded acceptor D for a context-free language L by working from the description of a nondeterministic pushdown acceptor N for L without constructing a grammar for L.

(*a*) Describe how to encode a sequence of moves of N as a sequence of integers.

(*b*) If string $\sigma \in L$ has length n, what is the maximum number of moves which N will make while accepting σ? (Other parameters required in the answer should be determined by the reader.)

(*c*) How many tracks on D's tape would be required to store the encoded move sequence?

(*d*) Find a tape format for D which stores (i) the instantaneous description of N, (ii) the move sequence of N, and (iii) the count of the number of attempts at recognition.

5.8 NORMAL FORMS FOR CONTEXT-FREE GRAMMARS

We now show that, for every nonerasing context-free grammar G, there exists another context-free grammar G' which generates the same language, where in G' the leftmost symbol on the right side of each production is a terminal symbol. Such grammars are known as *normal-form grammars*, or *normal grammars*. Grammars not in this form are called *nonnormal grammars*. The process of removing nonterminal symbols from the first position on the right side of the productions is similar to the process of modifying a pushdown acceptor to read an input symbol during every move. Such a machine must anticipate (nondeterministically, perhaps) a sequence of moves not using input symbols and skip over those moves. It may have to write a sequence of symbols on the pushdown list in one move to be able to store necessary information on the pushdown tape. Just as the modified machine may require many more states to perform the necessary anticipation, the normal-form grammar may require many more nonterminal symbols than were used in the original grammar. In this section we will discuss a computational procedure to transform a nonnormal context-free grammar into a normal one.

Normal context-free grammars are important because they describe the process of "real-time" checking of the syntax of strings in a context-free language. Many of the syntactic features of high-level programming languages can be described by context-free languages. The existence of a normal context-free grammar to describe the language implies that a real-time check of the syntax of a program written in a context-free language is possible.

First we should define our terms:

A *normal production* is one in which the replacement string begins with a terminal symbol. Any production which is not normal is nonnormal. A *normal grammar* is one in which every production is normal.

To perform the transformation from an arbitrary context-free grammar G to an equivalent normal grammar G', proceed as follows:

1. Separate the productions of G into a normal set and a nonnormal set.
2. Write the productions of G in matrix-equation form

$$x^T = x^T A + f^T \tag{1}$$

where x is a column vector whose components are the nonterminal symbols of G, f contains the right sides from the normal productions, and A contains the right sides from the nonnormal productions, with the initial nonterminal symbols deleted (they are obtained from x in the matrix multiplication).

3. The solution of Eq. (1) is

$$x^T = f^T A^* \tag{2}$$

Interpreting this equation as a set of productions, we see that the right-hand side of every production begins with some set from f^T, each component of which begins with a terminal symbol. Thus we have expressed each of the original nonterminal symbols in terms of normal productions. But the transformation is not complete, because we do not know how to express the sets denoted by A^*.

4. There are two ways to express A^* in the grammar:
   (*a*) Evaluate A^* to obtain regular expressions involving nonterminal symbols on the right-hand sides of the productions. The results of this evaluation may have complex structures. Furthermore, when one tries to write simpler productions not having the * operator on the right side, many manipulations may be required. Thus we avoid this approach and discuss an algebraic algorithm to find a set of rewriting rules which describe the components of A^*.
   (*b*) Use the result $A^* = \lambda + AA^*$ to obtain

$$x^T = f^T + f^T AA^* \tag{3}$$

which is equivalent to Eq. (2). Let $B = AA^*$. Then

$$x^T = f^T + f^T B \tag{4}$$

The components of B will become new nonterminal symbols in the grammar. We need normal productions to define the B's. We have

$$B = AA^* = A + AAA^* = A + AB \tag{5}$$

This defines the B's in terms of the A's and the B's. But some of these productions may not be in normal form. Therefore we may have to replace initial nonterminal symbols in the elements of A by expressions which begin with terminal symbols. The elements of A can contain nonterminal symbols from the set x only. Therefore we can replace each one by an equivalent normal expression from Eq. (3). After these substitutions are made, Eq. (5) will have been converted to normal form.

Example 1   Given the grammar G with rewriting rules

$S \rightarrow aSb$
$S \rightarrow XY$
$X \rightarrow YXc$
$X \rightarrow b$
$Y \rightarrow XS$
$S \rightarrow c$

Find a normal grammar G' equivalent to G.

First write the productions as equations:

$$x^T = [S \quad X \quad Y] = [S \quad X \quad Y] \begin{bmatrix} \varphi & \varphi & \varphi \\ Y & \varphi & S \\ \varphi & Xc & \varphi \end{bmatrix} + [aSb + c \quad b \quad \varphi] \tag{6}$$

Thus

$$A = \begin{bmatrix} \varphi & \varphi & \varphi \\ Y & \varphi & S \\ \varphi & Xc & \varphi \end{bmatrix} \tag{7}$$

and the solution to Eq. (6) is

$$x^T = f^T + f^T B \tag{8}$$

where $B = AA^*$. The results for the original nonterminal symbols are

$$[S \quad X \quad Y] = [aSb + c \quad b \quad \varphi] + [aSb + c \quad b \quad \varphi] \begin{bmatrix} B_{11} & B_{12} & B_{13} \\ B_{21} & B_{22} & B_{23} \\ B_{31} & B_{32} & B_{33} \end{bmatrix} \tag{9}$$

Now we need normal productions defining the B_{ij}'s, which come from Eq. (5):

$$\begin{bmatrix} B_{11} & B_{12} & B_{13} \\ B_{21} & B_{22} & B_{23} \\ B_{31} & B_{32} & B_{33} \end{bmatrix} = \begin{bmatrix} \varphi & \varphi & \varphi \\ Y & \varphi & S \\ \varphi & Xc & \varphi \end{bmatrix} + \begin{bmatrix} \varphi & \varphi & \varphi \\ Y & \varphi & S \\ \varphi & Xc & \varphi \end{bmatrix} \begin{bmatrix} B_{11} & B_{12} & B_{13} \\ B_{21} & B_{22} & B_{23} \\ B_{31} & B_{32} & B_{33} \end{bmatrix} \tag{10}$$

But these are still not in normal form. To simplify matters, notice that B_{11}, B_{12}, and B_{13} are null and can be removed. [A more general test can be used to remove all the null B_{ij}'s —see Rosenkrantz (1967)—but we need not be concerned with such refined techniques here.] To get the productions defining the B's into normal form, we substitute the solution for X, Y, and S from Eq. (9) into Eq. (10) to obtain (using $B_{11} = B_{12} = B_{13} = \varphi$)

$$S = aSb + c + bB_{21}$$
$$X = b + bB_{22}$$
$$Y = bB_{23}$$
$$B_{21} = bB_{23} + aSbB_{31} + cB_{31} + bB_{21}B_{31}$$
$$B_{22} = aSbB_{32} + cB_{32} + bB_{21}B_{32}$$
$$B_{23} = aSb + c + bB_{21} + aSbB_{33} + cB_{33} + bB_{21}B_{33}$$
$$B_{31} = bcB_{21} + bB_{22}cB_{21}$$
$$B_{32} = bc + bB_{22}c + bcB_{22} + bB_{22}cB_{22}$$
$$B_{33} = bcB_{23} + bB_{22}cB_{23}$$

These equations define a set of rewriting rules for the normal grammar G'. For example, the last equation represents the two rewriting rules

$$B_{33} \rightarrow bcB_{23}$$
$$B_{33} \rightarrow bB_{22}cB_{23}$$

Note that not only does the number of nonterminal symbols increase substantially but also the number of productions increases even more. ■

This procedure can be modified to work from the right-hand ends of the rules and produce an equivalent grammar in which the right side of each rule both begins and ends with a terminal symbol (Prob. 6).

These grammatical arguments can be translated into the machine domain to show that any context-free language is accepted by a nondeterministic pushdown acceptor which reads an input symbol in every move (Prob. 3). Unfortunately, the same statement cannot be made for languages accepted by deterministic pushdown acceptors; consider the language

$$L = \{a^i b^j c b^j a^i | i,j \geq 1\} \cup \{a^i b^j a^i | i,j \geq 1\}$$

Any deterministic pushdown acceptor for L must place the two counts i and j on the pushdown list. If a c appears after the sequence of b's, then the machine must match the numbers of b's and a's with the counts on the pushdown list. However, if an a occurs following the sequence of b's, the machine must erase the j count from the pushdown tape to uncover the i count, which is then used to check the length of the sequence of a's. This erasing must be performed without reading input symbols.

PROBLEMS

1. Find a normal-form grammar equivalent to the grammar of Example 1 of Sec. 5.5.

2. Show that the language

$$L_3 = \{\alpha\alpha | \alpha \in \{1,2\}^*\}$$

is not context-free. [*Hint:* It may help to show that

$$L'_3 = \{\alpha3\alpha | \alpha \in \{1,2\}^*\} \notin 1DPDA.]$$

3. In Sec. 5.5 we discussed a procedure to construct a nondeterministic pushdown acceptor for a given context-free language. Using the normal-form theorem, show how to construct a nondeterministic pushdown acceptor for a given context-free language which reads one input symbol in each move.

4. Let $L = \{a^i b^i c b^j a^i | i,j \geq 1\} \cup \{a^i b^j a^i | i,j \geq 1\}$.

(*a*) Find a deterministic pushdown acceptor for L.

(*b*) Find a nondeterministic pushdown acceptor for L which reads an input symbol during each move.

5. (P) A counter machine is similar to a pushdown machine except that the pushdown tape is replaced by a single counter which can contain a single arbitrarily large nonnegative integer. In one step the machine can do one of three things:

1. Not change the counter contents
2. Increase the counter contents by 1
3. Decrease the counter contents by 1, unless the contents are zero, in which case nothing is changed

In addition, the action of the machine in a given step can be affected by whether the counter contains a zero or a nonzero value.

(*a*) Give a mechanism for describing a counter machine. Define a condition for acceptance by a counter machine.

(*b*) Construct a counter machine to recognize the language

$$L_2 = \{1^n 2^m 3^n | n \geq 1, m \geq 1\}$$

(*c*) Let $1DC_1$ denote the set of languages accepted by deterministic (one) counter acceptors. Prove

Type 3 $\subset 1DC_1 \subseteq$ *type 2*

(*d*) Show that the set of counter machines is equivalent to the set of pushdown machines which have only one pushdown symbol in addition to the pushdown endmarker.

6. Find the algorithm to produce a grammar equivalent to a given normal grammar such that each production has a terminal symbol at the beginning and end of the right side. [*Hint:* Parallel the preceding development with transposed matrices and use $B = A + AA + ABA$ in place of Eq. (5). Explain why the different version of Eq. (5) is required.]

7. In Prob. 4 of Sec. 5.3 we defined pushdown machines which replaced single pushdown symbols by sequences of pushdown symbols in one move.

(*a*) By encoding sequences of up to m (a fixed, finite integer) pushdown symbols into a single pushdown symbol, argue that an equivalent replacing pushdown machine can be constructed such that it

(i) Writes only a single symbol on the pushdown tape in one move

(ii) Always reads at least p (a fixed, finite integer) input symbols between any two moves which do not read the input tape

(b) Why must p be finite?

(c) Let n be the length of the input sequence. Show that the machine constructed in this problem recognizes the string in $(1 + \epsilon) n$ moves. How is ϵ related to p?

5.9 COMMENTS

The practical uses of the pushdown model were recognized before the study of mathematical linguistics really began to relate linguistic models to machine models [see Newell and Shaw (1957)]. Consequently, a large number of papers and books discuss this model. For example, Ginsburg (1966) contains a detailed treatment of pushdown machines and the associated linguistic problems. Papers which discuss the practical uses of pushdown lists (mainly for compiling) abound in the literature. The Bibliography cites some of these. Floyd (1964b) and Feldman and Gries (1968) survey these applications.

Lemma 1 of Sec. 5.6 is due to Bar-Hillel, Perles, and Shamir (1961); an extension of this lemma to more complex languages appears in Brainerd (1967).

The construction of a deterministic linear-bounded machine to accept a given context-free language (Sec. 5.7) follows Kuroda (1964).

Normal-form theorems were given by Greibach (1965) and generalized by Rosenkrantz (1967), whose approach we have adopted.

6
Other Machine Models

In this chapter we will discuss some models which are constructed by modifying the pushdown machine. Many of these models were originally constructed by casting the structure of a useful computational algorithm into a machine configuration.

Four questions one might ask when studying a new machine model are: (1) What are the properties of the set of languages which are accepted by machines which fit the model? (2) How does the set of languages accepted by these machines compare with the sets of languages accepted by other classes of machines? (3) How does the model relate to the structure of useful algorithms? (4) Is there a grammatical description of the languages accepted by the class of machines? We have already discussed most cases for which an interesting answer to question 4 is known. Grammatical descriptions of some classes of languages not discussed in Chaps. 2 to 5 have been constructed by imposing constraints on the rewriting rules to force the derivations in the grammar to mimic the given acceptor of the language. We will not discuss these grammars in this book.

Some machine models are related to useful algorithms. The model discussed in this chapter that is quite closely related to a useful algorithm is the stack machine, which contains some features required by compiler programs. Except for this case, we will not discuss question 3 in this chapter.

To answer question 2, we must compare two sets of languages which may not be equivalent, so we must exhibit languages which are in one set but not in the other one. It is usually easy to show by construction that a given language is in a given set. The major difficulties in these constructions arise in the management of the infinite storage. Therefore we will concentrate on that aspect of the simulations.

It is more difficult to show that a particular language is not in a given set of languages. Usually, to show that a language is not in a given set, one develops a theorem which states some properties concerning the structure of the languages which are in the set. The important lemma concerning context-free languages (Lemma 1 of Sec. 5.6) is an example of this type of result. It would be very helpful to have such a "characterization theorem" for each new set of languages being considered, so that the relationships between the sets of languages could be formulated as strict inclusions rather than as weak inclusions. Unfortunately, characterization theorems are not known for some of the sets of languages to be discussed in this chapter. To relate these sets to other sets, we will state conjectures, showing the languages which we believe are in one set and not the other. The noninclusion parts of these relationships cannot be proved using only the results presented in this text.

An important relationship between two sets of languages is that of equivalence. An important equivalence is one between a set of languages and the set of recursive languages, because if a model is equivalent to a Turing machine, more complex elaborations of that model need not be considered, since they also will be equivalent to Turing machines. Thus, when we construct a new model, we must be careful to discover whenever the model is actually equivalent to a Turing machine. We will prove that a relatively simple machine with two counters is equivalent to a Turing machine.

New classifications of languages and machines are introduced each year; we describe only some of the simpler ones and some that seem to be most directly related to compilation processes. References to papers describing some other classes of languages are given in the Bibliography.

6.1 TWO-WAY PUSHDOWN AUTOMATA

A two-way pushdown machine has the same structure as a one-way pushdown machine (Fig. 5.1.1), except that in any move the head on the input tape can remain on the same square or can be moved to either adjacent square. A tuple description of these machines is a straightforward modification of the quintuple description of the one-way pushdown machine; the details are left as an exercise for the reader (Prob. 4). To denote the sets of languages accepted by two-way pushdown machines, we use *2DPDA* and *2NPDA* for the deterministic and nondeterministic cases, respectively.

Obviously,

$$2DPDA \supseteq 1DPDA$$
$$2NPDA \supseteq 1NPDA$$

and we already know (Theorem 1 of Sec. 5.4)

$$1NPDA \supset 1DPDA$$

In this section we will complete these relationships by showing that the first two inclusions are strict inclusions and that the sets *1NPDA* and *2DPDA* are not comparable.

The first two results are easy to prove by finding the proper examples. We write the results as a theorem and indicate the examples necessary for the proofs, but we leave the details of a proof to the reader.

Theorem 1   *2DPDA $\supset$ 1DPDA, 2NPDA $\supset$ 1NPDA*

Proof   Consider $\{a^n b^n c^n | n \geq 1\}$.

The third result must be a conjecture because a characterization theorem for the class *2DPDA* is not known.

Conjecture 1   *2DPDA* and *1NPDA* are incomparable.

Basis for conjecture   Consider

$$\{a^n b^n c^n | n \geq 1\} \text{ and } \{x2yx^R z | x, y, z \in \{0,1\}^*\}.$$

PROBLEMS

1. Show: $\{xx^R | x \in \{0,1\}^*\} \in 2DPDA$.
2. Show: $\{a^n b^n c^n | n \geq 1\} \in 2DPDA$.
3. Show: $\{x2yx^R z | x, y, z \in \{0,1\}^*\} \in 1NPDA$.
4. Give an exact definition of a two-way pushdown acceptor.
5. Prove that two-way pushdown machines do not need the option to not move the head on the input tape.
6. (R) State and prove characterization theorems for the classes *2DPDA*, *2NPDA*.
7. (R) Prove Conjecture 1.
8. (R) Is *2DPDA = 2NPDA*?

6.2 PUSHDOWN AUTOMATA WITH MANY PUSHDOWN TAPES

If an extra pushdown tape is added to a pushdown machine, a pushdown machine with two pushdown tapes is obtained. If its moves are not restricted, a one-way pushdown machine with two pushdown tapes is equivalent to a Turing machine:

Theorem 1   If moves which do not read the input tape are allowed, a one-way deterministic pushdown machine with two pushdown tapes is equivalent to a Turing machine.

> *Outline of proof*   Let L and R denote the two pushdown tapes. The two-tape pushdown machine will simulate the operations of T, a deletion-insertion Turing machine (Prob. 14 of Sec. 3.1). Let L' be the contents of T's tape to the left of the read/write head, and R' be the contents of T's tape to the right of the head. Now L' and R' can be stored on the L and R pushdown tapes, with one symbol per square, the symbols in the squares adjacent to the read/write head located at the top of the pushdown tapes (Fig. 6.2.1). The simple operations of the Turing machine correspond to simple operations of the pushdown machine. The general structure of the simulation is:
>
> 1. Copy the input tape onto the L pushdown list. During the remaining steps the machine will not read the input tape.
> 2. Copy the L tape onto the R tape, erasing L.
> 3. Simulate the Turing machine using the pushdown tapes to represent the Turing machine's tape. Moves of the Turing machine are simulated by changing the symbol in the control unit when writing and by reading or writing on pushdown tapes when the Turing machine makes a move.

This simulation would not be possible if the pushdown machine were forced to read an input symbol in every move. However, if the pushdown machine were a two-way machine, it could simulate a Turing machine and still be forced to read a symbol every move, by "rocking" on the input tape rather than remaining motionless. Finally, if the pushdown machine did not have endmarkers on the input tape, it would have to be nondeterministic for this simulation to work; the machine cannot deterministically decide when to begin phase 2 of the simulation process outlined above. If it made the wrong decision, it would move off the input tape, thereby rejecting the input sequence.

These observations limit the ways that the model can be modified to become less capable than a Turing machine. For example, in view of the

first observation, multitape one-way pushdown machines without λ-moves
may not be equivalent to Turing machines.   Machines which are forced to
move the input read head one square to the right every time interval could
accept the input sequence if it were presented as a time sequence of symbols
at an input terminal.   Machines which can operate in this way are known as
real-time machines.   We designate the sets of languages accepted by real-time
machines by writing *RT* in the designation.   The number of pushdown tapes
is written as a subscript.   For example, $DRTPD_n$ denotes the set of languages
accepted by deterministic real-time pushdown acceptors having n pushdown
tapes.

We state an obvious theorem without proof:

Theorem 2 (a) $DRTPD_n \subseteq NRTPD_n$
$\left.\begin{array}{l}(b)\;\; DRTPD_n \subseteq DRTPD_{n+1}\\(c)\;\; NRTPD_n \subseteq NRTPD_{n+1}\end{array}\right\} n \geq 1$

We can conjecture:

Conjecture 1 (a) $NRTPD_n \subset DLBA$
$\left.\begin{array}{l}(b)\;\; DRTPD_n \subset DRTPD_{n+1}\\(c)\;\; NRTPD_n \subset NRTPD_{n+1}\\(d)\;\; DRTPD_n \subset NRTPD_n\end{array}\right\} n \geq 1$

Bases for conjecture   Consider the statements
(a) $\{xx \mid x \in \{0,1\}^*\}$ is not in $NRTPD_n$ for any n.   Also see Prob. 2.

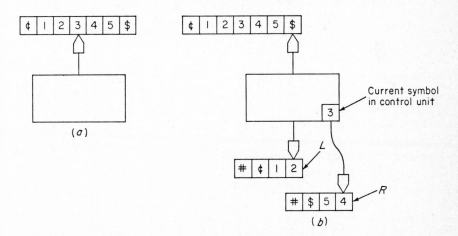

Fig. 6.2.1   The representation of a Turing machine's tape in a two-tape pushdown
machine. (a) Turing machine; (b) pushdown representation.

    (b) $\{x_1 2 x_2 2 x_3 \cdots 2 x_n 2 x_1{}^R 2 x_2{}^R 2 \cdots 2 x_n{}^R | x_i \in \{0,1\}^*, 1 \le i \le n\}$
         is in $DRTPD_n$ but not in $DRTPD_{n-1}$.

    (c) $\{x_1 x_2 x_3 \cdots x_n x_1{}^R x_2{}^R \cdots x_n{}^R | x_i \in \{0,1\}^*, 1 \le i \le n\}$
         is in $NRTPD_n$ but not in $NRTPD_{n-1}$.†

    (d) $\{x_1 x_2 x_3 \cdots x_n x_1{}^R x_2{}^R \cdots x_n{}^R | x_i \in \{0,1\}^*, 1 \le i \le n\}$
         is in $NRTPD_n$ but not in $DRTPD_n$.

Each of these statements might be shown by arguments similar to those used in the discussion of Theorem 1 of Sec. 5.2 and Theorem 1 of Sec. 5.4. However, the necessary characterization theorems are not available. At the end of the next section we will use another device to prove some of these statements. This will prove that there are an infinite number of nonequivalent classes of languages between the context-free and the context-sensitive languages.

PROBLEMS

1. Give a precise definition of an acceptor with n pushdown lists which accepts only if the pushdown lists are empty (except for endmarkers) and the machine is in a final state.

2. Find an algorithm which can be used to show: $NRTPD_n \subseteq DLBA$. (*Hint:* Simulate a given machine in $NRTPD_n$ on a $DLBA$. How long can each pushdown list become?)

3. In the list of bases for Conjecture 1, a number of statements are made. Each statement asserts that a given language is a member of some given set of languages, and that it is not a member of another set of languages. State and prove the membership claims which are made in bases b to d. (There are two of them.)

4. (R) State and prove characterization theorems for the sets $DRTPD_n$.

5. (R) Prove parts a, b, and d of Conjecture 1.

6.3 COUNTER MACHINES

If the pushdown-tape alphabet of a pushdown machine is restricted to the endmarker and one other symbol, each pushdown tape is equivalent to a counter. The count on such a pushdown tape is the number of squares between the endmarker and the read/write head on that tape. Since only the last (unary) digit of the count is examined by the read/write head, the action of the machine may depend upon whether a counter contains zero or not, but it may not depend upon the counter containing any other specific integer.

---

† This example seems quite reasonable. However, Book and Greibach (1970) have used a very complex simulation to show that the set $NRTPD_3$ is equivalent to the set of languages accepted by n-tape real-time nondeterministic Turing machines. Thus $NRTPD_3 = NRTPD_m$ $(m > 3)$. This result should serve as a warning to the reader to be very wary of "reasonable" conjectures.

Let $1DC_n$ ($1NC_n$) denote the sets of languages accepted by (non-) deterministic n-counter machines, and let $DRTC_n$ ($NRTC_n$) denote the sets of languages accepted by the real-time versions of the machines. In Prob. 5 of Sec. 5.8, it was proved that the sets $1DC_1$ and $1NC_1$ lie between the context-free languages and the regular languages. In the preceding section a trivial simulation was used to show that a pushdown machine with two pushdown tapes could simulate a Turing machine. Using a more complex encoding of the Turing machine's tape, a similar result can be obtained for machines with two counters! This section contains a proof of this statement. The complexity of the encoding suggests that we divide the proof into two parts.

First, using a simple encoding, we show that a three-counter machine can simulate a Turing machine ($1DC_3 = DTMA$). Then a further encoding is used to show that any three-counter machine can be simulated on a two-counter machine ($1DC_2 \supseteq 1DC_3$). Thus we have $1DC_2 = DTMA$.

The simulations depend on the ability of the counter machine to make moves without reading input symbols. Since the simulations will not work if this ability is removed, we consider the real-time operation of counter machines at the end of the section.

Three-counter machines   The result of Prob. 13 of Sec. 3.1 is that a Turing machine with two tape symbols is equivalent to a Turing machine with more symbols on the tape. We simplify this discussion without loss of generality by proving that any Turing machine with two tape symbols, denoted 0 and 1, can be simulated by a three-counter machine. We encode the contents of the tape into two binary numbers. The contents of the squares to the left of the read/write head are encoded into

$$L = \sum_{i=0}^{N} l_i 2^i$$

where l_i is the bit in the $(i + 1)$st square to the left of the read/write head. Similarly, encode the information about the contents of the tape to the right of the read/write head in

$$R = \sum_{j=0}^{M} r_j 2^j$$

where r_j is the bit in the $(j + 1)$st square to the right of the read/write head. The contents of the square under the read/write head will be stored in the control unit of the counter machines.

At the end of the simulation of one move of the Turing machine, two of the machine's counters will contain the current values of L and R. The third counter will not contain useful information just after a move has been simulated.   It is required for temporary storage during the move simulation. A finite amount of other information required for the simulation will be stored within the control unit of the counter machine.

The only operations involving the Turing machine's tape (and therefore the counters) are reading, writing, and moving the head along the tape. Reading and writing are trivial because the simulator stores the symbol currently under the head of the Turing machine within its control unit.   The only problem is simulating motion of the read write head.

Consider simulating a move left by one square.   Suppose that C_1 contains L and that C_2 contains R.   After the move left, the new value of L should be one-half of the old value of L.   The symbol under the head after the move is the remainder obtained from the division of L by 2.   We use the third counter to halve the value of L and determine the remainder of the division by 2.   The new value of L will be in C_3, and C_1 will be emptied. After that operation is completed, C_1 and C_2 can be used to manipulate R. The new value of R should be double the old value plus the value of the symbol which was previously under the read/write head.   The doubling operation can be performed using two counters, and the addition is trivial.

A move to the right can be handled in a similar way.

The remaining details of the simulation can be handled within the finite-state control of the counter machine.   We have sketched the simulation which proves

Theorem 1   A three-counter machine in which λ-moves are allowed is equivalent to a Turing machine ($IDC_3 = DTMA$).

Two counters   A further encoding can be used to prove that any deterministic three-counter machine M_3 can be simulated by a deterministic two-counter machine M_2.   As before, the two-counter machine must be able to make moves in which the input reading head is not moved.

Let m, n, and p denote the contents of the three counters of M_3.   Construct a new number q as follows:

$$q = 2^m 3^n 5^p$$

The two counters of M_2 will manipulate this number.   The complex part of the simulation of M_3 is the simulation of the manipulations of the infinite storage.   The three elementary operations for each counter are:

1. Add 1.
2. Test if zero.
3. Subtract 1 if not zero.

We must show that M_2 can perform each of these operations for each of the counters of M_3. Similar algorithms are used to manipulate each of the three counters, so we will discuss only the algorithms to manipulate the first counter, which contains m.

The following three procedures manipulate q to perform each of these three operations on m. Each procedure is written on the assumption that one counter of M_2 contains q and the other counter is empty. At the conclusion of each procedure, one counter is empty and the other contains q, though the new value of q may be in the other counter.

1. To add 1 to m, multiply q by 2.
2. To test if m is 0, divide q by 2, saving the quotient in the other counter. If there is no remainder, m is not 0. After determining the remainder, multiply the quotient by 2 and add back the remainder (so that q is not changed).
3. To subtract 1 from m, divide q by 2 and keep the quotient. If the remainder is not 0, an illegal move is being simulated and M_2 should reject the input string.

Combining Theorem 1 and the above simulation, we have

Theorem 2 A deterministic two-counter machine in which λ-moves are allowed is equivalent to a Turing machine.

Real-time counter languages Theorem 2 forces any study of counter languages to be limited to those counter machines on which the recognition time is bounded by some function of the length of the input tape. Now we discuss some results concerning real-time counter languages. We will show that adding another counter to real-time acceptors will increase the set of languages which the machines can accept and that adding nondeterminism to the machines also increases the set of languages which they accept.

All these results are related to one result concerning the languages:

$$L_1(n,p) = \{0^{m_1}10^{m_2}1 \cdots 10^{m_n}20^{m_1}10^{m_2}10^{m_3}1 \cdots 10^{m_p}10^q|$$
$$n \geq p, q \geq 0, m_i \geq 0, 1 \leq i \leq n\}$$

This one important result is based on the fact that the counter machine must have emptied its counters at the time it accepted the input string.

Consider the states of the counters and the control unit of an r-counter machine recognizing a string $x \in L_1(n,p)$ just after the machine reads the 2 in the input string. Let k be the number of symbols in the input string beyond that 2. If each counter is to be empty before the end of the input, it cannot contain more than k 1's. Therefore the number of possible states of the r

counters is not more than $(k + 1)^r$ (since some counters could be empty), and the number of possible states of the counters and the control unit considered together (total states) must be not more than $s(k + 1)^r = f(k,r)$.

Given that there are k remaining symbols in the input sequence and that they complete the last portion of a string in $L_1(n,p)$, how many ways can this sequence of symbols be constructed? There are (p) 1's and $(k - p)$ 0's in the sequence. The 1's can be inserted between the 0's in arbitrary ways. The number of ways that this insertion can be made is

$$g(k,p) = \frac{k!}{(k - p)!p!} > \frac{(k - p + 1)^p}{p!}$$

Thus there are $g(k,p)$ different ways that the string could end and still be in the language. Each of these endings must be matched by a similar beginning. Therefore the acceptor must be able to remember which of the $g(k,p)$ beginnings actually occurred. Since a different total state is required for each possible beginning segment, it must be true that

$$f(k,r) > g(k,p) \qquad \text{for all } k \tag{1}$$

For small k, statement (1) can be satisfied by adding more states to the control unit. Thus we are concerned only with satisfying statement (1) for large k.

Suppose that the acceptor had $p - 1$ counters. Then statement (1) becomes

$$f(k, p - 1) > g(k,p)$$

or

$$s(k + 1)^{p-1} > \frac{(k - p + 1)^p}{p!}$$

which is equivalent to

$$sp! > (k - p + 1)\left(\frac{k - p + 1}{k + 1}\right)^{p-1}$$

We will show that this inequality cannot be satisfied for arbitrarily large values of k. Thus a real-time recognizer with $p - 1$ counters cannot accept $L_1(n,p)$.

For large k we have

$$(k - p + 1)\left(\frac{k - p + 1}{k + 1}\right)^{p-1} > \tfrac{1}{2}(k - p + 1)$$

and if $k > 2sp! + p$ (a constant), we have

$$\tfrac{1}{2}(k - p + 1) > sp!$$

Therefore

$$(k - p + 1)\left(\frac{k - p + 1}{k + 1}\right)^{p-1} > sp!$$

for large k, and so

$$f(k, p - 1) < g(k,p)$$

for large k, and $L_1(n,p)$ cannot be recognized by a real-time $(p - 1)$-counter machine. But $L(n,p)$ can be recognized by a deterministic p-counter real-time acceptor. We have proved

Theorem 3 $DRTC_p \supset DRTC_{p-1}$
and $NRTC_p \supset NRTC_{p-1}$

To compare $NRTC_p$ with $DRTC_p$ we consider the languages

$$L_2(n,p) = \{0^{m_1}10^{m_2}1 \cdots 10^{m_n}10^q10^{i_1}10^{m_{i_1}}10^{i_2}10^{m_{i_2}}1 \cdots 10^{i_p}10^{m_{i_p}}|$$
$$q \geq 0, n > p, 1 \leq i_j \leq n \text{ for } 1 \leq j \leq p, m_k \geq 0 \text{ for } 1 \leq k \leq n\}$$

and the number of total states which an r-counter real-time machine can reach by the time the $(n + 1)$st 1 has been read. Let k be the number of symbols in this initial segment.

Since each counter is empty at the beginning of the string, the number of total states of the acceptor is limited to $f(k,r) = s(k + 1)^r$.

For each initial segment of the form $0^{m_1}10^{m_2}1 \cdots 10^{m_n}10^q1$, there is a different set of final segments which complete strings in $L_2(n,p)$. There are $g(k,n)$ such initial segments. If the acceptor can distinguish all these, we must have

$$g(k,n) < f(k,r)$$

But we just proved that

$$g(k,n) > f(k, n - 1) \qquad \text{for sufficiently large } k$$

Thus a deterministic real-time acceptor for $L_2(n,p)$ must have at least n counters. However, a nondeterministic acceptor for $L_2(n,p)$ having $p(<n)$ counters can be constructed (it nondeterministically chooses which counts to remember). Therefore we have shown

Theorem 4 $NRTC_n \supset DRTC_n$

Note that $L_2(p,1) \in NRTC_1$ for any p, and that $L_2(p,1) \notin DRTC_{p-1}$. Thus the sets $NRTC_n$ and $DRTC_p$ are incomparable if $n < p$.

PROBLEMS

1. (a) Show that $\{x \mid x = 1^m 0^m 1^m 0^m \cdots 1^m$ with $m \geq 0$ and length $(x) = mp, p \geq 1\}$ is in $DRTC_2$.

(b) Show that $\{0^n 1^m 0^{n+m} \mid m,n > 0\} \in DRTC_1$.

(c) Show that $\{0^n 1^m 0^{n-m} \mid n > m > 0\} \in DRTC_1$.

(d) Show that $\{0^n 1^m 0^{m-n} \mid m > n > 0\} \in DRTC_1$.

(e) Show that $\{0^n 1^m 0^{m \cdot n} \mid m,n \geq 0\} \in DRTC_3$.

(f) Show that $\{0^{n^2} \mid n \geq 0\} \in DRTC_2$.

(g) Prove that the sets $DRTC_n$ and $DRTPD_m$ are incomparable if $n > m$.

2. (a) Show that $\{(0 + 1)^{n_1}(1 + 2)^{n_2} 2 0^{n_1} 1^{n_2} \mid n_1,n_2 \geq 0\} \in NRTC_2$, but not in $DRTC_p$, for any p.

(b) Construct a language based on the language in part a such that it is in $NRTC_n$ and is not in $NRTC_{n-1}$, for any $n > 2$.

3. Show that $\{xx^R \mid x \in \{0,1\}^*\}$ is recognizable by a two-way deterministic one-counter machine.

4. Show that a one-way deterministic one-counter machine can be used to check a mathematical expression to determine whether it has a proper parentheses structure.

5. Consider a finite-state machine which moves on a two-dimensional tape (corresponding to the first quadrant of the plane). The machine can read the symbol in the square it is located in, and can change state and move to one of the eight neighboring squares in one move. It cannot write in any of the squares. All the squares contain 0, except those along the x axis, which contain 1, those along the y axis, which contain 2, and the square at the origin, which contains 3. Let the machine be able to receive an input sequence from some reading head which moves one-way on a one-dimensional tape. Prove that this machine is equivalent to a Turing machine. (*Hint:* Consider the x and y co-ordinates of the machine's location to be two integers.)

6. (a) Show that $NRTC_p$ is closed under the operation of reversal of the strings in the language.

(b) Show that $DRTC_p$ is not closed under reversal. Consider

$$L = \{0^{n_1} 1^{n_2} 0^{n_3} \cdots 1^{n_p} 2(0 + 1)^{n_1}(1 + 2)^{n_2}(0 + 1)^{n_3} \cdots (1 + 2)^{n_p} \mid n_i \geq 0\}$$

7. Pushdown and counter machines can be defined so that acceptance is indicated either by reaching an "accepting state" or by emptying the pushdown list(s) or counter(s).

(a) Give exact definitions of the machines and the accepting conditions for both cases.

Let $T(A)$ denote the set of strings accepted by machine A, when the acceptance is indicated by reaching an accepting state. Similarly, let $N(A)$ denote the set accepted by empty lists or counters. Let $T = \bigcup_A T(A)$, $N = \bigcup_A N(A)$.

(b) Prove that if λ-moves are allowed, $T \subseteq N$.

(c) Prove that if the machines are nondeterministic, $T \subseteq N$. (*Note:* λ-moves may not be allowed.)

(d) Prove that $N \subseteq T$ if the machine has an endmarker at the right end of the input tape.

8. For what class(es) of machines is $T \neq N$? (See Prob. 7 above and Prob. 5 of Sec. 6.1.)

9. Describe an algorithm which can be used by a three-counter simulator of a Turing machine to read the input tape and place the correct initial values in the counters before it simulates the first move of the Turing machine. Must the entire input tape be copied before the move simulation begins? Explain.

10.   (R) State and prove theorems analogous to Lemma 1 of Sec. 5.6 for one-way *n*-counter languages.

11.   (R) Find grammatical descriptions of one-way *n*-counter languages.

6.4   STACK AUTOMATA†

The pushdown machine models some aspects of the compilation process for a context-free programming language.   Most actual compiler languages contain some constraints which cannot be expressed within a context-free grammar.   Therefore most compiler languages are not context-free languages.

In ALGOL, variables are classified as real, integer, Boolean, and so on. The program is divided into blocks.   At the beginning of every block, declarations are made which state the classification of every variable to be used in the block.   The statement

if x **then** $y := z$

is illegal unless the variable x had been declared to be a Boolean variable. This type of constraint cannot be expressed in a context-free language because the number of declarations at the beginning of the block is not limited, and because the declarations and uses of the variables can appear in any order. To check the validity of the statement, an arbitrarily long list of declarations must be searched to discover whether a declaration that x is a Boolean variable appears in the list.   A pushdown machine could not search such a list more than once, because the list would be erased as it was searched.

A compiler program solves this problem by using the pushdown mechanism some of the time.   To handle the exceptional constraints it constructs a "symbol table" in which the declaration information is stored.   When the "if" statement is to be compiled, the symbol table is examined to determine whether x had been declared to be a Boolean variable.

A machine model which includes a pushdown list and some mechanism whereby symbol-table information could be stored and examined would model many aspects of the compilation process for actual computer languages. The stack machine is an attempt to provide this capability.   A stack automaton is a pushdown machine in which the read/write head can leave the top of the stack and examine symbols within the stack.   The machine may move the stack head right until a blank square is reached (the blank symbol b is in the squares that the machine has erased or has not yet written).   When the read/write head is within the stack, it cannot modify the contents of any of the squares.

In one step a stack machine uses the following information:

1. The symbol under the reading head (which is on the input tape)

† This section can be omitted at first reading.

2. The symbol under the read/write head (which is on the stack tape)
3. The internal state of the control unit

to determine:

    a. The direction of motion of the input reading head
    b. The stack action, which is one of the following steps:
        (1) Move the read/write head one square to the left (into the stack) if it is not at the bottom of the stack (i.e., over #).
        (2) Move the read/write head one square to the right, if it is not at the top of the stack (i.e., over *b*).
        (3) If the read/write head is at the top of the stack (i.e., over *b*), move the read/write head one square to the left and erase that square (write a *b* there).
        (4) If the read/write head is at the top of the stack (i.e., over *b*), write a specified sequence of stack symbols at the top of the stack; after writing, the read/write head will be at the new top of the stack.
        (5) Neither move the head nor change the contents of the stack.
    c. The next internal state

Various restrictions on these possible actions may be imposed to create differing models. The machine may allow one-way or two-way motion by the input head. The machine may be deterministic or nondeterministic. Finally, the machine may not be allowed to erase symbols from the stack tape.

Note that the stack machine may move one square on the stack beyond the sequence of squares on which it has written symbols. This capability is needed so that the machine can detect when it has reached the top of the stack without having to keep a special marking symbol at the top. If a marker were required, it would have to be erased as the stack expanded; this requirement would severely limit the capabilities of nonerasing machines.

The instantaneous description of the configuration of a stack machine is similar to the instantaneous description of a pushdown machine, except that the position of the stack head must be indicated. It is constructed as follows:

1. Write down the contents of the input tape, including the endmarkers.
2. Write the state of the finite-state control immediately to the left of the symbol being scanned by the input head of the machine.
3. Write down the contents of the stack to the right of the input tape's contents, placing the top of the stack to the right.
4. Place the mark ↑ to the left of the symbol being scanned by the stack head of the machine.

Example 1   The instantaneous description of the stack machine shown in Fig. 6.4.1 is

$$¢T_1S_1T_2T_3\$\#P_1{\uparrow}P_2P_3$$ ∎

Acceptance conditions for stack automata can be defined in a way similar to the way used for pushdown automata.   Those stack machines which cannot erase symbols from their stacks cannot be required to empty the stack before acceptance.   We can achieve a uniform definition of acceptance by defining it only in terms of the state of the machine when (and if) it halts with the reading head over the right endmarker of the input tape.   We start the acceptor in its initial state S_1 with the input head reading the left endmarker.   If the machine halts in a state from the set F of final states when the input head is over the right endmarker, the input string is accepted.

We will denote the sets of languages accepted by the eight classes of stack machines by sequences of symbols constructed as follows:

1. The first symbol is an integer equal to the number of directions the input head can move.
2. The second symbol is $D(N)$ if the machine is (non-)deterministic.
3. The next two symbols are NE if the machine is not allowed to erase symbols from the stack.   Otherwise there is no symbol for this step.
4. The last two symbols are SA.

For example, $INNESA$ denotes the set of languages accepted by one-way nondeterministic stack automata which cannot erase symbols on their stacks.

In this section we will discuss some results which locate the sets accepted by some two-way stack automata in the hierarchy of languages.   We will not discuss results concerning one-way stack automata because they are difficult to prove and the proofs do not use interesting constructions.   First we will show that two-way deterministic nonerasing stack automata can simulate the behavior of deterministic linear-bounded automata ($2DNESA \supseteq DLBA$). Then we will show that if either nondeterminism or erasing is allowed, nondeterministic linear-bounded machines can be simulated ($2NNESA \supseteq$ type 1,

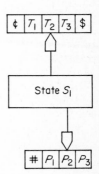

Fig. 6.4.1   A stack machine during a computation.

$2DSA \supseteq type\ 1$).   Finally, a diagonal argument will be used to show that
the set $2DSA$ is strictly larger than the set of context-sensitive languages.

6.4.1 SIMULATION OF LINEAR-BOUNDED AUTOMATA BY STACK AUTOMATA

Two-way stack machines can simulate linear-bounded automata.   The stack
is used to store the sequence of the instantaneous descriptions of the linear-
bounded machine.   Consecutive instantaneous descriptions correspond to
the conditions in the linear-bounded machine before and after a single move
is executed.

On the stack the instantaneous descriptions of the linear-bounded
machine are separated by special marking symbols (Fig. 6.4.2).   A number,
represented in unary notation, is associated with each instantaneous description.   This number will not be used during the simulation of a deterministic
linear-bounded machine, but it will be used for the nondeterministic case,
which is discussed later in this section.   It is convenient to use different
marking symbols for the two ends of the instantaneous descriptions, say ! for
the left end and * for the right end.

First the stack machine must write the proper initial description on the
stack.   Then it can start the simulation.   To simulate one move of the
linear-bounded machine, the simulator must copy the top instantaneous
description, making the changes which simulate the move of the linear-bounded machine.   It must also check each new instantaneous description to
determine whether it represents an accepting condition for the linear-bounded
machine.   The most difficult part of this simulation is the copying process,
so we will devote most of the discussion to this process.

Simulation details   How can the stack machine make a new copy (on the
top of the stack) of the instantaneous description on the top of the stack?
It cannot remember the entire instantaneous description within its control
unit, but it can remember short segments of the description.   We will describe an algorithm in which only one symbol is remembered at any time.
Suppose that i of the l symbols of the instantaneous description have been
copied and that the machine needs to copy the $(i + 1)$st symbol to the top
of the stack.   How can the machine know which of the symbols on the stack
is the $(i + 1)$st symbol of the previous instantaneous description?   When a
Turing machine simulator copies instantaneous descriptions, it marks the
symbols as they are copied; the last unmarked symbol is the first symbol
which has not yet been copied.   The stack machine cannot mark the symbols
which have been copied, because it is not allowed to change them.   It must

! –ID1– * $-n_1-$! –ID2– * $-n_2-$! –ID3– * $-n_3-$! . . .

Fig. 6.4.2 The contents of the stack of a stack machine simulating a linear-bounded
machine.

count squares to determine the position of the symbol to be copied. This count cannot be stored in the finite-state control unit. However, the position of the input head of the stack machine can be used to count the number of symbols which have been copied; then that count can be used to position the stack head within the stack to find the $(i + 1)$st symbol in the previous instantaneous description. A flow-chart description of the algorithm is shown in Fig. 6.4.3. The following example shows the conditions in the simulator as the copying algorithm is executed.

Example 2 A two-way deterministic stack machine is designed to simulate the linear-bounded machine of Example 1 of Sec. 3.2. When this machine is presented with the input sequence 111, the sequence of instantaneous descriptions of the stack machine begins as follows:†

$S_1 ¢111$\$$\uparrow$#
$S_1 ¢111$\$$#\uparrow S_1$
$S_2 ¢111$\$$#S_1 \uparrow$!
$¢S_2 111$\$$#S_1 ! \uparrow ¢$
$¢1 S_2 11$\$$#S_1 ! ¢\uparrow 1$
$¢11 S_2 1$\$$#S_1 ! ¢1 \uparrow 1$
$¢111 S_2$\$$#S_1 ! ¢11 \uparrow 1$
$¢111 S_3$\$$#S_1 ! ¢111 \uparrow$\$
$¢111 S_4$\$$#S_1 ! ¢111$\$$\uparrow$ *

} Create initial instantaneous description.

⋮

$S_5 ¢111$\$$#! S_1 ¢111$\$$*1! ¢S_1 111$\$$*1\uparrow$!
$S_6 ¢111$\$$#! S_1 ¢111$\$$*1! ¢S_1 111$\$$*\uparrow 1$!
$S_6 ¢111$\$$#! S_1 ¢111$\$$*1! ¢S_1 111$\$$\uparrow *1$!
$S_6 ¢111$\$$#! S_1 ¢111$\$$*1! ¢S_1 111\uparrow$\$$*1$!   Move to the left end of the previous *ID*.

⋮

$S_6 ¢111$\$$#! S_1 ¢111$\$$*1\uparrow ! ¢S_1 111$\$$*1$!
$S_7 ¢111$\$$#! S_1 ¢111$\$$*1! \uparrow ¢S_1 111$\$$*1$!   Move to counted position; remember
$S_{8,¢} ¢111$\$$#! S_1 ¢111$\$$*1! ¢\uparrow S_1 111$\$$*1$!   symbol found.
$S_{8,¢} ¢111$\$$#! S_1 ¢111$\$$*1! ¢S_1 \uparrow 111$\$$*1$!

⋮   Move to top of stack.

$S_{8,¢} ¢111$\$$#! S_1 ¢111$\$$*1! ¢S_1 111$\$$*1! \uparrow b$
$S_9 ¢111$\$$#! S_1 ¢111$\$$*1! ¢S_1 111$\$$*1! \uparrow ¢$ Write next symbol.
$¢S_{10} 111$\$$#! S_1 ¢111$\$$*1! ¢S_1 111$\$$*1\uparrow ! ¢$ Count i spaces on input tape.
$¢S_5 111$\$$#! S_1 ¢111$\$$*1! ¢S_1 111$\$$*\uparrow 1! ¢$ Start to copy next symbol by moving to left end of previous *ID*. ∎

This example shows the operation of the complex portion of the algorithm of Fig. 6.4.3. Not shown are the additional steps required when the

---

† Subscripted S's appear in two places in these descriptions, with two different meanings. The S before the \$ represents the state of the simulator; it is not a symbol known to the simulator. The S's after the \$ represent states of the simulated machine; they are stack symbols of the simulator.

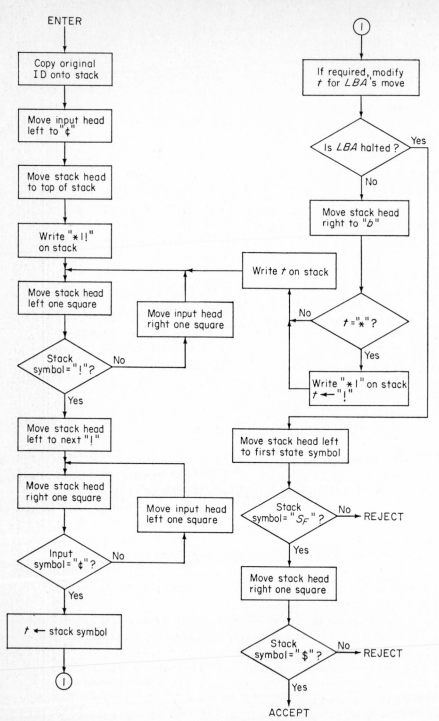

Fig. 6.4.3 Flow chart of the algorithm for the simulation of the operation of a linear-bounded machine by a two-way stack machine.

symbol being copied must be modified because it is changed by the action of the simulated machine or when the tests for halting and acceptance are made. Those details are straightforward but tedious; they are given by Knuth and Bigelow (1967).

This simulation proves

Theorem 1 $2DNESA \supseteq DLBA$

Context-sensitive languages   The simulation just described is performed by a deterministic two-way nonerasing stack machine; it mimics the behavior of a deterministic linear-bounded machine.   Since the question of the equivalence of deterministic and nondeterministic linear-bounded machines is open, we must expand the capabilities of the stack machine to obtain a machine model that we can be certain can accept any context-sensitive language. There are two ways to increase the power of the machine to make this possible: by allowing the stack machine to be nondeterministic or by allowing the stack machine to erase symbols from its stack.   In the first case the equivalence is obvious.   The simulation can proceed as before, except that the simulator nondeterministically chooses the moves to be simulated.   There will exist a sequence of choices leading to acceptance by the simulator if and only if there existed a sequence of choices leading the nondeterministic linear-bounded machine being simulated to an accepting configuration.   Thus we have

Theorem 2 $2NNESA \supseteq NLBA = type\ 1$

The second way to simulate nondeterministic linear-bounded automata with two-way stack automata is to use an erasing deterministic machine.   In this case the stack is used not only to store the instantaneous descriptions of the linear-bounded machine, but also to keep track of the sequence of choices which the simulator has tried for the simulated machine as it tries to accept the string in question.   The numbers n_i (Fig. 6.4.2) are used to keep a record of the choices.   The number indicating which choice was tried in a given move is placed between the instantaneous descriptions describing the conditions before and after the move.   If the jth alternative is taken on the ith move of the machine, then $n_i = j$.

The deterministic simulator searches the tree of possible moves using a left-to-right algorithm (see Sec. 3.4 for a discussion of tree-searching algorithms).   When a new node is added to the path (moving away from the root of the tree), the first option among the alternative moves is used.   When a node must be deleted from the path, the replacement node will correspond to the next untried choice at the previous node.   Whenever the simulated machine reaches a rejecting condition, the simulator must delete one node from the path.   To delete a node the simulator erases the last instantaneous description and increments the previous n_i.   If there exists a choice corresponding to the new value of n_i, that choice is used.   However, if there are no more choices at that point, another node must be deleted from the path and the process repeated.   The simulator rejects the input if the stack is ever completely erased, because then it knows that there does not exist a sequence of choices leading the linear-bounded machine to an accepting condition.

A machine using the preceding algorithm succeeds only if one is certain that the linear-bounded machine which is being simulated will halt and give a definite answer to the membership question for any input tape.   In Sec. 4.2 we discussed this problem and observed that an arbitrarily chosen linear-bounded machine may not halt, because it may enter an infinite loop.   If it is deterministic, it is easy to use a count to detect such looping.   When we proved that $DLBA$ was closed under complementation, we constructed a deterministic linear-bounded machine which simulated a given deterministic machine while counting its moves.   A similar construction can be used on any given nondeterministic linear-bounded machine M_1 to form M_2, another nondeterministic linear-bounded machine which counts the moves made by M_1 and simulates the actions of M_1.   The count is used to detect infinite loops: whenever the count overflows its limit, M_2 halts and rejects the input tape.   Thus M_2 halts for any input tape.   (This construction does not produce a recognizer for the complement of the language accepted by M_1. Why?)   If the stack simulator simulates M_2, the left-to-right search strategy will succeed.

In summary, given $M_1 \in NLBA$, construct $M_2 \in NLBA$ such that M_2 always halts and M_2 accepts the language that M_1 accepts.   Now construct a machine $M_3 \in 2DSA$ which simulates M_2.   Then M_1, M_2, and M_3 all accept the same language, and we have shown

Theorem 3 $2DSA \supseteq NLBA = type\ 1$

6.4.2 ERASING TWO-WAY STACK ACCEPTORS ACCEPT LANGUAGES WHICH ARE NOT CONTEXT-SENSITIVE

There exists at least one language in the set $2DSA$ which is not a context-sensitive language.   In this section we will use a diagonal argument coupled with a modified version of the previous simulation to prove this result.   In Sec. 3.7 we discussed diagonal arguments.   We saw that a diagonal argument cannot be used with context-sensitive languages without a coding procedure such that any input sequence specifies a linear-bounded machine, and furthermore, every linear-bounded acceptor is described by some string of symbols from the input alphabet.   This encoding is necessary so that each input sequence can be interpreted as the definition of a machine which accepts sequences over the same alphabet.   Then the diagonalization step of asking whether a string is in the language which it defines is possible.   We will discuss the encoding procedure and the diagonal construction before we discuss the required simulation.

Encodings We need a scheme to encode the description of an arbitrary linear-bounded acceptor M into a fixed alphabet. First we discuss how the individual quintuples of M are encoded into sequences of symbols over the alphabet $V = \{[,],s,t,L\}$. Then we give rules which describe how the encoded descriptions of the quintuples are used to form an encoded description of the entire machine. Finally, we state how an arbitrary string of symbols from V can be interpreted as the definition of a machine.

We will use the following encoding of a single quintuple of M:

1. If $S_i T_j T_k L S_l$ is a quintuple of M, place $[s^i t^j s^l t^k L]$ in the description.
2. If $S_i T_j T_k N S_l$ is a quintuple of M, place $[s^i t^j s^l t^k]$ in the description.
3. If $S_i T_j T_k R S_l$ is a quintuple of M, place $[s^i t^j s^l t^k LL]$ in the description.

Sequences such as s^i must be used, rather than new symbols, so that the alphabet used in the description of M is fixed, independent of the complexity of M. If some such coding device were not utilized, the described machine could not have more states or symbols than the number of symbols used in the description, and not all linear-bounded machines would be described by a string over the given alphabet. Unless all linear-bounded machines can be described in the coding scheme, that scheme cannot be used for a diagonal argument.

A description of M must specify not only its quintuples but also the set of its states, the set of its tape symbols, its initial state, and the set of its final states. The sets of symbols and states can be deduced by examining the quintuples, since every symbol and state which are used must appear in at least one quintuple. Without loss of generality, we fix the encoding of the endmarkers and the initial state of the linear-bounded machine as follows: Let the left and right endmarkers be T_1 and T_2, respectively (these symbols must always be in the set of symbols). Let S_1 be the starting state. The set of final states is listed in the description according to the following rule:

4. If S_i is a final state of M, include $[s^i]$ in the description of M.

A string describing M can be obtained from the substrings generated from rules 1 to 4 by concatenating them in any order.

Example 3 The linear-bounded acceptor with final state S_2, endmarkers (T_1,T_2), tape symbols (T_3,T_4), and quintuples

$S_1 T_1 T_1 R S_1$
$S_1 T_4 T_3 R S_2$
$S_2 T_4 T_3 R S_1$
$S_1 T_3 T_3 R S_1$
$S_2 T_3 T_3 R S_2$

can be described by the string

$[ststLL][sttttsstttLL][ssttttstttLL][stttstttLL][sstttsstttLL][ss]$

Another of its 6! = 720 descriptions is

$[ststLL][ss][sstttsstttLL][ssttttstttLL][stttstttLL][sttttsstttLL]$

Now we need a set of rules to interpret *any* sequence of the five symbols as the description of a linear-bounded machine. The easy solution to this problem is to ignore any subsequences of a string which are not in the format described by rules 1 to 4. Every subsequence which is in the format of one of the rules will be interpreted as though it had been generated by following that rule.

Example 4   Consider the string

$S = [st]][[ssttL][\ ][sttssttt]][ss]][s][t][$

Only three substrings have the correct format:

$[sttssttt]$
$[ss]$
$[s]$

Thus string S describes a linear-bounded machine with two states, which are both accepting states, three symbols (T_1, T_2, T_3), and one quintuple $(S_1 T_2 T_3 N S_2)$.

The diagonal construction   The alphabet of the machine to be constructed is $T = \{t_1, t_2, \ldots, t_7\}$. Introduce the mapping†

$$R = \langle (\not{c}, t_1), (\$, t_2), ([, t_3), (], t_4), (s, t_5), (t, t_6), (L, t_7) \rangle$$

which encodes the symbols of V into the symbols of T. The mapping R is extended to sequences of symbols by the rule $R(xy) = R(x)R(y)$, where x and y may be sequences or symbols. Thus, for example, $R(\not{c}[sst]\$) = t_1 t_3 t_5 t_5 t_6 t_4 t_2$. In the diagonal language to be constructed, V will be the set of terminal symbols and $\not{c}$, $\$$ will be the endmarkers. The machine whose description will be taken from the input string uses t_1, t_2 as endmarkers and $\{t_3, t_4, \ldots, t_7\}$ as the set of terminal symbols.

Let $M(\alpha)$ denote the linear-bounded machine described by string α according to the encoding described above, and let $L = \{x \mid x \in V^* \text{ and } R(x) \text{ is not accepted by } M(x)\}$. For every context-sensitive language L_i, there exists a string y_i which describes an acceptor for L_i. Thus L_i is accepted by $M(y_i)$. But y_i is not in L if it is in L_i, and vice versa. Since every context-sensitive language is in the set of languages described by the strings x, L is different from every context-sensitive language. Thus L is not a context-sensitive language.

† This notation denotes a mapping in which the first member of a pair is mapped into the second member of the pair. Thus $R(\not{c}) = t_1$, etc.

We need to show that L can be accepted by a two-way deterministic stack machine. A simulation very similar to the one described in the preceding section will be used. Let S be the simulator and M be the machine being simulated. There are three new difficulties which must be handled. First, M may enter an infinite loop and not accept the string. Second, S is not designed with a complete knowledge of M; rather, the input tape contains the description of M. Therefore S does not have a fixed, known bound on the number of states or symbols used by M. Finally, S does not know the maximum number of choices which are available in a nondeterministic move, or for that matter, whether M is deterministic. We consider each of these difficulties in turn.

Infinite loops   To avoid infinite loops, S places on its stack a count of the number of moves which it has simulated. This count is placed on the stack immediately following the instantaneous description of the conditions after the move (Fig. 6.4.4). Let n be the length of the input sequence, m be the number of states of M, and p be the number of tape symbols of M. The number of moves which M can make without entering an infinite loop is less than $(mp)^n$. Using the techniques described in Sec. 4.2, this count can be stored in n-tape squares. If the count overflows the n positions, M must be in an infinite loop. The base for the counting is the product of the number of symbols and the number of states of the simulated machine.

Since the base for the counting is not known when the simulator is designed, the contents of the n positions of the counter cannot be encoded in a simple way. Rather, we use unary notation (sequences of s's or t's) to represent the digits. Each position of the count must be represented by two such digits, one counting to m, the other counting to p. We use the symbol : to separate the digit positions of the counter and ; to separate the two components of each count position, as in

$$:sssss;tt:sss;t:\ \cdot\ \cdot\ \cdot$$

The s's will count up to m; the t's will count to p. The maximum number of states (symbols) in $M(\alpha)$ can be bounded above by the length of the longest sequence of s's (t's) in α. Therefore a component of the count overflows whenever the sequence of s's (t's) on the stack becomes longer than any sequence of s's (t's) on the input tape. It is difficult for S to find the longest sequence of s's on its input tape. The length of this sequence is being used to form an upper bound on the number of moves of M. Any higher upper

$$\#!-ID1-?:s^*;t^**n_1!-ID2-?:s^*;t^*:\ \cdot\ \cdot\ \cdot\ [:s^*;t^*]^**n_2!$$

Fig. 6.4.4 Stack format for the diagonal language simulation of Sec. 6.4.2.

limit could be used, at the expense of slowing down the operation of S. We know that the longest sequence on the input tape is shorter than the entire input sequence. If we use the length of the input tape as the upper bound, the algorithm will work and will be simpler, but S may be slower. But we do not care about speed. Therefore we use a check against the length of the input tape to generate the overflow condition which causes a carry to propagate into the next position of the counter; if a carry propagates out of the nth position of the counter, M must be in an infinite loop. Thus M would reject the input sequence.

The simulator must copy the count sequence from below the upper instantaneous description on the stack to the top of the stack and increment it. It could use the same algorithm as the one used to copy the instantaneous description but for the unfortunate fact that the length of the sequence of symbols representing the count may reach $n^2 + n$. That algorithm cannot be adapted unless the length of the sequence can be bounded by a fixed multiple of n. Moreover, if the sequence of length $n^2 + n$ could be any arbitrary sequence of symbols, S would not be able to copy it. But this particular sequence has a restricted form: It can be divided into not more than $2n$ sequences, and each sequence contains not more than n copies of the same character. The delimiters : and ; separate these sequences. Because the sequence to be copied has this format, the previous algorithm can be modified to copy the sequence, as follows:

Both copying algorithms use the position of the input head relative to an endmarker as a counter. Their structures are similar: In one cycle of moving into the stack and back to the top, one sequence of identical symbols will be copied. When the stack head moves into the stack, the position of the input head is used to count the location of the sequence to be copied (just as it counted the location of the symbol in the preceding algorithm). When the stack head moves back toward the top of the stack, the position of the input head is used to count the number of symbols in the sequence which is being copied.

Now we present a more detailed description of this algorithm. The reader may skip this discussion and continue with the section discussing the numbers of symbols and states. A detailed flow chart of the copying and incrementing algorithm is given in Fig. 6.4.5. At various points in the flow chart an italic letter in a circle is attached to a branch. These letters reference entries in Table 6.4.1, where the positions of the two heads when the machine reaches that point in the algorithm are shown.

We will describe the sequence of steps used to copy and increment (if necessary) one position of the counter. We assume that the stack head is initially at the top of the stack and that the input head is over the left endmarker (step a). The finite-state control contains information as to whether the next sequence to be copied is a sequence of s's or t's. As the stack head

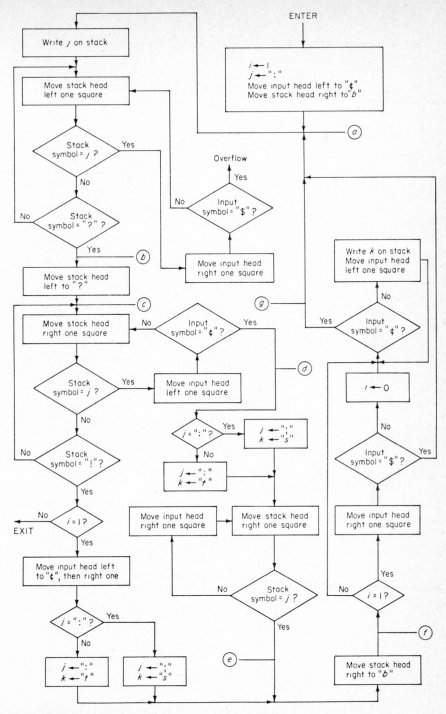

Fig. 6.4.5 Flow chart of the algorithm to copy and increment the move counter.

207

Table 6.4.1 The positions of the heads of the stack machine as it copies the next sequence of s's on the stack

Step	Position of input head	Position of stack head
a	left end (ϕ)	Top
b	n squares from ϕ (n = number of colons on stack between top and topmost ?)	Topmost ?
c	n squares from ϕ	Second topmost ?
d	ϕ	: beginning sequence to be copied
e	m squares from ϕ (m = number of s's in sequence to be copied)	; ending sequence to be copied
f	m squares from ϕ	Top
g	ϕ	Top (sequence having been copied)

moves into the stack, the input head moves right one square every time certain delimiters are read on the stack as follows: If a sequence of s's (t's) is to be copied, the head is moved whenever a colon (semicolon) is read by the stack head.   When the stack head reaches a question mark (step b), the input head remains stationary while the stack head moves left to the next question mark (step c).   The stack head then moves to the right to the ith colon (semicolon), where i is the count contained in the position of the input head (step d). When the next colon (semicolon) is reached, the input head, which is again on the left endmarker, is used to count the number of s's (t's) in the next sequence to the right on the stack (step e).   This count is saved while the stack head moves to the top of the stack (step f).   Then the correct number of s's (t's) is written, followed by the proper delimiter (step g).

When the count in the position being copied should be incremented, the input head is moved one extra square after the sequence of s's (t's) is counted.   If the right endmarker is read after that move, this counter position has overflowed; therefore no s's (t's) should be added to the top of the stack. The proper delimiter should be written there, and the control unit should remain in the incrementing mode of operation for the next count.   A similar test is used to detect when the machine being simulated is in a loop (Prob. 4).

Indefinite numbers of symbols and states   Since the numbers of symbols and states of M are not known to S when it is designed, sequences of s's and t's separated by commas are used to represent the symbols in the instantaneous description of M.   Each such sequence denotes a single element in the description of $M(\alpha)$.   Thus $t,ttt,tttt,sss,tt$ represents the instantaneous description $\phi t_3 t_4 S_3 \$$.

This encoding adds three complications to the simulation algorithm.

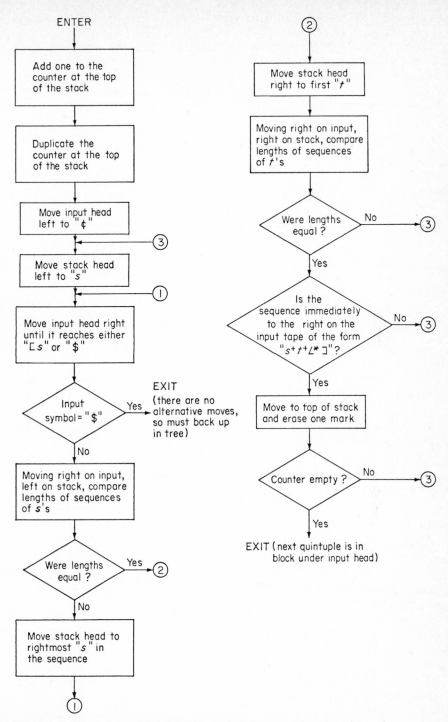

ENTER

Add one to the counter at the top of the stack

Duplicate the counter at the top of the stack

Move input head left to "¢"

Move stack head left to "s"

Move input head right until it reaches either "⌐s" or "$"

Input symbol = "$"? — Yes → EXIT (there are no alternative moves, so must back up in tree)

No

Moving right on input, left on stack, compare lengths of sequences of s's

Were lengths equal? — Yes → ②

No

Move stack head to rightmost "s" in the sequence

①

②

Move stack head right to first "t"

Moving right on input, right on stack, compare lengths of sequences of t's

Were lengths equal? — No → ③

Yes

Is the sequence immediately to the right on the input tape of the form "s⁺t⁺⌐*⌐"? — No → ③

Yes

Move to top of stack and erase one mark

Counter empty? — No → ③

Yes

EXIT (next quintuple is in block under input head)

Fig. 6.4.6 Flow chart of the algorithm to find the next quintuple to be used.

First, the instantaneous description is longer than the length of the input tape. Thus a copying algorithm similar to the count-copying algorithm must be used to copy the description. Second, the algorithm to find the applicable quintuple for a move is involved; we discuss this in more detail below. Third, when S starts, the encoding described by the mapping R must be performed during the process of copying the instantaneous description of S onto the stack.

Counting alternatives The count representing n_i, the number of the last choice which was explored, must be expressed in unary notation. Updating and copying this count are straightforward processes. This counter is used only in finding the quintuple to be applied during the next move of the simulated machine. Overflow is detected during the search for the next move.

Finding the quintuple to use The algorithm to find the quintuple to be used in the next move is described by the flow chart in Fig. 6.4.6. The structure of the algorithm is relatively simple. At the top of the stack, S keeps a copy of the count of the number of the next alternative to be tried. Let p denote that number. The machine scans the input tape from left to right, looking for subsequences that are in the correct format to describe a move which M could make next. As each move is found, p is reduced by one. When p becomes zero, the desired quintuple is under the reading head on the input tape. If the input head reaches the right endmarker during the search, there are no more choices for the next node on this path through the move tree. Therefore S must back up in the tree search, since the previous node cannot lie on an accepting path.

  Remember that our goal was to show that L, the diagonal language, could be recognized by a two-way deterministic stack machine. There were three difficulties with directly using the previous simulation algorithm. They were: (1) M might enter an infinite loop. (2) S does not know how many states and symbols M has. (3) S has difficulty finding the next move for M. Since we have shown how these difficulties can be overcome, we have

Theorem 4 $2DSA \supset NLBA = type\ 1$

PROBLEMS

1 Find algorithms which can be used to show the following relationships:

  (a) $\{x2x \mid x \in \{0,1\}^*\} \in 1DNESA$
  (b) $\{xx \mid x \in \{0,1\}^*\} \in 1NNESA$
  (c) $\{xx \mid x \in \{0,1\}^*\} \in 2DNESA$
  (d) $\{a^n b^{n^2} \mid n \geq 0\} \in 1DNESA$
  (e) $\{a^n b^m c^{m \cdot n} \mid m, n \geq 1\} \in 1DSA$
  (f) $\{a^n b^m c^{[m/n]} \mid m, n \geq 1\} \in 1DSA$, where $[m/n]$ is the greatest integer less than or equal to m/n.

(*g*) $\{a^n | n$ is a perfect number$\} \in 2DSA$.   (A perfect number is one which is equal to the sum of all its divisors, excepting itself.   For example, $6 = 1 + 2 + 3$ is perfect.)

2.   Find algorithms which can be used to show

   (*a*) $1DSA \subseteq DLBA$
   (*b*) $1NSA \subseteq NLBA = $ *type 1*

3.   Consider one-way deterministic nonerasing stack machines which have two heads on their stacks: one which is read-only, the other write-only.   (Note that the write-only head must be at the top of the stack.)   Prove that the set of languages accepted by these machines is equivalent to the set of recursive languages.   [*Hint:* Consider the string in the portion of the stack between the two heads to be the string of a Post normal system (Prob. 5 of Sec. 3.5).]

4.   When the two-way deterministic stack machine simulated a nondeterministic linear-bounded machine, it counted the number of moves which had been simulated to determine whether the simulated machine was in an infinite loop.   Draw a flow chart to describe the manipulations required to perform these tasks.

5.   Argue that

$$\{x2x2y2u2u2z2x | u, x, y, z \in \{0,1\}^* \text{ and } yz = x\}$$

cannot be accepted by a machine in the class $1DSA$.

6.   Use diagonal arguments to prove $2NSA \neq $ *type 0*.

7.   In this problem we will prove that each of the two classes of deterministic one-way stack languages is closed under complementation.

   (*a*) List the conditions which might cause a deterministic one-way stack machine to reject an input string.

   (*b*) Prove: Given a one-way stack machine A, there exists another one-way stack machine B such that

   (1) $L(A) = L(B)$
   (2) B does not enter infinite loops in which the machine writes symbols on the stack and does not move the input head.
   (3) The determinism and nonerasing properties of A are preserved in B.

   (*c*) Prove: Given a one-way stack machine C, there exists another one-way stack machine D such that

   (1) $L(C) = L(D)$
   (2) D does not enter infinite loops in which the machine reads the stack without either writing on the stack or moving the input head.
   (3) The determinism and nonerasing properties of C are preserved in D.

(*Hint:* See Sec. 2.6 and apply those arguments to the stack.)

   (*d*) Prove: Given a one-way stack machine E, there exists another one-way stack machine F such that

   (1) $L(E) = L(F)$
   (2) F never enters loops in which the input head is not moved, but the machine reads the stack, then writes on it, then reads it, etc.
   (3) The determinism and nonerasing properties of E are preserved in F.

   (*e*) Using the above results, prove that each of the two classes of one-way deterministic stack languages are closed under complementation.

8.   (R) Find diagonal arguments to show

   (*a*) $2DSA \neq 2DNESA$
   (*b*) $2NSA \neq 2NNESA$

6.5 COMMENTS

The major results of Chaps. 2 to 6 are summarized in Appendix 2. In these five chapters, four different classes of languages based on their grammars were introduced, and a larger number of machine models have been related to those classes of languages. Many machine models have been introduced in an effort to develop closer relationships between mathematical linguistics, automata theory, and the algorithms used in compiler programs. Every year it seems that other models are introduced; often some of these include some features of compilers which were not included in previous models.

The models discussed in this chapter first appeared in print as follows: Two-way pushdown machines, Gray, Harrison, and Ibarra (1967); counter machines, Schutzenberger (1962); stack machines, Ginsburg, Greibach, and Harrison (1967). Papers describing other more recent models and results are cited in the Bibliography.

The two complex algorithms in this chapter are the simulation of a Turing machine by a two-counter machine originally shown in Minsky (1961) and the stack automata simulations originally shown in Knuth and Bigelow (1967).

7
Operations on Languages

In Chap. 1 we discussed grammars from three points of view: first, as a set of rules for generating sentences in languages; second, as a set of rules for testing a string of symbols for membership in the language defined by the grammar; finally, we discussed transformational grammars, in which the set of rules specify a transformation applied to one sequence of symbols to produce a second sequence of symbols. Similarly, machines can be considered as acceptors of languages, as generators of languages, or as translators of languages. In this chapter we will discuss the latter two viewpoints. A translator of a language transforms the sentences of that language into other strings. We can consider that set of strings to be a language. Thus we ask questions like, "If a finite-state machine translates a regular language, what kind of language will be produced?" In most of this chapter we will discuss questions like this for various combinations of translators and languages.

Machine models of the generation and translation processes are useful in constructing intuitive proofs of important results which compare sets of languages with each other. For example, in Sec. 5.4 we gave intuitive, but not precise, reasons why the language $\{xx^R | x \in \{0,1\}^*\}$ is not in the set $1DPDA$. Some of the results discussed in this chapter can be used to provide a rigorous, but not too complex, proof of this result.

The properties of sets of languages are also important in showing that two sets of languages are not identical. For example, a set of languages which is closed under the operation of intersection cannot be equivalent to a set of languages which is not closed under intersection. We shall develop some of the properties which can be used to show the nonequivalence of two sets of languages.

In Sec. 7.1 we discuss the notion of a machine as a generator of strings in a language. The remainder of the chapter is devoted to transformations of languages. Most of the results concerning the properties which are preserved under various transformations hold because the set of languages is accepted by a machine with some type of finite-state control unit and a reading head which moves on an input tape. These essentials of the machine model are formalized in the structure of balloon automata, which are introduced in Sec. 7.2.

In Sec. 7.3 we consider the translation of languages by finite-state transducers. Most of the results are obtained by considering a finite-state transducer to be a portion of the finite-state control unit of an acceptor. The results can be "proved" by drawing a picture which depicts the construction so accurately that a further description of the proof is not necessary.

When machines with infinite memory are used as transducers, the languages produced by the translation process can be very complex; in fact, most sets of languages are not closed under the operation of translation by a pushdown machine. Sections 7.4 and 7.5 discuss some of the small number of statements which can be made about translations performed by machines with an infinite memory.

Finally, in Sec. 7.6, the operation of intersecting a language with a regular set is discussed. This operation is closely related to certain finite-state translations. It is used in a rigorous proof that $1NPDA \neq 1DPDA$.

7.1 GENERATORS

Suppose that we take the transition graph of a finite-state acceptor A and consider the symbols which were input symbols to be output symbols. Let the machine that we obtain be called G. Machine G does not have any input symbols, so it will be nondeterministic. If we require that G start in the initial state of A and finish in a final state of A, what sequences can be produced by G? If we connected G to A (Fig. 7.1.1), both machines would always be in the same state. It should be obvious that A reaches a final state whenever G does. Thus G generates strings from the language accepted by A.

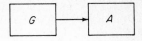

The specification of any one-way acceptor A can be changed to the specification of a generator G for the same language by changing the input symbols to output symbols, without changing the remainder of the specification of A. The output of G must be ignored unless the generator reaches some state which is a final state of G. If A has λ-moves, G will produce λ outputs; these should be ignored when the symbols produced by G are concatenated to form the output sequence.

The only interesting generators are nondeterministic. A deterministic generator could produce only a finite number of different output sequences (not more than the number of initial states of the generator). Since any finite set is regular, we have

Theorem 1   Any deterministic generator generates a regular language.

It is more difficult to construct a generator for a language accepted by a two-way machine. First, the acceptor has an input tape. The power of the two-way acceptor arises from its ability to reexamine squares of the input tape. A generator which is constructed by reversing the accepting process will have an input tape; it may visit some squares several times before the generation process terminates. On the first visit to a square, it may write a symbol of its own choosing in that square. During subsequent visits to the same square, it may read only the symbol that it previously wrote in the square. If these rules were not followed, the operation of the generator would not correspond to the operation of the acceptor. Therefore the generator must be constrained to never erase a nonblank symbol on the input tape, but rather to check the input tape's symbol whenever that symbol is nonblank. The details of a formal description of these rules are left to the reader (Probs. 2 and 6).

In the following sections we will find generators useful in proving certain results, particularly when finite-state acceptors are involved in the problem.

PROBLEMS

1. Write a specification of the generator G which corresponds to the machine M in Table 2.4.8. Simulate the actions of G and M as they generate and accept the string *xxyyy*.

2. A two-way generator as formulated in this section writes on a tape and can later read that tape. Therefore it is a Turing machine.

Is this statement true or false? Prove your answer.

3. Show that a nondeterministic acceptor for a one-way language L can be constructed from a generator G of L by using G to generate a string in L and then comparing that string with the input string (Fig. 7.1.2). Explain why this construction works only for languages accepted by one-way machines.

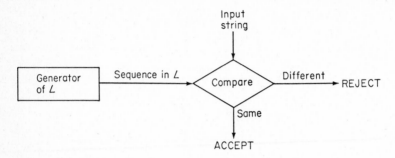

Fig. 7.1.2 An acceptor constructed from a generator.

4. Let L be a language over the alphabet A. Consider a string

$$s = a_1a_2a_3 \cdots a_n$$

in L. Let $B = \{0,1\}$, and let F be the mapping

$$F: A^* \to B^*$$

such that

$$F(s) = F(a_1a_2 \cdots a_n) = b_1b_2b_3 \cdots b_n$$

where

$$b_i = \begin{cases} 1 & \text{if the sequence } a_1a_2 \cdots a_i \text{ is in } L \\ 0 & \text{otherwise} \end{cases}$$

Let $F(L) = \{t \mid t = F(s) \text{ for some } s \in L\}$.

    (a) Prove that $F(L)$ is a regular language if L is a regular language. (*Hint:* Consider the machine in Fig. 7.1.3.)

    (b) If L is an arbitrary context-free language, what is the "simplest" type of machine which accepts $F(L)$?

    (c) If L is context-sensitive, prove that $F(L)$ is also.

    (d) Comment on the classification of $F(L)$ when L is a recursive language.

5. Give a formal definition of a finite-state generator.

6. Give a formal definition of a two-way pushdown generator.

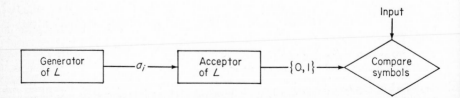

Fig. 7.1.3 An acceptor for $F(L)$; see Prob. 4.

7. Using Theorem 1, state a sufficient condition that an acceptor accepts a regular language. Your answer should be valid for an acceptor with any type of infinite memory.

7.2 BALLOON AUTOMATA

Most machine models include a finite-state control unit and an infinite storage. There are restrictions on how the machine may examine or modify the infinite storage. In previous chapters, we classified machines by the nature of the restrictions on their use of the infinite storage. The balloon automaton model allows a very general access to the infinite storage. Thus almost all the previous models are special cases of balloon automata.

The balloon automaton model provides a minimum framework for many results concerning the closure of sets of languages under various translation operations.

We will describe the balloon automaton model informally; the formal description is slightly more complex, and the additional precision obtained from the formal description is not necessary for our purposes.

A balloon acceptor always has a read-only input tape, a finite-state control, a set of final states, and a designated initial state. In addition, it may store an infinite amount of information with restricted access to that information. The infinite information is stored in the "balloon." At any instant the balloon contains a single positive integer. Let Z denote the set of positive integers. The restricted access to the infinite information is specified by three additional items:

1. A finite nonempty set of values M which can be "read" from the balloon.
2. A recursive procedure† r to read the balloon:

$$r: Z \to M$$

3. A recursive procedure w to write the balloon.

During one move the balloon machine examines

1. Its internal state
2. The symbol under the input reading head
3. The value read from the balloon

to determine

    a. The motion of the reading head
    b. The next internal state
    c. The new value to be stored in the balloon

† See Sec. 3.1 for the definition of a recursive procedure. In Prob. 1 of Sec. 9.6, we show that if this restriction is removed, the machine can recognize a language which is not recursive.

To simplify the discussion we take a Moore-like model, in which the information written in the balloon is determined by the state of the finite-state control only (but see Prob. 12). For this case the writing function w is specified by

$$w: S \times Z \to Z$$

The writing function w can be specified as a set of functions w_i; w_i is used to write the balloon whenever the machine is in state i. Each w_i maps Z into Z.

There are four types of balloon automata ($1DBA$, $1NBA$, $2DBA$, $2NBA$), depending upon whether the input head motion is one-way or two-way and whether the finite-state control unit is deterministic or nondeterministic. These sets of machines are too large to provide many results, and they do not correspond to the sets of machines which we have been discussing. Consequently, we need a finer classification of balloon automata such that the members of each class not only are of the same type (one-way nondeterministic, for example), but have some relationship to each other. We therefore introduce the concept of a closed class of balloon automata, as follows:

Let a closed class of balloon automata (or simply, a class of balloon automata) be a set of balloon automata of a certain type which contain:

1. All finite-state acceptors
2. If M_1 and M_2 are in the class, then so is any balloon automaton M_3 satisfying:
    a. In any move, M_3 writes its balloon by using either a writing function used by M_1 or a writing function used by M_2.
    b. When M_3 reads the balloon, it obtains different values from two different balloon states Z_1 and Z_2 only if either M_1 or M_2 can distinguish Z_1 and Z_2 (by reading different values from the balloon). In other words, if r_i is the function reading the balloon of M_i, then $r_3(Z_1) \neq r_3(Z_2)$ implies $r_1(Z_1) \neq r_1(Z_2)$ or $r_2(Z_1) \neq r_2(Z_2)$.

We use the symbol C to denote a closed class of balloon automata.

Classes of pushdown machines form classes of balloon automata
The set of all pushdown machines of a certain type ($1NPDA$, $1DPDA$, $2NPDA$, or $2DPDA$) forms a class of balloon automata. To prove this statement, we need to show (1) how the contents of the pushdown list can be encoded into an integer (which would be stored in the balloon) and (2) how this integer is manipulated to simulate reading and writing operations on the pushdown tape. An encoding procedure similar to the one used in Sec. 6.3 will be used here. Let r be the number of symbols in the pushdown-tape alphabet. Now encode the contents of the tape into a base-r integer with the top symbol of the pushdown tape in the least significant position of the

integer. This integer will be stored in the balloon. The balloon can be read and written by algorithms similar to those described in Sec. 6.3.

Similar constructions can be used to show that the classes of stack machines, Turing machines, counter machines, and finite-state machines form classes of balloon automata (Probs. 6 to 11). Unfortunately, the classes of Turing machines with space bounds (such as linear-bounded machines) do not form classes of balloon automata.

PROBLEMS

1. (P) Show that if $L \in C \subseteq 1DBA$, then $\sim L \in C$, where the complement is taken with respect to all words over the alphabet of L.

2. Show that if $L \in C \subseteq 1NBA$, then $L^R \in C$.

3. Show that the set of languages accepted by any closed class of balloon automata within $2DBA$ or $2NBA$ is closed under reversal.

4. If $L_i \in C \subseteq 1NBA$, $1 \leq i \leq n$, construct

$$L = \{x_{i_1}x_{i_2} \cdots x_{i_m} | x_{i_j} \in L_{i_j}, 1 \leq i_j \leq n, 1 \leq j \leq m\}$$

(a) Show that $L \in C$.

(b) Show that

$$L' = \{x_1 x_2 \cdots x_m | \text{for each } i, 1 \leq i \leq m, \text{there exists a } j, 1 \leq j \leq n, \text{such that } x_i \in L_j\} \in C$$

5. Prove that the set of languages accepted by machines in a closed class of nondeterministic balloon automata is closed under union.

6. Prove all the details necessary to show that the set $1NPDA$ is a closed class of balloon automata.

7. Show that the sets $1DPD_n$ and $1NPD_n$, for fixed n, form classes of balloon automata.

8. Prove that the set of Turing machines forms a closed class of balloon automata.

9. Prove that the sets of n-counter machines form closed classes of balloon automata.

10. Prove that the sets of stack machines form closed classes of balloon automata.

11. Prove that the sets of real-time n-counter and n-pushdown list machines do not form closed classes of balloon automata.

12. (P) Define a *Mealy balloon automaton* in which the information written into the balloon is determined not only by the state but also by the "input conditions" (which include the information read from the balloon). Show that a closed class of Mealy balloon automata is equivalent to a closed class of Moore balloon automata.

7.3 FINITE-STATE TRANSDUCERS

A transducer is a machine which has both inputs and outputs. The input and output symbols may be chosen from two different alphabets. Let $I = \{I_1, I_2, \ldots, I_n\}$ and $O = \{O_1, O_2, \ldots, O_m\}$ be the finite input and output alphabets, respectively. Also let T denote the mapping performed by a given transducer. If the transducer produces the output sequence $y \in O^*$ when presented with the input sequence $x \in I^*$, then we write $T(x) = y$. The mapping T can be extended to languages as follows:

> Let $T(L_1) = L_2$ if and only if $T(x) \in L_2$ for every x in L_1, and furthermore, for every y in L_2 there exists at least one $x \in L_1$ such that $y = T(x)$.

Also, we can extend the mapping to classes of languages:

> Let $T(C_1) = C_2$ if and only if $T(L_1) \in C_2$ for every language $L_1 \in C_1$, and for every language $L_2 \in C$ there exists at least one $L_1 \in C_1$ such that $L_2 = T(L_1)$.

We make another extension to the functional notation to relate a class of transducers C_T and two classes of languages C_1 and C_2 as follows:

> Let $C_T(C_1) = C_2$ if and only if $T(L_1) \in C_2$ for every language $L_1 \in C_1$ and every transducer $T \in C_T$, and furthermore, there exists a transducer $T_1 \in C_T$ and a language $L_3 \in C_1$ such that $T_1(L_3) = L_2$ for every language $L_2 \in C_2$.

This latter form of notation will be common in this section, since our results describe the effects of various types of translations upon various classes of languages.

In this section we consider the mappings performed by finite-state one-way transducers. We divide the problem into several cases, depending upon how many output symbols the transducer can produce for each input symbol, upon the determinism of the transducer, and so on. The word "transducer" is seldom used in the literature. Rather, certain conventional names have been used for the various versions of finite-state transducers. We will use these conventional names during our discussion.

Our objective is to prove something about the classes of languages which can be produced by a finite-state translation performed on a class of languages. In most cases, the class of languages will be closed under the translation operation. This result will be obtained by showing that either the translator itself or its inverse can be incorporated into the finite-state control of an acceptor for the original language, thereby constructing an acceptor for the translated language. Since the mechanisms dealing with the balloon will not be changed by this amalgamation, the new acceptor will be in the same class as the old acceptor. Unfortunately, not all interesting cases are that simple, and in some cases there are no strong results. But classes of languages in *INBA* are closed under most finite-state translations.

We will discuss the different forms of finite-state translations in separate subsections. Most of the results are based on simple constructions very similar to those used in the first two cases.

The last important result is based on the proof that a two-counter machine is equivalent to a Turing machine. We will show that a translation which simply erases certain symbols and allows all others to pass unchanged can be applied to the intersection of two $1NC_1$ languages to produce any recursive language. Therefore classes of translations which include this particular translation can produce recursive languages if they are applied to certain simple classes of languages. This result, though not very constructive, is quite important in delimiting the capabilities of various models for translation processes.

7.3.1 COMPLETE SEQUENTIAL MACHINES

A complete sequential machine (csm) is a one-way deterministic finite-state machine (transducer) that produces a single output symbol in each move in which it reads a single input symbol. Therefore, for any csm, the input and output sequences have the same length. A formal definition of a csm is as follows:

A *complete sequential machine* is a sextuple $\langle I,O,S,S_0,f,g \rangle$,

where $\quad I =$ the finite set of input symbols
$\quad O =$ the finite set of output symbols
$\quad S =$ the finite set of states
$\quad S_0 \in S =$ the initial state
$\quad f: I \times S \to S =$ the next state function
$\quad g: I \times S \to O =$ the output function

Let csm (L_1) represent the language which is the translation of L_1 by a particular complete sequential machine. Furthermore, let $\text{csm}^{-1}(L_1)$ be the language L_2 such that $L_1 = \text{csm}(L_2)$. Note that if $L_2 = \text{csm}^{-1}(L_1)$, it might not be true that $L_2 = \text{csm}(L_1)$ for some complete sequential machine, since the machine required to perform the inverse translation might be nondeterministic.

Suppose $L_2 = \text{csm}^{-1}(L_1)$ for some csm M. Also assume that L_1 is accepted by a one-way deterministic balloon machine M_1 in closed class C_1. An acceptor for L_1 is depicted in Fig. 7.3.1a, where C_1 is the control unit of M_1 and B_1 is the balloon of M_1. Consider placing M between the reading head of M_1 and its finite-state control (Fig. 7.3.1b). If the sequence on the input tape is in L_2, then the sequence which will be seen by M_1 will be in L_1; this string will be accepted by M_1. If we define acceptance in terms of the state of M_1 alone, the composite machine will accept L_2. Now machine M is a finite-state machine, and could have been merged with the finite-state

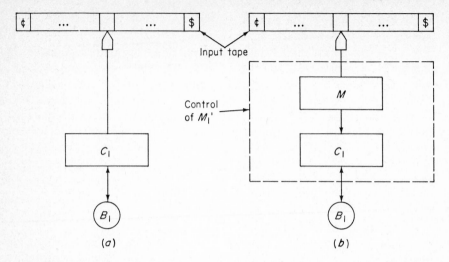

Fig. 7.3.1 Insertion of a transducer into the input information path. (*a*) Acceptor for L_1; (*b*) acceptor for $csm^{-1}(L_1)$.

control of M_1 to form M_1', which will be the finite-state control of another machine in class C_1 which accepts L_2. Therefore we have

Theorem 1 If $L_1 \in C_1 \subseteq 1DBA$, then $csm^{-1}(L_1) \in C_1$.

The same construction can be used to show

Theorem 2 If $L_1 \in C_1 \subseteq 1NBA$, then $csm(L_1) \in C_1$ and $csm^{-1}(L_1) \in C_1$.

Rewriting acceptors   Note that the classes of languages accepted by machines which can rewrite their input tapes (Turing machines, linear-bounded machines, etc.) are not included in the results stated in Theorems 1 and 2. A construction in which the csm is permanently placed between the reading head and the other part of the finite-state control does not work in these cases. However, these classes of languages are also closed under csm mappings. We construct an acceptor for $csm^{-1}(L_1)$ by having the rewriting transducer use the csm to translate the input tape before M_1 uses its own recognition algorithm on the translated tape. Thus

Theorem 3   (*a*) $csm^{-1}(DLBA) \subseteq DLBA$
             (*b*) $csm(NLBA) \subseteq NLBA$
             (*c*) $csm(TMA) \subseteq TMA$

The classes of languages in $2DBA$ are also closed with respect to the inverse csm mappings. The construction for this proof is more complicated; it is deferred to the next section, when a more general case is discussed.

7.3.2 GENERALIZED SEQUENTIAL MACHINES

A generalized sequential machine (gsm) is a one-way deterministic finite-state transducer which produces a (possibly empty) sequence of output symbols each time it reads an input symbol. Let gsm (L_1) and gsm^{-1} (L_1) denote the mappings performed by a gsm and its inverse, respectively.

The generalized sequential machine model is an extension of the complete sequential machine model in two directions. First, the gsm may produce many output symbols for each input symbol that it reads. Second, the machine may read input symbols (and change state) without producing output symbols. An upper bound in the length of the output sequence can be obtained by multiplying the length of the input sequence by the length of the longest output sequence which can be produced from each input symbol. A nontrivial lower bound on the length of the output sequence cannot be obtained because the translator can accept input symbols without producing output symbols. Therefore the output sequence from the translation can be much shorter than the input sequence.

We will show by construction that some classes of languages are closed under the gsm and gsm^{-1} mappings. The basic trick used with the csm can be used here. Consider placing a gsm M in the path between the reading head and the finite-state control of a machine M_1 which accepts $L_1 \in IDBA$. The gsm might produce a sequence of output symbols for each input symbol. The control of M_1 accepts one of these symbols at a time. Thus we must store the output sequence of M for later use by M_1. A "buffer" is inserted in the path to hold the sequence (Fig. 7.3.2). Whenever M_1 needs another symbol, it examines the buffer to see whether it contains a symbol which it has not yet read. If there are no unused symbols in the buffer, M_1 causes the gsm to read input symbols until a sequence of symbols is placed in the buffer. (This may require several moves by the gsm.) The finite buffer and the logic to control its use can be absorbed into the finite control of M_1', the machine which recognizes gsm^{-1} (L_1).

We have shown

Theorem 4 If $L_1 \in C_1 \subseteq IDBA$, then gsm^{-1} $(L_1) \in C_1$.

Similarly, we can use gsm^{-1} in place of gsm in Fig. 7.3.2; the machine constructed that way recognizes gsm (L_1) if $L_1 \in C_1 \subseteq INBA$. The gsm^{-1} machine reads (possibly empty) sequences of symbols from the input tape to produce symbols which are passed to M_1 for further processing. This construction proves

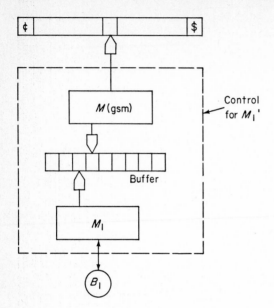

Fig. 7.3.2 The construction for the gsm^{-1} proof.

Theorem 5 If $L_1 \in C_1 \subseteq INBA$, then gsm $(L_1) \in C_1$.

A more complex construction is required to show that every class of two-way balloon languages is closed under gsm^{-1}. Again we use the construction shown in Fig. 7.3.2. A problem arises if M_1 wishes to move to the left. Then M must also be backed up. The problem is to determine the state of M before its last move to the right. In other words, we must deterministically run M backward for one input symbol.

Two items of information can be used to determine the previous state of M. First, the present state of M is known. Second, by moving the input head to the left, previous input symbols can be examined. However, if the input head is moved to the left to examine previous input symbols, its position must be restored. The restoration problem is nontrivial, because the finite-state control unit cannot count the number of squares over which the head has been moved. Figure 7.3.3 contains a flow chart of the algorithm that we will discuss.

Consider moving the input head one square to the left. It might happen that the present state of M and the previous input symbol uniquely determine the previous state of M. In this fortunate circumstance, the backup process is complete after the single move. Otherwise, the present state of M and the previous symbol determine a set of states any one of which might have been the previous state of M. Further left motions must be made to determine which state was the previous state. We continue to move M to the left until

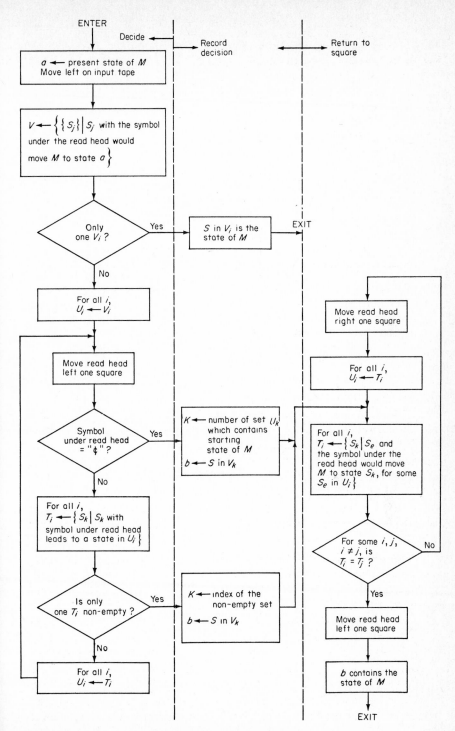

Fig. 7.3.3 Flow chart for backing up one square.

a square is reached where the state of M can be determined uniquely.   The next problem is to return the reading head to the proper square.   Remember that the number of squares passed over cannot be counted.   Consider the machine when it just resolves the state dilemma.   It knows that the conflict about the state of M could not be resolved until the square under the input head was examined.   This fact can be used to move the head forward to the proper square.   We illustrate with the following example.

Example 1   In this example we show the details of the algorithm used to resolve questions about the state of the gsm when it is moved to the left.   The state transitions of the gsm are all the information about the machine that can be used.   Table 7.3.1 specifies the transition table of the gsm for this example.

Suppose that the input sequence to the gsm is $\notin abccba\$$.   Then the gsm will be in state S_1 when the second a is reached.   Now suppose that M_1 wishes to move left (the gsm must back up to the second b in the input sequence).   Let k be the number of the square from which M_1 should back up (in this case $k = 7$).   Moving backward across the input tape, we can construct a table of the states which could have been the state of M when it reached each previous square (Table 7.3.2).   The first two columns of the table, containing the number of the square and the symbol in that square, are shown for illustrative purposes only; this information is not stored in the finite-state control of the machine.   In the third column of the table we write some sets of states.   The entries in the third column are generated as follows:

1. In the first row, write the set consisting of the state of the gsm before backing up.
2. In the second row, list sets of states, each set containing a single state S such that, if the gsm had been in state S when reading square $(k - 1)$, it would be in the state listed in the first row when reading square k.   A state will be listed at most once in this row.   Why?
3. In row i $(i \geq 3)$, the jth group of states $G_{i,j}$ contains those states S such that, if the gsm had been in state S when reading square $(k - i + 1)$, it would be in some state from the set $G_{(i-1),j}$ when reading square $(k - i + 2)$.   Some of these sets $G_{i,j}$ may be empty.

For example, $G_{3,1}$ contains both S_1 and S_2 because, with the input symbol c, the next state of M would be S_2 (a state in $G_{2,1}$) whether M were in S_1 or S_2.

At any time in the backing-up process, the finite-state control remembers the information from at most two of the entries in the third column of the table.

It should be clear that the information in any entry in the third column is

Table 7.3.1   The state transitions of the gsm in Example 7.3.1

	a	b	c	$\notin$	$\$$
$\to S_1$	S_2	S_2	S_2	S_1	S_1
S_2	S_3	S_1	S_2	S_2	S_2
S_3	S_1	S_1	S_3	S_3	S_3

Table 7.3.2 Tracing the states of M while running backward from square 7

Square no.	Input symbol	Possible sets of states of M
7	a	(S_1)
6	b	$(S_2), (S_3)$
5	c	$(S_1, S_2), (S_3)$
4	c	$(S_1, S_2), (S_3)$
3	b	$(S_1, S_2, S_3), (\quad)$

finite, and that it can be computed by a finite-state machine while the input head moves to the left. The way the table is constructed, the states in the set $G_{i,j}$ are those states having the property that, if the gsm were in one of them when on square $(k - i + 1)$, then it would be in the state in $G_{2,j}$ when on square $(k - 1)$.

The first problem is: When the gsm was reading square $(k - 1)$, what was its internal state? This state must be one of the entries in the second row of the table.

As the machine moves backward on the input tape trying to resolve this problem, one of the sets $G_{i,j}$ may become null. If this occurs, the machine knows that there could not exist a predecessor of $G_{2,j}$ for the given input sequence. Thus that possibility is eliminated. When all but one of the possibilities are eliminated in this way, the problem is resolved, and the state of M when it was on square $(k - 1)$ is known.

In some cases, the gsm may back up all the way to the left endmarker on the input tape without otherwise resolving the problem. It is known that the gsm started at the left endmarker in its initial state. Thus the problem is resolved; if set $G_{i,k}$ is the one which contains the initial state of M, the state in $G_{2,k}$ must be the answer.

The second problem is to get the reading head back to square $(k - 1)$. We will locate square k from our knowledge of exactly how far the machine had to back up before the first problem could be resolved.

Consider the information in the row just preceding the one where the question was resolved. Let S_i and S_j be two states in different groups on that row. Then consider two experiments in which M is run forward from the square where the first question was resolved. In one experiment we start the machine in state S_i. In the other we start the machine in state S_j. The machines in the two experiments will reach the same state for the first time when M reaches square k. Then the backing-up process can be completed by moving the reading head left one square. ∎

This discussion can be summarized in

Theorem 6   Let $L_1 \in C_1$, a class of balloon automata. Then $\text{gsm}^{-1}(L_1) \in C_1$.

This algorithm succeeds only because M is deterministic. (Why?)

7.3.3 SEQUENTIAL TRANSDUCERS

Sequential transducers (st) are one-way nondeterministic finite-state transducers in which a single step involves reading a (possibly empty) sequence of
input symbols and producing another (possibly empty) sequence of output
symbols. This generalization of a gsm introduces nondeterminism into the
translator. Note that any gsm^{-1} mapping is nondeterministic, and thus a
member of the class st, but the class of mappings defined by the class of sequential transducers is larger than gsm^{-1} because the inverse of a sequential
transducer may not be deterministic. We can use the proof of Theorem 5
to obtain

Theorem 7 If $L_1 \in C_1 \subseteq 1NBA$, then $st\,(L_1) \in C_1$.

7.3.4 ONE-STATE TRANSDUCERS

The spectrum of finite-state translations ranging from csm to st includes a
variety of machines, differing with respect to the restrictions on the use of
input symbols and the production of output symbols. The st class is so
large that it is difficult to find classes of languages which are closed under this
class of mappings. To obtain further results, other types of restrictions must
be considered. For example, we might restrict the number of states in the
transducer. In this section we discuss *one-state* transducers.

A large class of one-state translations is the class of substitutions; in a
substitution each symbol can be (nondeterministically) replaced by some
string from a set of strings—these sets may be different for different input
symbols. A homomorphism is a substitution in which each symbol is replaced by a unique string; it is a deterministic mapping. The most restricted
substitution is an erasure: An input symbol is either copied to the output without change or nothing is output (the symbol is erased). We will see that even
erasures can map many interesting classes of languages into the class of recursive languages. This result severely limits our hopes of obtaining numerous
results concerning more general translations.

Substitutions A *substitution* in a string is performed by a nondeterministic
machine which independently replaces each symbol I_i by a string from a set
$S_i \in O^*$; the set S_i may be infinite. The sets S_i can be different for different
input symbols. The particular string which replaces the jth symbol in the
input sequence may not depend on which sequence replaced the $(j - 1)$st
symbol (the substitution machine has no memory because it has only one
state). The complexity of the result of a substitution depends not only upon
the input language, but also upon the structure of the infinite sets (or languages) S_i. Let $sub\,(C_1,C_2)$ denote the class of languages obtained by substituting strings from languages of class C_1 for symbols in strings from the

languages in class C_2. The arguments used in proving Theorem 5 can be modified to prove

Theorem 8   sub $(1DFSM, C_1) \subseteq C_1$ if $C_1 \subseteq 1NBA$.

A substitution is so general that we cannot make more statements concerning the closure of classes of languages under substitutions.

Homomorphisms   Homomorphisms (homo) are substitutions in which each symbol of the input string is replaced by a unique (possibly empty) word. A homomorphism is a special case of a gsm mapping (with one state in the gsm), and the gsm results can be rephrased:

Theorem 9   If C_1 is accepted by a class of balloon automata, then
$\text{homo}^{-1}(C_1) = C_1$.

Theorem 10 $\text{homo}^{-1}(TMA) = TMA$

Erasures   An important case of a homomorphism is a selectively erasing homomorphism.   In an erasure the symbols in some set T are not erased, and the remaining symbols in the string are erased.   Let erase (L, T) be the set of strings which are formed from the strings of L by erasing all symbols not in T.   Any recursive language can be expressed as the erasure of the intersection of two $1DPDA$ languages.   This result is very important, because it allows one to show that certain mappings applied to certain classes of languages produce recursive languages.   Furthermore, any recursive language can be expressed as the result of these mappings applied to specific languages in the class.   Therefore many mappings of languages can be eliminated from further studies.

The proof of this result is divided into two lemmas.   We will discuss them first.   Next we will use them to prove the theorem.   Then we will discuss nonerasing homomorphisms, which become an important class of mappings in view of this theorem, because without erasing, the set of recursive languages cannot be produced by homomorphism operators applied to simple languages.   Finally, we will show that the erasure of the intersection of two nondeterministic one-counter languages is recursive.   The result gives information about the result of applying erasing mappings to almost every intersection of classes of languages, since most classes of languages include the set of nondeterministic one-counter languages.

Choose a sentence x in an arbitrary recursive language L_0.   Let $V = \{V_1, V_2, \ldots, V_m\}$ be the alphabet of L_0.   Consider a derivation of x in which the sequence of working strings is $S, s_1, s_2, \ldots, s_n$, with $s_n = x$.

Let L_0 be generated by a grammar G_0, with N_0 its set of nonterminal symbols and with p rewriting rules numbered $1, 2, \ldots, p$. Let φ_i denote the left side of the ith rule and ψ_i denote the corresponding right side. Each s_j can be subdivided as follows:

$$s_j = u_{j-1}\psi_{k_{j-1}}w_{j-1} = u_j\varphi_{k_j}w_j \qquad 1 \leq j \leq n$$

into three strings, where k_j is the number of the rule used in the jth step. The left subdivision shows the result of applying the rule for the $(j-1)$st step, and the right subdivision shows the conditions for applying the rule to be used in the jth step.

The derivation of x can be written

$$S \Rightarrow \psi_{k_1} = u_2\varphi_{k_2}w_2 \Rightarrow u_2\psi_{k_2}w_2 = u_3\varphi_{k_3}w_3 \Rightarrow \cdots \Rightarrow u_n\psi_{k_n}w_n = x$$

Consider this entire line to be one string y over an expanded alphabet. From y construct y' by writing the number of the production used in a step immediately to the right of the right side of the production:

$$y' = (S \Rightarrow \psi_{k_1}k_1 = u_2\varphi_{k_2}w_2 \Rightarrow u_2\psi_{k_2}k_2w_2 = u_3\varphi_{k_3}w_3 \Rightarrow \cdots$$
$$\Rightarrow u_n\psi_{k_n}k_nw_n = x)$$

The symbols k_i, chosen from the set $N = \{n_1, n_2, \ldots, n_p\}$, are distinct symbols denoting the rule numbers. Now introduce a new alphabet $\hat{V} = \{\hat{V}_1, \hat{V}_2, \ldots, \hat{V}_m\}$ of symbols which are not used elsewhere and let $\hat{\theta}$ be the string obtained from any string θ by the substitutions $(V_i \to \hat{V}_i, 1 \leq i \leq m)$. Also, let $\hat{G}_0$ denote the grammar obtained from G_0 by these same substitutions. Construct the string $z(x)$, which contains the derivation of x, as follows:

$$z(s) \equiv [S \Rightarrow (\hat{\psi}_{k_1}k_1)^R = \hat{u}_2\hat{\varphi}_{k_2}\hat{w}_2 \Rightarrow (\hat{u}_2\hat{\psi}_{k_2}k_2\hat{w}_2)^R$$
$$= \hat{u}_3\hat{\varphi}_{k_3}\hat{w}_3 \Rightarrow \cdots \Rightarrow (\hat{u}_n\hat{\psi}_{k_n}k_n\hat{w}_n)^R = x]$$

We will now discuss two lemmas concerning $z(x)$.

Lemma 1 Let $Z(G) = \{z(x)|x \in L(G)\}$ for any grammar G. Then erase $(Z(G),V)$ is the language L_0.

Proof Obvious, since the erasure erases all of $z(x)$ except the final x.

Lemma 2 $Z(G)$ is the intersection of two languages in the class $1DPDA$.

Proof (a) Let

$$L_A = \{u_2^R k_j u_1^R = u_1 u_2 \Rightarrow |u_1 u_2 \in \{N_0 \cup \hat{V}\}^*, k_j \in \{n_1, \ldots, n_p\}\}$$

and let

$$L_1 = \{S \Rightarrow x_1\hat{u}_3k_n\hat{u}_4 = x|x_1 \in L_A^*, u_3u_4 = x \in V^*, k_n \in \{n_1, \ldots, n_p\}\}$$

The set L_1 is a deterministic context-free language. In particular, the set L_A contains palindromes with centermarker ($=$) with exactly one symbol from a distinct set (N) inserted into the left-hand side of each palindrome. The set L_1 contains strings formed by a sequence x_1 of palindromes from L_1 separated by markers ($\Rightarrow$). Consider a deterministic pushdown acceptor for L_1. It checks the palindromes until it reaches a right side that begins with a symbol from V, then it checks that the entire right side of that palindrome contains the corresponding symbols from V. If the string terminates after that match, the string is accepted (Fig. 7.3.4).

(b) Let

$$L_B = \{u_1 u_2 u_3 \Rightarrow u_3{}^R k_j u_4{}^R u_1{}^R = |u_1, u_2, u_3, u_4 \in \{N_0 \cup \hat{V}\}^*,$$
$$k_j \in \{n_1, \ldots, n_p\} \text{ and rule } j \text{ of } \hat{G}_0 \text{ is } u_2 \to u_4\}$$

and let

$$L_2 = \{x_2 x_3 | x_2 \in L_B{}^*, x_3 \in V^*\}$$

The set L_2 is a deterministic context-free language. A deterministic pushdown acceptor for L_2 can operate like a recognizer of palindromes with centermarkers until it detects the occurrence of k_j. Then it checks for $\hat{\phi}_j{}^R$ on the pushdown list and for $\psi_j{}^R$ on the input tape; this process checks that the jth rule was applied correctly. Following that check, the normal palindrome matching continues. Whenever an $=$ is read, the pushdown tape must be empty and the palindrome checking is restarted. A string of symbols from V must complete the input string (Prob. 12).

(c) $Z(G) = L_1 \cap L_2$. Obvious, since each language constrains an adjacent pair of sequences from $\{N_0 \cup \hat{V}\}^*$ such that the entire string in $Z(G)$ must have the desired form.   Q.E.D.

These two lemmas directly give

Theorem 11 Every recursive language is the erasure of the intersection of two deterministic context-free languages.

In view of this result, one must restrict substitutions to nonerasing substitutions (sub_λ) in order to obtain interesting results. Some of these results are

Theorem 12 If $L \in C_1 \subseteq 1NBA$, then $\text{sub}_\lambda(L) \in C_1$.

Theorem 13 If $L \in C_1$ and $\text{gsm}^{-1}(L) \in C_1$, then $\text{sub}_\lambda(L) \in C_1$.

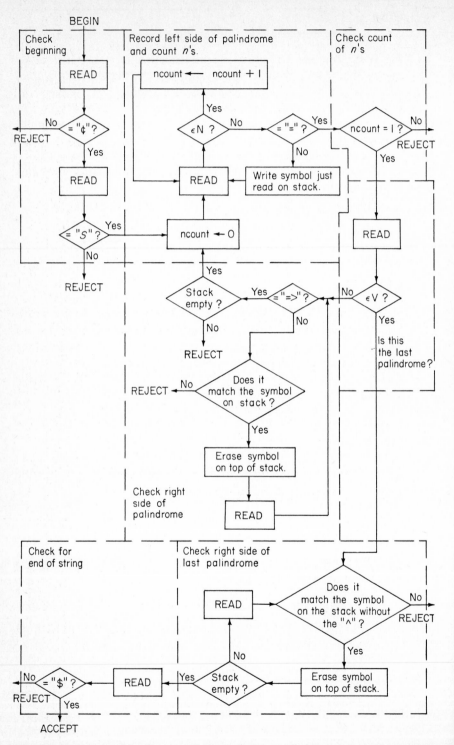

Fig. 7.3.4 The algorithm for recognizing L_1 in the proof of Lemma 2. All questions concern the symbol most recently read from the input tape.

Balloon automata with several balloons A theorem similar to Theorem 11 is true for nondeterministic one-counter languages. It is proved by a slightly different argument. We will prove it by using a more general lemma concerning balloon automata with several balloons. Let C_1 be a closed class of balloon automata in $1NBA$, and let $M_1, M_2, \ldots, M_n$ be n machines in class C_1. Also, let r_i and w_i be the balloon reading and writing functions of the ith machine. Let machine $M_{1,2,\ldots,n}$ be a one-way nondeterministic machine having n balloons, the ith balloon having reading and writing functions r_i and w_{ij}. In one move all the balloons may be read and rewritten.

Lemma 3 The language accepted by $M_{1,2,\ldots,n}$ is the erasure of the intersection of the languages accepted by machines in class $C_1 \subseteq 1NBA$.

Proof In this proof we consider machines which do not read an input symbol unless they also move the reading head to the right one square after using the symbol. This restriction does not reduce the generality of the results, since any machine M which does not meet the condition is equivalent to another machine M' which does meet the restriction (M' remembers the last symbol is read within its finite-state control).

Consider a Mealy machine (Prob. 12 of Sec. 7.2) M having n balloons. Let a move of M be described as a $(2n + 4)$-tuple $I_j, S_q, N_1, N_2, \ldots, N_n, S_k, w_1, w_2, \ldots, w_n$, where N_i is the integer read from the ith balloon and w_i specifies the function to be used in writing the ith balloon. The machine does not read any input symbol without also moving right in the same step. If there is no move, we write a λ in the first position of the tuple. Construct machines $P_i(M), 1 \leq i \leq n$, such that P_i is a nondeterministic acceptor which operates as follows:

1. P_i has the same set of states as M.
2. Suppose P_i is in state S_q, reading N from its balloon, and suppose that $I_j, S_q, N_1, N_2, \ldots, N_{i-1}, N, N_{i+1}, \ldots, N_n, S_r, w_{11}, w_{12}, \ldots, w_{1i}, \ldots, w_{1n}$ is a move of M. Then P_i can move to state S_r, writing in its balloon using w_{1i} while reading the following sequence of input symbols:

$$I_j S_q N_1 N_2 \cdots N_{i-1} N N_{i+1} \cdots N_n S_r w_{11} w_{12} \cdots w_{1i} \cdots w_{1n}$$

The input sequence contains a complete record of the moves made by P_i.

Consider the sequences accepted by $P = P_1 \cap P_2 \cap P_3 \cap \cdots \cap P_n$. A sequence will be accepted by P if and only if it is a complete record of a legitimate move sequence for machine M. If we erase all

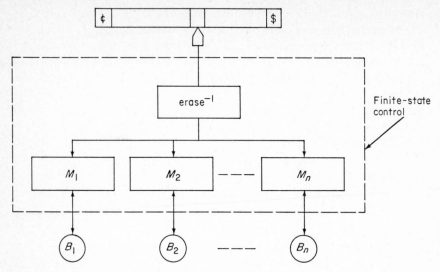

Fig. 7.3.5 An n-balloon acceptor.

the symbols in $L(P)$ but the symbols in I (the input symbols), we obtain the strings in $L(M)$. The constraint that the input head move when reading guarantees that each symbol on the input tape appears exactly once in the strings in P. An acceptor of $L(M)$ has the structure shown in Fig. 7.3.5.   Q.E.D.

Now consider nondeterministic one-counter machines. These form a closed class of *INBA*. Therefore we can apply Lemma 3. Every nondeterministic two-counter language must be the erasure of the intersection of two nondeterministic one-counter languages. But two-counter languages are recursive. Therefore we have

Theorem 14 Any recursive language is the erasure of the intersection of two nondeterministic one-counter languages.

In view of this result, the nonerasing homomorphisms (homo$_\lambda$) become most important. Many classes of languages are closed under homo$_\lambda$. For example, we have

Theorem 15 *INBA* is closed under homo$_\lambda$.

PROBLEMS

1. Find a procedure to generate a regular transformational grammar to describe the action of a given finite-state transducer. Show an example.

2. Prove: gsm $(C) = C$ if $C \subseteq 1NBA$.

3. Let $|x|$ be the number of symbols in a string x. Let $|L| = \{1^{|x|} | x \in L\}$. Show that $|L|$ is in the same class as L if L is accepted by a one-way nondeterministic balloon acceptor or by a two-way nondeterministic rewriting machine.

4. Let $L_2 \backslash L_1 = \{x | yx \in L_1$ for some $y \in L_2\}$; this language is commonly known as the left quotient of L_1 by L_2. Similarly, define $L_1/L_2 = \{x | xy \in L_1$ for some $y \in L_2\}$, the right quotient of L_1 by L_2.

    (a) Let $L_1 \in C_2 \subseteq 1NBA$, and $L_2 \in type\ 3$. Show $L_2 \backslash L_1 \in C_2$.

    (b) State and prove an analogous result concerning L_1/L_2.

    (c) Prove similar results for $L_2 \backslash L_1$ and L_1/L_2 if L_1 is regular.

5. Using the results of Prob. 4, prove that any class of languages accepted by one-way nondeterministic balloon automata having endmarkers can be accepted by another one-way nondeterministic machine of the same class without requiring endmarkers on the input tape.

6. Why cannot the proof of Theorem 6 be used to show gsm $(L_1) \in C_1$?

7. Prove Theorem 7. (*Hint:* Consider Fig. 7.3.6, where M_1 accepts L_1. Is the buffer finite?)

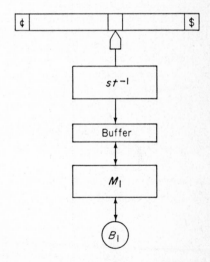

Fig. 7.3.6 A construction to prove Theorem 7.

8. Prove Theorems 9 and 10.

9. Use Theorem 11 to prove that $L_1 \cap L_2 \notin 1NPDA$ if L_1 and L_2 are in $1DPDA$.

10. Prove that if $C_1 \supset 1DPDA$ and C_1 is closed under both homomorphism and intersection, then $C_1 = TMA$.

11. Let C_1 be any closed class of balloon automata. Prove:

    (a) csm$^{-1}(C_1) \subseteq$ csm (C_1)

    (b) csm $(C_1) \subseteq$ gsm$^{-1}(C_1)$

    (c) gsm$^{-1}(C_1) \subseteq$ gsm (C_1)

12. Find a flow chart for the algorithm followed by an acceptor of L_2 in Lemma 2.

13. Why must the machines P_i in the proof of Lemma 3 be nondeterministic?

14. Can one modify the proof of Lemma 3 to cover two-way machines? Explain.

15. Prove: (*a*) st $(LBA) \not\subseteq LBA$

(*b*) gsm $(LBA) \not\subseteq LBA$

(*c*) st $(TMA) = TMA$

16. Let a length-preserving transducer be a transducer for which the length of its output sequence is the same as the length of its input sequence, for all input sequences.

(*a*) Show that a length-preserving sequential transducer preserves the class $NLBA$.

(*b*) Show: homo^{-1} $(DLBA) = DLBA$

homo^{-1} $(NLBA) = NLBA$

[*Hint:* Can you bound the length of homo (x), where x is the input string?]

17. Show: homo $(DLBA) = TMA$.

18. Consider the class of nonerasing homomorphisms (homo$_\lambda$). Let the alphabet of the original strings be V_1, and let V_2 be the alphabet of symbols used in the replacement sequences. Thus

$$\text{homo}_\lambda: V_1 \to V_2{}^+$$

Let $T = \{x | \text{homo}_\lambda\,(y) = x, y \in V_1\}$. We wish to determine the properties of $h \in \text{homo}_\lambda$ such that $h(L_1)$ is in C_1 when $L_1 \in C_1 \subseteq IDBA$. Show that

(*a*) $h^{-1}(L_1)$ is nondeterministic if one string in T is a prefix to another string in T (x is the prefix of y if $y = xu$).

(*b*) $h^{-1}(L_1)$ is deterministic whenever no string in T is the prefix of another string in T.

(*c*) For any h such that $h^{-1}(L)$ is deterministic, $h(C_1) \subseteq IDBA$.

(*d*) (R) What properties should h have so that $h(C_1) \subseteq 2DBA$ where $C_1 \subseteq 2DBA$?

19. Which of the results of this section can be applied to real-time counter and pushdown languages?

7.4 PUSHDOWN TRANSDUCERS

Now we return to the pushdown transducer, a pushdown machine with outputs. This model resembles simplified compilers that translate computer languages into forms understandable by the hardware of the computer. This model is not sufficiently complex to model actual compiler languages, such as

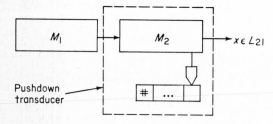

Fig. 7.4.1 A generator for a language produced by a pushdown transducer.

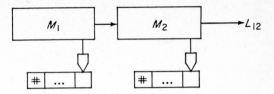

Fig. 7.4.2 A generator for a language in class *DRTPDT(1DPDA)*.

ALGOL—at least a stack machine is required for this purpose. Fortunately, most of the translation processes which take place in compilers can be described as a translation by a pushdown machine; usually, the additional complexity of the stack model is required only to detect violations of subtle constraints. Therefore many practical constraints on the capability of compilers can be ascertained from the theoretical limitations on the translations which can be performed by pushdown machines.

Paralleling the classes of finite-state transducers discussed in the preceding section, we could define several classes of pushdown transducers. In the simplest case the transducer is one-way deterministic and produces one output symbol for each input symbol. For a given language L and a given one-way-deterministic pushdown transducer T, let $DRTPDT(L)$ denote the set of all strings y such that y is the output of T when the input is a string in L. Let $DRTPDT^{-1}$ denote the inverse mapping.

Theorem 1 $DRTPDT(DFSM) \subseteq 1NPDA$

Proof Let M_1 be a finite-state generator for a particular regular language L_1. Let M_2 be the deterministic pushdown transducer. Consider the generator for $L_{21} = M_2(L_1)$ shown in Fig. 7.4.1. Now group M_1 with the finite-state control of M_2 to form a single finite-state control. The new machine is a nondeterministic pushdown generator of L_{21}. Thus $L_{21} \in 1NPDA$.   Q.E.D.

Now consider the pushdown translation of a context-free language. A picture of the generator of the translated language includes two pushdown tapes (Fig. 7.4.2). Thus the translated language is accepted by a pushdown acceptor with two pushdown tapes. If the two-tape acceptor is not allowed λ-moves, and if the two pushdown tapes must be empty for the input string to be accepted, we can almost state that $DRTPDT(DRTPD_1) \subseteq NRTPD_2$. This statement will be true only if the transducer is not considered to have produced an output unless it ends in an accepting condition. When we impose this condition, we must allow the pushdown translator not to translate certain strings over the input alphabet.

In an important special case the input language is context-free and the translator of the language and the generator of the language are "associated." This means that the translator would be an acceptor of the input language if the output symbols produced during the translation process were ignored. If the translator is deterministic, the two pushdown tapes can be merged into one tape, because the two tapes are always manipulated in the same way. Therefore we have

Theorem 2 $T_1(L_2) \subseteq 1DPDA$ if the translator T_1 and the acceptor of L_2 are associated deterministic pushdown machines.

Whenever either machine is nondeterministic, the definition of association between them is more complex (Prob. 1).

The requirement that two pushdown automata be associated may seem to be so strong that the restriction is never met in actual practice.   An interesting practical case is a compiler which is checking the structure of the input sequence at the same time that it is performing the translation.   The machine is simultaneously an acceptor and a translator.   We can apply Theorem 2 to this simple compiler and deduce that only context-free languages can be produced at their outputs.

PROBLEMS

1.   Let M_1 be a nondeterministic acceptor of L, a context-free language.   Let M_2 be a nondeterministic pushdown translator of L to L_1.

(*a*) Give conditions on the descriptions of M_1 and M_2 such that the two machines, when connected as in Fig. 7.4.3, have the same number of symbols on their pushdown tapes at every time, regardless of which string $s \in L$ is input.

(*b*) Modify the configuration in Fig. 7.4.3 to produce a nondeterministic pushdown acceptor for L_1.

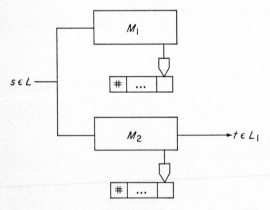

Fig. 7.4.3   An acceptor of a language in parallel with a translator of the language.

2. Prove: sub $(1NPDA,1NPDA) = 1NPDA$.

3. In what class is the pushdown translation of a $DLBA$ language?

4. Consider a deterministic pushdown transducer operating on the output of a pushdown generator. Suppose that the generator and transducer are not associated with each other. Can such a combination produce every recursive language if the transducer can make moves which do not produce output symbols? Explain.

5. Give a formal description of a pushdown transducer.

6. (*a*) Describe a procedure which can be used to find a transformational context-free grammar to describe the actions of a given pushdown translator.

(*b*) Can the transformational grammar of part *a* be used with a context-free generative grammar to prove $1NPDT(1NPDA) = 1NPDA$? Explain.

7. Define "association" between a one-way stack acceptor and a stack transducer such that the one-way stack translation of a one-way stack language by the associated transducer is in the same class of languages. For which varieties of one-way stack machines does your result hold?

8. Let a two-way pushdown transducer be defined to be similar to a one-way pushdown transducer, except that two-way motions are allowed. Show that a two-way pushdown transducer can translate from an infix representation of a mathematical expression to a prefix representation of the same expression. (*Hint:* See Sec. 5.1.)

7.5 REWRITING TRANSDUCERS

Transducers based on machines that can rewrite their input tapes must have tapes on which the input sequence is written. The output may be produced as the machine makes moves or by interpreting the contents of the input tape when the translator halts as the output. Let C be a class of rewriting machines, and let $T_C(C_1)$ represent the class of languages obtained by using transducers from class C to translate languages from class C_1. Translations by writing machines are complex, so not many closure results can be obtained. One is

Theorem 1   (*a*) $T_C(C_1) = C_1$ if $C \subseteq C_1 \subseteq 2NBA$
                   (*b*) $T_C(C_1) = C$ if $C_1 \subseteq C \subseteq 2NBA$

Proof Obvious, by considering a generator of the languages $T_C(C_1)$ as the combination of the translator and a generator of C_1 (similar to Fig. 7.4.2).   Q.E.D.

Rewriting machines with space or time bounds are not balloon automata, so Theorem 1 cannot be applied to them. Turing machines are the only rewriting machines that we have studied which form a closed class of balloon automata. Theorem 1*b* states that the Turing machine translation of a balloon language produces a recursive language. This is hardly surprising.

PROBLEMS

1. Prove: $T_{DLBA}(DLBA) \subseteq NLBA$ if the output is read from the tape when the transducer halts.

2. Prove: Let L_1 be accepted by a Turing machine with tape bound $f_1(n)$, and let T be a translator with tape bound $f_2(n)$. Show that $T(L_1)$ is accepted by a machine with tape bound max $\{f_1(n), f_2(n), f_1(f_2(n)), f_2(f_1(n))\}$.

7.6 INTERSECTIONS WITH REGULAR SETS

Given a language L_1 accepted by an acceptor A_1 and a regular set R accepted by an acceptor A. What kind of language is $L_2 = L_1 \cap R$?

Theorem 1 Let $L_2 = L_1 \cap R$, where R is a regular set. Then L_2 is in the same class of languages as csm^{-1} (L_1).

Proof An acceptor for csm^{-1} (L_1) can be constructed by including a finite-state transducer run forward in the control unit. An acceptor for L_2 can be constructed by including an acceptor A in parallel with an acceptor for L_1 (Fig. 7.6.1). Now call the machine A a csm (which passes its input symbols through to its output). Define the accepting states of A_2 such that both A_1 and A must be in accepting states for the input string to be accepted. A_2 accepts L_2.   Q.E.D.

By Theorem 6 of Sec. 7.3, most classes of languages are closed under gsm^{-1}, and thus under csm^{-1}. Therefore most classes of languages are closed under intersection with a regular set. To extend this result, we might consider intersecting languages with more complex languages. However, since many classes of languages are closed under homomorphisms, and most

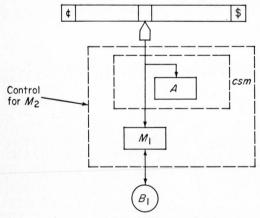

Fig. 7.6.1 An acceptor for $L_1 \cap R$.

include one-counter languages, Theorem 14 of Sec. 7.3 tells us that, if the classes were closed under such intersections, all recursive languages would be in the classes. Therefore intersections with more complex sets do not produce interesting results.

Theorem 1 can be used to form a simple proof that

$$L_4 = \{xx^R | x \in \{0,1\}^*\} \notin 1DPDA.$$

An auxiliary construction is required. Let $P_i(L) = \{y | y \in L$ and exactly $(i - 1)$ of the prefixes of y are in $L\}$.† We do not consider a string to be one of its own prefixes.

Lemma 1 If $L \in C_1 \subseteq 1DBA$, then $P_i(L) \in C_1$ for any i.

Proof To construct an acceptor for $P_i(L)$, equip an acceptor for L with a counter which counts the number of times that an accepting state was reached while the input string was processed. Now require that this counter contain exactly i for the input string to be accepted. The modified machine accepts $P_i(L)$. It is important to note that the counter need not count higher than $i + 1$, a known finite integer. Q.E.D.

Theorem 2 $L_4 = \{xx^R | x \in \{0,1\}^*\} \notin 1DPDA$

Proof Suppose the contrary (that $L_4 \in 1DPDA$). Then, by Lemma 1, $P_i(L_4) \in 1DPDA$. Also, by Theorem 1, $P_i(L_4) \cap R \in 1DPDA$ for any regular set R.

Consider $R = (01)^+(10)^+(01)^+(10)^+$, and let $i = 2$. Thus $L_5 = P_2(L_4) \cap R$ contains those even-length palindromes without centermarker that are contained in R and that have exactly one prefix which is also a palindrome. We wish to show that

$$L_5 = \{(01)^n(10)^n(01)^n(10)^n | n \geq 1\}.$$

There must be two identical symbols adjacent to each other at the center of an even-length palindrome without centermarker. There are only three places in sequences from R where the same symbol occurs in two consecutive positions. The first two are the only positions that could be the center of a palindrome beginning with the first symbol. For a string y to be in L_5, both of these sequences must be palindromes. Let the first of these be x. Since x is a palindrome, it must have the form $(01)^n(10)^n$. For y to be a palindrome, x must be matched by x^R. Therefore L_5 has the form

$$L_5 = \{(01)^n(10)^n(01)^n(10)^n | n \geq 1\}$$

† A prefix of a string y is any string x such that $xz = y$ for some nonempty string z.

Thus $L_5 \notin 1NPDA$, by Lemma 1 of Sec. 5.6.   But if $L_4 \in 1DPDA$, then $L_5 \in 1DPDA$ by Lemma 1 and Theorem 1.   The assumption $L_4 \in 1DPDA$ must be false.   Q.E.D

PROBLEMS

1. In the proofs of the csm^{-1} closure of classes of two-way languages, a complex backing-up algorithm had to be used (Fig. 7.3.3).   Show that a backing-up algorithm is not required for showing closure under intersection with a regular set.   (*Hint:* Consider checking the input string with the finite-state acceptor and then returning to the beginning to run the two-way machine on the input tape.)

2. Prove: $L_1 \cap L_2 \in DLBA$ if $L_1 \in DLBA$, $L_2 \in 1NPDA$.

3. Prove: $P_i(L) \in DLBA$ if $L \in DLBA$.

4. (R) Find an analog of Theorem 1 for intersections with counter languages.

5. (R) Prove: $\{x_1 x_2 x_3 \cdots x_n x_1^R x_2^R \cdots x_n^R | x_i \in \{0,1\}^*, 1 \le i \le n\} \notin DRTPD_n$. (See Conjecture $1d$ of Sec. 6.2.)

7.7 COMMENTS

The various operations described in this chapter have usually been discussed separately for each machine model as it was developed.   The unifying concept of the balloon automaton, which makes these results so easy to prove, was introduced by Hopcroft and Ullman (1967a).   In this chapter we used this unifying model to prove many closure results at one time.   We deferred our discussion of these results until this point to allow the use of this simple concept.

Many of the mappings performed by finite-state transducers first appeared in papers by Ginsburg and others.   The pushdown-transducer mappings are intimately related to compilation processes; these relationships have been studied by many authors.   The surveys by Floyd (1964b) and Feldman and Gries (1968) are especially comprehensive.   Evans (1965) and Lewis and Stearns (1966) formalized the pushdown translation process.   The notion of "association" is found in Ginsburg and Rose (1968).   Other papers related to the translation problem are closely allied with the ambiguity questions discussed in Chap. 9; we refer to those there.

Our proof of Theorem 2 of Sec. 7.6 is a modification of the proof in Ginsburg and Greibach (1966b); our modification eliminates the need for a complex intermediate result which they require.

8
Solvable Linguistic Questions

In Chaps. 2 to 6 we discussed the relationship between languages and machine models. The relationship was based on the idea of a machine as a device for answering the membership question. In Chap. 7 we discussed the effects of transformations on classes of languages. We used the relationship between machines and languages which was developed in the previous discussion.

In the final two chapters we will discuss some other interesting questions about languages. An important question is whether the languages described by two different grammars are equivalent. The writer of a language description would like to describe the language in the simplest way possible. Any proposed alternative description must be checked against the original description to determine whether the two descriptions do, in fact, describe the same language.

Another important question is whether a language is ambiguous. A computer program can be constructed to recognize an ambiguous language, but only one interpretation of a given statement will be found by most programs. This interpretation may not be the same as the one that the writer of the statement had in mind.   If the compiler program does not warn the programmer of this possibility, the programmer may be deceived into thinking that the computer is performing one algorithm while, in fact, it is performing a completely different one.   This situation is not tolerable, so it is essential to determine whether a language is unambiguous or not.   If a grammar is ambiguous, we should search for an equivalent unambiguous grammar. Thus we ask the following question: Given an arbitrary ambiguous grammar, is there an unambiguous grammar which is equivalent to it?

In Chap. 1 we showed that the membership question was solvable for context-sensitive languages.   Because the halting problem for Turing machines is recursively unsolvable, the membership question for recursive languages is recursively unsolvable.   In a similar way, many linguistic questions are solvable for "simple" languages, but as the languages become more complex, the question becomes recursively unsolvable.

One interesting problem is to determine the maximum complexity of a language such that a given question is always solvable, and to show that the question is recursively unsolvable for more complex languages.   In this chapter we introduce some of the questions which might be asked concerning languages, and we will discuss the solvable cases.   In Chap. 9 we will derive a basic unsolvability result and use it to prove certain unsolvability results concerning the same questions.

We discuss certain questions regarding simplifications and equivalence of languages first; then we turn to the most practical and, at the same time, most complex case—the ambiguity question.   The discussion of each question will begin with a concise statement of the question.

8.1   DERIVABILITY

This question is usually phrased in grammatical terms.   The question is

> *Derivability problem*   Given a type i language L generated by a phrase-structure grammar $G = \langle T,N,S,R \rangle$ and two strings $\psi_1, \psi_2 \in \{N \cup T\}^*$, does there exist a derivation in G such that $\psi_1 \Rightarrow^* \psi_2$?

Note that we do not require that $S \Rightarrow^* \psi_1$.

Since a context-sensitive grammar never contains rewriting rules that decrease the length of any string, this question can be answered for any context-sensitive language and any strings ψ_1, ψ_2.   A Turing machine which answers the question examines all derivations which begin with ψ_1.   Whenever a string longer than ψ_2 is produced, that attempt to derive ψ_2 can be abandoned.   Therefore the set of derivations which must be tested is finite. That set can be explored by the Turing machine in finite time.   If ψ_2 is derived, the answer to the question is yes.   On the other hand, if the set of derivations is exhausted before one is found to derive ψ_2, the answer is no.   In Sec. 9.2 we show that the question is unsolvable for recursive languages.

The machine version of a similar question is

> *Reachability problem*   Given a machine M of class C and two instantaneous descriptions ID_1 and ID_2 of M, will M, if started in configuration ID_1, ever reach configuration ID_2?

If M accepts a context-sensitive language, then the reachability question for M is solvable.   In fact, if M operates on a tape whose length is bounded by $f(n)$, where n is the length of the input sequence and f is a recursive function, the reachability question will be solvable (Prob. 1).   However, if M is a Turing machine, the question is unsolvable (Sec. 9.2).

PROBLEMS

1. Show that if M is a Turing machine whose tape length is bounded by $f(n)$, the reachability question is solvable for M if f is a recursive function.

2. Suppose that Turing machine M uses a tape whose length is bounded by $f(n)$, where f is a recursive function.   Let L denote the language accepted by M.   Show that the following questions are solvable:

(*a*) Given state $S_1 \in M$, does M ever reach S_1 in the course of accepting some given $x \in L$?

(*b*) Given a string x, is $x \in L$?

3. Describe a Turing machine which can answer the derivability question for an arbitrary context-sensitive language.   You must specify

(*a*) How the grammar is encoded on the tape (remember that the grammar may have an unlimited number of symbols)

(*b*) How the strings ψ_1 and ψ_2 are encoded

(*c*) The format of the information of items *a* and *b*

(*d*) The algorithm used

8.2 EQUIVALENCE

The language version of the problem is

> *Equivalence problem*   Given two type i grammars G_1 and G_2, do they define the same language?

When G_1 and G_2 are regular, one can show the solvability of the question by constructing two acceptors for the two languages and testing the finite-state machines for equivalence.   This test can be performed by finding the simplest machines equivalent to each of the acceptors and then testing these for equivalence by a straightforward technique, which is discussed in finite-state-machine theory.

If L_1 and L_2 are context-free languages, the equivalence question is unsolvable (Sec. 9.3).

PROBLEMS

1. What is the machine version of the *equivalence problem*?

2. (R) How can one test two regular grammars for equivalence without constructing acceptors for the languages?

3. (R) What can you say about the equivalence problem for two languages which are accepted by counter machines?

8.3 EMPTINESS, COMPLETENESS

These two related questions concern a grammar G and the language L_G it describes. The linguistic versions of the problems are

Emptiness problem Given a type i grammar G, is L_G empty?

Completeness problem Given a type i grammar G with terminal vocabulary T, is $L_G = T^*$?

Suppose that a class of languages were closed under complementation. Then these two problems would be both solvable or both unsolvable for languages in that class, because the complement of any empty language is complete, and vice versa. However, since many classes of languages are not closed under complementation, only one of the problems may be unsolvable for some classes of languages.

The *emptiness problem* is solvable for context-free languages. If there are n nonterminal symbols in the context-free grammar and the language is not empty, some string in the language must have a derivation whose tree is not deeper than $n + 1$ levels. (If there were more levels in the tree, the portion between two identical nonterminal symbols could be removed, creating a shorter tree which describes a derivation of some string in the language.) All trees which have not more than $n + 1$ levels and which represent derivations in G can be systematically searched by a Turing machine to find whether one of them derives a sentence.

For context-sensitive languages, the emptiness problem cannot be solved (Sec. 9.3).

The *completeness problem* is solvable for regular languages (Prob. 1), but not solvable for context-free languages. This result is consistent with the previous discussion because the set of context-free languages is not closed under the operation of complementation.

PROBLEMS

1. Prove that the completeness problem is solvable for regular languages
    (*a*) Using the closure of DFSA under complementation
    (*b*) Without using the closure under complementation

2. State machine versions of the emptiness and completeness problems.

3. Prove that if the emptiness problem is recursively unsolvable for languages in class C_1, then it is recursively unsolvable for languages in class $C_2 \supseteq C_1$.

4. What is wrong with the following reasoning: Since the set of context-free languages is closed under union, V^* is a context-free language, and the equivalence problem is unsolvable for context-free languages, the completeness problem is unsolvable for context-free languages.

5. Prove: If a class C of languages has a solvable emptiness problem and if C is closed under intersection with regular sets, then the *membership question* is solvable for languages in C. (*Hint:* A specific string is a regular set.)

8.4 INFINITENESS

The machine version of the problem is

> *Infiniteness problem*   Given an acceptor A of class C, does A accept an infinite number of different strings?

This problem is not equivalent to the completeness problem, since a language can be infinite without being complete.

The simplest approach to showing that the infiniteness problem is solvable for context-free languages is based on the reasoning used in the proof of Lemma 1 of Sec. 5.6. That lemma asserts the membership of a certain infinite set of strings in a context-free language, given that a string of length greater than some limit is in the language. The infiniteness problem can be solved by testing all strings less than twice that length for membership. This task can be accomplished by a Turing machine.

For context-sensitive languages the infiniteness problem is recursively unsolvable.

PROBLEMS

1. Explain why only strings of length up to $2n$ need be examined when solving the infiniteness problem for context-free languages. Can you place a smaller upper bound on the length of the strings to be examined?

2. Can you solve the infiniteness problem for regular languages by examining the structure of the transition graph of a finite-state acceptor for the language? Explain.

3. Describe a Turing machine to solve the infiniteness problem for context-free languages. You must find
    (a) An encoding to describe the grammar
    (b) An algorithm for the machine
Remember that the number of symbols used in the language is not known beforehand.

8.5 AMBIGUITY

A grammar G is *ambiguous* if there are two derivations of some string $x \in L_G$ which have different derivation trees (Sec. 1.4).   The question of ambiguity is very important when applied to programming languages for computing machines.   If the programming language is ambiguous, there are at least two ways to interpret some sentence in the language.   If the computer translated the statement using a different interpretation than the interpretation used by the programmer, the algorithm actually performed by the machine would not be the same as the algorithm that the programmer thought he had described. This undesirable possibility could not occur if G were unambiguous.   Unfortunately, the ambiguity problem cannot be solved for context-free grammars, which embody many features of most programming languages.

> *Ambiguity problem*   Given a type i grammar G, is there a string $x \in L_G$ which has at least two different derivation trees in G?

Now we prove that the ambiguity problem can be solved for regular grammars.   Let G be a regular grammar with n nonterminal symbols, and suppose that there is at least one string in L_G with two different derivations. Let x be the shortest string which has two different derivations.   Since each step in the derivation of x produces one terminal symbol, and since these terminal symbols are identical (both derivations produce x), the two derivations of x have the same length and can differ only in the nonterminal symbols which appear in the working strings of the derivation.   Construct a sequence of the nonterminal symbols in the order that they appear in the sequence of working strings.   Let the sequence of nonterminal symbols for each of the two nonequivalent derivations D_1 and D_2 of x be as follows:

$$D_1: SN_{11}N_{12} \cdots N_{1p}$$
$$D_2: SN_{21}N_{22} \cdots N_{2p}$$

If i and j represent the first and last positions at which the sequences differ, then

$$N_{1k} = N_{2k} \qquad 1 \le k < i$$
$$N_{1k} \ne N_{2k} \qquad k = i \text{ and } k = j$$
$$N_{1k} = N_{2k} \qquad j < k \le p$$

We will find bounds on the lengths of the three subsequences of symbols. These lengths are $i - 1$, $j - i + 1$, and $p - j$.   To find these bounds we use the fact that x is the shortest word having two derivations.   The first subsequence cannot contain the same symbol twice, because if it did, the symbols between them and one occurrence of the symbol could be removed, leaving one occurrence of the symbol.   This would produce an ambiguous derivation of a string shorter than x. Therefore $i \leq n + 1$. Similarly, $p - j \leq n$. Now consider the pairs of symbols (N_{1k}, N_{2k}) which appear in the middle subsequences. If any pair of symbols appeared twice, the symbols between them and one occurrence of the pair could be removed to produce an ambiguous derivation of a shorter string. Since there are n^2 such pairs, $j - i + 1 \leq n^2$. Combining the limits, we find

$$p \leq n^2 + 2n$$

This places an upper limit on the length of the shortest ambiguous string. By testing all strings of length less than $n^2 + 2n$ for ambiguity, the ambiguity of G can be determined.

The ambiguity problem is unsolvable for context-free languages (Sec. 9.4).

A related problem is

Inherent ambiguity problem   Given a type i language L, does there exist a type i grammar G describing L such that G is unambiguous?

This question is harder to discuss than the ambiguity question, because it is difficult to ascertain that there does not exist any grammar having the desired property. This problem is unsolvable for context-free languages (Sec. 9.5). It is solvable for regular languages (Prob. 2).

PROBLEMS

1. Prove that if L is accepted by a deterministic machine M, then L has an unambiguous grammar. (*Hint:* This grammar will be a member of the set used to describe languages accepted by machines of the same type as M.)

2. Prove that there are no regular languages which are inherently ambiguous. (*Hint:* See Prob. 1.)

3. (R) Is the ambiguity problem solvable for languages in the classes INC_1 and IDC_1?

8.6 COMMENTS

A summary of most of these results is given by Landweber (1964). In the next chapter we continue the discussion of the unsolvable cases of these problems.

9
Unsolvable Linguistic Questions

In Chap. 3 we discussed one unsolvable problem—the *halting problem* for Turing machines. The halting problem is not very useful for proving the unsolvability of linguistic questions. *Post's correspondence problem* is much more useful. Therefore, in this chapter, we first discuss the correspondence problem and prove that it is unsolvable. Unfortunately, there is no simple proof of this important unsolvability result.

After we obtain the basic unsolvability result, we will reduce other unsolvable questions to the correspondence problem. One significant result is that it is recursively unsolvable whether a context-free language is inherently ambiguous. Context-free languages are extremely important for modeling the structure of compiler languages. The negative result forces one to use ad hoc procedures to determine whether there is an unambiguous grammar for a given compiler language.

We close the chapter with a theoretically curious but practically uninteresting demonstration that there exists an infinite hierarchy of unsolvable problems, each one more difficult than all that precede it in the hierarchy.

9.1 POST'S CORRESPONDENCE PROBLEM

Post's correspondence problem is so important in proofs of the unsolvability of linguistic questions that we will discuss the proof of the unsolvability of the correspondence problem.   The proof, by reduction to a special case of the halting problem, is complex.

> *Post's correspondence problem*   Given an alphabet A which contains at least two letters and two sets $\{x_1, x_2, \ldots, x_m\}$ and $\{y_1, y_2, \ldots, y_m\}$ of m nonempty strings over A, does there exist an integer p and integers $i_1, i_2, \ldots, i_p$, with $1 \le i_k \le m$ (for $1 \le k \le p$), such that
>
> $$x_{i_1} x_{i_2} \cdots x_{i_p} = y_{i_1} y_{i_2} \cdots y_{i_p}$$

Post proved that this problem was recursively unsolvable by reducing it to another problem he had previously shown to be unsolvable.   Here we will prove the unsolvability of the correspondence problem from the unsolvability of the modified halting problem (Sec. 3.6.2).   Our proof is a modification of Post's proof.†

The general structure of the proof is as follows: First we show that the halting problem's unsolvability can be used to show the unsolvability of the problem "Does a Turing machine M (with endmarkers), when started with blank tape, ever halt with a blank tape?"   Then we introduce Post normal systems and construct a Post normal system which is related to the machine M.   By examining the set of Post normal systems which are related to all possible Turing machines, we conclude that the existence of a solution to the halting problem would give a solution to the correspondence problem, and vice versa.   Therefore the correspondence problem will be unsolvable.   The argument is divided into three sections: (1) construction of the blank-tape halting problem, (2) introduction of Post normal systems and their relationship to Turing machines and the correspondence problem, and (3) the Post normal system giving the unsolvability result.

The Blank-tape halting problem   In Sec. 3.6.2 we proved that the following problem is recursively unsolvable for the set of Turing machines.

> *Description halting problem*   Given a Turing machine M having its own description on its tape, does M halt?

Let M be a particular Turing machine in D, a set of machines for which the description halting problem is unsolvable.   Another machine M' having endmarkers on its tape can be constructed such that M' simulates M, and M' halts if and only if M halts.   Let D' be the set of all machines using endmarkers constructed from machines M in D.   For every machine M' in D'

---

† Readers who are not interested in the details of the proof may accept the unsolvability on faith and proceed to the next section.

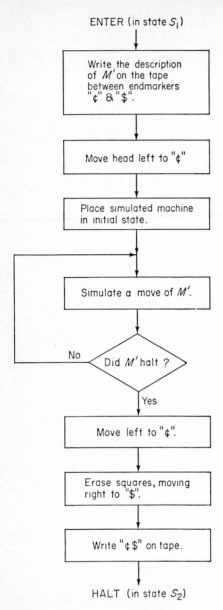

ENTER (in state S_1)

Write the description of M' on the tape between endmarkers "¢" & "$".

Move head left to "¢"

Place simulated machine in initial state.

Simulate a move of M'.

Did M' halt ?

No

Yes

Move left to "¢".

Erase squares, moving right to "$".

Write "¢ $" on tape.

HALT (in state S_2)

Fig. 9.1.1 Flow chart of the simulation used by machines in set D'' to simulate machines in set D'.

a machine M'' can be constructed such that M'' starts with a blank tape and erases the tape only if M' halts when M' is given its own description on the input tape. The set D'' contains all machines M'' constructed in this way from machines in set D'. Each machine in D'' uses the algorithm of Fig. 9.1.1 to simulate a machine in D'.

A machine from set D'' will halt when given a tape with two adjacent endmarkers if and only if the corresponding machine in D halts when given its own description on its input tape. Furthermore, every machine in set D'' transforms the instantaneous description $S_1 \not\in \$$ into $\not\in S_2 \$$ if it halts.

Now consider the

Blank-tape halting problem Given a Turing machine M, will M transform an instantaneous description $S_1 \not\in \$$ into an instantaneous description $\not\in S_2 \$$?

This problem is recursively unsolvable for the nonempty set D''.

Post normal systems A *Post normal system* is a set of rewriting rules for strings over a fixed, finite alphabet V. Each rewriting rule of a Post normal system has the form

$$\alpha_i P \rightarrow P \beta_i$$

where P is a variable which represents the original string with the string α_i deleted from the front end. If a string x has the form $\alpha_i y$, then the rule above can be used to transform it to the string $y \beta_i$. A Post normal system can be specified by a set of pairs of strings $\{(\alpha_1, \beta_1), (\alpha_2, \beta_2), \ldots, (\alpha_m, \beta_m)\}$, where each pair represents one rewriting rule.

Example 1 Let $P = \{(a,bc),(ab,a),(c,ab)\}$ be a Post normal system. A derivation in the Post normal system which begins with the string $aaba$ is as follows:

$x_1 =$ $aaba$		
$x_2 =$ $ababc$		(1)
$x_3 =$ $abca$		(2)
$x_4 =$ caa		(2)
$x_5 =$ $aaab$		(3)
$x_6 =$ $aabbc$		(1)
$x_7 =$ $abbcbc$		(1)
$x_8 =$ $bbcbcbc$		(1)

The numbers to the right of a string denote the number of the rule which was used to obtain that string from the previous one. Since no rules apply to x_8, the derivation must terminate with that string. ■

Let x_j represent the string before the jth step of a derivation, and suppose that the k_jth rule can be applied at step j. Then it must be true that

$$x_j = \alpha_{k_j} u_j \tag{1}$$

Use of the rule gives

$$x_{j+1} = u_j \beta_{k_j} \tag{2}$$

Since k_{j+1} is the number of the next rule applied, we also have

$$x_{j+1} = u_j\beta_{k_j} = \alpha_{k_{j+1}}u_{j+1} \tag{3}$$

and

$$x_{j+2} = u_{j+1}\beta_{k_j+1} \tag{4}$$

Therefore

$$x_j\beta_{k_j}\beta_{k_j+1} = \alpha_{k_j}u_j\beta_{k_j}\beta_{k_j+1} = \alpha_{k_j}\alpha_{k_j+1}u_{j+1}\beta_{k_j+1} = \alpha_{k_j}\alpha_{k_j+1}x_{j+2} \tag{5}$$

If a derivation from x_1 to x_{m+1} requires m steps in which rules $k_1, \ldots, k_m$ were used, then Eq. (6) must be satisfied.

$$x_1\beta_{k_1}\beta_{k_2} \cdots \beta_{k_m} = \alpha_{k_1}\alpha_{k_2} \cdots \alpha_{k_m}x_{m+1} \tag{6}$$

This equation is very similar to the equation which appears in the statement of the correspondence problem. However, the strings x_1 and x_{m+1} must be eliminated from Eq. (6) to make it identical with the equation in the correspondence problem. We return to this detail after we show how a Turing machine can be simulated by a Post normal system.

Post normal systems simulating Turing machines   Every simulation involves an encoding (often trivial) which is used to represent the conditions in the simulated machine in a format convenient for the simulator. When simulating a Turing machine M by a Post normal system $P(M)$, $P(M)$ uses the instantaneous description of M surrounded (for convenience) by the left and right endmarkers $\#_L$ and $\#_R$ to represent the conditions in M. Let w denote one of these strings.

A Post normal system can change only the beginning of the string, and the results of the change are appended to the end of the string. Between the simulations of consecutive moves of the Turing machine, the instantaneous description must be rotated until the neighborhood of the read/write head reaches the beginning of the string. The working string of the Post normal system will be w or a cyclic permutation of w.

Now we construct the rules of the Post normal system which simulates a given Turing machine M. The rules can be divided into three groups: (1) those to simulate moves of M, (2) those which are used to rotate the description to position the neighborhood to be changed near the left end, and (3) those which handle length changes.

The rules in the first group are constructed as follows:

1. If $S_iT_jT_kNS_l$ is a quintuple in M, place the rule (S_iT_j,S_lT_k) in $P(M)$.
2. If $S_iT_jT_kRS_l$ is a quintuple in M, place the rule (S_iT_j,T_kS_l) in $P(M)$.
3. If $S_iT_jT_kLS_l$ is a quintuple in M, place the rule $(T_pS_iT_j,S_lT_pT_k)$ in $P(M)$ for all T_p in the tape alphabet T of M, and for $T_p = \#_L$.

The rules in the second group are used to rotate the description to move the S_i symbol toward the left end so that the next move can be simulated. They are constructed as follows:

4. Place the rule (T_i,T_i) in $P(M)$ for all $T_i \in T$.
5. Place the rules $(\#_L,\#_L)$ and $(\#_R,\#_R)$ in $P(M)$.

The third group of rules deals with length changes. These rules are constructed as follows:

6. Place the rule $(S_i\#_L,\#_LS_ib)$ in $P(M)$ for all $S_i \in S$, where S is the set of states of M and b is the blank symbol.
7. Place the rule $(S_i\#_R,S_ib\#_R)$ in $P(M)$ for all $S_i \in S$.
8. Place the rule $(\$b\#_R,\$\#_R)$ in $P(M)$.
9. Place the rule $(\#_Lb\mathcal{c},\#_L\mathcal{c})$ in $P(M)$.

Example 2 Let a Turing machine M be described by

States: S_1, S_2, S_3
Tape symbols: $\mathcal{c}, \$, 0, 1$
Quintuples: $S_1\mathcal{c}1LS_2$
                 $S_20\mathcal{c}RS_3$
                 S_311RS_3

Let 0 be the blank symbol.

The corresponding Post normal system has the following rewriting rules:

Quintuples	Case used to find rule	Rule
$S_1\mathcal{c}1LS_2$	3	$(\mathcal{c}S_1\mathcal{c},S_2\mathcal{c}1)$
$S_1\mathcal{c}1LS_2$	3	$(\$S_1\mathcal{c},S_2\$1)$
$S_1\mathcal{c}1LS_2$	3	$(0S_1\mathcal{c},S_201)$
$S_1\mathcal{c}1LS_2$	3	$(1S_1\mathcal{c},S_211)$
$S_1\mathcal{c}1LS_2$	3	$(\#_LS_1\mathcal{c},S_2\#_L1)$
$S_20\mathcal{c}RS_3$	2	$(S_20,\mathcal{c}S_3)$
S_311RS_3	2	$(S_31,1S_3)$
—	4	$(\mathcal{c},\mathcal{c})$
—	4	$(\$,\$)$
—	4	$(0,0)$
—	4	$(1,1)$
—	5	$(\#_L,\#_L)$
—	5	$(\#_R,\#_R)$
—	6	$(S_1\#_L,\#_LS_10)$
—	6	$(S_2\#_L,\#_LS_20)$
—	6	$(S_3\#_L,\#_LS_30)$
—	7	$(S_1\#_R,S_10\#_R)$
—	7	$(S_2\#_R,S_20\#_R)$
—	7	$(S_3\#_R,S_30\#_R)$
—	8	$(\$0\#_R,\$\#_R)$
—	9	$(\#_L0\mathcal{c},\#_L\mathcal{c})$

Consider starting M with an instantaneous description $S_1\cent\$$. The corresponding string in the Post normal system is $\#_L S_1 \cent \$ \#_R$. The sequence of strings of the derivation in the normal system is

$$\#_L S_1 \cent \$ \#_R$$
$$\$ \#_R S_2 \#_L 1$$
$$\#_R S_2 \#_L 1 \$$$
$$S_2 \#_L 1 \$ \#_R$$
$$1 \$ \#_R \#_L S_2 0$$
$$\$ \#_R \#_L S_2 01$$
$$\#_R \#_L S_2 01 \$$$

.

.

.

$$\#_L \cent 1 S_3 \$ \#_R$$
$$\cent 1 S_3 \$ \#_R \#_L$$
$$1 S_3 \$ \#_R \#_L \cent$$
$$S_3 \$ \#_R \#_L \cent 1$$

At this point the derivation terminates because no rule can be applied to the string. The last string in the sequence is a cyclic permutation of the instantaneous description of the machine's terminating condition. ■

Rules 1 to 9 can be used to construct a Post normal system $P(M)$ to simulate any given Turing machine M. In particular, if M reaches instantaneous description ID_2 after starting with the instantaneous description ID_1, then $P(M)$ can derive ID_2 from ID_1. Let A and B represent ID_1 and ID_2, respectively. Then, by Eq. (6), there exists a sequence of integers $i_1, i_2, \ldots, i_m$ such that

$$A\beta_{i_1}\beta_{i_2} \cdots \beta_{i_m} = \alpha_{i_1}\alpha_{i_2} \cdots \alpha_{i_m}B \tag{7}$$

where the α's and β's represent the components of the rules of $P(M)$. Furthermore, if there is a solution to Eq. (7) such that A and B are two instantaneous descriptions of M, then M must be able to arrive at B by some sequence of moves which begins at A.

The unsolvability result   Let M'' be a Turing machine in a class D'' for which the blank-tape halting problem is unsolvable. Consider the P'' problem:

P'' problem   Given a Post normal system $P'' = \{(\alpha_1,\beta_1), \ldots, (\alpha_n,\beta_n)\}$, does there exist an integer k and a sequence of integers $i_1, i_2, \ldots, i_k$, $1 \le i_j \le n \, (1 \le j \le k)$, such that

$$\#_L S_1 \cent \$ \#_R \beta_{i_1}\beta_{i_2} \cdots \beta_{i_k} = \alpha_{i_1} \cdots \alpha_{i_k} \#_L \cent S_2 \$ \#_R \tag{8}$$

This problem is recursively unsolvable if P'' can range over the set $P(D'') = \{P(M) | M \in D''\}$, because if P'' were the description of some M'' in D'', a solution to this problem would be equivalent to a solution to the blank-tape halting problem for M''.

As noted above, the P'' *problem* is almost the same as the *correspondence problem*, but the extra sequences at the beginning and end of the equation in the P'' problem must be removed to make them the same. Because those sequences are fixed, they can be removed. The messy construction used to remove them can be divided into three steps.

1. Let x's and y's denote individual symbols. From P'', construct a new Post normal system $f(P'')$ as follows:

   a. For each $(\alpha_i, \beta_i) \in P''$, with $\alpha_i = x_{i_1} x_{i_2} \cdots x_{i_p}$ and $\beta_i = y_{i_1} y_{i_2} \cdots y_{i_m}$, construct

   $$\alpha_1' = :x_{i_1}:x_{i_2}:x_{i_3} \cdots :x_{i_p}$$

   and

   $$\beta_1' = y_{i_1}:y_{i_2}:y_{i_3}: \cdots y_{i_m}:$$

   where : is a symbol not used in the alphabet of P''.

   b. Let $f(P'')$ contain the rewriting rules

   $$(\alpha_1', \beta_1') \qquad 1 \le i \le n$$

   and the two rewriting rules

   $$(;,;:\#_L:S_1:\cent:\$:\#_R:) = (\alpha_{n+1}', \beta_{n+1}')$$
   $$(:\#_L:\cent:S_2:\$:\#_R:;,;) = (\alpha_{n+2}', \beta_{n+2}')$$

2. If the P'' problem can be solved with the sequence in Eq. (8), then the correspondence problem for $f(P'')$ can be solved with the sequences

   $$;:\#_L:S_1:\cent:\$:\#_R:\beta_{i_1}'\beta_{i_2}' \cdots \beta_{i_k}'; =$$
   $$;\alpha_{i_1}'\alpha_{i_2}' \cdots \alpha_{i_k}':\cent_L:\cent:\$:S_2\$:\#_R:; \quad (9)$$

   or

   $$\beta_{n+1}'\beta_{i_1}'\beta_{i_2}' \cdots \beta_{i_k}'\beta_{n+2}' = \alpha_{n+1}'\alpha_{i_1}'\alpha_{i_2}' \cdots \alpha_{i_k}'\alpha_{n+2}' \quad (10)$$

3. Furthermore, if the correspondence problem for $f(P'')$ is solved, say, with

   $$\beta_{j_1}'\beta_{j_2}' \cdots \beta_{j_p}' = \alpha_{j_1}'\alpha_{j_2}' \cdots \alpha_{j_p}' \quad (11)$$

   then

   a. $j_1 = n + 1$, because the only pair of corresponding sequences which begin the same way (with ;) is $(\alpha_{n+1}', \beta_{n+1}')$.

   b. Similarly, $j_p = n + 2$, because $(\alpha_{n+2}', \beta_{n+2}')$ is the only pair of sequences which end the same way.

Therefore, any solution to the correspondence problem in $f(P'')$ must have the form of Eq. (11), in which the sequences satisfy Eq. (9). The existence of a solution to Eq. (9) implies the existence of a solution to the blank-tape halting problem for P''. The correspondence problem for the set $F = f(P(D''))$ is unsolvable because the P'' problem is unsolvable for the set $P(D'')$.

The numerous symbols used in $P(D'')$ could be encoded into sequences of two symbols (Prob. 2), proving that the correspondence problem is unsolvable even when the alphabet contains only two letters.

PROBLEMS

1. Show that if there exists one solution to the correspondence problem for P, then there exists an infinite number of solutions to the problem. (*Hint:* If x is a string which solves the problem, consider x^n, $n \geq 1$.)

2. Let the alphabet of a Post normal system be $\{T_1, T_2, \ldots, T_n\}$. Using the encoding $T_i \rightarrow ba^ib$, show that the correspondence problem is unsolvable for the set of Post normal systems having two-letter alphabets.

3. Show that the correspondence problem is solvable if the alphabet contains only a single letter. (*Hint:* This problem reduces to the solution of a linear equation in integers.)

4. A monogenic normal system is a Post normal system in which not more than one production can be applied to any string over the alphabet. Show that any Turing machine can be simulated by a monogenic normal system. (*Hint:* Consider deterministic Turing machines.)

9.2 DERIVABILITY

The *derivability problem* for recursive languages is unsolvable because it can be reduced to the *halting problem* for Turing machines. In Sec. 3.5 we constructed a recursive language in which the sequence of strings in a derivation was the same as the sequence of instantaneous descriptions of a Turing machine. Therefore, if the derivability problem for recursive grammars were solvable, then the problem "Can a given recursive grammar derive $\#_L \mathcal{c} S_2 \$ \#_R$?" would be solvable. But the latter is the blank-tape halting problem, shown to be unsolvable in the preceding section.

The same argument can be used to show that the *reachability problem* is unsolvable for Turing machines.

PROBLEM

1. Explain why the halting problem as formulated in Sec. 3.6.2 cannot be used directly to prove the results of this section.

9.3 EMPTINESS, COMPLETENESS, EQUIVALENCE

The *completeness* and *equivalence problems* are recursively unsolvable for context-free languages. The emptiness problem is unsolvable for *DLBA* languages. To show the unsolvability result for these problems we define a class of context-free languages based on the correspondence problem. Let $\{\alpha_1, \alpha_2, \ldots, \alpha_n\}$ be a set of n nonnull sequences over the alphabet $\{a,b\}$. Let $R(i) = ba^i b$, the i a positive integer, be the representation of the integer i. Define the language $L(\alpha,n)$ as follows:

$$L(\alpha,n) = \{R(i_1)R(i_2) \cdots R(i_k)bb\alpha_{i_k}\alpha_{i_k-1} \cdots \alpha_{i_1} | k \geq 1,$$
$$1 \leq i_j \leq n \text{ for } 1 \leq j \leq k\}$$

This is a context-free language generated by a grammar with the rewriting rules

$$\left.\begin{array}{l} S \rightarrow R(i)A\alpha_i \\ A \rightarrow R(i)A\alpha_i \end{array}\right\} \text{ for all } 1 \leq i \leq n$$
$$A \rightarrow bb$$

Furthermore $L(\alpha,n) \in 1DPDA$. A deterministic acceptor for $L(\alpha,n)$ can use the occurrence of three b's in a row as a centermarker. Since $L(\alpha,n) \in 1DPDA$, $\sim L(\alpha,n) \in 1DPDA$ (Prob. 4 of Sec. 5.6 or Prob. 1 of Sec. 7.2).

Now consider the intersection problem:

Intersection problem Given two languages L_1 and L_2 of class C_1, is their intersection empty?

We now show that the intersection problem is recursively unsolvable for deterministic pushdown languages over a two-letter alphabet.

Consider the language

$$L_3(\alpha,\beta,n) = L(\alpha,n) \cap L(\beta,n)$$

Any string in L_3 must begin with a representation of a sequence $(i_1, \ldots, i_m)$ of the integers between 1 and n, inclusive, followed by a centermarker. Following the centermarker, there must be a word $w \in \{a,b\}^*$ satisfying

$$w = \alpha_{i_m}\alpha_{i_m-1} \cdots \alpha_{i_1} = \beta_{i_m}\beta_{i_m-1} \cdots \beta_{i_1}$$

The set $L_3(\alpha,\beta,n)$ is empty if and only if there is no solution to this equation defining w. This equation has a solution if and only if the correspondence problem for the sets (α,β) does. But that problem is unsolvable if the pairs (α,β) are allowed to range over the correspondence problems in set F (defined at the end of Sec. 9.1). Therefore the intersection problem is recursively unsolvable for the set of deterministic context-free languages. Since the intersection of any two context-free languages is in $DLBA$, the emptiness problem for $DLBA$ languages is recursively unsolvable, even if there are only two symbols in the alphabet of the language.

Now consider the *completeness problem*. By taking complements, the question

$$L_1 \cup L_2 = T^*?$$

can be reduced to

$$(\sim L_1) \cap (\sim L_2) = \varphi?$$

The language $\sim L(\alpha,n)$ is in the class $1DPDA$. Thus

$$L_4 = (\sim L(\alpha,n)) \cup (\sim L(\beta,n))$$

is context-free. The completeness problem for L_4 is the same as the intersection problem for $L(\alpha,n)$ and $L(\beta,n)$. That question is unsolvable. Therefore the completeness problem is recursively unsolvable for context-free languages over two-letter alphabets.

The equivalence problem is easily resolved. Since T^* is a context-free language and the question

$$L_4 = T^*?$$

is unsolvable, the equivalence problem for two context-free languages over two-letter alphabets must be recursively unsolvable. Therefore we cannot find an algorithm to determine in all cases whether two specifications of context-free programming languages do indeed specify the same language. If the two language specifications are sufficiently restricted, a solution to the equality problem may be found.

PROBLEMS

1. Find a flow-chart description of an algorithm which could be used by a deterministic pushdown machine to accept $L(\alpha,n)$ for a given set $\{\alpha_1, \ldots, \alpha_n\}$.

2. Prove: If the completeness problem is recursively unsolvable for the set of languages C_1, then it is also recursively unsolvable for the languages in any set $C_2 \supseteq C_1$.

3. Show that the intersection problem is recursively unsolvable for two languages in the class $2DPDA$.

4. Consider the problem: "Given a context-sensitive grammar, does there exist a context-free grammar to define the same language?" Construct

$$L_5(\alpha,\beta,n) = \{uu \mid u \in L_3(\alpha,\beta,n)\}$$

(*a*) Show that if L_5 is not empty, then it is not context-free. (*Hint:* Use Lemma 1 of Sec. 5.6.)

(*b*) Show that the emptiness problem is unsolvable for the set of languages of the form of L_5 when (α,β) ranges over the set F, and hence that the problem above is unsolvable.

(*c*) Is the result of Prob. 3 of Sec. 3.3 consistent with these results? Explain.

5. Show that the problem "Is $L_3(\alpha,\beta,n)$ finite?" is recursively unsolvable, and hence that the finiteness problem is recursively unsolvable for the set of $DLBA$ languages. (*Hint:* See Prob. 1 of Sec. 9.1.)

6. Consider the *inclusion problem:* Given two languages L_1 and L_2 in class C, is $L_1 \subseteq L_2$?

    (a) Show that the inclusion problem is equivalent to the equality problem.

    (b) Show that the inclusion problem is unsolvable for context-free languages.

7. Can one determine whether any pair of one-way nondeterministic pushdown acceptors are equivalent? Explain.

8.   (a) Show that the language $L(\alpha,n) \cap L(\beta,n) \in 2DSA$.

    (b) Show that the emptiness and finiteness (does a language contain only a finite number of strings?) problems are unsolvable for the class $2DSA$.

9. Consider the problem: "Given two Turing machine acceptors, do they accept the same language?" Show that this problem is recursively unsolvable.

10. Prove that the emptiness problem is recursively unsolvable for machines in the class $DRTPD_2$.

9.4 AMBIGUITY

The question of whether a context-free grammar is ambiguous will now be discussed. It is a very important question for computer-language specifications, as discussed in Chap. 8. We use the languages $L(\alpha,n)$ to construct another context-free language $L_6(\alpha,\beta,n)$ as follows:

$$L_6(\alpha,\beta,n) = L(\alpha,n) \cup L(\beta,n)$$

The language $L(\alpha,n)$ has an unambiguous grammar, since the grammar for $L(\alpha,n)$ specified in Sec. 9.3 is unambiguous for any α and n. A context-free grammar G_6 for $L_6(\alpha,\beta,n)$ can be constructed from the unambiguous grammars for $L(\alpha,n)$ and $L(\beta,n)$ by using S_1 and S_1' for the two sentence symbols of $L(\alpha,n)$ and $L(\beta,n)$ and adding the rules $S \to S_1$ and $S \to S_1'$, where S is the sentence symbol in the grammar for L_6. In this grammar a string x will have two derivations if and only if it is in both $L(\alpha,n)$ and $L(\beta,n)$. Thus G_6 will be unambiguous if and only if the intersection problem is solvable for the languages $L(\alpha,n)$ and $L(\beta,n)$. But if the pair (α,β) ranges over the set F, this question is recursively unsolvable. Therefore the ambiguity problem is recursively unsolvable for context-free languages.

PROBLEMS

1. Consider the grammar $G(\alpha,\beta,n)$ with the following rewriting rules:

$$S \to S_1 \qquad\qquad S \to S_2$$
$$S_1 \to \alpha_i S_1 R(i) \qquad S_2 \to \beta_i S_2 R(i) \qquad 1 \le i \le n$$
$$S_1 \to : \qquad\qquad S_2 \to :$$

Show that $L(G(\alpha,\beta,n))$ is ambiguous if and only if there is a solution to the correspondence problem for (α,β).

2. Is the following argument correct? Explain.

    Every context-free language is context-sensitive language. The ambiguity problem for context-free languages is recursively unsolvable. Therefore the ambiguity problem is recursively unsolvable for context-sensitive languages.

9.5 INHERENT AMBIGUITY

Another important question is whether a given grammar specifies a language which is inherently ambiguous.   A type i language is inherently ambiguous if there does not exist an unambiguous type i grammar for the language.   The major problem in any discussion of this question is to show that a grammar having the desired properties (that it be unambiguous and that it specify the given language) does not exist.

First, we prove that there does not exist an unambiguous context-free grammar for the context-free language

$$L_7 = \{a^i b^i c^j | i, j \geq 1\} \cup \{a^i b^j c^j | i, j \geq 1\}$$

Suppose that an unambiguous context-free grammar G exists such that $L(G) = L_7$.   We will show that this assumption leads to a contradiction.

Let N be the set of nonterminal symbols of G, with S the sentence symbol, and let x, y, z denote strings of terminal symbols from the set $\{a,b,c\}$.

A nonterminal symbol A is superfluous if either there do not exist strings x, y such that $S \Rightarrow^* xAy$ or there does not exist a string z such that $A \Rightarrow^* z$.   Form G' from G by eliminating any superfluous A along with any productions which contain any superfluous A.   The elimination of the superfluous nonterminal symbol A cannot change the derivations of strings in $L(G)$, since A cannot appear in any derivations of strings.   Thus G' is unambiguous and $L(G') = L(G) = L_7$.   In the remainder of the argument we consider only G'.

Let $N' = \{N_1, \ldots, N_l\}$ be the set of nonterminal symbols of G'.   We will divide the set N into five mutually exclusive sets A, B, C, D, and E.

The set $A = \{A_1, \ldots, A_{l_1}\}$ contains those nonterminal symbols A_i such that there do not exist x, y such that $A_i \Rightarrow^* xA_iy$ is a derivation in G'. Let an A-derivation be a derivation in G' which uses only nonterminal symbols from set A.   Any A-derivation must produce a finite-length string in $L(G')$. Let n_1, n_2, and n_3 denote the maximum numbers of a's, b's, and c's, respectively, which could be produced by an A-derivation.   (The n_1 a's may appear in a different derivation from the one in which the n_2 b's appears.)   Let $m = \max(n_1, n_2, n_3)$.

The set $B = \{B_1, \ldots, B_{l_2}\}$ contains those nonterminal symbols B_i such that there exists a derivation $B_i \Rightarrow^* xB_iy$ with $xy = a^p$ for some $p \geq 1$.

The set $C = \{C_1, \ldots, C_{l_3}\}$ contains those nonterminal symbols C_i such that there exists a derivation $C_i \Rightarrow^* xC_iy$ with $xy = c^p$ for some $p \geq 1$.

The set $D = \{D_1, \ldots, D_{l_4}\}$ contains those nonterminal symbols D_i such that there exists a derivation $D_i \Rightarrow^* a^{p_i} D_i b^{p_i}$ for some $p_i \geq 1$.

The set $E = \{E_1, \ldots, E_{l_5}\}$ contains those nonterminal symbols E_i such that there exists a derivation $E_i \Rightarrow^* b^{q_i} E_i c^{q_i}$ for some $q_i \geq 1$.

We now show that sets $A, \ldots, E$ are mutually exclusive and that every nonterminal symbol in N' is in one of these sets. In this discussion we rely on the fact that every string in L has the form $a^ib^jc^k$ ($i = j$ or $k = j$, $i, j, k \geq 1$). Set A is exclusive of the others because any symbol in the others cannot meet the condition for membership in A.

To show that B and C must be mutually exclusive, assume the contrary; then there exists $N_k \in N'$, which is in both B and C. Then the following derivations exist:

$$S \Rightarrow^* xN_ky \Rightarrow^* xzy = a^tb^uc^v$$

and

$$S \Rightarrow^* xN_ky \Rightarrow^* xx_1{}^{m_1}N_ky_1{}^{m_1}y \Rightarrow^* xx_1{}^{m_1}x_2{}^{m_2}N_ky_2{}^{m_2}y_1{}^{m_1}y \Rightarrow^*$$
$$xx_1{}^{m_1}x_2{}^{m_2}zy_2{}^{m_2}y_1{}^{m_1}y = w$$

for arbitrary integers m_1 and m_2. There are two symmetric cases to consider. In one case, suppose $x_1y_1 = a^r$ and $x_2y_2 = c^s$. Then it must be true that $y_1 = \lambda$, because otherwise in w those a's from y_1 would follow the c's from x_2 and/or y_2. Similarly, $x_2 = \lambda$, because otherwise c's would precede b's in w. Thus $w = a^{t+m_1r}b^uc^{v+m_2s}$ would be in the language for any m_1 and m_2. But not all these strings are in L. Hence B and C are disjoint. The mutual exclusivity between the other pairs of sets is shown by similar arguments.

Now we show that every nonterminal symbol $N_i \in N$ is in one of the sets $A, \ldots, E$. The only symbols which need to be considered are those which do not meet the condition for membership in set A. Thus consider N_i such that $N_i \Rightarrow *x_iN_iy_i$ for some $x_i, y_i \in \{a,b,c\}^*$. Since all superfluous nonterminal symbols have been removed from G', there must exist a derivation

$$S \Rightarrow^* xN_iy \Rightarrow^* xuy$$

Also, there exist derivations

$$S \Rightarrow^* xN_iy \Rightarrow^* xx_iN_iy_iy \Rightarrow^* xzy$$
$$S \Rightarrow^* xN_iy \Rightarrow^* xx_i{}^2N_iy_i{}^2y \Rightarrow^* xx_izy_iy$$

and

$$S \Rightarrow^* xN_iy \Rightarrow^* xx_i{}^3N_iy_i{}^3y \Rightarrow^* xx_i{}^2zy_i{}^2y$$

First, it must be true that $x_i \in \{a^*\} \cup \{b^*\} \cup \{c^*\}$, for otherwise the string $xx_i{}^2zy_i{}^2y$ would not be in $a^* b^* c^*$. Similarly, $y_i \in \{a^*\} \cup \{b^*\} \cup \{c^*\}$.

Second, it cannot be true that $x_i = y_i = \lambda$, because if so, there would be two derivations,

$$S \Rightarrow^* xN_iy \Rightarrow^* xzy$$
$$S \Rightarrow^* xN_iy \Rightarrow^* xN_iy \Rightarrow^* xzy$$

of different length for the same string xzy, contrary to the assumption that G' is unambiguous.

Now we must enumerate the remaining cases according to which symbols appear in x_i and y_i. The arguments for all cases are similar. We will discuss only the case $x_i \in a^*$. If $y_i \in a^*$, the symbol N_i is in set B. Thus $y_i \in b^*$ and $y_i \in c^*$ are the two other cases. Consider $x_i = a^r$, $y_i = b^s$. Then there exist derivations

$$S \Rightarrow^* xN_iy \Rightarrow^* xzy = a^tb^uc^v$$

and

$$S \Rightarrow^* xN_iy \Rightarrow^* xx_i{}^{m_1}N_iy_i{}^{m_1}y \Rightarrow^* xx_i{}^{m_1}zy_i{}^{m_1}y = a^{t+m_1r}b^{u+m_1s}c^v$$

which give strings in $L(G')$, for any $m_1 > 0$. Each of these strings must have either the same numbers of a's and b's or the same numbers of b's and c's. Thus, for all m_1, we must have either

$$t + m_1r = u + m_1s$$

or

$$u + m_1s = v$$

The latter cannot be true since m_1 is arbitrary. Therefore we must have $t = u$ and $r = s$. If $r = s$, then N_i is in set D. We conclude that if

$$N_i \Rightarrow^* x_iN_iy_i$$

with $x_i = a^r$ and $y_i = b^s$, then $r = s$ and N_i is in set D. A symmetric argument can be used to show that the case $x_i = b^r$, $y_i = c^s$, $r \neq s$, is impossible, and if $r = s$, N_i would be in set E. The argument that the case $x_i = a^r$, $y_i = c^s$ is impossible is similar to the argument we used to show that B and C are disjoint. The remaining possibilities such as $x_i = c^r$, $y_i = a^s$ are easily shown to be impossible.

Thus we have

Lemma 1 In an unambiguous context-free grammar for the language $L_7 = \{a^ib^ic^j | i, j \geq 1\} \cup \{a^ib^jc^j | i, j \geq 1\}$, every nonterminal symbol N satisfies one and only one of the following conditions:

(a) There do not exist $x, y \in \{a,b,c\}^*$ such that $N \Rightarrow^* xNy$.
(b) $N \Rightarrow^* xNy$, $xy = a^r$ for some $r \geq 1$.
(c) $N \Rightarrow^* xNy$, $xy = c^r$ for some $r \geq 1$.
(d) $N \Rightarrow^* a^{p_i}Nb^{p_i}$ for some $p_i \geq 1$.
(e) $N \Rightarrow^* b^{q_i}Nc^{q_i}$ for some $q_i \geq 1$.

Now let $Q = (\prod p_i)(\prod q_i)$, where the products are taken over all values of p_i and q_i for which the relationships in D or E hold for any N. By construction, every p_i and q_i divides Q. Remember that m is the maximum number of copies of one symbol which can occur in a string derived in an A-derivation. Let $M > m$ be a multiple of Q (and thus a multiple of every p_i and q_i).

Consider a derivation of the string $s_1 = a^M b^M c^{2M}$. Any derivation of s_1 must contain some occurrences of nonterminal symbols from sets D or E, because otherwise s_1 could not have more than m b's. Suppose that a nonterminal symbol $E_i \in E$ were used in the derivation. Then

$$S \Rightarrow^* xE_iy \Rightarrow^* xzy = a^M b^M c^{2M} = s_1$$

and

$$S \Rightarrow^* xE_iy \Rightarrow^* xb^M E_i c^M y \Rightarrow^* xb^M zc^M y = a^M b^{2M} c^{3M} = s_2$$

are derivations in G'. This is impossible, since the string s_2 is not in L_7. The derivation of s_1 must use some nonterminal symbols from set D, and none from set E. But then there exist derivations

$$S \Rightarrow^* D_iy \Rightarrow {}^*xzy = a^M b^M c^{2M} = s_1$$

and

$$S \Rightarrow^* xD_iy \Rightarrow^* xa^M D_i b^M y \Rightarrow^* xa^M zb^M y = a^{2M} b^{2M} c^{2M} = s_3$$

The latter derivation does not use any nonterminal symbols from set E, and does use some from set D.

Now consider a derivation of $s_4 = a^{2M} b^M c^M$. An argument which is symmetric to the preceding one shows that derivations of s_4 cannot use any nonterminal symbols from set D and must use some from set E. Also, there must be a derivation

$$S \Rightarrow^* xE_iy \Rightarrow^* xb^M E_i c^M y \Rightarrow^* xb^M zc^M y = a^{2M} b^{2M} c^{2M} = s_3$$

which uses nonterminal symbols from set E and does not use any nonterminal symbols from set D. This derivation of s_3 must be different from the previous derivation of s_3. Therefore G' is ambiguous. This contradiction to the assumption proves that there cannot exist an unambiguous context-free grammar for L_7. Thus we have shown

Theorem 1 L_7 is an inherently ambiguous context-free language.

The unsolvability of the *inherent ambiguity problem* is obtained by inserting $L(\alpha,q)$ and $L(\beta,q)$ into strings of L_7 to form a new language L_8:

$$L_8(\alpha,\beta,q) = \{a^n xb^n c^m \,|\, x \in L(\alpha,q); m, n \geq 1\} \cup$$
$$\{a^n yb^m c^m \,|\, y \in L(\beta,q); m, n \geq 1\}$$

If the correspondence problem for (α,β) does not have a solution, the intersection of the two sets in $L_8(\alpha,\beta,q)$ is empty, and there is an unambiguous grammar for $L_8(\alpha,\beta,q)$.

On the other hand, if the correspondence problem for (α, β) has a solution, the intersection of $L(\alpha, q)$ and $L(\beta, q)$ contains at least one string. Let x be one string in that intersection. Then some strings of the form $a^n x b^n c^n$ will have at least two derivations in any context-free grammar for $L_8(\alpha, \beta, q)$, and the language will be inherently ambiguous.

The inherent ambiguity problem is recursively unsolvable for any family of languages which contains the set of languages $L_8(\alpha, \beta, q)$, where (α, β) range over F. Thus the inherent ambiguity problem is recursively unsolvable for context-free languages.

In Prob. 2 we prove that there does exist an unambiguous recursive grammar for any recursive language.

PROBLEMS

1. Show that $L_8(\alpha, \beta, q)$ would have an unambiguous context-free grammar if the correspondence problem for (α, β) did not have a solution.

2. Show that there are no inherently ambiguous recursive languages. Comment on the relationship between this result and the unsolvability of the inherent ambiguity problem for context-free languages.

3. Show that the inherent ambiguity problem would be solvable for context-sensitive languages if $DLBA = NLBA$. (*Hint:* See Prob. 1 of Sec. 8.5.)

4. Is the following argument correct? Explain. (See Prob. 2 of Sec. 9.4.)
Every context-free language is a context-sensitive language. The inherent ambiguity problem is recursively unsolvable for context-free languages. Therefore the inherent ambiguity problem is recursively unsolvable for context-sensitive languages.

9.6 AN INFINITE HIERARCHY OF UNSOLVABLE PROBLEMS

Now we discuss a theoretical curiosity which is not of any practical value to the compiler-builder—an infinite hierarchy of unsolvable problems in which each problem is "harder" than its predecessors in the hierarchy.

Consider a class of Turing machines which have "oracles." A Turing machine with an oracle can consult the oracle to determine the answer to a specified true-false question concerning the string which is contained on that portion of the tape located to the right of the read/write head and to the left of a special endmarker !. Any move by the Turing machine can depend on the answer of the oracle rather than on the input symbol. In the quintuples of the machine, we describe this dependence by writing Y or N in place of the input symbol; Y means that the move can be made if the oracle answers yes and N specifies a move which can be made when the answer is no.

All the problems in the particular infinite family of problems that we will discuss are based on the halting problem. Let T_0 be the set of Turing machines which halt when given their own description on the input tape. Let the set T_i $(i \geq 1)$ contain those Turing machines with oracle i (to be defined in a moment) which halt when given their own descriptions on the input tape. Now suppose that we build a machine E_i with an oracle i such that E_i answers the question, "Is the input string a description of a machine in T_i?"†

We first show that E_i does not exist. Suppose otherwise. Then E_i halts for every input tape and gives an answer yes or no. Now construct a machine E'_i from E_i by causing E'_i to halt whenever E_i answers no, and to enter an infinite loop whenever E_i answers yes. Thus E'_i halts when given input tape x only if $x \notin T_i$. Suppose that E'_i were in T_i. Then E'_i would not halt when given its own description, by the construction of the machine. But by assumption, E'_i is in T_i, which is a contradiction. Similarly, suppose that $E'_i \notin T_i$. Then, by the construction of E'_i, it would halt, but by the assumption, it does not halt. Thus E'_i must not exist. Note that this argument does not depend on the definition of the oracle.

Now let oracle i answer the question "Is x in T_{i-1}?," where x is the string presented to the oracle. With this type of oracle, the set T_i contains a machine which answers the question, "Is the input string a description of a machine in T_{i-1}?" This machine is not in T_{i-1}. Thus T_i contains a machine that is not in T_{i-1}.

Let us call one unsolvable problem P_1 harder than another problem P_2 if a Turing machine with an oracle which answers P_2 cannot solve P_1. From the preceding argument, there exists an infinite sequence of unsolvable halting problems, each one harder than the one before.

An infinite hierarchy of sets of strings with members V_i $(i \geq 1)$ can be constructed as follows: Let

$$V_i = \bigcup_{k=0}^{i} T_k$$

where T_k is the set of languages accepted by machines in the set T_k.

Each set V_i contains descriptions of machines which can answer the membership question for V_{i-1}, but not for V_i. Thus the membership questions for the sets V_i increase in difficulty as i increases. These sets constitute an infinite set of classes of languages which are progressively larger than the set of recursive languages.

PROBLEMS

1. Show that a balloon automaton which is allowed to use a nonrecursive function to read or write the balloon can recognize a language which is not recursive. (*Hint:* Use the nonrecursive function as an oracle.)

2. (R) Is there an infinite hierarchy of Post correspondence problems corresponding to the hierarchy T_i? Can these problems be applied to linguistic questions?

† We still have not defined the oracle.

9.7 COMMENTS

The solvability-unsolvability results are summarized in Appendix 3.   Landweber (1964) summarizes most of these solvability-unsolvability results. Post (1946) described the correspondence problem and proved it to be unsolvable.   Hierarchies of unsolvable problems have been introduced by several writers.   Ours is similar to one used by Hartmanis and Hopcroft (1968) to compare the difficulties of some of the problems shown to be unsolvable earlier in this chapter.   Our proof of the inherent ambiguity of L_7 is based upon Maurer (1969).

Many workers have searched for machine models which accept only unambiguous languages.   Most of these models depend upon the determinism of the machine (Prob. 1 of Sec. 8.5)   Others use procedures in the model which are patterned after the mode of operation of most compiler programs.   References to many of these papers are listed in the Bibliography; the interested reader might start with Feldman and Gries (1968) for a survey of practical applications and some references to theoretical papers.

Appendix 1
Abbreviations

This appendix contains a listing of the abbreviations used in this book to denote sets of languages, in alphabetical and numerical order. We give a word description of each set of languages.

Abbreviation	Denotes the set of languages
DLBA	Accepted by deterministic linear-bounded acceptors
$DRTC_n$	Accepted by deterministic real-time acceptors which have n counters
$DRTPD_n$	Accepted by deterministic real-time pushdown acceptors which have n pushdown tapes
DTMA	Accepted by deterministic Turing machine acceptors
NLBA	Accepted by nondeterministic linear-bounded acceptors
$NRTC_n$	Accepted by nondeterministic real-time acceptors which have n counters
$NRTPD_n$	Accepted by nondeterministic real-time pushdown acceptors which have n pushdown tapes
NTMA	Accepted by nondeterministic Turing machine acceptors
Type 0	Defined by recursive grammars
Type 1	Defined by context-sensitive grammars
Type 2	Defined by context-free grammars
Type 3	Defined by regular grammars
1DBA	The set of one-way deterministic balloon automata
$1DC_n$	Accepted by one-way deterministic acceptors which have n counters
1DFSA	Accepted by one-way deterministic finite-state acceptors
1DNESA	Accepted by one-way deterministic stack acceptors which cannot erase symbols on the stack
1DPDA	Accepted by one-way deterministic pushdown acceptors
1DSA	Accepted by one-way deterministic stack acceptors
1NBA	The set of one-way nondeterministic balloon automata
$1NC_n$	Accepted by one-way nondeterministic acceptors which have n counters
1NFSA	Accepted by one-way nondeterministic finite-state acceptors
1NNESA	Accepted by one-way nondeterministic stack acceptors which cannot erase symbols on the stack
1NPDA	Accepted by one-way nondeterministic pushdown acceptors
1NSA	Accepted by one-way nondeterministic stack acceptors
2DBA	The set of two-way deterministic balloon automata
2DFSA	Accepted by two-way deterministic finite-state acceptors
2DNESA	Accepted by two-way deterministic stack acceptors which cannot erase symbols on the stack
2DPDA	Accepted by two-way deterministic pushdown acceptors
2DSA	Accepted by two-way deterministic stack acceptors
2NBA	The set of two-way nondeterministic balloon automata
2NFSA	Accepted by two-way nondeterministic finite-state acceptors
2NNESA	Accepted by two-way nondeterministic stack acceptors which cannot erase symbols on the stack
2NPDA	Accepted by two-way nondeterministic pushdown acceptors
2NSA	Accepted by two-way nondeterministic stack acceptors

Appendix 2
Relationships between
Classes of Languages

Tables A.2.1 and A.2.2 give a summary of the relationships between many classes of languages. In Table A.2.1 each nonequivalent class is listed in the first column; the classes which are equivalent are listed in the second column. The third and fourth columns summarize the hierarchy; the sets which strictly include the class or weakly include it are listed. The final column lists the class of balloon automata within which the class of languages belongs. Table A.2.2 specifies the class which includes languages obtained by performing Boolean operations and reversals on the language included in the set which labels the row.

Those results which were proved in this text are referenced to the text: T denotes theorem, P denotes problem, S denotes the section where the result was discussed, and C denotes conjecture.

Other results in the table are obvious (O), left as exercises (E), or can be found by reference (R) to the list of references below.

When a result is proved by using a property of a class of balloon automata, the reference at the result refers to the property of the class.

A triple-numbering system is used to indicate the section; e.g., T2.4.1 refers to Theorem 1 of Sec. 2.4.

The references corresponding to R1 to R7 are as follows:

R1: Ginsburg and Greibach (1966b)
R2: Ginsburg, Greibach, and Harrison (1966)
R3: Ginsburg, Greibach, and Harrison (1967)
R4: Gray, Harrison, and Ibarra (1967)
R5: Hopcroft and Ullman (1967b)
R6: Schkolnick (1968)
R7: Ullman (1969)

Table A.2.1   Inclusions among language classes

Class (x)	$x =$	$x \subset$	$x \subseteq$	Balloon class of x
$1DFSA$	$1NFSA$(T2.4.1) $2DFSA$(T2.6.1) $2NFSA$(P2.6.5) $Type\ 3$(T2.5.1)	$1DC_1$(P5.8.5)		$1DBA$(E)
$1DPDA$		$1NPDA$(T7.6.2) $2DPDA$(T6.1.1) $1DSA$(E)		$1DBA$(S7.2)
$1NPDA$	$Type\ 2$(T5.5.1)	$DLBA$(T5.7.1) $2NPDA$(T6.1.1)		$1NBA$(P7.2.6)
$DLBA$		$2DNESA$(R4)	$NLBA$(T4.3.1)	
$NLBA$	$Type\ 1$(T4.4.1)	$2DSA$(T6.4.4) $2NNESA$(T6.4.2)†		
$DTMA$	$NTMA$(S3.4) $Type\ 0$(T3.5.2)			
$1DC_1$		$1DPDA$(E) $1NC_1$(E) $1DC_2$(E) $2DC_1$(E)		$1DBA$(P7.2.9)
$1NC_1$		$1NC_2$(E) $2NC_1$(E)		$1NBA$(P7.2.9)
$2DC_1$			$2NC_1$(O) $2DPDA$(O)	$2DBA$(P7.2.9)
$2NC_1$			$2NPDA$(O)	$2NBA$(P7.2.9)
$1DC_2$	$DTMA$(T6.3.1)			
$DRTC_1$		$1DPDA$(E) $NRTC_1$(T6.3.4) $DRTC_2$(T6.3.3)		
$NRTC_1$		$1NPDA$(E) $NRTC_2$(T6.3.3)		
$DRTC_p$		$NRTC_p$(T6.3.4) $DRTC_{p+1}$(T6.3.3) $DLBA$(E) $DRTPD_p$(E)		

Table A.2.1 (*continued*)

Class (x)	$x =$	$x \subset$	$x \subseteq$	Balloon class of x
$NRTC_p$		$NRTC_{p+1}$(T6.3.3) $NLBA$(E) $NRTPD_p$(E)		
$2DPDA$		$DLBA$(R4)	$2NPDA$(O)	$2DBA$(P7.2.7)
$2NPDA$			$2NSA$(O)	$2NBA$(P7.2.7)
$1DPD_2$	$DTMA$(T6.2.1)			
$DRTPD_p$		$DLBA$(C6.2.1) $NRTPD_p$(C6.2.1) $DRTPD_{p+1}$(C6.2.1)		
$NRTPD_p$		$NLBA$(E)	$NRTPD_{p+1}$ (C6.2.1)	
$1DNESA$			$1DSA$(O)	$1DBA$(P7.2.10)
$1DSA$		$1NSA$(R2)		$1DBA$(P7.2.10)
$1NNESA$			$1NSA$(O)	$1NBA$(P7.2.10)
$1NSA$		$DLBA$(R6)		$1NBA$(P7.2.10)
$2DNESA$		$2NNESA$(R5)	$2DSA$(O)	$2DBA$(P7.2.10)
$2DSA$		$2NSA$(E)		$2NBA$(P7.2.10)
$2NNESA$			$2NSA$(O)	$2NBA$(P7.2.10)
$2NSA$		TMA(R3)		$2NBA$(P7.2.10)

†A recent result by O. Ibarra (personal communication) proves the strict inclusion.

Table A.2.2 Effects of operations on language classes

Class (x)	$L_1 \cap L_2 \in$	$L_1 \cup L_2 \in$	$\sim L_1 \in$	$L^R \in$
$1DFSA$	$1DFSA$(P2.5.6)	$1DFSA$(P2.5.6, T5.6.1)	$1DFSA$(P2.5.6)	$1DFSA$(P2.5.4)
$1DPDA$	$DLBA$(T4.2.1, T5.7.1) $2DPDA$(E)	$1NPDA$(T5.6.1) $2DPDA$(E)	$1DPDA$(P5.6.4)	$1NPDA$(R1)
$1NPDA$	$DLBA$(T4.2.1, T5.6.3)	$1NPDA$(T5.6.1)	$DLBA$(T4.2.2, T5.7.1)	$1NPDA$(P7.2.2)
$DLBA$	$DLBA$(T4.2.1)	$DLBA$(T4.2.2)	$DLBA$(T4.2.2)	$DLBA$(E)
$NLBA$	$NLBA$(T4.2.1)	$NLBA$(T4.2.3, T5.6.1)	$2DSA$(E)	$NLBA$(E)
$DTMA$	$DTMA$(P3.4.2, P3.5.3)	$DTMA$(P3.4.2, P3.5.3)	——(P3.6.1)	$DTMA$(P3.5.4)
$1DC_1$	$1DC_2$(E)	$1NC_1$(E)	$1DC_1$(P7.2.1)	$1NC_1$(E)
$1NC_1$	$1NC_2$(E)	$1NC_1$(P7.2.5)	$DLBA$(E)	$1NC_1$(P7.2.2)
$2DC_1$	$2DC_1$(E)	$2NC_1$(E)	$DLBA$(E)	$2DC_1$(P7.2.3)
$2NC_1$	$2NC_1$(E)	$2NC_1$(P7.2.5)	$DLBA$(E)	$2NC_1$(P7.2.3)
$DRTC_1$	$DRTC_2$(E)	$DRTC_2$(E) $NRTC_1$(E)	$DRTC_1$(P7.2.1)	$NRTC_1$(E)

Table A.2.2 *(continued)*

Class (x)	$L_1 \cap L_2 \in$	$L_1 \cup L_2 \in$	$\sim L_1 \in$	$L^R \in$
$NRTC_1$	$NRTC_2$(E)	$NRTC_1$(E)	$DLBA$(E)	$NRTC_1$(P7.2.2)
$DRTC_p$	$DRTC_{2p}$(E)	$NRTC_p$(E) $DRTC_{2p}$(E)	$DRTC_p$(P7.2.1)	$NRTC_p$(P6.3.6)
$NRTC_p$	$NRTC_{2p}$(E)	$NRTC_p$(P7.2.5)	$DLBA$(E)	$NRTC_p$(P6.3.6)
$2DPDA$	$2DPDA$(E)	$2NPDA$(E)	$DLBA$(E)	$2DPDA$(P7.2.3)
$2NPDA$	$2NPDA$(E)	$2NPDA$(P7.2.5)	$DTMA$(E)	$2NPDA$(P7.2.3)
$DRTPD_p$	$DRTPD_{2p}$(E)	$NRTPD_p$(E) $DRTPD_{2p}$(E)	$DRTPD_p$(P7.2.1)	$NRTPD_p$(E)
$NRTPD_p$	$NRTPD_{2p}$(E)	$NRTPD_p$(P7.2.5)	$DLBA$(E)	$NRTPD_p$(P7.2.2)
$1DNESA$	$DLBA$(E)	$1NNESA$(E)	$1DNESA$(P6.4.7)	$2DNESA$(E)
$1DSA$	$DLBA$(E)	$1NSA$(E)	$1DSA$(P6.4.7)	$2DSA$(E)
$1NNESA$	$DLBA$(E)	$1NNESA$(P7.2.5)	$DLBA$(E)	$1NSA$(E)
$1NSA$	$DLBA$(E)	$1NSA$(P7.2.5)	$DLBA$(E)	$1NSA$(P7.2.2)
$2DNESA$	$2DNESA$(E)	$2DNESA$(E)	$2DNESA$(R5)	$2DNESA$(P7.2.3)
$2DSA$	$2DSA$(E)	$2DSA$(E)	$2DSA$(R7)	$2DSA$(P7.2.3)
$2NNESA$	$2NNESA$(E)	$2NNESA$(P7.2.5)	$DTMA$(E)	$2NNESA$(P7.2.3)
$2NSA$	$2NSA$(E)	$2NSA$(P7.2.5)	$DTMA$(E)	$2NSA$(P7.2.3)

Solvability Results

In Table A.3.1 we list results concerning the solvability or unsolvability of linguistic questions. The symbols S and U are used to denote "solvable" and "recursively unsolvable," respectively. The word "never" in the inherent ambiguity question denotes that languages of that class are never inherently ambiguous. The notation for references is similar to the one used in Appendix 2. A separate list of references is given at the end of the table.

For statements of the questions, see Chaps. 8 and 9.

Many of the results listed in this table are the direct consequence of implications concerning the unsolvability or solvability of certain problems, based upon the inclusion of one set of languages within another. The sources of these results are not indicated in the table. Usually, the source is one of the following:

P8.3.3
P8.5.1
P9.3.2
Hopcroft and Ullman (1968a)

The blanks in the table indicate positions where it is not known whether or not the problem is unsolvable.

Table A.3.1 Solvability results

Class	Membership	Equality	Emptiness	Completeness	Infiniteness	Ambiguity	Inherent ambiguity
$1DFSA$	S	S(S8.2)	S	S(S8.3)	S	S(S8.5)	Never
$1DPDA$	S		S	S	S	S(R1)	Never
$1NPDA$	S	U(S9.3)	S(S8.3)	U(S9.3)	S(S8.4)	U(S9.4)	U(S9.5)
$DLBA$	S	U	U(S9.3)	U	U(S9.3)		Never
$NLBA$	S(S8.1)	U	U	U	U	U	
$DTMA$	U(S9.2)		U	S	S	U	Never
$1DC_1$	S		S		S		Never
$1NC_1$	S		S		S		
$2DC_1$	S						Never
$2NC_1$	S						
$DRTC_1$	S		S	S	S	U	Never
$NRTC_1$	S		S		S		U
$DRTC_p(p \geq 2)$	S						
$NRTC_p(p \geq 2)$	S						
$2DPDA$	S	U(R3)	U(R3)	U(R3)	U(R3)		Never
$2NPDA$	S	U(R3)	U(R3)	U(R3)	U(R3)		Never
$DRTPD_p(p \geq 2)$	S	U	U	U	U		Never
$NRTPD_p(p \geq 2)$	S		U	U	U		Never
$1DNESA$	S		S	S			Never
$1DSA$	S		S	S			Never
$1NNESA$	S	U	S	U			
$1NSA$	S	U	S	U			
$2DNESA$	S	U	U	U	U		Never
$2DSA$	S(R2)	U	U	U	U		Never
$2NNESA$	S	U	U	U	U		
$2NSA$	S	U	U	U	U		

R1: Ginsburg and Greibach (1966b)

R2: Ginsburg, Greibach, and Harrison (1967)

R3: Gray, Harrison, and Ibarra (1967)

Bibliography

This bibliography contains many, but certainly not all, of the important theoretical papers and books concerning those parts of automata theory which are discussed in this text. Additional references can be found in the bibliographies of these papers and books. Most of the new theoretical work in the field is published in one of the following journals:

Information and Control
Journal of the Association for Computing Machinery
Journal of Computer and System Science
Mathematical System Theory
Proceedings of the Annual Symposia on Switching and Automata Theory, sponsored by IEEE
Proceedings of the Annual Symposia on the Theory of Computing, sponsored by ACM

Each citation contains the name(s) of the author(s) and year of publication (the latter with letters when needed, to remove ambiguity); the pertinent text chapter and section number(s); the reference to the paper and a short description of the aspects of the paper most interesting to automata theorists. (The shorᵗ description is omitted in some cases when the title explains the contents.) The section number may be followed by letters, which should be interpreted as follows:

A   Application of the theory
B   Basic result; usually an original paper
E   Extension of the theory beyond the coverage in this text
G   General source on mathematical linguistics
L   Bibliography
S   Survey of a particular portion of the theory

In addition, some citations are followed by a reference to a published review in *Computing Reviews*, having the form CR7703 (shown in brackets). The number is the sequence number of the review; since all reviews in CR are numbered sequentially, we do not cite the particular volume or issue in which the review was published. *Computing Reviews* classifies every reviewed paper by content; the papers most relevant to the material of this text are catalogued in category 5.22.

The following abbreviations are used:

BSTJ	Bell System Technical Journal
Comm. ACM	Communications of the Association for Computing Machinery
CR	Computing Reviews (see above)
IBM Jour. R and D	IBM Journal of Research and Development
IEEE	Institute of Electrical and Electronics Engineers
Info. and Control	Information and Control
JACM	Journal of the Association for Computing Machinery
JCSS	Journal of Computer and System Science
MST	Mathematical System Theory

ACM Curriculum Committee (1968) [G]: CURRICULUM 68, *Comm. ACM*, vol. 11, no. 3, pp. 151–197, Mar. 1968. Details of a proposed curriculum in computer science at undergraduate and graduate levels.

Aho, A. V. (1967) [5E]: Indexed Grammars—An Extension of Context-free Grammars, *Proc. 8th Ann. Symp. on Switching and Automata Theory*, Oct. 1967, *IEEE Publ.* 16C56, pp. 21–31 [CR16745]. Also in *JACM*, vol. 15, no. 4, pp. 647–671, Aug. 1968. A family of languages between context-sensitive and context-free.

———— (1969) [6.4E]: Nested Stack Automata, *JACM*, vol. 16, no. 3, pp. 383–406, July 1969 [CR18314]. Describes a family of machines to accept the family of languages defined in Aho (1967).

————, J. E. Hopcroft, and J. D. Ullman (1968a) [5.7E]: Time and Tape Complexity of Pushdown Automaton Languages, *Info. and Control*, vol. 13, no. 3, pp. 186–206, Sept. 1968 [CR17545]. A recognition algorithm for languages in *2NPDA*.

Aho, A. V., and J. D. Ullman (1968b) [5A,E]: Automaton Analogs of Syntax Directed Translation Schemata, *Proc. 9th Ann. Symp. on Switching and Automata Theory*, Oct. 1968, *IEEE Publ.* 68-C-50-C, pp. 143–159. Formal models for pushdown translation processes.

——, ——, and J. E. Hopcroft (1970) [5E]: On the Computational Power of Pushdown Automata, *JCSS*, vol. 4, no. 2, pp. 129–136, Apr. 1970 [CR20378].

Amar, V., and G. Putzolu (1964) [5E]: On a Family of Linear Grammars, *Info. and Control*, vol. 7, no. 3, pp. 283–291, Sept. 1964 [CR7703]. A subset of the set of linear context-free languages is introduced.

——, and —— (1965) [2.3E]: Generalizations of Regular Events, *Info. and Control*, vol. 8, no. 1, pp. 56–63, Feb. 1965 [CR8331]. Also in E. R. Caianiello (ed.), "Automata Theory," Academic, New York, 1966, pp. 1–5. An extension of Amar and Putzolu (1964).

Arbib, M. A. (ed.) (1968) [2E,S]: "Algebraic Theory of Machines, Languages and Semigroups," Academic, New York, 1968 [CR16026]. Highly mathematical treatment of finite-state problems.

—— (1969) [G]: "Theories of Abstract Automata," Prentice-Hall, Englewood Cliffs, N.J., 1969.

Arden, D. N. (1960) [2.3B]: Delayed Logic and Finite State Machines, pp. 1–35, in "Theory of Computing Machine Design," University of Michigan Press, Ann Arbor, 1960. Solution of regular expression equations.

Bar-Hillel, Y., M. Perles, and E. Shamir (1961) [8,9, 5.6B]: On Formal Properties of Simple Phrase Structure Grammars, in Y. Bar-Hillel (ed.), "Language and Information," Addison-Wesley, Reading, Mass., 1964, pp. 116–150 [CR7178]. Basic results on context-free languages. Original source of Lemma 1 of Sec. 5.6.

Blum, M., and C. Hewitt (1967) [3E]: Automata on a Two-dimensional Tape, *Proc. 8th Ann. Symp. on Switching and Automata Theory*, *IEEE Publ.* 16C56, pp. 155–160, Oct. 1967. A finite-state machine on a two-dimensional tape. Several results related to pattern recognition and some unsolvable questions.

Bodnarchuk, V. G. (1965a) [2.3E]: The Metrical Space of Events, *Kibernetica*, vol. 1, no. 1, pp. 24–27, 1965. How a measure might be applied to sets of strings.

—— (1965b) [2.3E]: Analysis of Weighted Graphs by the Method of Solving Systems of Equations in Algebra of Events, MT-63-257, art. 27. Solution uniqueness in set equations having nonregular solutions.

Book, R. V., and S. A. Greibach (1970) [6.2E]: Quasi-realtime Languages, *MST*, vol. 4, no. 2, pp. 97–111, June 1970. Proof that the set of real-time definable n-tape nondeterministic Turing machine languages can be recognized by a nondeterministic machine with one stack and one pushdown tape (or three pushdown tapes without a stack).

Booth, T. (1967) [G]: "Sequential Machines and Automata Theory," Wiley, New York, 1967 [CR15238]. Material on sequential circuit problems; also several chapters on Turing machines and languages, but no proofs of relationships between machine models and linguistic models.

Brady, A. H. (1966) [3.6.1]: The Conjectured Highest Scoring Machines for Rado's $\sum(k)$ for the Value $k = 4$, *IEEE Trans.*, vol. PGEC-15, no. 5, p. 802, Oct. 1966. Some busy-beaver function evaluations.

Brainerd, B. (1967) [5.6E]: An Analog of a Theorem about Context-free Languages, *Info. and Control*, vol. 11, nos. 5–6, pp. 561–567, 1967 [CR15241]. Extensions of Lemma 1 of Sec. 5.6 to more general cases.

Brooker, R., and D. Morris (1962) [5A]: A General Translation Program for Phrase Structure Languages, *JACM*, vol. 9, no. 1, pp. 1–10, Jan. 1962. An early syntax-directed compiler is summarized.

Brzozowski, J. A. (1962) [2.3A,S]: A Survey of Regular Expressions and Their Applications, *IEEE Trans.*, vol. EC-11, pp. 324–335, June 1962.

——— (1963) [2.3A]: Canonical Regular Expressions and Minimal State Graphs for Definite Events, in "Mathematical Theory of Automata," Polytechnic Institute of Brooklyn, New York, 1963. Regular expressions for a subclass of finite-state machines.

——— (1964a) [2.3A,B]: Derivatives of Regular Expressions, *JACM*, vol. 11, no. 4, pp. 481–494, Oct. 1964 [CR7359]. How to get a transition table from a regular expression.

——— (1964b) [2.3A]: Regular Expressions from Sequential Circuits, *IEEE Trans.*, vol. EC-13, no. 6, pp. 741–744, Dec. 1964 [CR9796]. How to get a regular expression from a transition graph.

———, and E. J. McCluskey (1963) [2.3]: Signal Flow Graph Techniques for Sequential Circuit State Diagrams, *IEEE Trans.*, vol. EC-12, no. 2, pp. 67–76, Apr. 1963. How to get regular expressions from transition graphs by using flow-graph techniques.

Caianiello, E. R. (ed.) (1966) [G]: "Automata Theory," Academic, New York, 1966 [CR10935]. Various papers from this are separately referenced.

Chaitin, G. J. (1965) [2E]: An Improvement on a Theorem of E. F. Moore, *IEEE Trans.*, vol. EC-14, pp. 466–467, June 1965. Theorem is in Moore (1956).

Chartres, B. A., and J. J. Florentin (1968) [5A]: A Universal Syntax-directed Top-down Analyzer, *JACM*, vol. 15, no. 3, pp. 447–463, July 1968 [CR15766]. A parsing algorithm for any simplified context-free grammar; time bounds are placed on the recognition process.

Cheatham, T. E., Jr., and K. Sattley (1964) [5A]: Syntax-directed Compiling, *Proc. Spring Joint Computer Conf.*, vol. 25, pp. 31–57, Spartan Books, Baltimore, Md., 1964 [CR6304]. Basic paper, with detailed examples of syntax-directed compilation.

Chomsky, N. (1956) [1B]: Three Models for the Description of Language, *IRE Trans.*, vol. IT-2, pp. 113–124, 1956. Early paper on language classification.

——— (1959a) [1B]: On Certain Formal Properties of Grammars, *Info. and Control*, vol. 2, pp. 137–167, 1959. An early paper on the classification of languages.

——— (1959b) [1B]: A Note on Phrase Structure Grammars, *Info. and Control*, vol. 2, pp. 393–395, 1959. Simplified proof of result in Chomsky (1959a).

——— (1962) [5B]: Context-free Grammars and Pushdown Storage, *MIT Res. Lab. Electron. Quart. Progr. Rep. 65*, 1962, pp. 187–194.

——— (1963) [1B]: Formal Properties of Grammars, in Luce, Bush, and Galanter (eds.), "Handbook of Mathematical Psychology," vol. 2, Wiley, New York, 1963, pp. 323–418 [CR10731]. Modified version of Chomsky (1959a).

———, and M. P. Schutzenberger (1963) [1B]: The Algebraic Theory of Context-free Languages, in Braffort and Hirschberg (eds.), "Computer Programming and Formal Systems," North-Holland Publishing Company, Amsterdam, 1963, pp. 118–161. Use of formal power series to answer ambiguity questions.

Cohen, J. M. (1967) [1E]: The Equivalence of Two Concepts of Categorical Grammar, *Info. and Control*, vol. 10, pp. 475–484, May 1967. Grammars with cancellation rules are studied; see bibliography for the basic papers on this subject.

Cook, S. A. (1968) [4E]: Off-line Turing Machine Computations, *Proc. Hawaii Int. Conf. on System Sciences*, pp. 14–16, University of Hawaii Press, Honolulu, Jan. 1968 [CR16273]. Some space bounds are used to classify functions.

——— (1969) [6.2E]: Variations on Pushdown Machines, detailed abstract in *Proc. First Ann. Symp. on Theory of Computing*, pp. 229–231. Complete paper as Characterizations of Pushdown Machines in Terms of Time-bounded Computers,

JACM, vol. 18, no. 1, pp. 4–18, Jan. 1971. Introduces pushdown machines with Turing machine tapes and places interesting time bounds on some simulations they can perform.

Copi, I. M., C. C. Elgot, and J. B. Wright (1958) [2.3B]: Realization of Events by Logical Nets, *JACM*, vol. 5, pp. 181–196, 1958. Reprinted in Moore (1964). Equivalences between regular expressions and the sets of strings accepted by networks of AND, OR, NOT logical devices. Expansion on Kleene (1956).

Cudia, D. F. (1970) [9E]: General Problems of Formal Grammars, *JACM*, vol. 17, no. 1, pp. 31–43, Jan. 1970. Extension of Cudia and Singletary (1968) to examinations of the degrees of unsolvability of various problems.

———, and W. E. Singletary (1968) [9E]: Degrees of Unsolvability in Formal Grammars, *JACM*, vol. 15, no. 4, pp. 680–692, Oct. 1968 [CR16747]. A refinement of the correspondence problem and its application to some unsolvable questions.

Davis, M. (1958) [G]: "Computability and Unsolvability," McGraw-Hill, New York, 1958. Mathematical presentation of Turing machines and the associated theories.

——— (ed.) (1965) [3.6,9]: "The Undecidable: Basic Papers on Undecidable Propositions, Unsolvable Problems, and Computable Functions," Raven Press, Hewlett, N.Y., 1965 [CR9790]. A collection of various papers on unsolvability.

Dennis, J. B., and P. D. Denning (1972) [G]: "Machines, Languages, and Computation," Prentice-Hall, New York, to be published.

Earley, J. (1970) [5.1A]: An Efficient Context-free Parsing Algorithm, *Comm. ACM*, vol. 13, no. 2, pp. 94–102, Feb. 1970 [CR19258]. Good algorithm which does not depend on the class of the grammar.

Eilenberg, S., and J. B. Wright (1967) [2E]: Automata in General Algebras, *Info. and Control*, vol. 11, no. 4, pp. 452–470, Oct. 1967. Very abstract—old results in new formalism.

Elgot, C. C., and J. E. Mezei (1965) [2E]: On Relations Defined by Generalized Finite Automata, *IBM Jour. R and D*, vol. 9, pp. 47–68, 1965 [CR11632]. Some properties of multitape finite-state machines.

Evans, A., Jr. (1965) [5A]: Syntax Analysis by a Production Language, Carnegie Institute of Technology, Pittsburgh (thesis), 1965. A linguistic approach to specification of the translation of a context-free programming language.

Evey, J. (1963) [5B]: The Theory and Application of Pushdown Store Machines: Mathematical Linguistics and Automatic Translation, *Harvard Comput. Lab.*, *Rep.* NSF-10, Cambridge, Mass., 1963.

Feder, J. (1968) [A]: Languages of Encoded Line Patterns, *Info. and Control*, vol. 13, no. 3, pp. 230–244, Sept. 1968. A simple application of automata theory to pattern recognition.

Feldman, J., and D. Gries (1968) [5A]: Translator Writing Systems, *Comm. ACM*, vol. 11, no. 2, pp. 77–113, Feb. 1968 [CR14729]. A survey of the field of compiler-compilers and syntax-directed compilation, in which the syntax is given as input to a program which either produces a compiler (former case) or is the compiler (latter case). Extensive bibliography.

Fischer, M. J. (1968) [5A,E]: Grammars with Macro-like Productions, *Proc. 9th Ann. Symp. on Switching and Automata Theory, IEEE Publ.* 68-C-50-C, pp. 131–142, Oct. 1968. An attempt to give to the rewriting rules some of the features of modern assembly programs.

Fischer, P. C. (1965a) [3.1]: On Formalisms for Turing Machines, *Proc. 6th Ann. Symp. on Switching and Automata Theory*, 1965. Later version in *JACM*, vol. 12, no. 4, pp. 570–588, Oct. 1965 [CR10558]. See also Herman (1968). Simple results concerning restrictions in Turing machine moves.

Fischer, P. C. (1965b) [S]: Multi-tape and Infinite-state Automata: A Survey, *Comm. ACM*, vol. 8, 12, pp. 799–805, Dec. 1965 [CR10561]. Bibliography and survey.

—— (1966) [6S]: Turing Machines with Restricted Memory Access, *Info. and Control*, vol. 9, no. 4, pp. 364–379, Aug. 1966 [CR12414]. Proofs about *n*-counter and *n*-pushdown machines which allow λ-moves.

——, A. R. Meyer, and A. L. Rosenberg (1967) [6.3B]: Real Time Counter Machines, *8th Ann. Symp. on Switching and Automata Theory, IEEE Publ.* 16C56, pp. 148–154, Oct. 1967. See also Counter Machines and Counter Languages, *MST*, vol. 2, pp. 265–283, 1968. Time and space bounds on the complexity of counter languages. Results establishing that $n + 1$ counters give more languages than n counters do.

Floyd, R. W. (1962) [5A]: On the Non-existence of a Phrase Structure Grammar for ALGOL 60, *Comm. ACM*, vol. 5, no. 9, pp. 483–484, 1962. Discussion of how side constraints remove ALGOL from the class of context-free languages.

—— (1963) [5A]: Syntactic Analysis and Operator Precedence, *JACM*, vol. 10, no. 4, pp. 316–333, July 1963. One approach to practical compilation problems.

—— (1964a) [9.5E]: Bounded Context Syntactic Analysis, *Comm. ACM*, vol. 7, no. 2, pp. 62–67, 1964 [CR6074]. One way to restrict context-free languages so that the inherent ambiguity question is solvable. Practical applications.

—— (1964b) [5A,S]: The Syntax of Programming Languages: A Survey, *Trans. IEEE*, vol. EC-13, no. 4, pp. 346–353, Aug. 1964. Good survey.

—— (1967) [2.4A]: Nondeterministic Algorithms, *JACM*, vol. 14, no. 4, pp. 636–644, Oct. 1967 [CR14507]. Attempt to use concepts of nondeterminism in practical cases, mainly as a way to write programs.

Gardner, M. (1970) [5G]: Mathematical Games, *Sci. Amer.*, vol. 223, no. 2, pp. 110–113, Aug. 1970. Examples of various types of palindromes.

Garvin, P. L. (1967a) [A]: Language and Machines, *Int. Sci. Technol.*, May 1967, pp. 63–76 [CR12656]. Discussion of the probability of building a machine to recognize "natural" languages.

—— (1967b) [A]: Machine Translation—Fact or Fancy?, *Datamation*, pp. 29–31, Apr. 1967. General discussion of machine translation of natural languages.

Ghiron, H. (1962) [2.3]: Rules to Manipulate Regular Expressions of Finite Automata, *IRE Trans.*, vol. EC-11, no. 4, pp. 574–575, Aug. 1962. Some identities in the algebra of regular expressions.

Gilbert, P. (1966) [5A]: On the Syntax of Algorithmic Languages, *JACM*, vol. 13, no. 1, pp. 90–107, Jan. 1966 [CR9801]. An attempt to model how a compiler scans an input string.

Gill, A. (1961) [2.1E]: State-identification Experiments in Finite Automata, *Info. and Control*, vol. 4, pp. 132–154, 1961. Bounds on the length of adaptive state identification and homing experiments for finite-state machines.

—— (1962) [2G]: "Introduction to the Theory of Finite-state Machines," McGraw-Hill, New York, 1962. Sequential circuit synthesis text.

Ginsburg, S. (1962) [3G,S]: "An Introduction to Mathematical Machine Theory," Addison-Wesley, Reading, Mass., 1962 [CR5431]. Primarily finite-state machines.

—— (1966) [G]: "The Mathematical Theory of Context-free Languages," McGraw-Hill, New York, 1966 [CR12079]. More mathematical approach. Primary emphasis on pushdown and finite-state machines.

——, and S. A. Greibach (1966a) [5,7B]: Mappings Which Preserve Context Sensitive Languages, *Info. and Control*, vol. 9, no. 6, pp. 563–582, 1966. Translations by PDA and LBA acting on context-sensitive languages are considered.

—— and —— (1966b) [5.3]: Deterministic Context Free Languages, *Info. and Control*, vol. 9, no. 6, pp. 620–648, 1966. Some basic results about the set $1DPDA$.

Ginsburg, S., and S. A. Greibach (1967) [7E]: Abstract Families of Languages, *IEEE Conf. Record of 8th Ann. Symp. on Switching and Automata Theory*, IEEE Publ. 16-C-56, pp. 128–139, Oct. 1967. Classifications of languages based on closure properties.

——, ——, and M. A. Harrison (1966) [6.4B]: One-way Stack Automata, *JACM*, vol. 14, no. 2, pp. 389–418, Apr. 1967; summary in *Proc. 7th Ann. Symp. on Switching and Automata Theory*, 1966 [CR15819]. Some results to place the classes of one-way stack languages in the hierarchy.

——, ——, and —— (1967) [6.4B]: Stack Automata and Compiling, *JACM*, vol. 14, no. 1, pp. 172–201, Jan. 1967. Basic motivations, definitions, and results concerning stack automata.

——, and M. A. Harrison (1968a) [B,E]: On the Elimination of Endmarkers, *Info. and Control*, vol. 12, no. 2, pp. 103–115, 1968. Conditions for the elimination of endmarkers from the input tapes of various machine models.

——, and —— (1968b) [6.4E]: One-way Nondeterministic Real-time List-storage Languages, *JACM*, vol. 15, no. 3, pp. 428–446, July 1968 [CR15822]. An attempt to model useful data structures in an automaton.

——, and J. Hopcroft (1968) [7.2E]: Two-way Balloon Automata and AFL, *Proc. 9th Ann. Symp. on Switching and Automata Theory*, IEEE Publ. 68-C-50-C, pp. 292–297, Oct. 1968. Also in *JACM*, vol. 17, no. 1, pp. 3–13, Jan. 1970. Relationships between the two models.

——, and H. G. Rice (1962) [5A]: Two Families of Languages Related to ALGOL, *JACM*, vol. 9, no. 3, pp. 350–371, July 1962 [CR3880]. Two classifications based upon the structures of the grammatical rules.

——, and G. F. Rose (1966) [7.4B]: Preservation of Languages by Transducers, *Info. and Control*, vol. 9, no. 2, pp. 153–176, 1966. (See following entry for corrections.) Results on pushdown transduction of pushdown languages; linear-bounded transducers on context-sensitive languages.

——, and —— (1968) [7.4B]: A Note on Preservation of Languages by Transducers, *Info. and Control*, vol. 12, nos. 5–6, pp. 549–552, 1968 [CR16750]. Corrections to Ginsburg and Rose (1966).

Ginzburg, A. (1967) [2.3B]: A Procedure for Checking Equality of Regular Expressions, *JACM*, vol. 14, no. 2, pp. 355–362, Apr. 1967 [CR12858]. An algebraic procedure for the equality question. It is equivalent to a synthesis followed by an equality test, and could be implemented on a computer.

—— (1968) [G]: "Algebraic Theory of Automata," Academic, New York, 1968. Mathematical approach.

Graham, R. M. (1964) [5A]: Bounded Context Translation, *Proc. Spring Joint Computer Conf.*, vol. 25, pp. 17–29, Spartan Books, Baltimore, Md., 1964 [CR6663]. Discussion of an algorithm which might be used in a compiler.

Grau, A. A. (1961) [5A]: Recursive Processes and ALGOL Translation, *Comm. ACM*, vol. 4, no. 1, pp. 10–15, 1961. An early explanation of procedures which could be used to translate expressions in ALGOL.

Gray, J. N., M. A. Harrison, and O. H. Ibarra (1967) [6.1B,E]: Two-way Pushdown Automata, *Info. and Control*, vol. 11, nos. 1–2, pp. 30–70, July 1967. Basic results on the subject.

Greibach, S. A. (1963) [9.4E]: The Undecidability of the Ambiguity Problem for Minimal Linear Grammars, *Info. and Control*, vol. 6, no. 3, pp. 119–125, June 1963.

—— (1964) [5A]: Formal Parsing Systems, *Comm. ACM*, vol. 7, no. 8, pp. 499–504, Aug. 1964 [CR6878]. How to form the analyzer which is the inverse of a given generator.

—— (1965) [5.8B]: A New Normal-form Theorem for Context-free Phrase-structure

Grammars, *JACM*, vol. 12, no. 1, pp. 42–52, Jan. 1965 [CR7830]. Original statement of results in Sec. 5.8.

Greibach, S. A. (1966) [9E]: The Unsolvability of the Recognition of Linear Context-free Languages, *JACM*, vol. 13, no. 4, pp. 582–587, Oct. 1966. The question "Is a given context-free language linear?" is recursively unsolvable.

—— (1968) [6E]: Independence of AFL Operations, *Proc. Hawaii Int. Conf. on System Sciences*, pp. 8–9, University of Hawaii Press, Honolulu, Jan. 1968 [CR16271]. Discussion of the interrelationships between the operations used in the definition of an abstract family of languages (AFL).

—— (1969) [9.6E]: An Infinite Hierarchy of Context-free Languages, *JACM*, vol. 16, no. 1, pp. 91–106, Jan. 1969 [CR17547]. A hierarchy of languages based upon bounding the number of reversals of direction in a pushdown stack between complete erasures.

Griffiths, T. V. (1968) [9.3E]: The Unsolvability of the Equivalence Problem for $\varLambda$-free Nondeterministic Generalized Machines, *JACM*, vol. 15, no. 3, pp. 409–413, July 1968 [CR15619].

——, and S. R. Petrick (1965) [5A]: On the Relative Efficiencies of Context-free Grammar Recognizers, *Comm. ACM*, vol. 8, no. 5, pp. 289–300, May 1965 [CR7999]. Comparisons of various algorithms for syntax checking in context-free languages. Examples.

Gruska, J. (1966) [5,9E]: On Sets Generated by Context-free Grammars, *Kybernetica*, vol. 2, no. 6, pp. 483–492, 1966 [CR14560, CR19661]. Classifications within the context-free class are introduced to prove some solvability results.

—— (1967) [5E]: On a Classification of Context-free Languages, *Kybernetica*, vol. 3, no. 1, pp. 22–29, 1967 [CR14561, CR19662]. A classification aimed at removing some of the difficulties of the inherent ambiguity questions for context-free languages.

—— (1968) [9.4E]: Unambiguity and Ambiguity of Context-free Grammars and Languages, *Proc. IFIP Cong.* 1968, Mathematics, Booklet A, North-Holland Publishing Company, Amsterdam, pp. 135–139 [CR15818]. Classifications of context-free grammars based on the numbers of nonterminal symbols, etc.

—— (1969) [5E]: Some Classifications of Context-free Languages, *Info. and Control*, vol. 14, no. 2, pp. 152–179, Feb. 1969 [CR17714]. Classifications similar to those in Gruska (1968), described in more detail.

Gusev, L. A., and I. M. Smirnova (1968) [S]: Languages, Grammars and Abstract Automaton Models (Survey), *Automat. Telemekh.*, 1968, no. 4, pp. 72–94, and no. 5, pp. 73–94, English trans., pp. 587–605, 757–774. Survey of basic results. Some Russian references.

Haines, L. H. (1965) [4.2B]: Generation and Recognition of Formal Languages, Ph.D. thesis, MIT, Cambridge, Mass., 1965. Results about context-sensitive languages.

Harrison, M. A. (1965) [G]: "Introduction to Switching and Automata Theory," McGraw-Hill, New York, 1965 [CR10203]. Primarily finite-state problems, but the last chapter discusses context-free languages. Long bibliography.

—— (1968) [2E]: On Infinite Linear Automata, *Proc. Hawaii Int. Conf. on System Sciences*, pp. 5–7, University of Hawaii Press, Honolulu, Jan. 1968 [CR16270]. A generalization of finite-state linear machines to fields with an infinite number of elements (states).

——, and O. H. Ibarra (1968) [6.1E]: Multi-tape and Multi-head Pushdown Automata, *Info. and Control*, vol. 13, no. 5, pp. 433–470, Nov. 1968 [CR19999]. Basic results on the sets of strings accepted by pushdown machines with various multiple inputs.

Hartmanis, J. (1967) [5E]: On Memory Requirements for Context-free Language Recognition, *JACM*, vol. 14, no. 4, pp. 663–665, Oct. 1967 [CR14342]. It is impossible to determine how much space is required to recognize context-free languages. See Lewis et al. (1965).

Hartmanis, J. (1968) [3E]: Computational Complexity of One-tape Turing Machine Computations, *JACM*, vol. 15, no. 2, pp. 325–339, Apr. 1968 [CR15240]. Proves space and time bounds for some recognition problems.

——— (1969) [9.6E]: On the Complexity of Undecidable Problems in Automata Theory, *JACM*, vol. 16, no. 1, pp. 160–167, Jan. 1969 [CR16897]. How undecidability changes with space requirements for recognition.

———, and J. E. Hopcroft (1968) [9.6B]: Structure of Undecidable Problems in Automata Theory, *Proc. 9th Ann. Symp. on Switching and Automata Theory, IEEE Publ.* 68-C-50-C, pp. 327–333, Oct. 1968. Relationship between the difficulties of various unsolvable problems; uses "oracles."

——— and ——— (1971) [4E]: An Overview of the Theory of Computational Complexity, *JACM*, vol. 18, no. 3, pp. 444–475, July 1971. Review of results relating to time-bounded and space-bounded Turing machines.

———, P. M. Lewis, II, and R. E. Stearns (1965) [5B,E]: Classifications of Computations by Time and Memory Requirements, *Proc. IFIP Cong.*, vol. 1, pp. 31–35, Spartan Books, Washington, D.C., 1965 [CR9076]. Early paper on the subject.

———, and H. Shank (1968) [5E]: On the Recognition of Primes by Automata, *JACM*, vol. 15, no. 3, pp. 382–389, July 1968. The set $\{x^n \mid n$ is prime$\}$ is context-sensitive but not context-free. See bibliography for references to other papers dealing with number-theoretic properties of input lengths.

———, and R. E. Stearns (1965) [5E]: On the Computational Complexity of Algorithms, *Trans. Amer. Math. Soc.*, vol. 117, no. 5, pp. 285–306, May 1965. Results on the complexity of the problem of recognizing context-free languages.

Hayes, J. P. (1968) [2.3]: On the Equivalence of Regular Expressions, *Univ. Ill. Coord. Sci. Lab. Rep.* R-374, April 1968. An algebraic technique to test equality of regular expressions.

Heistand, R. E. (1964) [2A]: An Executive System Implemented as a Finite-state Automaton, *Comm. ACM*, vol. 7, no. 11, pp. 669–677, Nov. 1964 [CR7282]. An executive program in a command and control system viewed as a finite-state machine.

Hennie, F. C. (1965) [3E]: One-tape, Off-line Turing Machine Computations, *Info. and Control*, vol. 8, no. 6, pp. 553–578, Dec. 1965. Discussion of time bounds on certain Turing machine computations.

——— (1968) [2S]: "Finite-state Models for Logical Machines," Wiley, New York, 1968 [CR15053]. Survey of finite-state-machine theory.

———, and R. E. Stearns (1966) [3E]: Two-tape Simulation of Multi-tape Turing Machines, *JACM*, vol. 13, no. 4, pp. 533–546, Oct. 1966. How to use two-tape Turing machines to simulate k-tape machines while bounding the time required for the calculation.

Herman, G. T. (1968) [3.1E]: Simulation of One Abstract Computing Machine by Another, *Comm. ACM*, vol. 11, no. 12, pp. 802, 813, Dec. 1968. Precise definition of simulation suggested by discussion in Fischer (1965a).

Hibbard, T. (1967) [5.3E]: A Generalization of Context-free Determinism, *Info. and Control*, vol. 11, no. 1, pp. 196–238, 1967. A study of the effects of limiting the number of visits to a square on a Turing machine tape during which the square can be rewritten.

———, and J. Ullian (1966) [7.3, 7.5E]: The Independence of Inherent Ambiguity from Complementedness among Context-free Languages, *JACM*, vol. 13, no. 4, pp. 588–593, 1966. The set of context-free languages with context-free complements and the set of inherently unambiguous context-free languages are incomparable.

Hooper, P. K. (1966) [3.2E]: The Immortality Problem for Post Normal Systems, *JACM*, vol. 13, no. 4, pp. 594–599, Oct. 1966 [CR11627]. The problem is, "Does there exist a word such that a given system does not halt?" Shown to be recursively unsolvable if the normal system is polygenic (nondeterministic).

Hopcroft, J. E. (1969) [9.3E]: On the Equivalence and Containment Problems for Context-free Languages, *MST*, vol. 3, no. 2, pp. 119–124, 1969.

———, and J. D. Ullman (1967a) [7.2B]: An Approach to a Unified Theory of Automata, *BSTJ*, vol. 46, no. 8, pp. 1793–1829, 1967 [CR14097]. Introduction of the balloon automaton formalism.

———, and ——— (1967b) [6.4B]: Nonerasing Stack Automata, *JCSS*, vol. 1, no. 2, pp. 166–186, Aug. 1967 [CR14098]. The relationship between two stack automaton models and space bounds on Turing machine tapes.

———, and ——— (1968a) [9B]: Decidable and Undecidable Questions about Automata, *JACM*, vol. 15, no. 2, pp. 317–324, Apr. 1968 [CR17717]. The relationships between decidability and undecidability questions about various types of balloon automata.

———, and ——— (1968b) [3E]: Relations between Time and Tape Complexities, *JACM*, vol. 15, no. 3, pp. 414–427, July 1968 [CR15620]. An investigation of some trade-offs between time and tape space.

———, and ——— (1968c) [6.4E]: Sets Accepted by One-way Stack Automata Are Context Sensitive, *Info. and Control*, vol. 13, no. 2, pp. 114–133, Aug. 1968. Proof that $1NSA \subseteq DLBA$.

———, and ——— (1969a) [3E]: Some Results on Tape-bounded Turing Machines, *JACM*, vol. 16, no. 1, pp. 168–177, Jan. 1969 [CR18540]. Extensions of some tape complexity results to nondeterministic and nonhalting machines. Some closure results are also discussed.

———, and ——— (1969b) [G]: "Formal Languages and Their Relation to Automata," Addison-Wesley, Reading, Mass., 1969 [CR20188]. A general book with a similar coverage to this work. It includes some results on computational complexity, but does not use balloon automata.

Huffman, D. A. (1954) [2.1B]: The Synthesis of Sequential Circuits, *Jour. Franklin Inst.*, vol. 257, nos. 3–4, pp. 161–190, 275–303, Mar. and Apr. 1954. Reprinted in Moore (1964). Basic paper on the concept of state.

Irland, M. I. (1970) [L]: Computational Complexity: A Bibliography, *ACM SIGACT News*, June 1970, no. 6, pp. 17–37. No annotations. Concentration on computational complexity. See Irland and Fischer (1970) for more complete listings.

———, and P. C. Fischer (1970) [L]: A Bibliography on Computational Complexity, *Univ. Waterloo, Dept. Appl. Anal. Comput. Sci., Res. Rep.* CSRR2028, Waterloo, Ontario. No annotations.

Irons, E. T. (1961) [5A]: A Syntax-directed Compiler for ALGOL 60, *Comm. ACM*, vol. 4, no. 1, pp. 51–55, Jan. 1961. A summary of how a translation performed by a compiler can be specified and implemented. Implementation and the semantic descriptions are discussed briefly.

Johnston, J. B. (1965) [9.4E]: A Class of Unambiguous Computer Languages, *Comm. ACM*, vol. 8, no. 3, pp. 147 149, March 1965 [CR7998]. A condition on context-free languages to ensure unambiguity.

Jones, N. D. (1967) [G,E]: Formal Languages and Rudimentary Attributes (thesis), Western Ontario University, London, Ont., 1967 [CR13676]. An approach to language classification through mathematical logic.

——— (1969) [5E]: Context-free Languages and Rudimentary Attributes, *Math. Systems Theory*, vol. 3, no. 2, pp. 102 109, 1969.

Kameda, T., and P. Weiner (1970) [2.4E]: On the State Minimization of Nondeterministic

Finite Automata, *IEEE Trans.*, vol. C-19, no. 7, pp. 617–626, July 1970. An algorithm that will find a set of machines which contains the minimum machine equivalent to a given nondeterministic finite-state machine is presented.

Kaplan, D. M. (1969) [2E]: Regular Expressions and the Equivalence of Programs, *JCSS*, vol. 3, no. 4, pp. 361–386, Nov. 1969 [CR19125]. An attempt to solve a restricted form of the program equivalence problem.

Kleene, S. C. (1952) [3G]: "Introduction to Metamathematics," Van Nostrand, Princeton, N.J., 1952. Some sections on recursive function theory relate to Turing machine computations.

——— (1956) [2.3B]: Representation of Events in Nerve Nets and Finite Automata, in C. E. Shannon and J. McCarthy (eds.), "Automata Studies," Princeton University Press, Princeton, N.J., pp. 3–42, 1956 [CR8330]. Introduction of regular expressions and proof of their equivalence with finite-state machines.

——— (1967) [3G]: "Mathematical Logic," Wiley, New York, 1967. A less sophisticated version of some of Kleene (1952).

——— (1969) [3.6G]: The New Logic, *Amer. Scientist*, vol. 57, no. 3, pp. 333–347, 1969. A popularized discussion of some computability results, condensed from Kleene (1967).

Knuth, D. E. (1965) [9.4E]: On the Translation of Languages from Left to Right, *Info. and Control*, vol. 8, no. 6, pp. 607–639, 1965 [CR10162]. One restriction on context-free languages to guarantee that they be unambiguous. Parallels the operation of some deterministic translators.

——— (1967) [5.2E]: A Characterization of Parenthesis Languages, *Info. and Control*, vol. 11, no. 3, pp. 269–289, Sept. 1967 [CR14350]. Some decision problems concerning a class of languages are discussed. This class is the largest one for which crucial equality questions are solvable.

——— (1968) [G]: "The Art of Computer Programming," vols. 1–7, Addison-Wesley, Reading, Mass., 1968 [CR14505, CR15182]. A series of volumes which promise to include a large amount of information on computer software. Volume 6 will cover mathematical linguistics.

———, and R. H. Bigelow (1967) [6.4B]: Programming Languages for Automata, *JACM*, vol. 14, no. 4, pp. 615–635, Oct. 1967 [CR13675]. Original proofs of some results in Sec. 6.4. Uses an ALGOL-like language to prove the results.

Kobayashi, K. (1968) [9E]: Some Unsolvable Problems on Context-free Languages and Their Application to On-line Language Recognizers, *Info. and Control*, vol. 13, no. 3, pp. 245–253, Sept. 1968 [CR17546]. Some unsolvability results in which the set of possible arguments is small.

Korenjak, A. J. (1969) [5.1E]: A Practical Method for Constructing *LR(k)* Processors, *Comm. ACM*, vol. 12, no. 11, pp. 613–623, Nov. 1969 [CR18722]. A more efficient algorithm than the one given in Knuth (1965) is described.

Kuroda, S. Y. (1964) [4B]: Classes of Languages and Linear Bounded Automata, *Info. and Control*, vol. 7, no. 2, pp. 207–223, 1964 [CR7705]. Basic results concerning closure under complement of *DLBA*; other results about *DLBA*, *NLBA*.

Landweber, P. S. (1963) [8,9S]: Three Theorems on Phrase Structure Grammars of Type 1, *Info. and Control*, vol. 6, no. 2, pp. 131–136, 1963. Basic paper on context-sensitive languages; closure under intersection, removal of endmarkers, and existence of a context-sensitive grammar describing the set accepted by an LBA are shown.

——— (1964) [8,9S]: Decision Problems of Phrase-structure Grammars, *IEEE Trans.*, vol. EC-13, no. 4, pp. 354–362, Aug. 1964. Survey of many problems concerning grammars and their solvability or unsolvability for various classes of grammars.

Lewis, P. M., II, and R. E. Stearns (1966) [7.4A]: Syntax Directed Transduction, *Proc.*

7th Ann. Symp. on Switching and Automata Theory, 1966. Also in *JACM*, vol. 15, no. 3, pp. 464–488, July 1968 [CR15621]. Automaton models of some translation processes used for compiler languages.

Lewis, P. M., II, R. E. Stearns, and J. Hartmanis (1965) [3,4E]: Memory Bounds for Recognition of Context-free and Context-sensitive Languages, *IEEE Conf. Record on Switching Circuit Theory and Logical Design, IEEE Publ.* 16C13, pp. 191–202, 1965. Space bounds on Turing machine recognition of context-free languages.

Lin, S., and T. Rado (1965) [3.6]: Computer Studies of Turing Machine Problems, *JACM*, vol. 12, no. 2, pp. 196–212, Apr. 1965 [CR8651]. Busy-beaver problems.

Loeckx, J. (1970) [5.1E]: An Algorithm for the Construction of Bounded-context Parsers. *Comm. ACM*, vol. 13, no. 5, pp. 297–307, May 1970. This algorithm finds a bounded-context parser whenever one exists for an arbitrary context-free language.

Maurer, H. A. (1969) [9.5B]: A Direct Proof of the Inherent Ambiguity of a Single Context-free Language, *JACM*, vol. 16, no. 2, pp. 256–260, Apr. 1969.

McNaughton, R. (1961) [2S]: Theory of Automata: A Survey, in "Advances in Computers," vol. 2, Academic, New York, 1961 [CR3920]. Many references to early work.

—— (1968) [G]: Automata, Formal Languages, Abstract Switching and Computability in a Ph.D. Computer Science Program, *Comm. ACM*, vol. 11, no. 11, pp. 738–740, 746, Nov. 1968 [CR16327]. Proposed course outlines. This text matches best with course 6, but also includes material from courses 4 and 5.

——, and H. Yamada (1960) [2.3B]: Regular Expressions and State Graphs for Automata, *IRE Trans.*, vol. EC-9, no. 1, pp. 39–47, 1960. Reprinted in Moore (1964). Procedures to find regular expressions from transition graphs.

Mealy, G. H. (1955) [2.1B]: A Method for Synthesizing Sequential Circuits, *BSTJ*, vol. 34, pp. 1045–1079, Sept. 1955. Introduces the Mealy model of sequential machines.

Meyer, A. R., and D. M. Ritchie (1968) [3E]: A Classification of Functions by Computational Complexity, *Proc. Hawaii Int. Conf. on System Sciences*, pp. 17–19, University of Hawaii Press, Honolulu, Jan. 1968 [CR16274]. Another means of classifying functions in a hierarchy.

Minsky, M. L. (1961) [7.2, 9B,E]: Recursive Unsolvability of Post's Problem of "Tag" and Other Topics in Theory of Turing Machines, *Ann. Math.*, vol. 74, no. 3, pp. 437–455, Nov. 1961. Some basic unsolvability results; constructions of "simple" universal Turing machines. Proof that a two-counter machine can simulate a Turing machine.

—— (1967) [2,3G]: "Computation: Finite and Infinite Machines," McGraw-Hill, New York, 1967. A good informal discussion of finite-state and Turing machines.

Moore, E. F. (1956) [2.1B]: Gedanken-experiments on Sequential Machines, in C. E. Shannon and J. McCarthy (eds.), "Automata Studies," Princeton University Press, 1956, pp. 129–153 [CR8330]. Basic paper on state-identification and machine-identification experiments on finite-state machines. The Moore model.

—— (1964) [2S]: "Sequential Machines: Selected Papers," Addison-Wesley, Reading, Mass., 1964. Collection of early papers about finite-state machines.

Myhill, J. (1957) [2B]: Finite Automata and the Representation of Events, *Wright Air Develop. Center Tech. Rep.* 57-624, 1957. An early paper showing many equivalent formulations of the set *DFSA*.

—— (1960) [4B]: Linear-bounded Automata, *Wright Air Develop. Div. Tech. Note* 60-165, 1960. Original introduction of the linear-bounded model.

Naur, P. (ed.) (1960) [5A]: Report on the Algorithmic Language ALGOL 60, *Comm. ACM*, vol. 3, pp. 299–314, May 1960 [CR4540]. Original specification of a compiler language by syntactic structure.

Nelson, R. J. (1965) [G]: Basic Concepts of Automata Theory, *Proc. ACM 20th Nat. Conf.*, pp. 138–161, 1965 [CR9072]. A formal approach.

—— (1968) [G]: "Introduction to Automata," Wiley, New York, 1968 [CR14096]. Primarily finite-state and Turing machines.

Newell, A., and J. C. Shaw (1957) [5.1B]: Programming the Logic Theory Machine, *Proc. West. Joint Comput. Conf.*, pp. 230–240, 1957. Early use of pushdown lists in computer programming.

Oettinger, A. G. (1961) [5A]: Automatic Syntactic Analysis and the Pushdown Store, in Structure of Language and Its Mathematical Aspects, *Proc. Symp. Appl. Math.*, vol. 12, pp. 104–129, 1961. An attempt at natural-language application of pushdown machines.

Ogden W. (1969) [6.4E]: Intercalation Theorems for Stack Languages, *Conf. Record of ACM Symp. on Theory of Computing*, pp. 31–42, 1969. Results which generalize Lemma 1 of Sec. 5.6 to stack languages.

Ott, E. H., and N. H. Feinstein (1961) [2.3A]: Design of Sequential Machines from Their Regular Expressions, *JACM*, vol. 8, no. 4, pp. 585–600, 1961. How to synthesize sequential machines by inspection of the regular expression. Also see Brzozowski (1964a).

Parikh, R. J. (1961) [9.5B]: On Context-free Languages, *JACM*, vol. 13, no. 4, pp. 570–581, Oct. 1966 [CR11431]. Reprint of original report, Language Generating Devices, *MIT Res. Lab. Electron., Quart. Progr. Rep.* 60, pp. 199–212, Jan. 15, 1961. Basic ambiguity and inherent ambiguity results for context-free languages.

Paull, M. C., and S. H. Unger (1968) [5E]: Structural Equivalence of Context-free Grammars, *JCSS*, vol. 2, no. 4, pp. 427–463, Dec. 1968. Defines structural equivalence in terms of similar derivation trees and discusses algorithms for finding structurally equivalent grammars.

Paz, A., and B. Peleg (1968) [2.3E]: On Concatenative Decompositions of Regular Events, *IEEE Trans.*, vol. C-17, no. 3, pp. 229–237, Mar. 1968 [CR15018]. The problem is: Given a regular set R, can one find two regular sets R_1, R_2 such that $R = R_1 R_2$?

Post, E. L. (1936) [3B]: Finite Combinatory Processes: Formulation I, *Jour. Symb. Logic*, vol. 1, pp. 103–105, 1936. Original paper on Post normal systems.

—— (1946) [9.1B]: A Variant of a Recursively Unsolvable Problem, *Bull. Amer. Math. Soc.*, vol. 52, no. 4, pp. 264–268, Apr. 1946. Original paper on the correspondence problem.

Rabin, M. O., and D. Scott (1959) [2B]: Finite Automata and Their Decision Problems, *IBM Jour. R and D.*, vol. 3, no. 2, pp. 114–125, Apr. 1959. Reprinted in Moore (1964). Many basic results concerning finite-state machines with input tapes.

Rado, T. (1962) [3.6B]: On Non-computable Functions, *BSTJ*, vol. 41, pp. 877–884, May 1962. Original statement of the busy-beaver problems.

Rahimi, M. A. (1970) [L]: Key-word Index Bibliography of Automata, Formal Languages and Computability Theory, *ACM SIGACT News*, May 1970, no. 5, pp. i–171. Extensive unannotated bibliography.

Ritchie, R. W., and F. N. Springsteel (1968) [2.6E]: Recognition of Languages by Marking Automata, *Proc. Hawaii Int. Conf. on System Sciences*, pp. 20–22, University of Hawaii Press, Honolulu, Jan. 1968 [CR16275]. Considers the sets of strings recognizable by two-way finite automata which can leave a finite number of markers on the input tape. May be related to Brainerd (1967).

Rogers, H., Jr. (1967) [3G,E]: "Theory of Recursive Functions and Effective Computability," McGraw-Hill, New York, 1967 [CR16025]. Basic text on recursive function theory.

Rose, G. F. (1964) [5.1E]: An Extension of ALGOL-like Languages, *Comm. ACM*, vol. 7, no. 2, pp. 52–61, Feb. 1964. An extension of the set of context-free languages to try to get more features of ALGOL. Very abstract.

Rosenberg, A. L. (1966) [2E]: On Multi-head Finite Automata, *IBM Jour. R and D*, vol. 10, no. 5, pp. 388–394, Sept. 1966 [CR14352]. Some results on finite-state machines with one tape and many heads. See the review for a criticism of the proofs.

———— (1967) [5E]: A Machine Realization of the Linear Context-free Languages, *Info. and Control*, vol. 10, no. 2, pp. 175–188, Feb. 1967 [CR12860]. Some results on linear context-free languages in which not more than one nonterminal symbol appears on the right side of a rule. Also discusses finite-state machines with several input tapes.

Rosenkrantz, D. J. (1967) [5.8B]: Matrix Equations and Normal Forms for Context-free Grammars, *JACM*, vol. 14, no. 3, pp. 501–507, July 1967 [CR13261]. Results of Sec. 5.8 proved by the methods used in this text.

———— (1969) [5E]: Programmed Grammars and Classes of Formal Languages, *JACM*, vol. 16, no. 1, pp. 107–131, Jan. 1969 [CR16992]. A programmed grammar is a set of rewriting rules which have sequencing constraints on their use. A language specification thus looks a bit like a SNOBOL program.

Rozenberg, G. (1968) [2E]: Some Remarks on Rabin and Scott's Notion of Multitape Automaton, *Bull. Acad. Polonaise Sci., Sér. Sci. Math., Astron. Phys.*, vol. 16, no. 3, pp. 215–218, 1968. Adds additional precision to the results of Rabin and Scott (1959) concerning finite-state machines with multiple input tapes.

Salomaa, A. (1966) [2.3]: Two Complete Axiom Systems for the Algebra of Regular Events, *JACM*, vol. 13, no. 1, pp. 158–169, Jan. 1966 [CR9794]. An axiomatic approach to the algebra of regular sets.

———— (1969) [G]: "Theory of Automata," Pergamon, New York, 1969 [CR18717]. General coverage of automata theory.

Samelson, K., and F. L. Bauer (1960) [5A,E]: Sequential Formula Translation, *Comm. ACM*, vol. 3, no. 2, pp. 76–83, 1960 [CR6015]. The use of a pushdown stack to translate arithmetic statements.

Savitch, W. J. (1970) [5E]: Relationships between Nondeterministic and Deterministic Tape Complexities, *JCSS*, vol. 4, no. 2, pp. 177–192, Apr. 1970.

Scheinberg, S. (1960) [5.6B]: Note on the Boolean Properties of Context-free Languages, *Info. and Control*, vol. 3, no. 4, pp. 372–375, 1960. An early paper containing some closure results for context-free languages.

Schkolnick, M. (1968) [6.4E]: Two-type Bracketed Grammars, *Proc. 9th Ann. Symp. on Switching and Automata Theory*, IEEE Publ. 68-C-50-C, pp. 315–326, Oct. 1968. Introduces a family of grammars to generate languages in *INSA*.

Schutzenberger, M. P. (1962) [6.3B]: Finite Counting Automata, *Info. and Control*, vol. 5, no. 2, pp. 91–107, 1962. First statements concerning counter machines.

———— (1963) [5]: On Context-free Languages and Push-down Automata, *Info. and Control*, vol. 6, no. 3, pp. 246–264, 1963. An abstract paper showing some results about unambiguous context-free languages.

Scott, D. (1967) [G]: Some Definitional Suggestions for Automata Theory, *JCSS*, vol. 1, no. 2, pp. 187–212, 1967. Attempt to give a unified formalism for machine models.

Shannon, C. E. (1956) [3B,E]: A Universal Turing Machine with Two Internal States, in C. E. Shannon and J. McCarthy (eds.), "Automata Studies," Princeton University Press, Princeton, N.J., pp. 129–153, 1956 [CR8330]. Coding procedures to minimize the numbers of symbols or states in universal Turing machines are shown.

————, and J. McCarthy (eds.) (1956) [2,3B]: "Automata Studies," Princeton University Press, Princeton, N.J., 1956. A collection of basic papers on finite-state and Turing machines.

Shepherdson, J. C. (1959) [2.6B]: The Reduction of Two-way Automata to One-way Automata, *IBM Jour. R and D*, vol. 3, pp. 198–200, 1959. Reprinted in Moore (1964). First proof that $2DFSA = 1DFSA$.

Stearns, R. E. (1967) [5E,B]: A Regularity Test for Pushdown Machines, *Info. and Control*, vol. 11, no. 3, pp. 323–340, Sept. 1967 [CR14774]. A test to determine whether a language in $1DPDA$ is regular.

————, and J. Hartmanis (1963) [7.3E]: Regularity Preserving Modifications of Regular Expressions, *Info. and Control*, vol. 6, no. 1, pp. 55–69, 1963. Some nonmachine types of modifications which preserve regularity are discussed.

————, and P. M. Lewis, II (1968) [5E]: Property Grammars and Table Machines, *Proc. 9th Ann. Symp. on Switching and Automata Theory*, Oct. 1968, *IEEE Publ.* 68-C-50-C, pp. 106–119. Also *Info. and Control*, vol. 14, no. 6, pp. 524–549, June 1969 [CR18205]. An extension of pushdown machines to model some compiler features, including infinite input alphabets.

Steel, T. B., Jr. (ed.) (1966) [5A]: "Formal Language Description Languages for Computer Programming," North-Holland Publishing Company, Amsterdam, 1966 [CR10465]. A collection of papers which formally describe some programming languages.

Tixier, V. (1967) [2.3E]: Recursive Functions of Regular Expressions in Language Analysis (thesis), Stanford University, Stanford, Calif., 1967 [CR13684]. Regular expressions and some extensions of that notion.

Tokura, N., and T. Kasami (1968) [5.3]: A Class of Context-free Grammars Which Generate Deterministic Languages, *Electron. Commun. in Japan*, vol. 51C, no. 8, Aug. 1968. Another way to obtain unambiguous context-free languages.

Trakhtenbrot, B. A. (1963) [3S]: "Algorithms and Automatic Computing Machines," transl. by J. Kristian, J. D. McCawley, and S. A. Schmitt, Heath, Boston, 1963. An elementary introduction to Turing machines.

Turing, A. M. (1936) [6.2B]: On Computable Numbers, with an Application to the Entscheidungsproblem, *Proc. London Math. Soc.*, ser. 2, vol. 42, pp. 230–265, 1936–1937; correction vol. 43, pp. 544–546, 1937. Original paper on Turing machines.

Ullian, J. S. (1966) [5E]: Failure of a Conjecture about Context Free Languages, *Info. and Control*, vol. 9, no. 1, pp. 61–65, Jan. 1966 [CR10160]. The conjecture is the converse of a statement in Haines (1965) concerning whether a particular language is context-free.

Ullman, J. D. (1969) [6.4E]: Halting Stack Automata, *JACM*, vol. 16, no. 4, pp. 550–563, Oct. 1969 [CR18316]. Proof that a time bound can be placed on computations by two-way stack acceptors, with the corollary that $2DSA$ is closed under complementation.

Unger, S. H. (1968) [5A]: A Global Parser for Context-free Phrase Structure Grammars, *Comm. ACM*, vol. 11, no. 4, pp. 240–246, Apr. 1968; corrigendum, *Comm. ACM*, vol. 11, no. 6, pp. 427, June 1968 [CR15190]. A top-to-bottom parser of context-free languages; also used to produce the parsing portion of a compiler for a given context-free language.

Vere, S. (1970) [5E]: Translation Equations, *CACM*, vol. 13, no. 2, pp. 83–89, Feb. 1970. Discusses the use of equations to describe the translation of context-free languages, and a procedure for generating a description of the translator from the equations. The techniques are similar to those used by Brzozowski (1964a,b) for the realization of finite-state machines.

Wang, H. (1957) [3.1B]: A Variant of Turing's Theory of Computing Machines, *JACM*, vol. 4, no. 1, pp. 63–94, Jan. 1957. A programming-language description of Turing machines.

Wood, D. (1970) [L]: Bibliography 23, Formal Language Theory and Automata Theory, *CR*, vol. 11, no. 7, pp. 417–430, July 1970.   Large bibliography without annotations.

Younger, D. H. (1967) [3E]: Recognition and Parsing of Context-free Languages in Time n^3, *Info. and Control*, vol. 10, no. 2, pp. 189–208, Feb. 1967 [CR12257].   A parsing algorithm which works for any context-free language and produces a parse in n^3 steps, where n is the number of symbols in the input string.

Index